COMPREHENSIVE ENGLISH PREFIX AND

探源英语前缀和后缀，轻松扩大英语词汇

- EXPAND ENGLISH VOCABULARY IN UNIQUE SMART WAY! PART 1 OUT OF 4 VERSION 2022

CW01337818

Contents

Many English words are formed by taking basic words and adding combinations of prefixes and suffixes to them. A basic word to which affixes (prefixes and suffixes) are added is called a root word because it forms the basis of a new word. The root word are mostly from Latin and Greek. This is very similar to Chinese language, which contains Radical. Radicals normally give you some hints in meaning, for example：

木　　mù　（名）1 tree: 2 wood:（木 is a root word, resemble the shape of tree）

本　　běn　1 the root or stem of a plant (the line at the bottom of 木 highlights the root of a tree)

末　　mò　（名）1 tip; end (the line at the top of 木 highlights the top of a tree)

林　　lín　1（名）wood; grove;

森　　sēn　1（形）full of trees (big forest)

树　　shù　（名）1 tree:（木 is used at radical here, indicating the relation with tree, or plants）

By decoding the root words from Latin and Greek, you will find most deep words such as biology and medical term are easier to remember, you can even sense out a new word meaning even it is new to you or it is even French, Germain or Italian. You will not be intimidated by English words, on the opposite, you will enjoy the "decoding" approach as a fun way to expand your English vocabulary. Applying such skills, I remember I can cram more than 100 difficulty GRE words in one or two hours! I will share my amazing secrets with you in this book!

I am a native Chinese grow up in China in the darkest era in China history-Culture revolution. We began our first English lesson in trial at grade 3, I just remember the frustrated teacher slam the door walk away. Then we won and continue play what we like and learn nothing. We began our first English alphabet lesson in Grade 6, which I enjoyed the chaos as a playful rebellious boy. I remember I just repeated a sentence "You are monkey" to my friends in whole grade seven. My English result at the end of that year was astonishing: 15 out of 100!

I realized the English is the compulsory subject if I can go to university, the honour you can bring to your family the most at my time, the only way can change your fate. The university entry exam is challenging, only less than 1% can successfully enter the college. I began to cram English and scored 87% in the high school entry exam at Grade eight and keep this result in the University Entry Exam.

When I resides in Malaysia after university in China, I realised I can not speak proper English and my English spelling was awful even I scored 620 in TOEFL reading! Through observation my kids English learning, I realised the phenetic in English, the prefix, appendix etc. As a Chinese who never learn Japanese, but I can understand 60% of Japanese newspaper in front of the Japanese restaurants I passed every day. Since promoting Mandarin Chinese is part of my business, I am very curious to explore more in languages, such as Malay language, Korean etc. I tried to read some French, German, Spanish and Italian article, the feeling is just like I am reading Japanese, I can decode some meaning! I use word "decode"! "Decoding is the ability to apply your knowledge of letter-sound relationships, including knowledge of letter patterns, to correctly pronounce written words. Understanding these relationships gives children (and you) the ability to recognize familiar words quickly and to figure out words they haven't seen before.

In the past decades, I create a Chinese-English vocabulary database. My Ph.D. dissertation area was "Data Mining", I gave up my Ph.D. research but apply the skills and concept of data base and data mining in my language business. Nearly one million entries enable me to find out the vocabulary with the derive from the same root. The List of Greek and Latin roots in English are referred Wikipedia[1] and online resource[2].

---

[1] https://en.wikipedia.org/w/index.php?oldid=516380353
[2] Reference 1: https://www.msdmanuals.com/professional/eye-disorders/eyelid-and-lacrimal-disorders/canaliculitis

The following is a comprehensive alphabetical list of Prefix and Suffix.

Some of those used in medicine and medical terminology are specially marked with (Medical).   Please refer to our "Decoding Greek and Latin roots in English 探源英语词根，轻松扩大英语词汇 - Expand English Vocabulary in Unique Smart Way! Part 1 out of 4 Version 2022".

The Latin and Greek roots, suffix and prefix are the gene of modern English vocabulary. Decoding the gene will expand your English Vocabulary in Unique Smart Way!

Best regards

David Yao

SEPTEMBER 4, 2022

Reference 2: https://www.genome.gov/genetics-glossary

Reference 3: https://dictionary.cambridge.org/dictionary/

About the Author:

David Yao, the founder of www.LegooMandarin.com and Educational Video Courses Online (www.Edeo.biz), born in china, resides in Kuala Lumpur, Malaysia, holding Master degree from University Malaya, has 25 years' experience in mandarin teaching for foreigners, creating a SYSTEM (more than 200 mandarin courses) designed for foreigners to study Chinese as secondary language. He expands his interest and expertise to English and Malaysian Language, editing a series of trilingual textbooks and vocabulary books. He practices Tai Chi for almost 30 years and establishes Tai Chi Fitness Organization (http://taichifitness.org/) to modernize and promote Tai Chi for fitness and health.

Scan QR code for Lifetime Access to Full Video course together with this book

@ the best price in Udemy:

Our Story

"Share with You What We Know Best" is our Slogan. We start with LEGOO Mandarin and now expand the system into other topics: Bahasa Malaysia, IT eCommerce, Accounting and Finance, Tai Chi Fitness and Qi Gong. You can learn anytime anywhere!

In addition to be a **Contents Provider**, we also provide **Online Systems,** which can be easily integrated with your school or company online system or use separately. We are using Udemy and other more than 10 similar platforms for video courses marketing. The Amazon KDP, Google Books and Apple iBooks are platforms we publishing our textbooks in addition to our own platform. We provide consultancy service to save your time and give you the best tips on how to leverage your efforts using all these amazing platforms. Please contact us for quotations (very reasonable price).

We can assign our trained teachers to conduct **live lesson** through Webinar, Skype and YouTube, Facebook at reasonable price.

Licencing Program to schools & Resellers

We offer Licencing Program to schools! More schools are using our system! You can use quiz, video course, PPT and PDF under our Licencing Program. Customized course development with your own LOGO can be done. Please contact us for details and quotations (very reasonable price).

Licencing Program to Resellers

We offer Licencing Program to Resellers, book stores and other Platforms (Websites, Google stores, Groupons, Facebook stores). We provide contents such PDF books, online Quiz and Video Courses. You can list our contents in your platform. We will share on 50-50 sales basis. We can provide technical assistance to integrate our contents with your system and help response within 24 hours.

Please contact us by whatsapp +60163863716.

David Yao Amazon Kindle Author Central page

For Hardcopy or paperback books at best price with reduced postage, please visit:
David Yao Amazon Kindle Author Central page:

http://bit.ly/david-amazon-kdp (USA)

https://www.amazon.co.uk/-/e/B07PR3LTMQ (UK)

https://www.amazon.de/-/e/B07PR3LTMQ (German)

http://www.amazon.fr/-/e/B07PR3LTMQ (France)

https://www.amazon.co.jp/~/e/B07PR3LTMQ (Japan)

https://www.amazon.com/-/e/B07PR3LTMQ (USA)

Preview and download books by David YAO at Apple Book Store:

https://books.apple.com/us/author/david-yao/id584331956

Part 1: Prefixes

AAA
Prefix: a- on/ in/ to
Meaning in English: on/ in/ to

Origin language: Anglo-Saxon/ Latin

English examples:

across　　adverb, preposition UK　/əˈkrɒs/ US　/əˈkrɑːs/ A2 从一边到另一边；穿过；横过 from one side to the other of something with clear limits, such as an area of land, a road, or a river

aboard　　adverb, preposition UK　/əˈbɔːd/ US　/əˈbɔːrd/ C1 上船（或飞机、公共汽车、火车等）；在船（或飞机、公共汽车、火车等）上 on or onto a ship, aircraft, bus, or train

aside 1 adverb UK　/əˈsaɪd/ US　/əˈsaɪd/ aside adverb (TO ONE SIDE) 在旁边；到（或向）一边 B2 on or to one side

Prefix: a- without/ not
Meaning in English: without/ not

Origin language: Anglo-Saxon/ Latin

English examples:

abiotic　　adjective UK　/ˌeɪ.baɪˈɒt.ɪk/ US　/ˌeɪ.baɪˈɑː.t̬ɪk/ 与生物无关的；非生物的 relating to things in the environment that are not living

Analgia　　noun [U] Medical Specialized　(medicine) state of painlessness, absence of pain

apathy   noun [U] UK /ˈæp.ə.θi/ US /ˈæp.ə.θi/无兴趣，懈怠；（尤指对重要事情的）漠不关心，无动于衷 behaviour that shows no interest or energy and shows that someone is unwilling to take action, especially over something important

anomaly   noun [C or U] UK /əˈnɒm.ə.li/ US /əˈnɑː.mə.li/ formal 异常的人（或事物）；不规则；（同一种类中的）畸形 a person or thing that is different from what is usual, or not in agreement with something else and therefore not satisfactory

atypical   adjective UK /ˌeɪˈtɪp.ɪ.kəl/ US /ˌeɪˈtɪp.ɪ.kəl/非典型的；异常的；不同寻常的 different from all others of the same type

amoral   adjective UK /ˌeɪˈmɒr.əl/ US /ˌeɪˈmɔːr.əl/毫无道德观念的；没有道德的 without moral principles

asocial   adjective UK /ˌeɪˈsəʊ.ʃəl/ US /ˌeɪˈsoʊ.ʃəl/ 不喜社交的，不合群的 not interested in forming social groups or connections with others

这本书描写了一个保守褊狭、缺乏信任、互不往来的社会。   The book depicts an insular, distrustful, asocial society.

Prefix: ab- from/ away

Meaning in English: from/ away

Origin language: Latin

English examples:

abdicate   1 verb UK /ˈæb.dɪ.keɪt/ US /ˈæb.də.keɪt/ (KING/QUEEN) 逊位；退（位），让（位），正式放弃（王位）[I or T] If a king or queen abdicates, he or she makes a formal statement that he or she no longer wants to be king or queen. [GRE]

abduct 1 verb [T] UK /æbˈdʌkt/ US /æbˈdʌkt/ [T] (TAKE A PERSON) 绑架；劫持；诱拐 to force someone to go somewhere with you, often using threats or violence

absent 1 adjective UK /ˈæb.sənt/ US /ˈæb.sənt/ (NOT PRESENT) B1 （尤指上课或工作）缺勤的；缺席的；不在场的 not in the place where you are expected to be, especially at school or work [GRE]

absence 1 noun UK /ˈæb.səns/ US /ˈæb.səns/ (NOT BEING PRESENT) 缺席；缺勤；不在场 B2 [U or C] the fact of not being where you are usually expected to be

abstain 1verb [I] UK /æbˈsteɪn/ US /æbˈsteɪn/ [I] (NOT DO) 节制；戒绝（尤指不好的享乐） to not do something, especially something enjoyable that you think might be bad

absorb 1 verb [T] UK /əbˈzɔːb/ US /əbˈzɔːrb/ [T] (TAKE IN) （尤指逐渐）吸收 B2 to take something in, especially gradually

abnormal adjective UK /æbˈnɔː.məl/ US /æbˈnɔːr.məl/ C1 反常的；异常的；变态的（尤指不好的） different from what is usual or average, especially in a way that is bad

Prefix (Medical): abdomin(o)- Of or relating to the abdomen, fat around the belly

Meaning in English: Of or relating to the abdomen

Latin: (abdōmen), abdomen, fat around the belly

Origin language: Latin

English examples:

abdomen noun [C] UK /ˈæb.də.mən/ US /ˈæb.də.mən/ specialized （人或动物的）腹（部）；（昆虫的）腹部 the lower part of a person's or animal's body, containing the stomach, bowels, and other organs, or the end of an insect's body

abdominals   noun [plural] UK /æbˈdɒm.ɪ.nəlz/ US /æbˈdɑː.mə.nəlz/ informal abs 腹肌 muscles in the abdomen

abdominis   adjective UK /æbˈdɒm.ɪ.nɪs/ US /æbˈdɑː.mə.nɪs/ specialized（拉丁语）肌肉的（用于腹部肌肉名称中，如 transversus abdominis muscle"腹横肌"） a Latin word meaning "of the abdomen", used in the names of abdominal muscles, for example the transverse abdominis muscle

Prefix (Medical): acanth(o)- thorn or spine

Meaning in English: thorn or spine

Origin language: Greek ἄκανθα (akantha), thorn

English examples:

acanthion   noun [C] (medicine) A point lying near the base of the nose; specifically, the point at the base of the anterior nasal spine that lies on the mesial line; tip of the anterior nasal spine.

Acanthocytes   noun [C] 棘紅細胞 Acanthocytes are also called spur cells. They are dense, shrunken, and irregularly shaped red blood cells with spikes on the outside. These cells form from changes in the fats and proteins on red blood cells' outer layers. Most adults have a small number of acanthocytes in their blood. Wikipedia

acanthoma   noun [C] 棘皮瘤 An acanthoma is a skin neoplasm composed of squamous or epidermal cells. It is located in the prickle cell layer. Types of acanthoma include pilar sheath acanthoma, a benign follicular tumor usually of the upper lip; clear cell acanthoma, a benign tumor found most frequently on the legs; and Degos acanthoma, often confused with but unrelated to Degos disease. Wikipedia

Prefix (Medical): acous(io)- Of or relating to hearing

Meaning in English: Of or relating to hearing

Origin language: Greek ἀκουστικός (acoustikos), of or for hearing

English examples:

acoustic 1 adjective UK /əˈkuː.stɪk/ US /əˈkuː.stɪk/ 声音的；听觉的 relating to sound or hearing

The microphone converts acoustic waves to electrical signals for transmission.

麦克风把声波转换成电信号进行传送。

acoustic 2 adjective （乐器）原声的，自然声的，不用电传音的 used to refer to a musical instrument that is not made louder by electrical equipment

an acoustic guitar 原声吉他

acoustic 3 noun [C usually plural] UK /əˈkuː.stɪk/ US /əˈkuː.stɪk/ （建筑物、房间的）传音效果，音响效果 the way in which the structure of a building or room affects the qualities of musical or spoken sound

The concert was recorded in a church that is famous for its acoustics.

这场音乐会是在一座以音响效果闻名的教堂内录制的。

acoumeter noun [C] (plural acoumeters) (physics) 听力测度计 An instrument for measuring the acuteness of the sense of hearing.

acoustician noun [C] 声学家 an expert in the branch of physics concerned with the properties of sound.

Prefix (Medical): acr(o)- extremity, topmost

Meaning in English: extremity, topmost；highest or farthest point

Origin language: Greek ἄκρον (akron), highest or farthest point

English examples:

Acrocranial   noun [U]Acrocranial is being pyramidal or pointed at the top with a breadth-height index of 98 or above.

acromegaly   noun [U]肢端肥大症 Acromegaly is a rare condition where the body produces too much growth hormone, causing body tissues and bones to grow more quickly. Over time, this leads to abnormally large hands and feet, and a wide range of other symptoms. Acromegaly is usually diagnosed in adults aged 30 to 50, but it can affect people of any age.

Acro-osteolysis   noun [U] 肢端骨质溶解 Acro-osteolysis is a radiographic finding which refers to bone resorption of the distal phalanges. Acro-osteolysis is associated with various conditions and its presence should prompt the clinician to search for the underlying etiology.

Prefix (Medical): ad- increase, adherence, motion toward, very

Meaning in English: increase, adherence, motion toward, very

Origin language: Latin

English examples:

adduct   verb [T] UK /əˈdʌkt/ US /əˈdʌkt/ specialized 内收（使身体的某一部分向身体中部或身体另一部分移动） to move a part of the body towards the middle of the body or towards another body part

The patient is unable to adduct her right eye. 患者右眼无法内收。

adduction   noun [U] UK /əˈdʌk.ʃən/ US /əˈdʌk.ʃən/ specialized 内收（使身体的某一部分向身体中部或身体另一部分移动） the movement of a part of the body towards the middle of the body or towards another body part

An abduction pillow is used to prevent adduction of the hip.   外展枕头被用来防止髋关节内收问题。

adductor   noun [C] UK /əˈdʌk.tər/ US /əˈdʌk.tɚ/ specialized 内收肌，内转肌（使身体的某一部分向身体中部或身体另一部分移动的肌肉，通常指

三种大腿肌）a muscle that moves a part of the body towards the middle of the body or towards another body part, often used to refer to the three large thigh muscles

When you move your leg toward the midline of the body, you are using adductor muscles. 当你将腿向身体中部移动时，使用的便是内收肌。

Prefix (Medical): aden(o)-, aden(i)- Of or relating to a gland

Meaning in English: Of or relating to a gland

Origin language: Ancient Greek ἀδήν, ἀδέν- (adēn, aden-), an acorn; a gland

English examples:

Adenocarcinoma　　　noun [U] 腺癌 (A-deh-noh-KAR-sih-NOH-muh) Cancer that forms in the glandular tissue, which lines certain internal organs and makes and releases substances in the body, such as mucus, digestive juices, and other fluids.

adenology　　　noun [U] 腺病学 the branch of medicine dealing with the development, structure, function, and diseases of glands.

adenotome　　　noun [U] 一种手术切除腺样体的器械 an instrument for the surgical excision of the adenoids.

adenine　　noun [U] UK　/ˈæd.ə.niːn/ US　/ˈæd.ən.iːn/ specialized 腺嘌呤 （存在于去氧核糖核酸和核糖核酸中的一种物质）　a substance that is found in DNA and RNA

adenoids　　noun [plural] UK　/ˈæd.ən.ɔɪdz/ US　/ˈæd.ən.ɔɪdz/腺样体，腺样增殖体 the soft mass of flesh between the back of the nose and the throat. Adenoids can sometimes become enlarged and make breathing difficult.

adenoma hyperplastic nodules　　　noun [plural] UK　/æd.ɪˌnəʊ.mə haɪ.pəˌplæs.tɪk ˈnɒdʒ.uːlz/ US　/æd.ənˈoʊ.mə ˌhaɪ.pɚˈplæs.tɪk ˈnɑː.djuːlz/ also

adenomatous nodules, hyperplastic nodules specialized 腺癌，增生性结节
（通常为良性） tumours that are formed by an unusual increase in thyroid
tissue. They are benign (= not likely to cause death).

Prefix (Medical): adip(o)- Of or relating to fat or fatty tissue
Meaning in English: Of or relating to fat or fatty tissue

Origin language: Latin (adeps, adip-), fat

English examples:

Adipocytes   noun [C] 脂肪細胞 Aipocytes, also known as lipocytes and
fat cells, are the cells that primarily compose adipose tissue, specialized in
storing energy as fat. Adipocytes are derived from mesenchymal stem cells
which give rise to adipocytes through adipogenesis. Wikipedia

adipose   adjective [before noun] UK   /ˈæd.ɪ.pəʊs/ /ˈæd.ɪ.pəʊz/ US
/ˈæd.ə.poʊs/ specialized 动物脂肪的 relating to animal fat

adipose tissue (= fat)   脂肪组织

Prefix (Medical): adren(o)- Of or relating to adrenal glands
Meaning in English: Of or relating to adrenal glands

Origin language: Latin

English examples:

adrenal   adjective UK   /əˈdriː.nəl/ US   /əˈdriː.nəl/ specialized 肾上的；肾
旁的；肾上腺的 used to refer to two glands situated above the kidneys (the
adrenal glands)

adrenal cortex   noun [C] UK   /əˌdriː.nəl ˈkɔː.teks/ US   /əˌdriː.nəl
ˈkɔːr.teks/ plural cortices UK   US   specialized 肾上腺皮质 the outer part of the
adrenal gland

adrenal gland   noun [C] UK /əˈdriː.nəl ˌɡlænd/ US /əˈdriː.nəl ˌɡlænd/ specialized 肾上腺（肾脏上方产生肾上腺素的一对腺体） one of a pair of glands that produce adrenalin, found just above the kidneys

adrenal medulla   noun [C] UK /əˌdriː.nəl medˈʌl.ə/ US /əˌdriː.nəl məˈdʌl.ə/ specialized 肾上腺髓质 the inner part of the adrenal gland that produces adrenaline

adrenalectomy   noun [C or U] UK /əˌdriː.nəlˈek.tə.mi/ US /əˌdriː.nəlˈek.tə.mi/ specialized 肾上腺切除（术） an operation to remove the adrenal gland, often because of a tumour

adrenalin   noun [U] also adrenaline UK /əˈdren.əl.ɪn/ US /əˈdren.əl.ɪn/肾上腺素 a hormone produced by the body, for example when you are frightened, angry, or excited, that makes the heart beat faster and prepares the body to react to danger

epinephrine   noun [U] UK /ˌep.ɪˈnef.rɪn/ US /ˌep.əˈnef.rɪn/ specialized 肾上腺素 a hormone that is made naturally in the body and may be given as a drug

adrenocortical   adjective UK /əˌdriː.nəˈkɔː.tɪ.kəl/ US /əˌdriː.noʊˈkɔr.tə.kəl/ specialized 肾上腺皮质的 relating to the adrenal cortex (= the outer part of the adrenal gland)

adrenoleukodystrophy noun [U] UK /əˌdriː.nə.luː.kəʊˈdɪs.trə.fi/ US /əˌdriː.noʊ.luː.koʊˈdɪs.trə.fi/ specialized 大脑白质退化症；肾上腺白质退化症；肾上腺脑白质营养不良 a rare genetic disease that increases the amount of a particular type of fatty acid in the brain and adrenal glands, affecting their normal activity

adrenal artery   noun [C] 肾上腺动脉 The adrenal arteries are arteries in the human abdomen that supply blood to the adrenal glands.

Prefix: aero- of the air or of air travel

Meaning in English: of the air or of air travel

Origin language: Anglo-Saxon/ Latin

English examples:

aero-   prefix UK /eə.rəʊ-/ US /er.oʊ-/空气的，空中的；航空的 of the air or of air travel

aerobatics noun [plural] UK /ˌeə.rəˈbæt.ɪks/ US /ˌer.oʊˈbæt̬.ɪks/特技飞行 skilful changes of position of an aircraft, such as flying upside down or in a circle

aerobics   noun [U] UK /eəˈrəʊ.bɪks/ US /erˈoʊ.bɪks/有氧健身法；有氧运动 energetic physical exercises, often performed with a group of people to music, that make the heart, lungs, and muscles stronger and increase the amount of oxygen in the blood

aerodrome noun [C] UK /ˈeə.rə.drəʊm/ US /ˈer.ə.droʊm/ uk 飞机场 old-fashioned for airfield

aerodynamic   adjective UK /ˌeə.rəʊ.daɪˈnæm.ɪk/ US /ˌer.oʊ.daɪˈnæm.ɪk/空气动力学的 relating to or using aerodynamics

aeronautics   noun [U] UK /ˌeə.rəˈnɔː.tɪks/ US /ˌer.əˈnɑː.t̬ɪks/ 航空学 the science of designing, building, and operating aircraft

aeroplane   noun [C] UK /ˈeə.rə.pleɪn/ US /ˈer.ə.pleɪn/ uk us airplane 飞机 A2 a vehicle designed for air travel that has wings and one or more engines

aerospace   adjective [before noun] UK   /ˈeə.rə.speɪs/ US /ˈer.oʊ.speɪs/航空航天工业的；航空航天器制造的 producing or operating aircraft or spacecraft

Aerosinusitis   noun [U] 气鼻窦炎 Aerosinusitis, also called barosinusitis, sinus squeeze or sinus barotrauma is a painful inflammation and sometimes bleeding of the membrane of the paranasal sinus cavities, normally the frontal sinus. It is caused by a difference in air pressures inside and outside the cavities

Aerotitis   中耳急性炎症 Aerotitis is an acute inflammation of the middle ear caused by the difference in air pressure between the airplane cabin and the middle-ear space.

Prefix (Medical): aesthesio- (BrE) sensation

Meaning in English: sensation

Origin language: Greek αἴσθησις

English examples:

anesthesia   noun [U] UK   /ˌæn.əsˈθiː.zi.ə/ /ˌæn.əsˈθiːʒə/ US /ˌæn.əsˈθiː.zi.ə/ /ˌæn.əsˈθiːʒə/（anaesthesia 的美式拼写 us spelling of anaesthesia（通常指被施用药物后的）麻醉状态 a state in which someone does not feel pain, usually because of drugs they have been given

anaesthesia 1 noun [U] mainly uk us usually anesthesia UK   /ˌæn.əsˈθiː.zi.ə/ /ˌæn.əsˈθiːʒə/ US /ˌæn.əsˈθiː.zi.ə/ /ˌæn.əsˈθiː.zi.ə/（通常指被施用药物后的）麻醉状态 a state in which someone does not feel pain, usually because of drugs they have been given

anesthesiology   noun [U] UK   /æn.əsˌθiː.ziˈɒl.ə.dʒi/ US /ˌæn.əsˌθiː.ziˈɑ ː.lə.dʒi/ us spelling of anaesthesiology（anaesthesiology 的美式拼写）麻醉学

anaesthetic noun [U or C] mainly uk us usually anesthetic UK /ˌæn.əsˈθet.ɪk/ US /ˌæn.əsˈθet̬.ɪk/ 麻醉剂 a substance that makes you unable to feel pain

Prefix: Afro- of or connected with Africa

Meaning in English: of or connected with Africa

Origin language: Anglo-Saxon/ Latin

English examples:

Afro- prefix UK /æf.rəʊ-/ US /æf.roʊ-/非洲的 of or connected with Africa

Afro-Caribbean culture　加勒比黑人文化

Afro-American literature 美国黑人文学

Prefix: after- coming after

Meaning in English: coming after

Origin language: Anglo-Saxon/ Latin

English examples:

after-　　6 prefix …之后的 UK /ɑːf.tər-/ US /æf.tɚ-/ coming after

an after-dinner speech　　　　宴会后的讲话

an after-hours club　　　　　深夜营业的夜总会

after-sales service　　　　　售后服务

afterbirth　　noun [S] UK /ˈɑːf.tə.bɜː θ/ US /ˈæf.tɚ.bɜː θ/胞衣；胎盘及羊膜 the material, including the placenta, that is pushed out of a woman's or female animal's body soon after she has given birth

aftercare　　noun [U] UK /ˈɑːf.tə.keər/ US /ˈæf.tɚ.ker/ （病人出院后的）护理；犯人出狱后的安置 the care of people after they have left a hospital or prison

aftereffect　　　noun [C usually pl] UK　/ˈɑː.f.tər.ɪˌfekt/ US /ˈæf.tɚ.əˌfekt/事后影响；余波；后遗症 an unpleasant effect that follows an event or accident, sometimes continuing for a long time or happening some time after it

头痛是这种事故的一种后遗症。　　Headaches are an aftereffect of this sort of accident.

afterlife　　　noun [S] UK　/ˈɑː.f.tə.laɪf/ US　/ˈæf.tɚ.laɪf/死后（灵魂）的生活 the life, for example in heaven, that some people believe begins after death

afternoon　　　noun [C or U] UK　/ˌɑː.f.təˈnuːn/ US　/ˌæf.tɚˈnuːn/下午，午后 A1 the period that starts at about twelve o'clock or after the meal in the middle of the day and ends at about six o'clock or when the sun goes down

aftershock　　　noun [C] UK　/ˈɑː.f.tə.ʃɒk/ US　/ˈæf.tɚ.ʃɑːk/（地震后的）余震 a sudden movement of the earth's surface that often follows an earthquake and is less violent than the first main movement

aftertaste　　　noun [C usually singular] UK　/ˈɑː.f.tə.teɪst/ US /ˈæf.tɚ.teɪst/（饮食等在口中留下的）后味，余味，回味 the taste that a particular food or other substance leaves in your mouth when you have swallowed it

afterthought　　　noun [C usually singular] UK　/ˈɑː.f.tə.θɔːt/ US /ˈæf.tɚ.θɑːt/事后想法；事后添加的事物 an idea, thought, or plan that was not originally intended but is thought of at a later time

afterwards　　　adverb UK　/ˈɑː.f.tə.wədz/ US　/ˈæf.tɚ.wɚdz/ mainly uk us usually afterward A2 过后，以后，后来 after the time mentioned

Meaning in English: Denoting a white or pale color

Origin language: Latin albus, white

English examples:

albino   noun [C] UK   /æl'biː.nəʊ/ US   /æl'baɪ.noʊ/ plural albinos 患白化病的人（或动物） a person or animal with white skin and hair and pink eyes

albinism   noun [U]   MEDICAL   specialized UK /'æl.bɪ.nɪ.zəm/ US /'æl.bɪ.nɪ.zəm/ 白化病 a condition in which a person or animal lacks pigment (= colour), so that they have white skin and hair and pink eyes

Meaning in English: pain

Origin language: Greek ἄλγος

English examples:

analgesic   noun [C] UK /ˌæn.əl'dʒiː.zɪk/ US /ˌæn.əl'dʒiː.zɪk/ Medical Specialized 止痛剂，镇痛药 a type of drug that stops you from feeling pain

Analgia   Noun [U] Medical Specialized (medicine) state of painlessness, absence of pain

Meaning in English: Denoting something as different, or as an addition

Origin language: Ancient Greek ἄλλος (allos), another, other

English examples

allopathy   noun [U] UK /ə'lɒp.ə.θi/ US /ə'lɑː.pə.θi/对抗疗法（针对症状进行直接对抗治疗） a name for conventional (= traditional and ordinary) medicine used by some followers of alternative medicine

allopathic adjective UK /ˌæl.əˈpæθ.ɪk/ US /ˌæl.əˈpæθ.ɪk/ 对抗疗法的 relating to traditional western medicine

Alloantigen noun [U] 同种异体抗原 a genetically determined antigen present in some but not all individuals of a species (as those of a particular blood group) and capable of inducing the production of an alloantibody by individuals which lack it. — called also isoantigen.

Alloantigen recognition noun [U] 同种异体抗原识别 Alloantigen recognition refers to immune system recognition of genetically encoded polymorphisms among the genetically distinguishable members of same species. Post-transplant recognition of alloantigens occurs in secondary lymphoid organs. Wikipedia

Prefix: all-"every", "every type of", or "the whole of"

Meaning in English: "every", "every type of", or "the whole of"

Origin language: Anglo-Saxon/ Latin

English examples:

all- 5 prefix UK /ɔːl-/ US /ɑːl-/ （用在很多名词前，构成形容词）每，各种，全部 used in front of many nouns to form adjectives meaning "every", "every type of", or "the whole of" that particular thing

an all-night bar (= a bar that is open for the whole night) 通宵营业的酒吧

all- 6 prefix （用在很多形容词和现在分词前）所有，任何 used in front of many adjectives and present participles to mean "everything" or "everyone"

an all-inclusive price 包括所有费用的价格

all-conquering armies 攻无不克的军队

all- 7 prefix （用在很多名词和形容词前）完全，十分 used in front of many nouns and adjectives to mean "completely"

纯棉短袜 all-cotton socks (= socks that are made completely of cotton)

When cooking the sauce, don't forget that all-important (= most or very important) ingredient, fresh basil.　做调味汁时，不要忘了加上最重要的配料——新鲜的罗勒。

Do you believe in an all-powerful god (= one with unlimited power)? 你相信存在一个全能的神吗？

all-American　1 adjective UK /ˌɔːl.əˈmer.ɪ.kən/ US /ˌɑːl.əˈmer.ɪ.kən/ (TYPICALLY AMERICAN) 典型美国式的；具有典型的美国理念的；为美国人所崇尚的 considered to be typical of the US, and respected and approved of by Americans

He was the perfect image of a clean-cut, all-American boy.　他代表了一个俊美的典型美国男孩的完美形象。

all-around adjective [before noun] UK /ˌɔːl.əˈraʊnd/ US /ˌɑːl.əˈraʊnd/ us 多才多艺的；全能的（同 all-round）used to say that a person has many different types of skills and abilities

all-round adjective [before noun] UK /ˌɔːlˈraʊnd/ US /ˌɑːlˈraʊnd/ uk us all-around 多才多艺的；全能的 used to say that a person has many different types of skills and abilities

She's a fantastic all-round sportswoman.　她是个非常了不起的全能运动员。

all-rounder　noun [C] UK /ˌɔːlˈraʊn.dər/ US /ˌɑːlˈraʊn.də/ uk 多才多艺的人，多面手；全才；通才 a person who has many different types of skills and abilities

all-consuming　adjective UK /ˌɔːl.kənˈsjuː.mɪŋ/ US /ˌɑːl.kənˈsuː.mɪŋ/ 耗尽时间（或精力）的；全身心投入的 taking almost all of your attention and time

all-in-one   1 adjective UK   /ˌɔːl.ɪnˈwʌn/ US   /ˌɑːl.ɪnˈwʌn/ 多用途的，多功能的；几合一的 doing the work of two or more usually separate parts

all-inclusive   adjective UK   /ˌɔːl.ɪnˈkluː.sɪv/ US   /ˌɑːl.ɪnˈkluː.sɪv/ 全部包括的，包括一切的 including everything

all-night   adjective [before noun] UK   /ˌɔːlˈnaɪt/ US   /ˌɑːlˈnaɪt/ 通宵，彻夜的 continuing all night

all-purpose   adjective [before noun] UK   /ɔːlˈpɜː.pəs/ US /ɑːlˈpɝː.pəs/ 通用的，多用途的 able to be used in many different ways or situations

all-seater   adjective [before noun] uk 每位观众都有座位的 in which every member of the crowd or audience sits on a seat, and none of them stand

all-singing   adjective UK   /ˌɔːlˈsɪŋ.ɪŋ/ US   /ˌɑːlˈsɪŋ.ɪŋ/ all-singing, all-dancing humorous （设备）先进的，现代的 An all-singing, all-dancing piece of equipment or system has a lot of advanced technical features, and therefore is able to do many things.

all-star   adjective [before noun] UK   /ˈɔːl.stɑːr/ US   /ˈɑːl.stɑːr/ 全明星的，众星云集的 having or including famous actors or players

an all-star baseball team   全明星棒球队

all-terrain vehicle   noun [C] UK   /ˌɔːl.tə.reɪn ˈvɪə.kəl/ US   /ˌɑːl.tə.reɪn ˈviː.ə.kəl/ abbreviation ATV 适合各种地形的车辆 a small vehicle with a seat and handlebars like a motorcycle but with three or four wheels, that can travel over very rough ground

all-time adjective [before noun] UK /ˌɔːlˈtaɪm/ US /ˌɑːlˈtaɪm/前所未有的，空前的 An all-time high, low, best, etc. is the highest, lowest, best, etc. level that has ever been.

all-wheel drive noun [C or U] UK /ˌɔːl.wiːl ˈdraɪv/ US /ˌɑːl.wiːl ˈdraɪv/ us 四轮驱动系统；四轮驱动车辆（前后四个车轮均有动力，即使在恶劣路面上也可行驶自如） a system in which a vehicle's engine supplies power to all its wheels instead of just to two, so that the vehicle can travel over very rough ground, or a vehicle that uses this system

all-you-can-eat 1 adjective [before noun] UK /ˌɔːl.jə.kənˈiːt/ US /ˌɑːl.jə.kənˈiːt/随意吃的，吃到饱的（一餐） used to describe a meal at a restaurant where people can serve themselves as much food as they want 2 随意用，无上限的（服务、下载量等） used to describe an arrangement in which a company allows customers to use a service as much as they like or to download as much as they like from the internet for a fixed amount of money

all/the four corners of the world/earth 四面八方，五湖四海；世界的各个角落 many different parts of the world

Prefix (Medical): ambi- Denoting something as positioned on both sides

Meaning in English: Denoting something as positioned on both sides; Describing both of two

Origin language: Latin (ambi-, ambo), both, on both sides

English examples:

ambidextrous adjective UK /ˌæm.bɪˈdek.strəs/ US /ˌæm.bɪˈdek.strəs/双手都很灵巧的；左右开弓的 able to use both hands equally well

ambidexterity 两手同利，或称双撇子 Ambidexterity is the ability to use both the right and left hand equally well. When referring to objects, the term indicates that the object is equally suitable for right-handed and left-handed people. When referring to humans, it indicates that a person has no marked preference for the use of the right or left hand.Wikipedia 两手同利，或称双撇子，指左右两手或左右两脚均善于日常活动，此类人比较罕见。

ambivalence　　noun [U] UK　/æmˈbɪv.ə.ləns/ US　/æmˈbɪv.ə.ləns/矛盾心理 the state of feeling of being ambivalent

ambivert　noun [C] /ˈæm.bɪ.vɜːt/ /-vɝːt/ specialized （兼具内向性格和外向性格特征的）綜向性格的人，中间性格的人 a person whose personality has features typical of both introverts and extroverts

Prefix (Medical): amnio- Pertaining to the membranous fetal sac (amnion)
Meaning in English:　Pertaining to the membranous fetal sac

Origin language: Greek ἄμνιον

English examples:

amnion　　noun [C] US　UK　/ˈæm.ni.ən/ plural amnions or amnia UK　/-ə/ US　specialized （哺乳动物、鸟类或爬行动物胎儿的）羊膜 a bag made of thin skin that contains amniotic fluid and surrounds the embryo of a mammal, bird, or reptile inside its mother

amniotic fluid　　noun [U] UK　/ˌæm.ni.ɒt.ɪkˈfluː.ɪd/ US　/- ɑː.t̬ɪkˈ-/ specialized 羊水（哺乳动物、鸟类或爬行动物羊膜中的液体）　the liquid that surrounds the embryo of a mammal, bird, or reptile

amniocentesis　　noun [U or S] UK　/ˌæm.ni.əʊ.senˈtiː.sɪs/ US /ˌæm.ni.oʊ.senˈtiː.sɪs/羊膜穿刺术（从孕妇腹中吸出液体检查胎儿健康状况）　a medical test in which a needle is used to remove a small amount of the liquid that surrounds a baby in the mother's womb in order to examine the baby's condition

Prefix (Medical): amph-, amphi- on both sides
Meaning in English: on both sides

Origin language: Greek ἀμφί (amphi)

English examples:

Amphicrania   noun [U] 两侧头痛 pain affecting both sides of the head — compare hemicrania.

Hemicrania   noun [U] 偏头痛 Hemicrania continua is a headache disorder. It causes constant pain in one side of the face and head. Unlike other headache disorders, environmental or lifestyle factors don't trigger hemicranial headaches. People may also have migraine-like symptoms, such as nausea or sensitivity to light.

amphismela   noun [U] 双刃解剖刀 An amphismela is an anatomical knife, edged on both sides. The term comes from the Greek α μ φ ι (utrinque, "on both sides"), and μ ε λ ι ζ ω (incido, "I cut")

amphomyci   noun [U] Amphomycin is an antibiotic with the molecular formula C58H91N13O20 which is produced by the bacterium Streptomyces canus

amphibian   noun [C] UK /æmˈfɪb.i.ən/ US /æmˈfɪb.i.ən/ [C] (ANIMAL) 两栖动物 an animal, such as a frog, that lives both on land and in water but must produce its eggs in water

amphibious   1 adjective UK /æmˈfɪb.i.əs/ US /æmˈfɪb.i.əs/（动物）水陆两栖的 of or relating to a type of animal that lives both on land and in water

Prefix (Medical): an- not, without

Meaning in English: not, without

Origin language: Greek

English examples:

Analgesics   noun [U] 止痛药 Analgesics (Analgesia) are medications that relieve pain. Unlike medications used for anesthesia during surgery, analgesics don't turn off nerves, change the ability to sense your surroundings or alter consciousness. They are sometimes called painkillers or pain relievers.

analgesic   noun [C] UK /ˌæn.əlˈdʒiː.zɪk/ US /ˌæn.əlˈdʒiː.zɪk/ Medical Specialized 止痛剂，镇痛药 a type of drug that stops you from feeling pain

Analgia   Noun [U] Medical Specialized (medicine) state of painlessness, absence of pain

Prefix (Medical): ana- back, again, up

Meaning in English: back, again, up

Origin language: Greek

English examples:

Anaplasia   noun [U] 逆行性生长 Anaplasia (from Ancient Greek: ἀνά ana, "backward" + πλάσις plasis, "formation") is a condition of cells with poor cellular differentiation, losing the morphological characteristics of mature cells and their orientation with respect to each other and to endothelial cells.

anaphylaxis   noun [U] UK /ˌæn.ə.fɪlˈæk.sɪs/ US /ˌæn.ə.fɪlˈæk.sɪs/ also anaphylactic shock, /ˌæn.ə.fɪlˌæk.tɪk ˈʃɒk/ /ˌæn.ə.fɪlˌæk.tɪk ˈʃɑːk/ specialized 过敏性反应 an extreme and dangerous allergic reaction to something that a person has eaten or touched

anaphase   noun [U or C] UK /ˈæn.ə.feɪz/ US /ˈæn.ə.feɪz/ 细胞分裂的后期 the stage during cell division in which the two sets of chromosomes divide and move apart

Meaning in English: pertaining to a man

Origin language: Greek ἀνήρ, ἀνδρ-

English examples:

Andrology noun [U]男科学 Andrology (from Ancient Greek: ἀνήρ, anēr, genitive ἀνδρός, andros, "man"; and -λογία, -logia) is a name for the medical specialty that deals with male health, particularly relating to the problems of the male reproductive system and urological problems that are unique to men. It is the counterpart to gynaecology, which deals with medical issues which are specific to female health, especially reproductive and urologic health. Wikipedia

android noun [C] UK /ˈæn.drɔɪd/ US /ˈæn.drɔɪd/仿真机器人 a robot (= machine controlled by computer) that is made to look like a human

androgynous 1 adjective UK /ænˈdrɒdʒ.ən.əs/ US /ænˈdrɑː.dʒən.əs/ 没有明显性别区分的；男女不分的；兼有两性特征的 not clearly male or female

伦诺克斯体型瘦削，头发剪得很短，那副中性模样倒也很时髦。 With her lean frame and cropped hair, Lennox had a fashionably androgynous look.

androgynous 2 adjective 雌雄同体的；雌雄同株的 specialized biology having both male and female features

Meaning in English: blood vessel

Origin language: Greek ἀγγεῖον

English examples:

Angiography Medical imaging；Angiography or arteriography is a medical imaging technique used to visualize the inside, or lumen, of blood vessels and organs of the body, with particular interest in the arteries, veins, and the heart chambers. Wikipedia

Angiogram An angiogram is a diagnostic procedure that uses imaging to show your provider how your blood flows through your blood vessels or heart. An injected contrast material makes it easy to see where blood is moving and where blockages are. Your provider can use X-rays or other types of imaging for your angiogram.

Prefix (Medical): angi(o)- blood vessel

Meaning in English: blood vessel

Origin language: Greek ἀγγεῖον

English examples:

Angiography   Medical imaging; Angiography or arteriography is a medical imaging technique used to visualize the inside, or lumen, of blood vessels and organs of the body, with particular interest in the arteries, veins, and the heart chambers. Wikipedia

Angiogram   An angiogram is a diagnostic procedure that uses imaging to show your provider how your blood flows through your blood vessels or heart. An injected contrast material makes it easy to see where blood is moving and where blockages are. Your provider can use X-rays or other types of imaging for your angiogram.

angina   noun [U] UK /ænˈdʒaɪ.nə/ US /ænˈdʒaɪ.nə/ also specialized angina pectoris, /ænˌdʒaɪ.nəˈpek.tə.rɪs/ 心绞痛 a condition that causes strong chest pains because blood containing oxygen is prevented from reaching the heart muscle by blocked arteries

angioma   noun [C] UK /ˌæn.dʒiˈəʊ.mə/ US /ˌæn.dʒiˈoʊ.mə/ specialized 血管瘤；淋巴管瘤 a benign (= not likely to cause death) tumour consisting of a mass of blood or lymph vessels

angioplasty   noun [U or C] UK /ˈæn.dʒi.əʊˌplæs.ti/ US /ˈæn.dʒi.oʊˌplæs.ti/ specialized 血管成形术 a medical operation to remove something blocking an artery (= thick tube carrying blood from the heart) in a person who has angina

angiosarcoma   noun [C or U] UK /ˌæn.dʒi.əʊ.s ɑ ːˈkəʊ.mə/ US /ˌæn.dʒi ̩oʊ.s ɑ ːrˈkoʊ.mə/ specialized 血管肉瘤 a tumour of the cells that line small blood vessels that is malignant (= is likely to lead to death if not treated)

Prefix (Medical): aniso- Describing something as unequal

Meaning in English: Describing something as unequal

Origin language: Ancient Greek ἄνῑσος (anīsos), unequal

English examples:

anisotropic   adjective PHYSICS   specialized /ˌæn.aɪ.səˈtrɒp.ɪk/ /ˌæn.aɪ.səˈtr ɑ ː.pɪk/ 各向异性的 Something that is anisotropic changes in size or in its physical properties according to the direction in which it is measured.

Anisocytosis   noun [U] 异红细胞增多症； 红血球大小不同 Anisocytosis is the medical term for having red blood cells (RBCs) that are unequal in size. Normally, a person's RBCs should all be roughly the same size. Anisocytosis is usually caused by another medical condition called anemia. It may also be caused other blood diseases or by certain drugs used to treat cancer.

Prefix: Anglo- relating to England or the UK

Anglo-   prefix UK /æŋ.gləʊ-/ US /æŋ.gloʊ-/ 英国的；英格兰的 relating to England or the UK

an Anglophile (= someone who loves England)   （热爱英国的）亲英派

Anglo-American   adjective UK /ˌæŋ.gləʊ.əˈmer.ɪ.kən/ US /ˌæŋ.gloʊ.əˈmer.ɪ.kən/ 英美的 used to refer to something involving the UK and US

an Anglo-American agreement   英美协议

Anglo-Indian   1 noun [C] UK   /ˌæŋ.gləʊˈɪn.di.ən/ US /ˌæŋ.gloʊˈɪn.di.ən/英印混血儿 a person with British and Indian parents or grandparents

Anglo-Saxon   1 adjective UK   /ˌæŋ.gləʊˈsæk.sən/ US /ˌæŋ.gloʊˈsæk.sən/盎格鲁-撒克逊人的 used to refer to the people who lived in England from about AD 600 and their language and customs 2 adjective 基于英国习俗的；受英国习俗影响的 used to describe modern societies that are based on or influenced by English customs

Prefix (Medical): ankyl(o)-, ancyl(o)- Denoting something as crooked or bent

Meaning in English: Denoting something as crooked or bent

Origin language: Ancient Greek ἀγκύλος (ankýlos), crooked, curved

English examples:

Ankylosis   noun [U] 关节僵硬 ankylosis, in medicine, stiffness of a joint as the result of injury or disease. The rigidity may be complete or partial and may be due to inflammation of the tendinous or muscular structures outside the joint or of the tissues of the joint itself.

Ankylosing spondylitis   强直性脊柱炎 Ankylosing spondylitis is an inflammatory disease that, over time, can cause some of the bones in the spine (vertebrae) to fuse. This fusing makes the spine less flexible and can result in a hunched posture.

Prefix: anthropo- (anthrop-) relating to humans

anthropo-   prefix UK   /æn.θrə.pə-/ US   /æn.θrə.pə-/ also anthrop- 人的；人类的 relating to humans

anthropocentric   adjective UK   /ˌæn.θrə.pəˈsen.trɪk/ US /ˌæn.θrə.pəˈsen.trɪk/ formal 人类中心说的 considering humans and their existence as the most important and central fact in the universe

anthropogenic   adjective UK /ˌæn.θrə.pəˈdʒen.ɪk/ US /ˌæn.θrə.pəˈdʒen.ɪk/ 由人类活动引起的，人为的 caused by humans or their activities

anthropoid   adjective [before noun] UK /ˈæn.θrə.pɔɪd/ US /ˈæn.θrə.pɔɪd/似人的，类人的；似猿的，类猿的 like a human being or an ape

anthropologist   noun [C] UK /ˌæn.θrəˈpɒl.ə.dʒɪst/ US /ˌæn.θrəˈpɑː.lə.dʒɪst/ 人类学家 someone who scientifically studies humans and their customs, beliefs, and relationships

anthropology   noun [U] UK /ˌæn.θrəˈpɒl.ə.dʒi/ US /ˌæn.θrəˈpɑː.lə.dʒi/ 人类学 the study of the human race, its culture and society, and its physical development

anthropomorphic   adjective UK /ˌæn.θrə.pəˈmɔː.fɪk/ US /ˌæn.θrə.pəˈmɔːr.fɪk/ 拟人化的；人格化的 treating animals, gods, or objects as if they are human in appearance, character, and behaviour:

anthropomorphism   noun [U] UK /ˌæn.θrə.pəˈmɔː.fɪ.zəm/ US /ˌæn.θrə.pəˈmɔːr.fɪ.zəm/ 拟人化，人格化；拟人观 the showing or treating of animals, gods, and objects as if they are human in appearance, character, or behaviour

The books "Alice in Wonderland", "Peter Rabbit", and "Winnie-the-Pooh" are classic examples of anthropomorphism.   像《爱丽斯漫游奇境记》、《兔子彼得》和《小熊维尼》这些书都是拟人创作手法的经典例子。

Prefix: ante- before or in front of
Meaning in English: in front of/before (Fun information – antepenultimate means next to the next to the last…this word can usually be found on the SAT.)

Origin language: Latin

English examples

ante- 2 prefix UK /æn.ti-/ US /ˈæn.t̬i-/ 在…前，在…前面 before or in front of

antebellum adjective [before noun] UK /ˌæn.tiˈbel.əm/ US /ˌæn.t̬əˈbel.əm/ mainly us 战前的；尤指美国南北战争之前的 relating to the time before a war, especially the American Civil War

antecedent 1 noun [C] UK /ˌæn.tiˈsiː.dənt/ US /ˌæn.t̬əˈsiː.dənt/（尤指作为后来存在或发生之事的起因或起源的）前事，前情，先例；祖先 formal someone or something existing or happening before, especially as the cause or origin of something existing or happening later

antechamber noun [C] UK /ˈæn.tiˌtʃeɪm.bər/ US /ˈæn.t̬iˌtʃeɪm.bɚ/ 前厅 an anteroom

antedate verb [T] UK /ˌæn.tiˈdeɪt/ US /ˈæn.t̬i.deɪt/ 早于…存在 formal for predate [GRE]

antegrade adjective MEDICAL specialized /ˈæn.ti.greɪd/ /ˈæn.t̬ə.greɪd/ 顺行的 used to describe a forward direction or movement, for example the normal flow of blood in the body

antenatal adjective [before noun] UK /ˌæn.tiˈneɪ.təl/ US /ˌæn.tiˈneɪ.t̬əl/ uk us prenatal 产前的；出生前的 relating to the medical care given to pregnant women before their babies are born

antenna 1 noun UK /ænˈten.ə/ US /ænˈten.ə/ (ORGAN) 触须，触角 [C] plural antennae UK /-iː/ US either of a pair of long, thin organs that are found on the heads of insects and crustaceans (= animals with hard outer shells) and are used to feel with 2 noun (NOTICING) 感觉；直觉 [C usually plural]

plural antennae or antennas the natural ability to notice things and understand their importance

anterior   1 adjective [before noun] UK   /ænˈtɪə.ri.ər/ US /ænˈtɪr.i.ɚ/ 前部的，前面的；向前的 specialized anatomy positioned at or towards the front

anteriorly   adverb UK   /ænˈtɪə.ri.ə.li/ US   /ænˈtɪr.i.ɚ.li/ specialized 身体前部的 towards the front of the body

anterius   adjective UK   /ænˈtɪə.ri.əs/ US   /ænˈtɪr.i.əs/ specialized (拉丁语，用于医学术语中)前 a Latin word meaning "front", used in medical names and descriptions

anteroom   noun [C] UK   /ˈæn.ti.ruːm/ /ˈæn.ti.rʊm/ US   /ˈæn.t̮i.ruːm/ /ˈæn.t̮i.rʊm/ also antechamber formal （通往较大、较重要房间的）前厅，接待室，候见室 a small room, especially a waiting room, that leads into a larger, more important room

Prefix (Medical): ante- Describing something as positioned in front of another thing

Meaning in English: Describing something as positioned in front of another thing

Origin language: Latin (āntē), before, in front of

English examples:

antepartum   产前 relating to the period before parturition

antebrachial   adjective UK   /æn.tiˈbreɪ.ki.əl/ US   /æn.tiˈbreɪ.ki.əl/ specialized 前臂的 relating to the forearm

the antebrachial vein   前臂静脉

antenatal   adjective [before noun] UK   /ˌæn.tiˈneɪ.təl/ US   /ˌæn.ti'neɪ.t̬əl/ uk us prenatal 产前的；出生前的 relating to the medical care given to pregnant women before their babies are born

antenatal care/classes   产前保健／学习班

the antenatal clinic   产前检查诊所

anterius   adjective UK   /ænˈtɪə.ri.əs/ US   /ænˈtɪr.i.əs/ specialized (拉丁语，用于医学术语中)前 a Latin word meaning "front", used in medical names and descriptions

anterolateral   adjective UK   /ˌæn.tə.rəʊˈlæt.ər.əl/ US /ˌæn.tə.roʊˈlæt̬.ɚ.əl/ specialized 前外侧的 in front of and to one side of another part of the body

Prefix: anti- opposed to or against
Meaning in English: opposite/ against

Origin language: Greek

English examples:

anti- 2 prefix UK   /æn.ti-/ US   /æn.t̬i/ /æn.taɪ-/ 反（对） opposed to or against

anti-abortion   adjective UK   /ˌæn.ti.əˈbɔː.ʃən/ US   /ˌæn.t̬i.əˈbɔːr.ʃən/ 反对堕胎的；反对流产的 supporting the belief that abortion (= the intentional ending of pregnancy) is morally wrong

anti-abortion activists/groups   反堕胎积极分子／团体

anti-ageing   adjective [before noun] uk us anti-aging UK /ˌæn.tiˈeɪ.dʒɪŋ/ US   /ˌæn.t̬iˈeɪ.dʒɪŋ/ 防衰老的 Anti-ageing substances are intended to prevent or limit the process of becoming old.

anti-ageing creams　　　　防衰老护肤霜

anti-aircraft　　　adjective UK　/ˌæn.tiˈeə.krɑːft/ US　/ˌæn.t̬iˈer.kræft/ 防空的
Anti-aircraft weapons, equipment, or activities are intended to destroy or defend against enemy aircraft.

an anti-aircraft missile/gun/weapon　　防空导弹 / 高射炮 / 防空武器

anti-aircraft defences/fire　　防空工事 / 炮火

anti-choice　　　adjective UK　/ˌæn.tiˈtʃɔɪs/ US　/ˌæn.t̬iˈtʃɔɪs/ disapproving 反对自由堕胎的 opposing the idea that a pregnant woman should have the freedom to choose an abortion (= the intentional ending of pregnancy)

the anti-choice lobby　　反对自由堕胎的游说团

anti-consumerist adjective UK　/ˌæn.ti.kənˈsjuː.mər.ɪst/ US
/ˌæn.t̬i.kənˈsuː.mɚ.ɪst/ 反消费主义的；反对过度消费的 opposed to the idea that people should be able to buy an unlimited amount of goods, and to the effect that such freedom has on the physical and social conditions in which people live

anti-federalist　　adjective UK　/ˌæn.tiˈfed.ər.əl.ist/ US　/ˌæn.t̬iˈfed.ɚ.əl.ist/ uk also mainly us anti-federal 反联邦主义的；反联邦制度的 opposed to a federalist system of government (= one in which power is divided between a central government and several local ones)

anti-federalist　　noun [C] UK　/ˌæn.tiˈfed.ər.əl.ist/ US
/ˌæn.t̬iˈfed.ɚ.əl.ist/ 反联邦主义者 someone who is opposed to a system of government in which power is divided between a single central government and several regional ones

Many voters are staunch anti-federalists.　　很多选民是坚定的反联邦主义者。

anti-football   noun [U] UK /ˈæn.tiˌfʊt.bɔːl/ US /ˈæn.tiˌfʊt.bɑːl/ 反足球（一种踢足球的风格，认为阻止对方球队进球比自己进球更重要。许多人认为这种风格不仅乏味而且有悖于比赛原则。）a style of playing football in which trying to prevent the opposing team from scoring is more important than scoring goals yourselves. Many people consider this style to be boring and against the principles of the game.

anti-inflammatory   1 adjective UK /ˌæn.ti.ɪnˈflæm.ə.tər.i/ US /ˌæn.tj.ɪnˈflæm.ə.tɔːr.i/ 消炎的，抗炎的；止痛消肿的 An anti-inflammatory drug is one that is used to reduce pain and swelling.

治疗关节炎的消炎药   anti-inflammatory drugs for arthritis

anti-inflammatory   2 noun [C] UK /ˌæn.ti.ɪnˈflæm.ə.tri/ US /ˌæn.tj.ɪnˈflæm.ə.tɔːr.i/ 止痛消炎药 an anti-inflammatory drug

Aspirin is an anti-inflammatory.

anti-life   adjective UK /ˌæn.tiˈlaɪf/ US /ˌæn.tjˈlaɪf/ disapproving 赞成堕胎的 supporting the idea that a pregnant woman should have the freedom to choose an abortion (= the intentional ending of pregnancy)

赞成堕胎的游说团体   the anti-life lobby

anti-lock   adjective [before noun] UK /ˌæn.tiˈlɒk/ US /ˌæn.tjˈlɑːk/（刹车装置）防抱死的 used to describe a type of brake that prevents the uncontrolled sliding of a vehicle by reducing the effects of braking suddenly

anti-noise   noun [U] UK /ˈæn.ti.nɔɪz/ US /ˈæn.tj.nɔɪz/（用于抵消有害噪声的）抗噪声 sound that is produced in such a way that it matches exactly and removes the effect of loud and possibly harmful noises, such as those produced by large engines in factories

anti-nuclear   adjective UK /ˌæn.tiˈnjuː.klɪər/ US /ˌæn.tjˈnuː.klɪr/ 反对生产和使用核武器的；反对使用核能的 opposed to the production and use of nuclear weapons, or to the production of electricity from nuclear power the anti-nuclear lobby/movement 反核游说团体 / 运动

anti-personnel adjective [before noun] UK /ˌæn.ti.pɜː.sənˈel/ US /ˌæn.t̬i.pɜː.sənˈel/（武器）用于杀伤人的；杀伤性的 Anti-personnel weapons are weapons that are intended to kill or injure people rather than damage weapons or buildings.

anti-personnel mines   杀伤性地雷

anti-racist   adjective UK /ˌæn.tiˈreɪ.sɪst/ US /ˌæn.t̬iˈreɪ.sɪst/ 反种族主义的；反对种族歧视的 opposed to the unfair treatment of people who belong to other races

反种族歧视立法 anti-racist legislation

anti-racist   noun [C] UK /ˌæn.tiˈreɪ.sɪst/ US /ˌæn.t̬iˈreɪ.sɪst/ 反种族主义者 an anti-racist person

anti-Semitic   adjective UK /ˌæn.ti.səˈmɪ.tɪk/ US /ˌæn.t̬i.səˈmɪ.tɪk/ 反犹太主义，排犹主义 having or showing a strong dislike of Jewish people, or treating them in a cruel and unfair way

anti-spam adjective [before noun] UK /ˌæn.tiˈspæm/ US /ˌæn.t̬iˈspæm/ 反垃圾邮件的 produced and used to prevent people sending and receiving unwanted emails, especially advertisements

anti-spam legislation/policies/resources/tools   反垃圾邮件立法 / 政策 / 资源 / 工具

anti-static adjective UK /ˌæn.tiˈstæt.ɪk/ US /ˌæn.t̬iˈstæt̬.ɪk/ 抗静电的 relating to devices or methods for preventing damage when electricity collects on the surface of objects

anti-tank   adjective [before noun] UK   /ˌæn.tiˈtæŋk/ US   /ˌæn.t̬iˈtæŋk/（武器）反坦克的 Anti-tank weapons are weapons that destroy or damage enemy tanks (= large military fighting vehicles).

反坦克导弹／火箭   anti-tank missiles/rockets

anti-terrorist   adjective UK   /ˌæn.tiˈter.ə.rɪst/ US   /ˌæn.t̬iˈter.ɚ.ɪst/反恐怖主义（活动）的 Anti-terrorist laws or activities are intended to prevent or reduce terrorism (= violent acts for political purposes).

Several governments have adopted tough new anti-terrorist legislation in the wake of the attacks.   袭击事件发生后，数国政府已经通过新的立法，严厉打击恐怖主义。

anti-virus   adjective [before noun] UK   /ˌæn.tiˈvaɪə.rəs/ US   /ˌæn.t̬iˈvaɪ.rəs/杀计算机病毒的 produced and used to protect the main memory of a computer against infection by a virus

anti-virus software/programs   杀毒软件／程序

an anti-virus company/product/package   计算机杀毒软件公司／产品／软件包

anti-war   adjective UK   /ˌæn.tiˈwɔːr/ US   /ˌæn.t̬iˈwɔːr/ 反战争的 opposed to a particular war or to all wars

反战抗议者 anti-war protestors

反战示威   an anti-war demonstration

antibacterial   adjective UK   /ˌæn.ti.bækˈtɪə.ri.əl/ US   /ˌæn.t̬i.bækˈtɪr.i.əl/（尤指用于皮肤）抗菌的，杀菌的 intended to kill or reduce the harmful effects of bacteria especially when used on the skin

抗菌洁面液 an antibacterial facial wash

antibiotic noun [C] UK /ˌæn.ti.baɪˈɒt.ɪk/ US /ˌæn.t̬i.baɪˈɑː.t̬ɪk/ 抗生素，抗菌素 C2 a medicine or chemical that can destroy harmful bacteria in the body or limit their growth

antibody noun [C] UK /ˈæn.tiˌbɒd.i/ US /ˈæn.t̬iˌbɑː.di/ 抗体 a protein produced in the blood that fights diseases by attacking and killing harmful bacteria

母乳中含有的抗体可保护新生婴儿免受感染。 Antibodies found in breast milk protect newborn babies against infection.

anticlimax noun [C or U] UK /ˌæn.tiˈklaɪ.mæks/ US /ˌæn.t̬iˈklaɪ.mæks/ 扫兴，扫兴的结局 an event or experience that causes disappointment because it is less exciting than was expected or because it happens immediately after a much more interesting or exciting event

anticlockwise adjective, adverb UK /ˌæn.tiˈklɒk.waɪz/ US /ˌæn.t̬iˈklɑːk.waɪz/ uk us counterclockwise 逆时针方向的（地） in the opposite direction to the movement of the hands of a clock

antidepressant 1 noun [C] UK /ˌæn.ti.dɪˈpres.ənt/ US /ˌæn.t̬i.dɪˈpres.ənt/ 抗抑郁药 a drug used to reduce feelings of sadness and worry

antidote 1 noun [C] UK /ˈæn.ti.dəʊt/ US /ˈæn.t̬i.doʊt/ 解毒剂；（尤指）解毒药 a chemical, especially a drug, that limits the effects of a poison 2 矫正方法；缓解办法；对抗手段 a way of preventing or acting against something bad

antifreeze noun [U] UK /ˈæn.ti.friːz/ US /ˈæn.t̬i.friːz/ 防冻剂，阻冻剂；抗凝剂；（尤指用于汽车散热器中的）防冻液 a liquid that is added to water in order to lower the temperature at which it freezes, used especially in car radiators (= cooling systems) in very cold weather

antigen   noun [C] UK   /ˈæn.tɪ.dʒən/ /ˈæn.tɪ.dʒen/ US   /ˈæn.t̬ɪ.dʒən/ /ˈæn.t̬ɪ.dʒen/ specialized 抗原 a substance that causes the production of antibodies in the body

antipathy   noun [C or U] UK   /ænˈtɪp.ə.θi/ US   /ænˈtɪp.ə.θi/ 憎恶，厌恶；反感 a feeling of strong dislike, opposition, or anger [GRE]

Antipsychotics   noun [U]   抗精神病药 Antipsychotics, also known as neuroleptics, are a class of psychotropic medication primarily used to manage psychosis, principally in schizophrenia but also in a range of other psychotic disorders. They are also the mainstay together with mood stabilizers in the treatment of bipolar disorder. Wikipedia

Prefix (Medical): aort(o)- aorta

Meaning in English: aorta

Origin language: Latin / Greek

English examples:

aorta noun [C] UK   /eɪˈɔː.tə/ US   /eɪˈɔːr.t̬ə/ 大动脉，主动脉 the main artery (= thick tube carrying blood from the heart) that takes blood to the other parts of the body

endaortitis. Noun [U]   动脉内膜炎 inflammation of the tunica intima of the aorta

aortic stenosis   1 noun [C or U] UK   /eɪˌɔː.tɪk stɪˈnəʊ.sɪs/ US   /eɪˌɔːr.t̬ɪk stəˈnoʊ.sɪs/ plural stenoses specialized 主动脉瓣狭窄 a narrowing of the heart valve that supplies the aorta (= the body's largest artery), reducing the blood flow to the aorta

He had been suffering from aortic stenosis and died of heart failure in his sleep.

他主动脉瓣狭窄，在睡梦中死于心脏衰竭。

aortic aneurysm noun [C] UK /eɪˌɔː.tɪk ˈæn.jə.rɪ.zəm/ US /eɪˌɔːr.t̬ɪk ˈæn.jɚ.ɪ.zəm/ specialized 主动脉瘤 a dangerous swelling of the wall of the aorta (= the body's largest artery)

Less than half the people with ruptured aortic aneurysms survive.

主动脉瘤破裂的病人只有不到一半的存活率。

aortic coarctation noun [U] UK /eɪˌɔː.tɪk kəʊ. ɑ ːkˈteɪ.ʃən/ US /eɪˈɔːr.t̬ɪk ˌkoʊ. ɑ ːrkˈteɪ.ʃən/ also coarctation of the aorta specialized 主动脉缩窄 a physical problem present from birth in which a part of the aorta (= the body's largest artery) is too narrow

With aortic coarctation, pulses in the arms are stronger than those in the legs.主动脉缩窄情况发生时，手臂脉搏比腿部的有力。

aortic root surgery noun [U or C] UK /eɪˌɔː.tɪk ˈruːt ˌsɜː.dʒər.i/ US /eɪˌɔːr.t̬ɪk ˈruːt ˌsɜː.dʒər.i/ specialized 主动脉根部瘤手术 an operation to treat an aortic aneurysm (= a dangerous swelling of the wall of the aorta) at a point where the aorta leaves the heart

aortic valve disease noun [C or U] UK /eɪˌɔː.tɪk ˈvælv dɪˌziːz/ US /eɪˈɔːr.t̬ɪk ˈvælv dɪˌziːz/ specialized 主动脉瓣疾病 a condition in which the valve between the heart and the aorta (= the body's largest artery) does not work properly

主动脉瓣疾病如不及时治疗可能引起心脏衰竭。　　　Untreated aortic valve disease can lead to heart failure.

valve-preserving aortic root repair noun [U] MEDICAL specialized UK /vælv.prɪˌzɜːv.ɪŋ eɪˌɔː.tɪk ˈruːt rɪˌpeər/ US /vælv.prɪˌzɜː.vɪŋ eɪˌɔːr.t̬ɪk ˈruːt rɪˌper/ 瓣膜保留主动脉根部重建 an operation to replace a section of the aorta (= the largest blood vessel) at a point where it leaves the heart, but keeping the heart valve

在瓣膜保留主动脉根部重建术中，一根人工血管支架被置入，取代主动脉受损的部分。 In valve-preserving aortic root repair an artificial graft is used to replace the damaged section of the aorta.

Prefix (Medical): apo- separated from, derived from

Meaning in English: separated from, derived from

Origin language: Ancient Greek ἀπό

English examples:

Apoptosis noun [U] 细胞凋亡 Apoptosis is a form of programmed cell death that occurs in multicellular organisms. Biochemical events lead to characteristic cell changes and death. These changes include blebbing, cell shrinkage, nuclear fragmentation, chromatin condensation, DNA fragmentation, and mRNA decay. Wikipedia

apoplectic adjective UK /ˌæp.əˈplek.tɪk/ US /ˌæp.əˈplek.tɪk/ 勃然大怒的；暴跳如雷的 extremely and obviously angry

apoplexy 1 noun [U] UK /ˈæp.ə.plek.si/ US /ˈæp.ə.plek.si/ [U] (ANGER) 勃然大怒 very great anger

apophatic adjective RELIGION specialized UK /ˌæp.əˈfæt.ɪk/ US /ˌæp.əˈfæt.ɪk/ （对有关上帝的）用否定方法所得的；用否定进路的 Apophatic theology involves defining or knowing God through negative statements.

apostasy noun [U] UK /əˈpɒs.tə.si/ US /əˈpɑː.stə.si/ formal 叛教；变节；脱党 the act of giving up your religious or political beliefs and leaving a religion or a political party

apostate noun [C] UK /əˈpɒs.teɪt/ US /əˈpɑː.steɪt/ formal 叛教者；变节者；脱党者 someone who has given up their religion or left a political party

Prefix: arch- most important

Meaning in English: most important

Origin language: Anglo-Saxon/ Latin

English examples:

arch- 7 prefix UK /ɑːtʃ-/ US /ɑːrtʃ-/ (MAIN) 主要的；最重要的 most important

an archbishop 　　　大主教

an archduke 　　　大公

archaic adjective UK /ɑːˈkeɪ.ɪk/ US /ɑːrˈkeɪ.ɪk/ 古老的，古代的；原始的 of or belonging to an ancient period in history

an archaic system of government 　　古老的政体

an archaic law/rule/language 　古代法律 / 法规 / 语言

archaism noun [C] UK /ɑːˈkeɪ.ɪ.zəm/ US /ɑːrˈkeɪ.ɪ.zəm/ specialized （一般不再使用的）古词，古语 a word or expression that is not generally used any more

archinephros noun [U] 原肾 The archinephros, or holonephros, is a primitive kidney that has been retained by the larvae of hagfish and some caecilians. A recent author has referred to this structure as "the hypothetical primitive kidney of ancestral vertebrates

Prefix: arch- greater or especially worse than others of the same type

Meaning in English: greater or especially worse than others of the same type

Origin language: Anglo-Saxon/ Latin

English examples:

arch- 8 prefix (EXTREME) 极度的；为首的；（尤指）极恶劣的 greater or especially worse than others of the same type

an arch-criminal 首犯

his arch-enemy 他的死敌

He's always been an arch-opponent of the project. 他一直是这个计划最强硬的反对者。

arch-enemy noun [C] UK /ˌɑːtʃˈen.ə.mi/ US /ˌɑːrtʃˈen.ə.mi/ 主要敌人；大敌；死敌 an especially bad enemy

arch-villain noun [C] UK /ˌɑːtʃˈvɪl.ən/ US /ˌɑːrtʃˈvɪl.ən/ 超级反派，大魔头 an especially bad villain (= an evil character in a story, film, etc.)

Prefix (Medical): arthr(o)- Of or pertaining to the joints, limbs
Meaning in English: Of or pertaining to the joints, limbs

Origin language: Ancient Greek αρθρος (arthros), a joint, limb

English examples:

arthritic 1 adjective UK /ɑːˈθrɪt.ɪk/ US /ɑːrˈθrɪt̬.ɪk/ 患有关节炎的 suffering from or affected by arthritis

arthritis noun [U] UK /ɑːˈθraɪ.tɪs/ US /ɑːrˈθraɪ.t̬əs/ 关节炎 a serious condition in which a person's joints (= the places where two bones are connected) become painful, swollen, and stiff

arthrodesis noun [U] UK /ɑːˈθrɒd.ə.sɪs/ US /ɑːrˈθrɑːd.ə.sɪs/ specialized 关节固定术，人为关节强硬术 the surgical process of joining together the bones of a joint to reduce pain or to help a patient who has problems walking

arthropod　noun [C] UK /ˈɑ:.θrə.pɒd/ US /ˈɑ:r.θrə.pɑ:d/ specialized 节肢动物（无脊椎动物，体外覆盖坚硬表皮，附肢的外骨骼具关节，身体成结状，比如蜘蛛，螃蟹或蚂蚁）a type of animal with no spine, a hard outer skin, legs with bones joined together, and a body divided into different parts, for example a spider, crab, or ant

arthroscopy　noun [C or U] UK /ɑ:ˈθrɒs.kə.pi/ US /ɑ:rˈθrɑ:s.kə.pi/ specialized 关节镜检查，关节内窥镜检查 a type of surgery in which a very small hole is made in a person's body in order to look at a joint using a special instrument and sometimes to repair the joint at the same time

arthrosis　noun [U]　MEDICAL　specialized UK /ɑ:ˈθrəʊ.sɪs/ US /ɑ:rˈθroʊ.sɪs/ 关节病 disease of the joints (= places where two bones join together)

arthrotomy　noun [C or U] UK /ɑ:ˈθrɒt.ə.mi/ US /ɑ:rˈθrɑ:t.ə.mi/ specialized 关节切开术 a surgical cut into a joint before performing an operation to replace the joint

Prefix (Medical): arteri(o)- Of or pertaining to an artery

Meaning in English: Of or pertaining to an artery

Origin language: Ancient Greek ἀρτηρία (artēría), a wind-pipe, artery (used distinctly versus a vein)

English examples:

arteria　noun [C] UK /ɑ:ˈtɪə.ri.ə/ US /ɑ:rˈtɪr.i.ə/ plural arteriae specialized (拉丁语) 动脉（用于医学术语中，复数形式为 arteriae) a Latin word meaning "artery", used in medical names and descriptions

arteriole　noun [C] UK /ɑ:ˈtɪə.ri.əʊl/ US /ɑ:rˈtɪr.iˌoʊl/ specialized 小动脉 a very small artery that often joins onto a capillary

arteriovenous malformation   noun 动静脉畸形 [C or U] UK
/ ɑ :.tɪə.ri.əʊˈviː.nəs mæl.fɔːˌmeɪ.ʃən/ US   / ɑ :rˌtɪr.i.oʊˈviː.nəs mæl.fɔːrˈmeɪ.ʃən/
abbreviation AVM specialized a condition present from birth in which there is
a problem with the connection between the arteries and veins in the brain,
causing blood from the arteries to flow directly into the veins without passing
through the capillaries

artery   1 noun [C] UK   /ˈ ɑ :.tər.i/ US   /ˈ ɑ :r.t̬ɚ.i/ [C] (IN BODY) 动
脉 one of the thick tubes that carry blood from the heart to other parts of the
body 2 noun [C] (ROUTE) 要道；干道；干线 an important road or railway
line

Prefix (Medical): articul(o)- joint

Meaning in English: joint

Origin language: Latin articulum

English examples:

articular   adjective UK   / ɑ :ˈtɪk.jə.lər/ US   / ɑ :ˈtɪk.jə.lɚ/ specialized 关节
的 relating to a joint (= a place in the body where two bones are connected)

articularis   combining form UK   / ɑ :ˌtɪk.jəˈl ɑ :.rɪs/ US
/ ɑ :rˌtɪk.jəˈler.ɪs/ also musculus articularis specialized （拉丁语）关节的（用
于与关节相连的肌肉名称中，如 articularis cubiti muscle"肘关节肌"）。
a Latin word meaning "articular ", used in the names of muscles that join with a
joint. For example, the articularis cubiti muscle is a muscle of the elbow.

articulate   1 adjective UK   / ɑ :ˈtɪk.jə.lət/ US   / ɑ :rˈtɪk.jə.lət/ 能表达
清楚的，善于表达的；口齿伶俐的，有口才的 able to express thoughts and
feelings easily and clearly, or showing this quality 4 verb [T] (FORM A
JOINT) 分成关节，结成关节 specialized medical to connect two bones by
forming a joint

articulation   1 noun UK /ɑ:ˌtɪk.jəˈleɪ.ʃən/ US /ɑ:rˌtɪk.jəˈleɪ.ʃən/ (PRONUNCIATION) 发音的方式 [U] the way in which you pronounce words or produce sounds 4 noun [C] 关节 the point where two bones connect to allow movement

Prefix: astro- relating to space, the planets, stars

Meaning in English: relating to space, the planets, stars

Origin language: Anglo-Saxon/ Latin

English examples:

astro-   prefix UK /æs.trəʊ-/ US /æs.troʊ-/ 星的；天体的；宇宙的；外层空间的；星形的 relating to space, the planets, stars, or other objects in space, or to a structure in the shape of a star

astrology   noun [U] UK /əˈstrɒl.ə.dʒi/ US /əˈstrɑː.lə.dʒi/ 占星术；占星学 the study of the movements and positions of the sun, moon, planets, and stars in the belief that they affect the character and lives of people

astronaut   noun [C] UK /ˈæs.trə.nɔːt/ US /ˈæs.trə.nɑːt/ 宇航员，航天员 a person who has been trained for travelling in space

astronautics   noun [U] UK /ˌæs.trəˈnɔː.tɪks/ US /ˌæs.trəˈnɑː.tɪks/ 航天学，宇宙航行学 the technology relating to space travel

astronomical   1 adjective UK /ˌæs.trəˈnɒm.ɪ.kəl/ US /ˌæs.trəˈnɑː.mɪ.kəl/ (SCIENTIFIC) 天文学的；天文的，天体的 [before noun] connected with astronomy

the Royal Astronomical Society   皇家天文学会

astronomical observations/instruments   天文观测 / 仪器

astronomical   2 adjective (LARGE) 极为巨大的；天文数字的 informal also astronomic, An astronomical amount is extremely large.

an astronomical rent/bill/price/fee 巨额租金／天文数字般的账单／天价／极高的收费

astronomically   1 adverb UK /ˌæs.trəˈnɒm.ɪ.kəl.i/ US /ˌæs.trəˈnɑː.mɪ.kəl.i/ 和天文学有关地 (SCIENTIFIC) in a way that is connected with astronomy

astronomy   noun [U] UK /əˈstrɒn.ə.mi/ US /əˈstrɑː.nə.mi/ C2 天文学 the scientific study of the universe and of objects that exist naturally in space, such as the moon, the sun, planets, and stars

astrophysics   noun [U] UK /ˌæs.trəʊˈfɪz.ɪks/ US /ˌæs.troʊˈfɪz.ɪks/ 天体物理学 the type of astronomy that uses physical laws and ideas to explain the behaviour of the stars and other objects in space

Prefix (Medical): atel(o) - imperfect or incomplete development

Meaning in English: imperfect or incomplete development

Origin language: Latin

English examples:

atelocardia   noun [U] imperfect development of the heart; An obsolete, nonspecific term for cardiac malformation; e.g., congenital heart disease.

Prefix (Medical): ather(o)- fatty deposit, Soft gruel-like deposit

Meaning in English: fatty deposit, Soft gruel-like deposit

Origin language: Latin

English examples:

atheroma   noun [C] UK   /ˌæθ.əˈrəʊ.mə/ US   /ˌæθ.əˈroʊ.mə/ plural atheromas or atheromata UK Medical Specialized /-tə/ US specialized 动脉粥样化，动脉粥状硬化斑块，粉瘤 a substance containing a lot of fat that forms on the inside wall of an artery and causes it to become hard or blocked；Atheroma is the medical term for the buildup of materials that adhere to arteries. Among others, these include: fat. cholesterol. calcium. (Root: ather- Meaning in English: gruel 粥)

atherogenic   adjective Medical Specialized /ˌaθərə(ʊ)ˈdʒɛnɪk/ PHYSIOLOGY 致动脉粥样硬化 tending to promote the formation of fatty deposits in the arteries.

Atherosclerosis   noun [U] Medical Specialized 动脉粥样硬化 Atherosclerosis is the buildup of fats, cholesterol and other substances in and on the artery walls. This buildup is called plaque. The plaque can cause arteries to narrow, blocking blood flow. The plaque can also burst, leading to a blood clot.

Prefix (Medical): atri(o)- an atrium (esp. heart atrium)

Meaning in English: an atrium (esp. heart atrium)

Origin language: Latin

English examples:

atrial   adjective /ˈeɪ.tri.əl/ specialized （心脏）前房的 relating to or happening in an atrium of the heart

atrial fibrillation   noun [U] UK   /ˌeɪ.tri.əl fɪb.rɪˈleɪ.ʃən/ US   /ˌeɪ.tri.əl ˌfɪb.rəˈleɪ.ʃən/ abbreviation AF specialized 心房颤动，心房纤颤 a problem in which the heart beats faster than normal and in a way that is not regular, resulting in the atria (= the top spaces) of the heart not emptying properly

atrial flutter   noun [U or C] UK   /ˌeɪ.tri.əl ˈflʌt.ər/ US   /ˌeɪ.tri.əl ˈflʌt̬.ɚ/ specialized 心房扑动 a problem in which the heart beats very fast and often in a way that is not regular, so that it does not send out blood effectively. Atrial flutter is often found with other types of heart disease and frequently develops into atrial fibrillation.

atrial septal defect   noun [C] UK /ˌeɪ.tri.əl ˈsep.təl diː.fekt/ US /ˌeɪ.tri.əl ˈsep.təl diː.fekt/ abbreviation ASD specialized 房间隔缺损，心房间隔缺损 a problem, present from birth, in which blood from the left atrium (= one of the top spaces) of the heart passes directly into the right atrium resulting in too much fluid in the right side of the heart and possible heart failure

atrioventricular   adjective UK /ˌeɪ.tri.əʊ.venˈtrɪk.jə.lər/ US /ˌeɪ.tri.oʊ.venˈtrɪk.jə.lɚ/ specialized 房室的（心房和心室的） relating to the connection between the atrium (= upper space) and ventricle (= lower space) of the heart

atrioventricular nodal reentrant tachycardia   noun [U] UK /ˌeɪ.tri.əʊ.venˌtrɪk.jə.lə ˌnəʊ.dəl riːˌen.trənt tæk.ɪˈk ɑ ː.di.ə/ US /ˌeɪ.tri.oʊ.venˌtrɪk.jə.lɚ ˌnoʊ.dəl riˌen.trənt tæk.ɪˈk ɑ ːr.di.ə/ abbreviation AVNT specialized 房室结折返性心动过速 an unusually fast heart rate caused by an extra electrical connection that forms through the AV node (= area of the heart that transmits electrical impulses)

atrium   1 noun [C] UK /ˈeɪ.tri.əm/ US /ˈeɪ.tri.əm/ plural atria or atriums [C] (ROOM) （尤指大商店或办公楼的）中庭，天井 a very large room, often with glass walls or roof, especially in the middle of a large shop or office building 2 noun [C] (HEART) 心房 specialized anatomy also auricle one of the two spaces at the top part of the heart that receive blood from the veins and push it down into the ventricles (= lower spaces)

Prefix: audio- relating to hearing or sound
Meaning in English: relating to hearing or sound

Origin language: Anglo-Saxon/ Latin

English examples:

audio- 2 prefix UK /ɔː.di.əʊ-/ US /ɑː.di.oʊ-/听力的，听觉的，声音的 relating to hearing or sound

audiobook noun [C] UK /ˈɔː.di.əʊ.bʊk/ US /ˈɑː.di.oʊ.bʊk/（配有光盘或网上录音资料的）有声读物 a recording, on a CD or made available on the internet, of a book being read aloud

audiology noun [U] UK /ˌɔː.diˈɒl.ə.dʒi/ US /ˌɑː.diˈɑː.lə.dʒi/ specialized 听力学 the area of science and medicine that is concerned with hearing and balance

audiovisual adjective [before noun] UK /ˌɔː.di.əʊˈvɪʒ.u.əl/ US /ˌɑː.di.oʊˈvɪʒ.u.əl/ abbreviation AV 视听的 used to refer to something that involves seeing and hearing

audiovisual equipment/aids/software 视听设备 / 辅助材料 / 软件

Prefix (Medical): aur(i)- Of or pertaining to the ear

Meaning in English: Of or pertaining to the ear

Origin language: Latin (auris), the ear

English examples:

aural adjective UK /ˈɔː.rəl/ US /ˈɔːr.əl/ 听力的，听觉的 relating to hearing

auricle 2 noun [C] (EARS) 耳廓 also pinna the part of the ear on the outside of the head

auricular 1 adjective UK /ɔːˈrɪk.jə.lər/ US /ɔːrˈɪk.jə.lə/ specialized (EARS) 耳（廓）的 relating to the external part of the ear

auricularis noun [C] UK /ˌɔː.rɪk.jəˈl ɑ ː.rɪs/ US /ɔːˌrɪk.jəˈler.ɪs/ plural auriculares specialized 耳肌 any of the three muscles that are attached to the external part of the ear and help to move the scalp or the external part of the ear itself

aurinasal 耳鼻的 relating to the ear and nose.

auscultate verb /ˈɔːskəlteɪt/ 听诊 examine a patient by listening to sounds from (the heart, lungs, or other organs), typically using a stethoscope.

Auscultation Auscultation is listening to the internal sounds of the body, usually using a stethoscope. Auscultation is performed for the purposes of examining the circulatory and respiratory systems, as well as the alimentary canal. The term was introduced by René Laennec. Wikipedia

Prefix: auto- of or by yourself, or operating independently

Meaning in English: self

Origin language: Greek

English examples:

auto- prefix UK /ɔː.təʊ-/ US /ɑː.t̬oʊ-/ 自己的；本身的；自己做的；自动的 of or by yourself, or operating independently and without needing help

an autofocus camera 自动聚焦照相机

an auto-immune disease 自身免疫疾病

autoimmune disease noun [C or U] UK /ɔː.təʊ.ɪˈmjuːn dɪˌzi:z/ US /ˌɔː.t̬oʊ.ɪˈmjuːn dɪˌzi:z/ specialized 自身免疫性疾病 a disease in which a person's immune system wrongly attacks its own healthy tissues

autoimmune liver disease noun [U] UK /ˌɔː.təʊ.ɪˈmjuːn ˈlɪ.və dɪˌziːz/ US /ˌɔː.t̬oʊ.ɪˈmjuːn ˈlɪv.ɚ dɪˌziːz/ specialized 自身免疫性肝病 a disease in which someone's immune system attacks their liver, making it swollen and painful and perhaps causing the person to develop hepatitis

autoimmune pancreatitis noun [U] UK /ˌɔː.təʊ.ɪˈmjuːn pæŋ.kri.əˈtaɪ.tɪs/ US /ˌɔː.t̬oʊ.ɪˈmjuːn ˌpæŋ.kri.əˈtaɪ.t̬əs/ specialized 自身免疫性胰腺炎 a condition in which someone's pancreas becomes swollen and painful, making them lose weight and develop jaundice (= a disease in which the skin turns yellow)

autograph 1 noun [C] UK /ˈɔː.tə.ɡrɑːf/ US /ˈɑː.t̬ə.ɡræf/（名人的）亲笔签名 a signature (= your name written by yourself), especially of a famous person

autoimmune adjective [before noun] UK /ˌɔː.təʊ.ɪˈmjuːn/ US /ˌɑː.t̬oʊ.ɪˈmjuːn/ specialized 自身免疫的 relating to a condition in which someone's antibodies attack substances that are naturally found in the body

One type of diabetes is an autoimmune disease/disorder that may be triggered by a virus. 有一类糖尿病可能是由一种病毒引起的自身免疫疾病／紊乱。

automat noun [C] UK /ˈɔː.tə.mæt/ US /ˈɑː.t̬ə.mæt/ us （用自动售货机出售食品的）自助餐馆 a restaurant where you buy food from boxes whose doors open when money is put in

automate verb [T] UK /ˈɔː.tə.meɪt/ US /ˈɑː.t̬ə-/ 使自动化 to make a process in a factory or office operate by machines or computers, in order to reduce the amount of work done by humans and the time taken to do the work

Massive investment is needed to automate the production process. 要实现生产过程的自动化需要大量的投资。

automatic   1 adjective UK   /ˌɔː.təˈmæt.ɪk/ US   /ˌɑː.t̬əˈmæt̬.ɪk/ (INDEPENDENT) B2 自动的；自动化的 An automatic machine or device is able to operate independently of human control.

automatic doors   自动门

an automatic rifle 自动步枪

automatic focus on a camera   照相机的自动调焦装置

automaton   noun [C] UK   /ɔːˈtɒm.ə.tən/ US   /ɑːˈtɑː.mə.tən/ plural automatons or automata UK   /-tə/ US 自动操作装置，机器人；机械行事的人 a machine that operates on its own without the need for human control, or a person who acts like a machine, without thinking or feeling

I take the same route to work every day, like some sort of automaton. 我每天按同一路线去上班，就像个机器人一样。

autonomy   1 noun [U] UK   /ɔːˈtɒn.ə.mi/ US   /ɑːˈtɑː.nə.mi/ 自治，自治权 the right of an organization, country, or region to be independent and govern itself

autonomous   1 adjective UK   /ɔːˈtɒn.ə.məs/ US   /ɑːˈtɑː.nə.məs/ 自主的，有自主权的 independent and having the power to make your own decisions

autopilot   noun [C or U] UK   /ˈɔː.təʊˌpaɪ.lət/ US   /ˈɑː.t̬oʊˌpaɪ.lət/ （飞机等的）自动驾驶仪 a device that keeps aircraft, spacecraft, and ships moving in a particular direction without human involvement

Prefix (Medical): aux(o)- increase; growth

Meaning in English: increase; growth

Origin language: Latin

English examples:

auxocardia   enlargement of the heart

Prefix (Medical): axill- Of or pertaining to the armpit

Meaning in English: Of or pertaining to the armpit

Origin language: Latin (axilla), armpit

English examples:

axilla noun [C] UK /ækˈsɪl.ə/ US /ækˈsɪl.ə/ plural axillae specialized 腋，腋窝 a technical word for the armpit (= the hollow place under your arm where your arm joins your body)

Prefix (Medical): azo(to)- nitrogenous compound

Meaning in English:

Origin language: Latin

English examples:

azothermia raised temperature due to nitrogenous substances in blood 血液中含氮物质导致体温升高

BBB

Prefix (Medical): balano- Of the glans penis or glans clitoridis

Meaning in English: Of the glans penis or glans clitoridis

Origin language: Greek βάλανος - balanos, acorn, glans

English examples:

Balanitis noun [U] 龟头炎 Balanitis is pain and inflammation (swelling and irritation) of the glans (head) of the penis that happens most often in uncircumcised males. Circumcision is a procedure performed to remove skin (the foreskin) from the head of the penis (the glans).

Prefix: bi- twice, or once every two

Meaning in English: twice, or once every two

Origin language: Anglo-Saxon/ Latin

English examples:

bi- 2 prefix UK /baɪ-/ US /baɪ-/ 两次；每…两次；两…一次 bi- prefix (TWICE) twice, or once every two

We meet bi-monthly (= twice every month or once every two months). 我们每月见两次面／两个月见一次面。

biannual adjective [before noun] UK /baɪˈæn.ju.əl/ US /baɪˈæn.ju.əl/ 一年两次的，一年两度的；半年一次的 happening twice a year

The committee has just published its biannual report. 委员会刚刚公布了半年报告。

bicentenary noun [C] uk UK /ˌbaɪ.senˈtiː.nər.i/ US /ˌbaɪ.senˈten.ɚ.i/ (us bicentennial, UK /ˌbaɪ.senˈten.i.əl/ /-sən-/) 200 周年；200 周年纪念日 the day or year that is 200 years after a particular event, especially an important one

A statue was erected to mark the bicentenary of the composer's birth. 们建了一尊塑像以纪念这位作曲家诞辰 200 周年。

bicentenary celebrations 200 周年庆祝活动

biennial 1 adjective UK /baɪˈen.i.əl/ US /baɪˈen.i.əl/两年一次的 happening once every two years 2 noun [C] UK /baɪˈen.i.əl/ US /baɪˈen.i.əl/（第二年开花的）两年生植物 a plant that lives for two years, producing seeds and flowers in its second year

Prefix: bi- having two
Meaning in English: two / having two

Origin language: Latin

English examples:

bi- 3 prefix (TWO) 双 having two

a biped (= an animal that walks on two legs)　两足动物

a biplane (= an old-fashioned aircraft with two wings)　双翼飞机

bicameral adjective politics specialized UK /ˌbaɪˈkæm.ər.əl/ US /ˌbaɪˈkæm.ɚ.əl/（政体）两院制的 (of a parliament, congress, etc.) having two parts, such as the Senate and the House of Representatives in the US

biceps noun [C] UK /ˈbaɪ.seps/ US /ˈbaɪ.seps/ plural biceps 肱二头肌 the large muscle at the front of the upper arm

bicipital 1 adjective anatomy specialized UK /baɪˈsɪp.ɪ.təl/ US /baɪˈsɪp.ɪ.təl/肱二头肌的 relating to the biceps muscle

bicycle noun [C] UK /ˈbaɪ.sɪ.kəl/ US /ˈbaɪ.sə.kəl/ A2 自行车，单车，脚踏车 a two-wheeled vehicle that you sit on and move by turning the two pedals (= flat parts you press with your feet)

binary adjective mathematics, computing, science specialized UK /ˈbaɪ.nər.i/ US /ˈbaɪ.nɚ.i/ 双的；由两部分组成的 consisting of two parts

binocular adjective science specialized UK /bɪˈnɒk.jʊ.lə/ US /-ˈnɑː.kjʊ.lɚ/ 同时用双目的；双目并用的 using both eyes to see things; made for use with both eyes

These fish have humanlike binocular vision. 这些鱼有类似人类的双目视力。

a binocular microscope　双目显微镜

binoculars   noun [plural] UK /bɪˈnɒk.jə.ləz/ US /bəˈnɑː.kjə.lɚz/双目镜，双筒望远镜 a pair of tubes with glass lenses at either end that you look through to see things far away more clearly

a pair of binoculars   一副双筒望远镜

binomial   1 noun [C] specialized UK /baɪˈnəʊ.mi.əl/ US /baɪˈnoʊ.mi.əl/ 二项式 mathematics an expression (= a mathematical statement) that has two terms (= numbers or symbols) that are not the same

Prefix: bio- connected with life and living things

Meaning in English: life

Origin language: Greek

English examples:

bio-   prefix UK /baɪ.əʊ-/ US /baɪ.oʊ-/ 生命的；生物的；生物学的 connected with life and living things

abiotic   adjective UK /ˌeɪ.baɪˈɒt.ɪk/ US /ˌeɪ.baɪˈɑː.t̬ɪk/与生物无关的；非生物的 relating to things in the environment that are not living

antibiotic   noun [C] UK /ˌæn.ti.baɪˈɒt.ɪk/ US /ˌæn.t̬i.baɪˈɑː.t̬ɪk/ 抗生素，抗菌素 C2 a medicine or chemical that can destroy harmful bacteria in the body or limit their growth

autobiography   1 noun UK /ˌɔː.tə.baɪˈɒg.rə.fi/ US /ˌɑː.t̬ə.baɪˈɑː.grə.fi/ 自传 [C] a book about a person's life, written by that person

biochemical   adjective UK /ˌbaɪ.əʊˈkem.ɪ.kəl/ US /ˌbaɪ.oʊˈkem.ɪ.kəl/ 生物化学的 connected with the chemistry of living things

biochemistry noun UK /ˌbaɪ.əʊˈkem.ɪ.stri/ US /ˌbaɪ.oʊˈkem.ɪ.stri/生物化学 [U] the scientific study of the chemistry of living things

bioclastic adjective geology specialized UK /ˌbaɪ.əʊˈklæs.tɪk/ US /ˌbaɪ.oʊˈklæs.tɪk/生物碎屑的 used to refer to a type of rock consisting of very small pieces of animals and plants

biodata noun [U] UK /ˈbaɪ.əʊˌdeɪ.tə/ US /ˈbaɪ.oʊˌdeɪ.t̬ə/（有关个人情况的）详细资料 details about someone's life, job, and achievements

biodefence noun [U] us biodefense UK /ˌbaɪ.əʊ.dɪˈfens/ US /ˌbaɪ.oʊ.dɪˈfens/生物武器防卫 the development and use of equipment and systems that protect against bioterrorism (= violent action using living matter, such as bacteria, to harm or kill people for political reasons)

bioenergy noun [U] UK /ˌbaɪ.əʊˈen.ə.dʒi/ US /ˌbaɪ.oʊˈen.ə.dʒi/生物质能，生物能源 energy that is produced from a biofuel (= a fuel that is made from living things or their waste)

biographer noun [C] UK /baɪˈɒg.rə.fər/ US /baɪˈɑː.grə.fɚ/传记作者 someone who writes the story of a particular person's life

biography noun [C or U] UK /baɪˈɒg.rə.fi/ US /baɪˈɑː.grə.fi/传记 B1 the life story of a person written by someone else

biologic adjective mainly us UK /ˌbaɪ.əˈlɒdʒ.ɪ.k/ US /ˌbaɪ.əˈlɑː.dʒ.ɪk/ → biological （同 biologic）

biological 1 adjective UK /ˌbaɪ.əˈlɒdʒ.ɪ.kəl/ US /ˌbaɪ.əˈlɑː.dʒɪ.kəl/ B2 生物的；与生命过程有关的 connected with the natural processes of living things the biological sciences   生物科学

biology   noun [U] UK /baɪˈɒl.ə.dʒi/ US /baɪˈɑː.lə.dʒi/ A2 生物学 the scientific study of the natural processes of living things

Prefix (Medical): blast(o)- germ or bud

Meaning in English: germ or bud

Origin language: Greek βλαστός

English examples:

Blastomere   noun [U] 卵裂球 In biology, a blastomere is a type of cell produced by cell division (cleavage) of the zygote after fertilization; blastomeres are an essential part of blastula formation.

blastula   blastula, hollow sphere of cells, or blastomeres, produced during the development of an embryo by repeated cleavage of a fertilized egg. The cells of the blastula form an epithelial (covering) layer, called the blastoderm, enclosing a fluid-filled cavity, the blastocoel.

Blastulation   noun [U] 囊胚 Blastulation is the stage in early animal embryonic development that produces the blastula. The blastula is a hollow sphere of cells known as blastomeres surrounding an inner fluid-filled cavity called the blastocoel. Wikipedia

Prefix (Medical): blephar(o)- Of or pertaining to the eyelid

Meaning in English: Of or pertaining to the eyelid

Origin language: Ancient Greek βλέφαρον (blépharon), eyelid

English examples:

Blepharoplast   noun [U] 眼睑 eyelid

Blepharoplast   noun [U] 基体，尤指有鞭毛的细胞 a basal body especially of a flagellated cell.

blepharospasm   noun [U] medical specialized UK /ˈblef.ə.rəʊˌspæz.əm/ US /ˈblef.ə.roʊˌspæz.əm/ （眼）睑痉挛 movement of the eyelid that cannot be controlled, where the eyelid closes tightly and makes sudden small movements

Prefix (Medical): brachi(o)- Of or relating to the arm

Meaning in English: Of or relating to the arm

Origin language: Latin (brachium), from Ancient Greek βραχίων (brachiōn), arm

English examples:

brachial   adjective anatomy specialized UK /ˈbreɪ.ki.əl/ US /ˈbreɪ.ki.əl/ 臂的，肱的 relating to the arm

brachial plexus injury   noun [C] medical specialized UK /ˌbreɪ.ki.əl ˈplek.səs ˌɪn.dʒər.i/ US /ˈbreɪ.ki.əl ˈplek.səs ˌɪn.dʒər.i/ 臂神经丛损伤 an injury in which the nerves that send out signals from the spine to the shoulder, arm, and hand are damaged

brachialis   noun [S] anatomy specialized UK /ˈbreɪ.ki.ə.lɪs/ US /ˌbreɪ.kiˈæl.ɪs/ 肱肌 a muscle of the upper arm that is used when bending the elbow

brachii   adjective anatomy specialized UK /ˈbreɪ.ki.aɪ/ US /ˈbreɪ.ki.aɪ/ （拉丁语）臂的，肱的 a Latin word meaning "of the arm", used in medical names and descriptions

brachiocephalic   adjective anatomy specialized UK /ˌbreɪ.ki.əʊ.səˈfæl.ɪk/ US /ˌbreɪ.ki.oʊ.səˈfæl.ɪk/ 头臂的，头肱的（用来指给头、颈和手臂输送血液的血管） relating to the arm and head, used when referring to blood vessels that supply blood to the head, neck, and arms

brachioradialis   noun [U] anatomy specialized UK /ˌbreɪ.ki.əʊˌreɪ.diˈ ɑ ːl.ɪs/ US /ˌbreɪ.ki.oʊˌreɪ.diˈæl.ɪs/ 肱桡肌 a muscle of the bottom part of the arm that helps to bend that part of the arm at the elbow

brachiosaurus   noun [C] UK /ˌbræk.i.əˈsɔː.rəs/ US /ˌbræk.i.əˈsɔːr.əs/ 腕龙（一种大型草食性恐龙，有四条腿，脖子和尾巴很长，头很小，前肢长于后肢）a very large plant-eating dinosaur with four legs, a very long neck and tail, and a small head. Its front legs were longer than its back legs.

Brachium of inferior colliculus   noun [U] 下丘臂 The brachium of the inferior colliculus is a pathway carrying fibers between the inferior colliculus and the ipsilateral medial geniculate body, which is located in the metathalamus, the caudal subpial portion of the thalamus.

brachium   noun [C] anatomy specialized UK /ˈbreɪ.ki.əm/ US /ˈbreɪ.ki.əm/臂，尤指肩至肘之间的上臂 plural brachia /ˈbreɪ.ki.ə/ US the arm, especially the upper arm from the shoulder to the elbow

臂状物   any body structure that looks like an arm

Prefix (Medical): brachy- Indicating 'short' or less commonly 'little'

Meaning in English: Indicating 'short' or less commonly 'little'

Origin language: Ancient Greek βραχύς (brachys), short, little, shallow

English examples:

brachytherapy   noun [C or U] medical specialized UK /bræk.iˈθe.rə.pi/ US /bræk.iˈθe.rə.pi/ 近距（放射）治疗 a treatment for cancer in which very small radioactive objects are put inside or near a tumour

Brachycephaly   Brachycephaly (derived from the Ancient Greek βραχύς, 'short' and κεφαλή, 'head') is the shape of a skull shorter than typical for its species. It is perceived as a desirable trait in some domesticated dog and cat breeds, notably the pug and Persian, and can be normal or abnormal in other animal species.

brachycephalic dogs   Brachy means shortened and cephalic means head. Therefore, brachycephalic dogs have skull bones that are shortened in length, giving the face and nose a pushed-in appearance. Due to the shorter bones of the face and nose, the anatomy and relationship with the other soft tissue structures are altered; some of these changes can cause physical problems for the affected dog.

Brachycephalic airway syndrome refers to a particular set of upper airway abnormalities that affect brachycephalic dogs. This syndrome is also called brachycephalic respiratory syndrome, brachycephalic syndrome, or congenital obstructive upper airway disease.

Prefix (Medical): brady- 'slow'

Meaning in English: slow

Origin language: Ancient Greek βραδύς (bradys), slow

English examples:

Bradykinesia   运动迟缓 Bradykinesia means slowness of movement and is one of the cardinal manifestations of Parkinson's disease. Weakness, tremor and rigidity may contribute to but do not fully explain bradykinesia.

bradycardia   noun bra·dy·car·dia | \ ˌbrā-di-ˈkär-dē-ə also ˌbra- \ r 心动过缓 elatively slow heart action. Bradycardia (brad-e-KAHR-dee-uh) is a slow heart rate. The hearts of adults at rest usually beat between 60 and 100 times a minute. If you have bradycardia, your heart beats fewer than 60 times a minute. — compare TACHYCARDIA

tachycardia   noun tachy·car·dia | \ ˌta-ki-ˈkär-dē-ə \ relatively rapid heart action whether physiological (as after exercise) or pathological; Tachycardia (tak-ih-KAHR-dee-uh) is the medical term for a heart rate over 100 beats a minute. Many types of irregular heart rhythms (arrhythmias) can cause tachycardia. A fast heart rate isn't always a concern. For instance, the heart rate typically rises during exercise or as a response to stress. — compare BRADYCARDIA

Meaning in English: bronchus

Origin language: Latin

English examples:

bronchial adjective UK /ˈbrɒŋ.ki.əl/ US /ˈbrɑːŋ.ki.əl/ 支气管的 of the pipes that carry air from the windpipe (= tube in the throat) to the lungs

bronchiole noun [C] anatomy specialized UK /ˈbrɒŋ.ki.əʊl/ US /ˈbrɑːŋ.ki.oʊl/ 细支气管 in the lungs, one of the very small tubes that branch out from the bronchi and connect to the alveoli (= little air bags)

bronchitis noun [U] UK /brɒŋˈkaɪ.tɪs/ US /brɑːŋˈkaɪ.t̬əs/ 支气管炎 an illness in which the bronchial tubes become infected and swollen, resulting in coughing and difficulty in breathing

bronchus noun [C] anatomy specialized UK /ˈbrɒŋ.kəs/ US /ˈbrɑːŋ.kəs/ plural bronchi UK /-kaɪ/ US 支气管 one of the two tubes that branch from the trachea (= tube that carries air from the throat to the lungs) and carry air into the lungs

Bronchiolitis obliterans noun [U] 闭塞性细支气管炎 Bronchiolitis obliterans (BO), also known as obliterative bronchiolitis, constrictive bronchiolitis and popcorn lung, is a disease that results in obstruction of the smallest airways of the lungs (bronchioles) due to inflammation. Symptoms include a dry cough, shortness of breath, wheezing and feeling tired. Wikipedia

Meaning in English: Of or pertaining to the cheek

Origin language: Latin (bucca), cheek

English examples:

buccal   adjective anatomy specialized UK /ˈbʌk.əl/ US /ˈbʌk.əl/面颊的，颊的 relating to the inside of the mouth, especially the cheek

Buccolabial adj. [bŭkʹ ō -lāʹ bē-əl] Relating to the cheek and the lip. Relating to the aspect of the dental arch or the surfaces of the teeth that are in contact with the mucosa of the lip and cheek.

buccolabial muscles   The facial muscles, also called craniofacial muscles, are a group of about 20 flat skeletal muscles lying underneath the skin of the face and scalp. Most of them originate from the bones or fibrous structures of the skull and radiate to insert on the skin.

Meaning in English: bursa (fluid sac between the bones)

Origin language: Latin

English examples:

bursa   noun [C] medical specialized UK /ˈbɜː.sə/ US /ˈbɝː.sə/ plural bursae 囊 a sac (= part of the body like a bag) that is filled with fluid and protects tissue from injury due to friction

bursitis   noun [U] medical specialized UK /bɜːˈsaɪ.tɪs/ US /bɝːˈsaɪ.t̬əs/ 滑囊炎，粘液囊炎 a condition in which the bursa (= sacs filled with fluid that protect tissue from injury due to friction) becomes swollen and painful

CCC

Meaning in English: Of or pertaining to hair

Origin language: Latin (capillus), hair

English examples:

capillary   noun [C] UK /kəˈpɪl.ər.i/ US /kəˈpɪl.ɚ.i/ specialized 毛细管；（尤指）毛细血管 a very thin tube, especially one of the smaller tubes that carry blood around the body

capillary telangiectasia   noun [U] UK /kəˌpɪl.ər.i tel.ændʒ.i.ekˈteɪ.ʒə/ US /ˈkæp.əˌler.i teˌlændʒ.i.ekˈteɪ.ʒə/ specialized 毛细血管扩张 a condition that produces raised dark red areas on the skin as a result of capillaries (= small blood vessels) being larger than normal

systemic capillary leak syndrome   noun [U]   MEDICAL specialized UK /sɪˌstem.ɪk keˌpɪl.ər.i ˈliːk ˌsɪn.drəʊm/ US /sɪˌstem.ɪk ˌkæp.əˌler.i ˈliːk ˌsɪn.droʊm/ (abbreviation SCLS); (Clarkson's disease) 系统性毛细管渗漏综合症 a rare condition where large amounts of blood begin to leak from blood vessels into the surrounding tissue, causing dangerously low blood pressure and sometimes organ failure and death

Clarkson's disease   noun [U] medical specialized UK /ˈklɑːk.sənz dɪˈziːz/ US /ˈklɑːrk.sənz dɪˌziːz/ (also systemic capillary leak syndrome) 毛细血管渗漏综合症，克拉克森综合症 a rare condition in which large amounts of blood flows from blood vessels into the surrounding tissue, causing dangerously low blood pressure and sometimes organ failure and death

Capillus   noun [U] hair

Capillus   Capillus Laser Therapy stimulates the follicle and helps reboot blood supply so hair can grow thicker and stronger.

Meaning in English: Pertaining to the head (as a whole)

Origin language: Latin (caput, capit-), the head

English examples:

capital   1 noun UK /ˈkæp.ɪ.təl/ US /ˈkæp.ə.t̬əl/ (CITY) 首都；首府；省会 A2 [C] a city that is the centre of government of a country or smaller political area

capitate   adjective anatomy specialized UK /ˈkæp.ɪ.teɪt/ US /ˈkæp.ə.ˌteɪt/（用于医学术语中）头状的 used in medical contexts to describe a body part that is shaped like a head

The end of the wrist bone is capitate, as it is rounded and larger than the rest. 腕骨末端呈头状，因为这里比其余部分大且圆。

capitation   noun [C or U] finance & economics specialized UK /ˌkæp.ɪˈteɪ.ʃən/ US /ˌkæp.əˈteɪ.ʃən/ 人头税；按人数均摊的费用 a tax, charge, or amount that is fixed at the same level for everyone

Doctors receive capitation of £33.85 per patient.   医生收到的均摊费用为每名病人 33.85 英镑。

capitis   adjective anatomy specialized UK /ˈkæp.ɪ.tɪs/ US /ˈkæp.ə.t̬ɪs/（拉丁语，用于命名一些连向头部的肌肉）头的 a Latin word meaning "of the head", used in the names of some muscles that are connected to the head

capitulum   1 noun [C] anatomy specialized UK /kəˈpɪtʃ.ə.ləm/ US /kəˈpɪtʃ.ə.ləm/ plural capitula （骨的）小头 the top part of a bone

Meaning in English: cancer

Origin language: Greek καρκίνος (karkinos), crab

English examples:

carcinogen   noun [C] UK   /kɑːˈsɪn.ə.dʒən/ US   /kɑːrˈsɪn.ə.dʒən/ 致癌物质 a substance that causes cancer

carcinogenesis   noun [U] medical specialized UK   /ˌkɑː.sɪn.əˈdʒen.ə.sɪs/ US   /ˌkɑːr.sə.nəˈdʒen.ə.sɪs/ 致癌过程 the process by which normal cells become cancer cells

carcinogenic   adjective UK   /ˌkɑː.sən.əˈdʒen.ɪk/ US /ˌkɑːr.sən.oʊˈdʒen.ɪk/ 致癌的 used to refer to a substance that causes cancer

carcinoid   noun [C] medical specialized UK   /ˈkɑː.sɪ.nɔɪd/ US /ˈkɑːr.səˌnɔɪd/ (also carcinoid tumour) 类癌 a type of small tumour that grows slowly and is most commonly found in the stomach or intestines. It can be benign (= harmless) or malignant (= likely to cause death if untreated)

carcinoma   noun [C] medical specialized UK   /kɑː.sɪˈnəʊ.mə/ US /kɑːr.səˈnoʊ.mə/ 癌；肿瘤 a cancerous growth that forms on or inside the body

Prefix: cardi- (cardio-) of the heart
Meaning in English: of the heart

Origin language: Anglo-Saxon/ Latin

English examples:

cardi-   prefix medical specialized UK   /kɑː.di-/ US   /kɑːr.di-/ → cardio- 心脏的；心脏病的（同 cardio-）

cardio-   prefix UK   /kɑː.di.əʊ-/ US   /kɑːr.di.oʊ-/ (also cardi-) 心脏的；心脏病的 of the heart

cardiac   adjective UK   /ˈkɑː.di.æk/ US   /ˈkɑːr.di.æk/ 心脏的；心脏病的 of the heart or heart disease

cardio   noun [U] informal UK   /ˈkɑː.di.əʊ/ US   /ˈkɑːr.di.oʊ/ 可提高心跳频率的运动；有氧运动 physical exercise that increases the rate at which your heart works

cardiograph   noun [C] medical specialized UK   /ˈkɑː.di.ə.grɑːf/ /ˈkɑː.di.ə.græf/ US   /ˈkɑːr.di.ə.græf/心电图仪 a machine for recording the beating of the heart

cardiography   noun [U] medical specialized UK   /ˌkɑː.diˈɒg.rə.fi/ US /ˌkɑːr.diˈɑː.grə.fi/ 心电图技术 the use of a machine to record the beating of the heart

cardiologist   noun [C] medical specialized UK   /ˌkɑː.diˈɒl.ə.dʒɪst/ US /ˌkɑːr.diˈɑː.lə.dʒɪst/ 心脏病专家 a doctor who specializes in treating diseases of the heart

cardiology   noun [U] UK   /ˌkɑː.diˈɒl.ə.gi/ US   /ˌkɑːr.diˈɑː.lə.gi/ 心脏病学 the study and treatment of medical conditions of the heart

cardiomyopathy   noun [U] medical specialized UK /ˌkɑː.di.əʊ.maɪˈɒp.ə.θi/ US   /ˌkɑːr.di.oʊ.maɪˈɑːp.ə.θi/心肌病 a disease in which the muscle of the heart is much thicker, bigger, or stiffer than normal

cardiopulmonary   adjective medical specialized UK /ˌkɑː.di.əʊˈpʊl.mə.nər.i/ US   /ˌkɑːr.di.oʊˈpʊl.mə.ner.i/ 心肺的 relating to the heart and lungs

cardiorespiratory   adjective medical specialized UK /ˌkɑː.di.əʊ.rɪˈspɪr.ə.tri/ US /ˌkɑːr.di.oʊˈres.pə.ə.tɔːr.i/ 心脏与呼吸的 relating to the heart, the lungs, and the tubes and muscles in the body used for breathing

cardiorespiratory fitness 心脏与呼吸的健康

cardiothoracic   adjective medical specialized UK /ˌkɑː.di.əʊ.θeˈræs.ɪk/ US /ˌkɑːr.di.ˌoʊ.θəˈræs.ɪk/心脏与胸腔的 relating to the heart and chest

cardiovascular   adjective medical specialized UK /ˌkɑː.di.əʊˈvæs.kjə.lər/ US /ˌkɑːr.di.oʊˈvæs.kjə.lɚ/ 心血管的 relating to the heart and blood vessels (= tubes that carry blood around the body)

cardioversion   noun [U] medical specialized UK /ˌkɑː.di.əˈvɜː.ʒən/ US /ˌkɑːr.di.oʊˈvɜː.ʒən/ 心律转变，心脏复律 a process in which electricity is used to make someone's heart beat regularly again after it has been beating too fast and not regularly. It is done under anaesthetic (= when the person has been given drugs to make them sleep and feel no pain).

Prefix (Medical): carp(o)- Of or pertaining to the wrist
Meaning in English: Of or pertaining to the wrist

Origin language: Latin (carpus) < Ancient Greek καρπός (karpós), wrist; NOTE: This root should not be confused with the mirror root carp(o)- meaning fruit.

English examples:

carpal   adjective anatomy specialized UK /ˈkɑː.pəl/ US /ˈkɑːr.pəl/ 腕的 relating to the carpus (= the wrist bones)

carpal bursitis   腕关节滑囊炎

carpal tunnel syndrome   noun [U] medical specialized UK /ˌkɑː.pəl ˈtʌn.əl ˌsɪn.drəʊm/ US /ˌkɑːr.pəl ˈtʌn.əl ˌsɪndroʊm/ 腕管综合征（腕部神经

受压引发的手部疼痛乏力）a medical condition of pain and weakness in the hand, caused by repeated pressure on a nerve in the wrist

Carpopedal adj. [kär′ pə-pĕd′ l] 腕足 Of, relating to, or involving the wrists and feet or the fingers and toes.

Prefix (Medical): cata- down, under

Meaning in English: down, under

Origin language: Greek κατά (kata)

English examples:

cataract 1 noun [C] UK /ˈkæt.ə.rækt/ US /ˈkæt̬.ə.rækt/ [C] (DISEASE) 白内障 a disease in which an area of someone's eye becomes less clear so that they cannot see clearly, or the area affected in this way 2 noun [C] (WATER FEATURE) 大瀑布 literary a large waterfall

catabolic adjective cat·a·bol·ic | \ ˌka-tə-ˈbä-lik \ 分解代谢 marked by or promoting metabolic activity concerned with the breakdown of complex molecules (such as proteins or lipids) and the release of energy within the organism : relating to, characterized by, or stimulating catabolism

Catabolism 分解代谢 Catabolism is the set of metabolic pathways that breaks down molecules into smaller units that are either oxidized to release energy or used in other anabolic reactions. Catabolism breaks down large molecules into smaller units. Wikipedia

cataclysm noun [C] literary UK /ˈkæt.ə.klɪ.zəm/ US /ˈkæt̬.ə.klɪ.zəm/ 剧变；大灾难；大变动 an event that causes a lot of destruction, or a sudden, violent change

catacomb   noun [C usually plural] UK   /ˈkæt.ə.kuːm/ US   /ˈkæt̬.ə.kuːm/ （旧时由纵横通道和若干房室构成的）地下墓穴 a series of underground passages and rooms where bodies were buried in the past

catalepsy   noun [U] UK   /ˈkæt.ə.lep.si/ US   /ˈkæt̬.ə.lep.si/ Medical Specialized 强直性昏厥；僵住症 a medical condition in which a person's body becomes stiff and stops moving, as if dead

cataleptic   adjective UK   /ˌkæt.əˈlep.tɪk/ US   /ˌkæt̬.əˈlep.tɪk/ 强直性昏厥的；僵住症 relating to or similar to catalepsy (= a medical condition in which a person's body becomes stiff and stops moving, as if dead):

catalyse   1 verb [T] uk (us catalyze) UK   /ˈkæt.əl.aɪz/ US   /ˈkæt̬.əl.aɪz/ 催化 chemistry specialized to make a chemical reaction happen or happen more quickly by acting as a catalyst

catalysis   noun [U] chemistry specialized UK   /kəˈtæl.ə.sɪs/ US /kəˈtæl.ə.sɪs/ 催化作用 the process of making a chemical reaction happen more quickly by using a catalyst

catalyst   1 noun [C] UK   /ˈkæt.əl.ɪst/ US   /ˈkæt̬.əl.ɪst/ 催化剂 chemistry specialized something that makes a chemical reaction happen more quickly without itself being changed

catapult   1 noun [C] UK   /ˈkæt.ə.pʌlt/ US   /ˈkæt̬.ə.pʌlt/ 投射器；石弩；弹射器 a device that can throw objects at a high speed

catastrophe   1 noun [C] UK   /kəˈtæs.trə.fi/ US   /kəˈtæs.trə.fi/ 大灾难；大灾祸 C2 a sudden event that causes very great trouble or destruction

catastrophic   adjective 1 UK /ˌkæt.əˈstrɒf.ɪk/ US /ˌkæt̬.əˈstrɑ:.fɪk/ 大灾难的；大灾祸的 causing sudden and very great harm or destruction:

catatonia   noun cat·a·to·nia | \ ˌka-tə-ˈtō-nē-ə \ 紧张症 a psychomotor disturbance that may involve muscle rigidity, stupor or mutism, purposeless movements, negativism, echolalia, and inappropriate or unusual posturing and is associated with various medical conditions (such as schizophrenia and mood disorders); 紧张性抑郁障碍 Catatonia is a group of symptoms that usually involve a lack of movement and communication, and also can include agitation, confusion, and restlessness. Until recently, it was thought of as a type of schizophrenia.; Catatonia is a complex neuropsychiatric behavioral syndrome that is characterized by abnormal movements, immobility, abnormal behaviors, and withdrawal. Wikipedia

catatonic   adjective UK /ˌkæt.əˈtɒn.ɪk/ US /ˌkæt̬.əˈtɑ:.nɪk/ 患紧张症的，患紧张性精神分裂症的 If someone is catatonic, they are stiff and not moving or reacting, as if dead.

Prefix: centi- 0.01 or one hundredth of the stated unit

Meaning in English: 100

Origin language: Latin

English examples:

centi-   prefix science UK /sen.tɪ-/ US /sen.t̬ə-/ 百分之一…；厘… 0.01 or one hundredth of the stated unit

centigrade   noun [U] adjective UK /ˈsen.tɪ.greɪd/ US /ˈsen.t̬ə.greɪd/ 摄氏温度 → Celsius 摄氏温度 (of) a measurement of temperature on a standard in which 0° is the temperature at which water freezes, and 100° the temperature at which it boils

centilitre   noun [C] uk (us centiliter) UK   /ˈsen.tiˌliː.tər/ US   /ˈsen.təˌliːtˌ/ (written abbreviation cl) 厘升 a unit of measurement of liquid equal to 0.01 of a litre

centimetre   noun [C] uk (us centimeter) UK   /ˈsen.tɪˌmiː.tər/ US /ˈsen.təˌmiː.tˌ/ (written abbreviation cm) 厘米，公分 A2 a unit of length equal to 0.01 of a metre

centipede   noun [C] UK   /ˈsen.tɪ.piːd/ US   /ˈsen.tə.piːd/ 蜈蚣，百足虫 a small, long, thin animal with many legs

centigram   noun [C] (uk also centigramme) UK   /ˈsen.tɪ.græm/ US /ˈsen.tə.græm/ 厘克 a unit of mass equal to 0.01 of a gram

Prefix (Medical): cephal(o)- Of or pertaining to the head (as a whole)

Meaning in English: Of or pertaining to the head (as a whole)

Origin language: Ancient Greek κεφαλή (képhalē), the head

English examples:

Cephalalgy   noun RARE•MEDICINE 头痛 a headache.

brachiocephalic   adjective anatomy specialized UK   /ˌbreɪ.ki.əʊ.səˈfæl.ɪk/ US /ˌbreɪ.ki.oʊ.səˈfæl.ɪk/ 头臂的，头肱的（用来指给头、颈和手臂输送血液的血管）relating to the arm and head, used when referring to blood vessels that supply blood to the head, neck, and arms

Brachycephaly   Brachycephaly (derived from the Ancient Greek βραχύς, 'short' and κεφαλή, 'head') is the shape of a skull shorter than typical for its species. It is perceived as a desirable trait in some domesticated dog and cat breeds, notably the pug and Persian, and can be normal or abnormal in other animal species.

brachycephalic dogs   Brachy means shortened and cephalic means head. Therefore, brachycephalic dogs have skull bones that are shortened in length, giving the face and nose a pushed-in appearance. Due to the shorter bones of the face and nose, the anatomy and relationship with the other soft tissue structures are altered; some of these changes can cause physical problems for the affected dog.

brachiocephalic   adjective UK /ˌbreɪ.ki.əʊ.səˈfæl.ɪk/ US /ˌbreɪ.ki.oʊ.səˈfæl.ɪk/ specialized 头臂的，头肱的（用来指给头、颈和手臂输送血液的血管） relating to the arm and head, used when referring to blood vessels that supply blood to the head, neck, and arms

cephalic   adjective medical specialized UK /sɪfˈæl.ɪk/ US /səˈfæl.ɪk/ 头的 relating to the head

cephalopod   noun [C] biology specialized UK /ˈsef.əl.əʊ.pɒd/ US /ˈsef.əl.ə.pɑːd/头足类动物（触须与头直接相连，如乌贼、章鱼） an animal such as an octopus or squid, that has tentacles (= long parts like arms) around the head

encephalitis   noun [U] MEDICAL specialized UK /ˌen.kef.əˈlaɪ.tɪs/ US /enˌsef.əˈlaɪ.təs/ 脑炎（一种严重疾病，由感染造成的大脑肿胀） a serious illness caused by an infection that makes the brain swell

encephalopathy   noun [C or U] MEDICAL specialized UK /ˌen.kef.əˈlɒp.ə.θi/ US /enˌsef.əˈlɑːp.ə.θi/ 脑病 inflammation affecting the surface of the brain that may be caused by infection or poisonous substances

encephalogram   noun en·ceph·a·lo·gram | \ in-ˈse-fə-lə-ˌgram \ an X-ray picture of the brain made by encephalography

hydrocephalus   noun [U]   MEDICAL   specialized UK /ˌhaɪ.drəˈsef.ə.ləs/ US /ˌhaɪ.drəˈsef.ə.ləs/ (also water on the brain) 脑积水 an abnormal increase in the amount of fluid in the skull that results in an increase in pressure inside the skull and an increase in the size of the head

myalgic encephalomyelitis   noun [U]   MEDICAL   UK specialized UK /maɪˌæl.dʒɪk enˌsef.ə.ləʊ.maɪ.əˈlaɪ.tɪs/ US /maɪˌæl.dʒɪk enˌsef.ə.loʊ.maɪ.əˈlaɪ.ţəs/ ➔ chronic fatigue syndrome 慢性疲劳综合征（同 chronic fatigue syndrome）(uk also ME); (abbreviation CFS) 慢性疲劳综合征 an illness, sometimes lasting for several years, in which a person's muscles and joints (= places where two bones are connected) hurt and they are generally very tired

plagiocephaly   斜头畸形 Deformational, or positional, plagiocephaly is when a baby develops a flat spot on one side of the head or the whole back of the head. It happens when a baby sleeps in the same position most of the time or because of problems with the neck muscles that result in a head-turning preference.

Prefix: cerebro- of or connected with the brain

Meaning in English: of or connected with the brain

Origin language: Anglo-Saxon/ Latin

English examples:

cerebro-   prefix medical specialized UK /ser.ɪ.brəʊ-/ US /sə.riː.broʊ-/ 脑 的 of or connected with the brain

cerebrospinal　　adjective medical specialized UK　/ˌser.ɪ.brəʊˈspaɪ.nəl/ US /səˌriː.broʊˈspaɪ.nəl/ 脑脊髓的 relating to both the brain and the spine

脑脊髓液　cerebrospinal fluid

cerebrovascular　adjective medical specialized UK　/ˌser.ɪ.brəʊˈvæs.kjə.lər/ US　/səˌriː.broʊˈvæs.kjə.lɚ/ 脑血管的 relating to the blood vessels, especially the arteries, that supply the brain

Passive smoking is considered a major cause of cerebrovascular disease, which causes strokes.　　吸二手烟被认为是造成脑血管病，导致中风的主要原因。

Prefix (Medical): cerat(o)- Of or pertaining to the cornu; a horn

Meaning in English: Of or pertaining to the cornu; a horn

Origin language: Ancient Greek κέρας, κερατ- (kéras, kerat-), a horn

English examples

Ceratoid　　adjective. having the shape or texture of animal horn.

Prefix (Medical): cerebell(o)- Of or pertaining to the cerebellum

Meaning in English: Of or pertaining to the cerebellum

Origin language: Latin (cerebellum), little brain

English examples:

cerebellar　　adjective medical specialized UK　/ˌser.ɪˈbel.ər/ US /ˌser.ɪˈbel.ɚ/ 小脑的 relating to the cerebellum (= the part of the brain that controls muscles, movement, and balance)

cerebellar ectopia　　　noun [U] medical specialized UK　/ser.ɪˌbel.ər ekˈtəʊ.pi.ə/ US　/ˌser.ɪˈbel.ɚ ekˈtoʊ.pi.ə/ 小脑外疝 a condition in which part of the cerebellum (= the part of the brain that controls muscles, movement, and balance) pushes through a hole in the base of the skull

cerebelli   adjective medical specialized UK /ˌser.ɪˈbel.i/ US /ˌser.ɪˈbel.i/
（拉丁语，用于医学术语中）小脑的 a Latin word meaning "of the cerebellum", used in medical names and descriptions

cerebellomedullary malformation syndrome   noun [U] medical specialized UK /ser.ɪˌbel.əʊ.medˌʌl.ər.i mæl.fɔːˈmeɪ.ʃən ˌsɪn.drəʊm/ US /ˌser.əˌbel.oʊ.meˈdʌl.ər.i ˌmæl.fɔːrˈmeɪ.ʃən ˌsɪn.droʊm/ (also Arnold-Chiari syndrome) 小脑髓质畸形综合症 a physical problem present from birth in which part of the brain is pushed through the opening for the spinal cord at the base of the skull, blocking the flow of fluid into the brain and spinal cord

cerebellum   noun [C] anatomy specialized UK /ˌser.əˈbel.əm/ US /ˌser.əˈbel.əm/ plural cerebella cerebellums 小脑（位于大脑的后方，控制肌肉，运动和保持平衡） a large part at the back of the brain that controls your muscles, movement, and balance

Prefix (Medical): cerebr(o)- Of or pertaining to the brain
Meaning in English: Of or pertaining to the brain

Origin language: Latin (cerebrum), brain

English examples:

cerebrology   noun [C] 脑科 The science that deals with the cerebrum or brain.

cerebral   1 adjective UK /ˈser.ə.brəl/ US /ˈser.ə.brəl/ 脑的，大脑的 medical specialized relating to the brain or the cerebrum 2 adjective 理智的；理性的 formal demanding or involving careful thinking and mental effort rather than feelings

cerebral cortex   noun [C] anatomy specialized UK /ˌser.ɪ.brəl ˈkɔː.teks/ US /ˌser.ɪ.brəl ˈkɔːr.teks/ 大脑皮层（大脑的灰色外层，多皱褶，管理语言、思维活动和创造性技能等） the grey outer layer of the cerebrum, responsible for language, thinking, creating new ideas, etc.

cerebral hemisphere   noun [C] anatomy specialized UK /ˌser.ɪ.brəl ˈhem.ɪ.sfɪər/ US /ˌser.ɪ.brəl ˈhem.ɪ.sfɪr/ 大脑半球（位于脑的前部，左右两边两个大脑半球分别控制对侧部分的身体） one of the two halves of the cerebrum, each of which controls the opposite side of the body

cerebral palsy   noun [U] US UK /ˌser.ə.brəlˈpɔːl.zi/ 大脑性麻痹；脑瘫 a physical condition involving permanent tightening of the muscles that is caused by damage to the brain around or before the time of birth

cerebration   1 noun [U] UK /ˌser.ɪˈbreɪ.ʃən/ US /ˌser.əˈbreɪ.ʃən/ 大脑的运作，用脑 medical specialized the operation of the brain 2 noun 思考，思考过程 formal the process of thinking

cerebro-   prefix medical specialized UK /ser.ɪ.brəʊ-/ US /sə.riː.broʊ-/ 脑的 of or connected with the brain

cerebrospinal   adjective medical specialized UK /ˌser.ɪ.brəʊˈspaɪ.nəl/ US /səˌriː.broʊˈspaɪ.nəl/ 脑脊髓的 relating to both the brain and the spine

脑脊髓液   cerebrospinal fluid

cerebrovascular   adjective medical specialized UK /ˌser.ɪ.brəʊˈvæs.kjə.lər/ US /səˌriː.broʊˈvæs.kjə.lɚ/ 脑血管的 relating to the blood vessels, especially the arteries, that supply the brain

cerebrum   noun [C] anatomy specialized UK /səˈriː.brəm/ US /səˈriː.brəm/ plural cerebra UK /-brə/ US cerebrums 大脑 the front part of the brain, that is involved with thought, decision, emotion, and character

Meaning in English: Of or pertaining to the neck, the cervix

Origin language: Latin (cervix, cervīc-), neck, cervix

English examples:

Cervicodorsal   noun [U] 颈背 (anatomy) Relating to the neck and the back.

cervical   1 adjective UK /səˈvaɪ.kəl/ US /ˈsɝː.vɪ.kəl/ 子宫颈的 relating to the cervix (= the narrow, lower part of the uterus) 2 adjective 颈椎的 medical specialized relating to the cervical vertebrae (= the bones in the neck)

cervical smear   noun [C] uk UK /səˌvaɪ.kəl ˈsmɪər/ US /ˌsɜr.vɪ.kəl ˈsmɪr/ (us Pap smear) 宫颈涂片检查（是否有癌变） a medical test in which some cells are taken from a woman's cervix (= the opening of her womb) and then tested to discover if she has cancer

cervicalis   adjective anatomy specialized UK /ˌsɜː.vɪˈkɑːl.ɪs/ US /ˌsɝː.vɪˈkæl.ɪs/ （拉丁语，用于命名一些颈部的神经和肌肉）颈的 a Latin word meaning "relating to the neck", used in the names of some nerves or muscles in the neck, for example the ansa cervicalis

cervicis   adjective anatomy specialized UK /ˈsɜː.vɪ.sɪs/ US /ˈsɝː.vɪ.sɪs/ （拉丁语，用于命名一些肌肉）颈的 a Latin word meaning "of the neck", used in the names of some muscles, for example the transversalis cervicis

cervix   noun [C] UK /ˈsɜː.vɪks/ US /ˈsɝː.vɪks/ plural cervices UK /-vɪs.iːz/ US 子宫颈 the narrow lower part of the womb that leads into the vagina

Meaning in English: chemistry, drug

Origin language: Greek χημεία

English examples:

chemotherapy   noun [U] UK   /ˌkiː.məʊˈθer.ə.pi/ US   /ˌkiː.moʊˈθer.ə.pi/ 化学疗法，化疗 the treatment of diseases using chemicals

化疗常用于治疗癌症。 Chemotherapy is often used in the treatment of cancer.

chems   noun [plural] slang UK   /kemz/ US   /kemz/ 毒品 drugs, often illegal ones, that are taken for enjoyment rather than for medical reasons

chemsex   noun [U] slang UK   /ˈkem.seks/ US   /ˈkem.seks/ （使用毒品寻求快感的）药物性爱 the use of drugs, often illegal ones, to increase pleasure during sex

Prefix (Medical): chir(o)-, cheir(o)- Of or pertaining to the hand

Meaning in English: Of or pertaining to the hand

Origin language: Ancient Greek χείρ, χειρο- (cheir, cheiro-), hand

English examples:

chiropractor   noun [C] UK   /ˈkaɪ.rəʊ.præk.tər/ US   /ˈkaɪ.roʊ.præk.tɚ/ 手疗法医师，按摩师；（尤指）脊椎指压治疗师 a person whose job is to treat diseases by pressing a person's joints (= places where two bones are connected), especially those in the back

chiral   手性 In chemistry, a molecule or ion is called chiral if it cannot be superposed on its mirror image by any combination of rotations, translations, and some conformational changes. This geometric property is called chirality. Wikipedia

Chiroptera 翼手目 The name "Chiroptera" is derived from Greek and literally means "hand wing" ("chiro" + "ptera"). Bats are mammals of the order Chiroptera. With their forelimbs adapted as wings, they are the only mammals capable of true and sustained flight.

Meaning in English: Of or pertaining to bile 胆汁

Origin language: Ancient Greek χολή (cholē), bile

English examples:

Cholemia   noun [U] 胆血症 Cholemia is a condition caused by the presence of excess bile in the blood. Its symptoms can include somnolence (drowsiness), yellow tinge to skin and whites of eyes, fatigue, nausea and, in extreme cases, coma. It is often an early sign of liver disease.

cholera   noun [U] UK /ˈkɒl.ər.ə/ US /ˈkɑː.lɚ.ə/ 霍乱 a serious infection of the bowels caused by drinking infected water or eating infected food, causing diarrhoea, vomiting, and often death

choleric   adjective formal UK /kɒlˈer.ɪk/ US /kəˈler.ɪk/ 暴怒的；易怒的，性情暴躁的 very angry or easily annoyed

cholesterol noun [U] chemistry, biology UK /kəˈles.tər.ɒl/ US /kəˈles.tə.rɑːl/ 胆固醇 C1 a substance containing a lot of fat that is found in the body tissue and blood of all animals, thought to be part of the cause of heart disease if there is too much of it

Meaning in English: Of or pertaining to the gallbladder

Origin language: Ancient Greek χοληκύστις (cholēkýstis), gallbladder < χολή (cholē), bile, gall + κύστις (kýstis), bladder

English examples:

Cholecystectomy noun [U] 胆囊切除术 Cholecystectomy is the surgical removal of the gallbladder. Cholecystectomy is a common treatment of symptomatic gallstones and other gallbladder conditions. In 2011, cholecystectomy was the eighth most common operating room procedure performed in hospitals in the United States. Wikipedia

---

Meaning in English: cartilage 软骨, gristle 软骨, granule 颗粒, granular 粒状

Origin language: Ancient Greek χονδρός (chondros)

English examples:

Chondrocalcinosis   noun [U] 软骨钙质沉积病, 又称为软骨钙化 Chondrocalcinosis, also known as calcium pyrophosphate deposition disease, is a rheumatic disease characterized by the excessive accumulation of calcium crystals in the cartilage of joints. The knee is the area that is most often affected by this disease, although it is also common in other joints and bone areas.

chondroid   adjective medical specialized UK   /ˈkɒn.drɔɪd/ US   /ˈkɑːn.drɔɪd/ 软骨样的 similar to cartilage

chondroid chordoma   noun [C or U] medical specialized UK   /ˌkɒn.drɔɪd kɔːˈdəʊ.mə/ US   /ˌkɑːn.drɔɪd kɔrˈdoʊ.mə/ 软骨样脊髓瘤 a rare type of bone tumour found in the brain that has some characteristics of bone tumours and some of cartilage tumours

chondrosarcoma   noun [C or U] medical specialized UK /ˌkɒn.drəʊ.sɑːˈkəʊ.mə/ US   /ˌkɑːn.droʊ.sɑːrˈkoʊ.mə/ 软骨肉瘤 a type of bone cancer that develops in the cartilage cells and usually affects the bones of the arms, legs, and pelvis and sometimes also the joints. It is malignant (= likely to cause death if not treated)

Meaning in English: color

Origin language: Ancient Greek χρῶμα

English examples:

Hemochromatosis   noun [U] 血色素沉着症 Hemochromatosis is a disorder in which extra iron builds up in the body to harmful levels. Without treatment, hemochromatosis can cause iron overload, a buildup of iron that can damage many parts of the body, including your liver, heart, pancreas, endocrine glands, and joints.

chromatid   noun [C] biology specialized UK   /ˈkrəʊmətɪd/ US   /ˈkroʊmətɪd/ 染色单体 either of the parts into which a chromosome divides during mitosis (= when one cell divides into two identical cells)

chromosomal   adjective UK   /ˌkrəʊ.məˈzəʊ.məl/ US   /ˌkroʊ.məˈsoʊ.məl/ 染色体的 medical specialized relating to chromosomes (= the parts of the cell that carry genetic information)

chromosome   noun [C] UK   /ˈkrəʊ.mə.səʊm/ US   /ˈkroʊ.mə.soʊm/ 染色体 any of the rod-like structures found in all living cells, containing the chemical patterns that control what an animal or plant is like

Prefix (Medical): cili- Of or pertaining to the cilia, the eyelashes; eyelids

Meaning in English: Of or pertaining to the cilia, the eyelashes; eyelids

Origin language: Latin (cilium), eyelash; eyelid

English examples:

ciliary   1 adjective medical, biology specialized UK   /ˈsɪl.i.ə.ri/ US /ˈsɪl.i.er.i/ 睫毛的 relating to the eyelashes 2 adjective 纤毛的 relating to cilia (= the very small parts like hairs on the surface of a cell that move regularly) 3 adjective 睫状体的 relating to the eye's ciliary body (= a circular structure behind the eye)

ciliary muscle   noun [C] anatomy specialized UK   /ˈsɪl.i.ə.ri ˌmʌs.əl/ US /ˈsɪl.i.er.i ˌmʌs.əl/ 睫状肌（晶状体周围的一块肌肉，作用是改变晶状体形状以获得清楚的映像） one of the muscles around the lens of the eye that can change the shape of the lens in order to produce a clear image

cilium   noun [C] biology specialized UK   /ˈsɪl.i.əm/ US   /ˈsɪl.i.əm/ plural cilia UK   /-ə/ US 纤毛（细胞表面上伸出的微小毛状突起，其有节律的运

动可产生其周围的液体移动，或帮助单细胞生物的移动） one of the very small parts like hairs on the surface of a cell that move regularly and keep the surrounding liquid moving around it or help an organism with only one cell to move

Prefix (Medical): cirrh- red-orange

Meaning in English:

Origin language: Latin / Greek

English examples:

cirrhosis   noun [U] UK /sɪˈrəʊ.sɪs/ US /səˈroʊ.sɪs/ 肝硬化 a serious disease of the liver that usually causes death

The commonest cause of cirrhosis is alcohol consumption.

引起肝硬化最常见的原因是饮酒。

cirrhosis of the liver   肝硬化

cirrocumulus   noun [U] environment specialized UK /ˌsɪr.əʊˈkjuː.mjə.ləs/ US /ˌsɪr.oʊˈkjuː.mjə.ləs/ 卷积云（一种稀薄的高空云，由一系列规则排列的白云堆积形成,底部扁平） a type of cumulus (= a tall, rounded, white cloud with a flat base) formed in a very thin layer and often in a regular pattern

Prefix (Medical): circum- Denoting something as 'around' another

Meaning in English: Denoting something as 'around' another

Origin language: Latin (circum), around

English examples:

circumcision   noun [C or U] UK /ˌsɜː.kəmˈsɪʒ.ən/ US /ˌsɝː.kəmˈsɪʒ.ən/ 包皮切除；割礼 the act of cutting the protecting loose skin off a boy's penis, for medical, traditional, or religious reasons, or an occasion when this is done

circumcise   verb [T] UK /ˈsɜː.kəm.saɪz/ US /ˈsɝː.kəm.saɪz/ （出于医疗、传统或宗教原因）割去（男孩的）包皮，对（男孩）行割礼；割除（女孩的）阴蒂 to cut the protecting loose skin off a boy's penis, for medical, traditional, or religious reasons

Prefix: co- together/with

Prefix: co-, con-, com-

Meaning in English: together/ with (Concrete – meaning to harden or to grow together)

Origin language: Latin

English examples:

co-   1 prefix UK /kəʊ-/ US /koʊ-/ 一起，共同 together; with

co-ownership   共同所有权

a co-writer/co-author   合著者

co-author   1 noun [C] UK /kəʊˈɔː.θer/ US /koʊˈɑː.θɚ/ （书、文章或报告等的）合著者 one of two or more people who write a book, article, report, etc. together 2 verb [T] UK /kəʊˈɔː.θer/ US /koʊˈɑː.θɚ/ 共同执笔，共同撰写，合著 to write a book, article, report, etc. together with another person or other people

co-brother   noun [C] indian english UK /ˈkəʊˌbrʌð.er/ US /ˈkoʊˌbrʌð.ɚ/ 自己妻子姐姐（或妹妹）的丈夫, 连襟 (YAO) the husband of your wife's sister

co-exist   verb [I] (also coexist) UK /ˌkəʊ.ɪgˈzɪst/ US /ˌkoʊ.ɪgˈzɪst/ 共生；共处；共存 to live or exist together at the same time or in the same place

co-opt   1 verb [T] UK /kəʊˈɒpt/ US /koʊˈɑːpt/ （指由现有成员）增选…为新成员，推举…为新成员 (of an elected group) to make someone a member through the choice of the present members 2 verb 强行拉进；拉拢，笼络 to include someone in something, often against their will 3 verb 借鉴，借用（别人的观点） to use someone else's ideas

co-parent　　　　1 verb [I or T]（尤指作为非亲生父母或不与小孩同住父母）共同承担抚养子女的义务 to be one of the people that takes responsibility for raising a child, especially when you are not the biological parent or you do not live with the child all of the time

co-pilot　　noun [C] UK　/ˈkəʊˌpaɪ.lət/ US　/ˈkoʊˌpaɪ.lət/（飞机的）副驾驶员 a pilot who helps the main pilot on an aircraft

co-star　　noun [C] UK　/ˈkəʊ.stɑːr/ US　/ˈkoʊ.stɑːr/ 合演者；联合主演者 a famous actor appearing with another famous actor in a film or a play, when both have parts of equal importance

co-worker　　　　noun [C] UK　/ˌkəʊˈwɜː.kər/ US　/ˌkoʊˈwɜː.kɚ/ 同事，同僚；（尤指）共同工作者，帮手 a person who you work with, especially someone with a similar job or level of responsibility

cooperate　　　　verb [I] (uk also co-operate) UK /kəʊˈɒp.ər.eɪt/ US /koʊˈɑː.pə.reɪt/ B2 合作，协作；配合 to act or work together for a particular purpose, or to be helpful by doing what someone asks you to do

cooperation　　　　noun [U] (uk also co-operation) UK /kəʊˌɒp.ərˈeɪ.ʃən/ US /koʊˌɑː.pəˈreɪ.ʃən/ B2 合作，协作；配合 the act of working together with someone or doing what they ask you

coordinate　　　　1 verb UK　/kəʊˈɔː.dɪ.neɪt/ US　/koʊˈɔːr.dən.eɪt/ (COMBINE) 协调；使相配合 [T] (uk also co-ordinate) to make many different things work effectively as a whole

coordinated　　　1 adjective UK　/kəʊˈɔ:.dɪ.neɪ.tɪd/ US　/koʊˈɔ:r.dən.eɪ.t̬ɪd/ (WELL ORGANIZED) 协调一致的 effectively organized so that all the parts work well together

coordination　　　1 noun [U] UK　/kəʊˌɔ:.dɪˈneɪ.ʃən/ US　/koʊˌɔ:r.dənˈeɪ.ʃən/ 协调，调节 the act of making all the people involved in a plan or activity work together in an organized way

Prefix: col- together; with

Meaning in English:

Origin language: Latin

English examples:

col-　　　prefix UK　/kɒl-/ US　/kɑ:l-/ 共；同；合 together; with

同事　colleagues

协作　collaborate

collaborate　　　1 verb [I] UK　/kəˈlæb.ə.reɪt/ US　/kəˈlæb.ə.reɪt/ [I] (WORK WITH) 合作；协作 C1 to work with someone else for a special purpose

collaborator　　　1 noun [C] UK　/kəˈlæb.ə.reɪ.tər/ US　/kəˈlæb.ə.reɪ.t̬ɚ/ [C] (ENEMY SUPPORTER) disapproving 通敌分子，卖国贼 a person who works with an enemy who has taken control of their country

collaboration　　　1 noun UK　/kəˌlæb.əˈreɪ.ʃən/ US　/kəˌlæb.əˈreɪ.ʃən/ (WORKING WITH) C1 合作；协作 [C or U] the situation of two or more people working together to create or achieve the same thing

collaborative adjective [before noun] UK /kəˈlæb.ər.ə.tɪv/ US /kəˈlæb.ɚ.ə.t̬ɪv/ 合作的；协作的 involving two or more people working together for a special purpose

collage noun [C or U] UK /ˈkɒl.ɑːʒ/ US /ˈkɑː.lɑːʒ/ 拼贴画；拼贴艺术 (the art of making) a picture in which various materials or objects, for example paper, cloth, or photographs, are stuck onto a larger surface

collapse 1 verb UK /kəˈlæps/ US /kəˈlæps/ (FALL) （由于压力、无力或缺乏支持而）倒塌，坍塌；崩溃，垮掉 B2 [I] to fall down suddenly because of pressure or having no strength or support

Prefix (Medical): colp(o)- Of or pertaining to the vagina

Meaning in English: Of or pertaining to the vagina

Origin language: Ancient Greek κόλπος (kólpos), bosom, womb; hollow, depth

English examples:

colposcopy noun [C or U] MEDICAL specialized /kɒl.pɒs.kə.pi/ /kɑːl.pɑː.skə.pi/ 阴道镜检查 a medical examination of the cervix (= the lower part of the womb that leads into the vagina) using a special instrument

If the results are positive, the patient will be sent for a colposcopy. 如果结果阳性，患者将会被送去做阴道镜检查。

Further evaluation is by colposcopy if required. 如果有要求的话，可进一步做阴道镜检查。

Prefix: com- together; with
Meaning in English:

Origin language: Latin

English examples:

com- prefix UK /kɒm-/ US /kɑːm-/ 共；同；合；公 together; with

combine   1 verb UK   /kəmˈbaɪn/ US   /kəmˈbaɪn/ （使）结合；（使）联合；（使）合并；（使）综合 B2 [I or T] to (cause to) exist together, or join together to make a single thing or group

combination   1 noun UK   /ˌkɒm.bɪˈneɪ.ʃən/ US   /ˌkɑːm.bəˈneɪ.ʃən/ 联合；混合；结合；综合 B2 [C or U] the mixture you get when two or more things are combined

commiserate   verb [I] UK   /kəˈmɪz.ə.reɪt/ US   /kəˈmɪz.ə.reɪt/ 表示同情（或惋惜） to express sympathy to someone about some bad luck [GRE]

committee   noun [C, + sing/pl verb] UK   /kəˈmɪt.i/ US   /kəˈmɪt̬.i/（代表较大的组织决策或搜集信息的）委员会 B2 a small group of people chosen to represent a larger organization and either make decisions or collect information for it

commotion   noun [S or U] UK   /kəˈməʊ.ʃən/ US   /kəˈmoʊ.ʃən/ 喧闹；喧嚣；混乱；骚动 a sudden, short period of noise, confusion, or excited movement [GRE]

communicate   1 verb UK   /kəˈmjuː.nɪ.keɪt/ US   /kəˈmjuː.nə.keɪt/ (SHARE INFORMATION) 交流，沟通（信息） B1 [I or T] to share information with others by speaking, writing, moving your body, or using other signals

communication   1 noun UK   /kəˌmjuː.nɪˈkeɪ.ʃən/ US   /kəˌmjuː.nəˈkeɪ.ʃən/ B1 交流；沟通；交际；传达；传播；通讯 [U] the act of communicating with people

Prefix: con- together; with

Meaning in English:

Origin language: Latin

English examples:

con-　　　5 prefix UK　/kɒn-/ US　/kɑːn-/共；与同 together; with

共谋　conspiracy

财团　consortium

concatenate　　　verb [T] computing formal or specialized UK /kənˈkæt.ə.neɪt/ US　/kənˈkæt̬.ə.neɪt/ 使连接,使连锁，把…连成一串 to put things together as a connected series [GRE]

concatenation　　　noun [C] formal UK　/kənˈkæt.ə.neɪ.ʃən/ US /kənˈkæt̬.ə.neɪ.ʃən/ 一连串有关联的事件、想法或事物 a series of events, ideas, or things that are connected [GRE]

concede　　　1 verb UK　/kənˈsiːd/ US　/kənˈsiːd/ (ADMIT) （常指不情愿地）承认 C2 [T] to admit, often unwillingly, that something is true

concentric　　　adjective UK　/kənˈsen.trɪk/ US　/kənˈsen.trɪk/ （指圆）同心的，同轴的 Concentric circles and rings have the same centre.

concentration camp　　　noun [C] UK　/kɒn.sənˈtreɪ.ʃən ˌkæmp/ US /kɑːn.sənˈtreɪ.ʃən ˌkæmp/ 集中营 a place where large numbers of people are kept as prisoners in extremely bad conditions, especially for political reasons

concrete　　　noun /ˌkɒŋ.kriːt ˈnaʊn/ US　/ˌkɑːn.kriːt ˈnaʊn/ 具体名词，实义名词 a noun that refers to a real physical object [GRE]

concrete   1 noun [U] UK /ˈkɒŋ.kriːt/ US /ˈkɑːn.kriːt/ 混凝土 B2 a very hard building material made by mixing together cement, sand, small stones, and water

Prefix: contra- against or opposite

Meaning in English: against or opposite

Origin language: Anglo-Saxon/ Latin

English examples:

contra-   prefix UK /kɒn.trə-/ US /kɑːn.trə-/ 与…相反；反对；对抗 against or opposite

contraband   noun [U] UK /ˈkɒn.trə.bænd/ US /ˈkɑːn.trə.bænd/ 违禁品；走私货 goods that are brought into or taken out of the country secretly and illegally

contraception   1 noun [U] UK /ˌkɒn.trəˈsep.ʃən/ US /ˌkɑːn.trəˈsep.ʃən/ C2 避孕（法）；节育（法）(the use of) any of various methods intended to prevent a woman becoming pregnant

contradict   verb [I or T] UK /ˌkɒn.trəˈdɪkt/ US /ˌkɑːn.trəˈdɪkt/ 反驳，否定；（事实或声明）（与…）相矛盾，（与…）有抵触 C1 (of people) to say the opposite of what someone else has said, or (of one fact or statement) to be so different from another fact or statement that one of them must be wrong [GRE]

contradiction   noun [C or U] UK /ˌkɒn.trəˈdɪk.ʃən/ US /ˌkɑːn.trəˈdɪk.ʃən/ C2 矛盾 the fact of something being the complete opposite of something else or very different from something else, so that one of them must be wrong

contradictory   adjective UK /ˌkɒn.trəˈdɪk.tər.i/ US /ˌkɑːn.trəˈdɪk.tɚ.i/ 对立的；相互矛盾的；不一致的 C2 If two or more facts, pieces of advice, etc. are contradictory, they are very different from each other.

contraflow   noun [C] mainly uk UK /ˈkɒn.trə.fləʊ/ US /ˈkɑːn.trə.floʊ/（由于公路另一侧修缮而暂时实行的）一侧双向行驶 a temporary traffic arrangement, usually on a main road, in which traffic travelling in both directions uses one side of the road while the other side is being repaired

contrast   1 noun [C or U] UK /ˈkɒn.trɑːst/ US /ˈkɑːn.træst/ B2 差别，差异；对照，对比 an obvious difference between two or more things

contravene   verb [T] formal UK /ˌkɒn.trəˈviːn/ US /ˌkɑːn.trəˈviːn/违反，违犯（法律或规则） to do something that a law or rule does not allow, or to break a law or rule [GRE]

Prefix: cor- together; with

Meaning in English: together; with

Origin language: Anglo-Saxon/ Latin

English examples:

cor-   prefix UK /kər-/ US /kɚ-/ 一起，共同，与...一起 together; with

corral   3 verb 把（一群人）集中起来（尤指控制起来）to bring a group of people together and keep them in one place, especially in order to control them

correlate   verb [I or T] UK /ˈkɒr.ə.leɪt/ US /ˈkɔːr.ə.leɪt/ 相互关系；联系；相关 If two or more facts, numbers, etc. correlate or are correlated, there is a relationship between them. [GRE]

correspond   1 verb [I] UK /ˌkɒr.ɪˈspɒnd/ US /ˌkɔːr.əˈspɑːnd/ [I] (MATCH) 相称；相类似；相当 B2 to match or be similar or equal

correspondence   1 noun UK /ˌkɒr.ɪˈspɒn.dəns/ US /ˌkɔːr.əˈspɑːn.dəns/ (WRITING) 信件，信函（尤指公函或商业信函）[U] letters, especially official or business letters

corroborate   verb [T] formal UK /kəˈrɒb.ə.reɪt/ US /kəˈrɑː.bə.reɪt/ 证实，确证 to add proof to an account, statement, idea, etc. with new information [GRE]

Prefix (Medical): cor-, core-, coro- Of or pertaining to eye's pupil

Meaning in English: Of or pertaining to eye's pupil

Origin language: Ancient Greek κόρη (kórē), girl, doll; pupil of the eye

English examples:

Iridectomy noun [U] 虹膜切除术 An iridectomy, also known as a surgical iridectomy or **corectomy**, is the surgical removal of part of the iris. These procedures are most frequently performed in the treatment of closed-angle glaucoma and iris melanoma. Wikipedia

Prefix (Medical): cordi- Of or pertaining to the heart

Meaning in English: Of or pertaining to the heart

Origin language: Latin (cor, cordi-), heart

English examples:

Commotio cordis   noun [U] 胸部的钝性撞击导致猝死 Commotio cordis is a phenomenon in which a sudden blunt impact to the chest causes sudden death in the absence of cardiac damage.

cordial   1 adjective formal UK /ˈkɔː.di.əl/ US /ˈkɔːr.dʒəl/ (FRIENDLY) 友好的，热诚的，诚挚的 friendly, but formal and polite

cordiality   noun [U] formal UK /ˌkɔː.diˈæl.ə.ti/ US /ˌkɔːrˈdi.æl.ə.t̬i/ 友好而庄重的表现；亲切而客气的行为 behaviour that is friendly, but formal and polite

Prefix (Medical): cornu- parts of the body describing them likened or similar to horns

Meaning in English: Applied to processes and parts of the body describing them likened or similar to horns

Origin language: Latin (cornū), horn

English examples:

Cornu   noun [C] medical specialized UK /ˈkɔːn.juː/ US /ˈkɔr.nuː/ plural cornua （人体）角状突起 any part of the body that is shaped like a horn (= a hard curved part on the heads of some animals)

cornucopia   noun [S] formal UK /ˌkɔː.njuˈkəʊ.pi.ə/ US /ˌkɔːr.nəˈkoʊ.pi.ə/ 丰盛，大量 a large amount or supply of something; 1 a curved, hollow goat's horn or similarly shaped receptacle (such as a horn-shaped basket) that is overflowing especially with fruit and vegetables (such as gourds, ears of corn, apples, and grapes) and that is used as a decorative motif emblematic of abundance. (merriam-webster) [GRE]

Prefix (Medical): cost(o)- Of or pertaining to the ribs

Meaning in English: Of or pertaining to the ribs

Origin language: Latin (costa), rib

English examples:

Costochondral   noun [U] 肋软骨炎 Costochondritis is a self-limited condition defined as inflammation of costochondral junctions of ribs or chondrosternal joints, usually at multiple levels and lacking swelling or induration. Pain is reproduced by palpation of the affected cartilage segments and may radiate on the chest wall.

Prefix (Medical): cox- Of or relating to the hip, haunch, or hip-joint

Meaning in English: Of or relating to the hip, haunch, or hip-joint

Origin language: Latin (coxa), hip

English examples:

coxopodite   noun/kɒkˈsɒpədʌɪt/ ZOOLOGY 节肢动物，尤指甲壳类动物腿上最靠近身体的部分。the segment nearest the body in the leg of an arthropod, especially a crustacean.

Prefix (Medical): crani(o)- Belonging or relating to the cranium

Meaning in English: Belonging or relating to the cranium

Origin language: Latin (cranium) < Ancient Greek κρᾱνίον (krānion), the cranium, skull, bones enclosing the brain

English examples:

craniology   noun /ˌkreɪnɪˈɒlədʒi/ 颅骨学 HISTORICAL the scientific study of the shape and size of the skulls of different human races.

craniofacial implant   noun [C] medical specialized UK   /kreɪ.ni.əʊˌfeɪ.ʃəl ˈɪm.pl ɑ :nt/ US /ˌkreɪ.ni.oʊˈfeɪ.ʃəl ˈɪm.plænt/ （人造眼、耳、鼻等用于整容手术的）颅面植入物 artificial eyes, ears, or noses used in plastic surgery (= medical operations to improve someone's appearance)

craniopharyngioma   noun [C] medical specialized UK /ˌkreɪ.ni.əʊ.fər.ɪn.dʒiˈəʊ.mə/ US /ˌkreɪ.ni.oʊ.fəˌrɪn.dʒiˈoʊ.mə/颅咽管瘤 a harmless tumour that forms near the pituitary gland in the brain

craniosynostosis noun [U] medical specialized UK
/ˌkreɪ.ni.əʊ.sɪn.əˈstəʊ.sɪs/ US /ˌkreɪ.ni.oʊˌsɪn.əˈstoʊ.sɪs/ 颅缝早闭 a medical condition in which one or more of the joins on a baby's head closes earlier than normal；Craniosynostosis is a condition in which one or more of the fibrous sutures in a young infant's skull prematurely fuses by turning into bone (ossification), thereby changing the growth pattern of the skull. Because the skull cannot expand perpendicular to the fused suture, it compensates by growing more in the direction parallel to the closed sutures.

cranium noun [C] anatomy specialized UK /ˈkreɪ.ni.əm/ US /ˈkreɪ.ni.əm/ plural craniums or crania 颅，头颅；头盖骨 the hard bone case that gives an animal's or a human's head its shape and protects the brain

Prefix: counter- opposing or as a reaction to something
Meaning in English: opposing or as a reaction to something

Origin language: Anglo-Saxon/ Latin

English examples:

counter- prefix UK /kaʊn.tər-/ US /kaʊn.tɚ-/ 反，逆 opposing or as a reaction to something

counter-culture noun [C or U] UK /ˈkaʊn.təˌkʌl.tʃər/ US /ˈkaʊn.təˌkʌl.tʃɚ/ 反正统文化，反主流文化（反对主流社会的生活方式和价值观念）；反主流文化的群体 a way of life and a set of ideas that are completely different from those accepted by most of society, or the group of people who live this way

counter-espionage noun [U] UK /ˌkaʊn.tərˈes.pi.ə.nɑːʒ/ US /ˌkaʊn.tɚˈes.pi.ə.nɑːʒ/ 反间谍活动 secret action taken by a country to prevent another country from discovering its military, industrial, or political secrets

counter-intuitive adjective UK /ˌkaʊn.tər.ɪnˈtʃuː.ɪ.tɪv/ US /ˌkaʊn.t̬ɚ.ɪnˈtuː.ɪ.t̬ɪv/ 反直觉的；与预期相反的 Something that is counter-intuitive does not happen in the way you would expect it to.

counter-revolution noun [C] UK /ˌkaʊn.tə.rev.əˈluː.ʃən/ US /ˌkaʊn.t̬ɚ.rev.əˈluː.ʃən/ 反革命

counter-suit noun [C] UK /ˈkaʊn.tə.suːt/ /ˈkaʊn.tə.sjuːt/ US /ˈkaʊn.t̬ɚ.suːt/ 反诉，抗辩，抗诉 a legal claim that you make as a reaction to a claim made against you

counteract verb [T] UK /ˌkaʊn.tərˈækt/ US /ˌkaʊn.t̬ɚˈækt/ 抵消；对抗；减少 to reduce or remove the effect of something unwanted by producing an opposite effect

counterattack noun [C] UK /ˈkaʊn.tər.ə.tæk/ US /ˈkaʊn.t̬ɚ.ə.tæk/ 反击；反攻 an attack intended to stop or oppose an attack by an enemy or competitor

counterattraction noun [C] UK /ˌkaʊn.tər.əˈtræk.ʃən/ US /ˌkaʊn.t̬ɚ.əˈtræk.ʃən/ 反吸引物，反诱惑物（相竞争的地方或娱乐形式）a place or type of entertainment that competes with another for visitors' or people's attention

counterbalance verb [T] UK /ˈkaʊn.təˌbæl.əns/ US /ˈkaʊn.t̬ɚˌbæl.əns/ 使平衡；抵消；弥补 to have an equal but opposite effect on something so that it does not have too much of a particular characteristic

counterclockwise adjective, adverb us UK /ˌkaʊn.təˈklɒk.waɪz/ US /ˌkaʊn.t̬ɚˈklɑːk.waɪz/ (uk anticlockwise) 逆时针方向的 in the opposite direction to the movement of the hands of a clock

counterfactual   adjective formal UK /ˌkaʊn.təˈfæk.tʃu.əl/ US /ˌkaʊn.tɚˈfæk.tʃu.əl/ 违实的，反事实的，与事实相反的 thinking about what did not happen but could have happened, or relating to this kind of thinking

counterfeit   adjective UK /ˈkaʊn.tə.fɪt/ US /ˈkaʊn.tɚ.fɪt/ 伪造的；仿造的；假冒的 made to look like the original of something, usually for dishonest or illegal purposes [GRE]

countermand   verb [T] formal UK /ˌkaʊn.təˈmɑːnd/ US /ˌkaʊn.tɚˈmænd/ 取消，撤回（命令）；重新发布（命令）to change an order that has already been given, especially by giving a new order [GRE]

countermeasure   noun [C] UK /ˈkaʊn.təˌmeʒ.ər/ US /ˈkaʊn.tɚˌmeʒ.ɚ/ 对策；反措施，应对措施 an action taken against an unwanted action or situation

countermove   noun [C] (also counter-move) UK /ˈkaʊn.tə.muːv/ US/ˈkaʊn.tɚ.muːv/ 对抗手段；反击；反制手段 (YAO) an action by one person that is a reaction to an action by someone else:

Prefix: cross- across

Meaning in English: across

Origin language: Anglo-Saxon/ Latin

English examples:

cross-   13 prefix UK /krɒs-/ US /krɑːs-/ 横过；越过 across

cross-border   adjective [before noun] UK /ˌkrɒsˈbɔː.dər/ US /ˌkrɑːsˈbɔːr.dɚ/ 跨越国界的；跨国的 between different countries, or involving people from different countries

cross-border trade   跨国贸易

cross-country   1 adjective UK /ˌkrɒsˈkʌn.tri/ US /ˌkrɑːsˈkʌn.tri/ 越野的 Cross-country sports involve people moving over long distances through the countryside. 2 adverb UK /ˌkrɒsˈkʌn.tri/ US /ˌkrɑːsˈkʌn.tri/ 横穿全国地 across the length of a country

cross-field   adjective UK /ˌkrɒsˈfiːld/ US /ˌkrɑːsˈfiːld/ 横传踢球/横传 /横传球 a kick, pass, or ball that goes from one side of a sports field to another during a game

cross-section   1 noun [C] UK /ˈkrɒs.sek.ʃən/ US /ˈkrɑːs.sek.ʃən/ 横截面（图），横断面（图），剖面（图） something that has been cut in half so that you can see the inside, or a model or picture of this

Prefix: cross- including different groups or subjects

Meaning in English: including different groups or subjects

Origin language: Anglo-Saxon/ Latin

English examples:

cross-   14 prefix 由不同群体或学科组成的 including different groups or subjects
subjects

cross purposes   adverb UK /ˌkrɒs ˈpɜː.pə.sɪz/ US /ˌkrɑːs ˈpɜˑ.pə.sɪz/ （两人因未意识到彼此谈论的事物不同而）相互误解，相互矛盾，各说各的 If two or more people are at cross purposes, they do not understand each other because they are talking about different subjects without realizing this.

cross-dresser   noun [C] UK /ˌkrɒsˈdres.ər/ US /ˌkrɑːsˈdres.ɚ/ 穿异性服装的人；女扮男装的人；男扮女装的人 a person who sometimes wears clothes usually associated with the opposite sex, as a form of self-expression; usually a heterosexual (= not gay) man who sometimes wears women's clothes, make-up, jewellery, etc.

cross-dressing   noun [U] UK /ˌkrɒsˈdres.ɪŋ/ US /ˌkrɑːsˈdres.ɪŋ/ 穿异性服装；女扮男装；男扮女装 the act of wearing clothes usually worn by the opposite sex

cross-examine   verb [T] UK /ˌkrɒs.ɪgˈzæm.ɪn/ US /ˌkrɑːs.ɪgˈzæm.ɪn/ (also cross-question) 盘问，诘问（尤指证人）to ask detailed questions of someone, especially a witness in a trial, in order to discover if they have been telling the truth

cross-legged   adverb UK /ˌkrɒsˈlegd/ /ˌkrɒsˈleg.ɪd/ US /ˌkrɑːsˈlegd/ /ˌkrɑːsˈleg.ɪd/ （通常指席地而坐时）盘腿地 having your feet crossed over each other, but your knees wide apart, usually while sitting on the floor

cross-party   adjective [before noun] UK /ˌkrɒsˈpɑː.ti/ US /ˌkrɑːsˈpɑːr.ti/ 跨党的，涉及多个党派的 mainly uk including different political parties

cross-reference   noun [C] UK /ˌkrɒsˈref.ər.əns/ US /ˌkrɑːsˈref.ɚ.əns/ 互见，相互参照 a note in a book that tells you to look somewhere else in the book for more information about something

cross-selling   noun [U] UK /ˌkrɒsˈsel.ɪŋ/ US /ˌkrɑːsˈsel.ɪŋ/ 交叉销售（向已经购买某公司产品的顾客出售其他产品的行为）the activity of selling a different product to someone who is already buying a product from the same company

cross-stitch   noun [U] UK /ˈkrɒs.stɪtʃ/ US /ˈkrɑːs.stɪtʃ/ 十字缝，十字形针法 a decorative style of sewing that uses stitches that cross each other to form an X

cross-trainer   1 noun UK /ˈkrɒsˌtreɪ.nər/ US /ˈkrɑːsˌtreɪ.nɚ/ 多功能训练器材，综合训练器材 [C] (also elliptical trainer) a piece of exercise equipment designed to exercise all of the body's main groups of muscles 2 noun 多用途运动鞋，综合训练鞋 [C usually plural] (also cross-training shoe) a sports shoe that is suitable for wearing in the gym (= a room or building where you can exercise) and also for running and other sports

cross-training   noun [U] UK /ˈkrɒsˌtreɪ.nɪŋ/ US /ˈkrɑːsˌtreɪ.nɪŋ/ 多项目 交叉训练 exercise that makes your whole body stronger by combining several different activities

crossfire   noun [U] UK /ˈkrɒs.faɪər/ US /ˈkrɑːs.faɪr/ 交叉火力 bullets fired towards you from different directions

crossroads   noun [C] UK /ˈkrɒs.rəʊdz/ US /ˈkrɑːs.roʊdz/ plural crossroads B2 十字路口 a place where two roads meet and cross each other

crosswalk   noun [C] us UK /ˈkrɒs.wɔːk/ US /ˈkrɑːs.wɑːk/ (uk zebra crossing) 人行横道 a place on a road, especially one where there is a lot of traffic, across which wide, black and white lines are painted, and at which vehicles must stop to allow people to walk across the road

Prefix (Medical): cry(o)- cold

Meaning in English: cold

Origin language: Greek κρύος

English examples:

Cryoablation   noun [U] 冷冻消融 Cryoablation is a process that uses extreme cold to destroy tissue. Cryoablation is performed using hollow needles through which cooled, thermally conductive, fluids are circulated. Cryoprobes are positioned adjacent to the target in such a way that the freezing process will destroy the diseased tissue. Wikipedia

cryogenic   adjective 1 UK /ˌkraɪ.əʊˈdʒen.ɪk/ US /ˌkraɪ.əˈdʒen.ɪk/ PHYSICS specialized 低温学的 related to the scientific study of very low temperatures and how to produce them 2 （在极低温度下冷冻人体，希望将来可能使其复活）深冻冷藏的 related to the freezing of dead human bodies at very low temperatures, hoping that it may be possible to bring them back to life in future

cryogenically   adverb 1 UK /ˌkraɪ.əʊˈdʒen.ɪ.kli/ US /ˌkraɪ.əˈdʒen.ɪ.kli/（在极低温度下冷冻人体，希望将来可能使其复活）深冻冷藏地 in a way that relates to the freezing of dead human bodies, cells, or body parts at very low temperatures

cryogenics   noun [U] physics specialized UK /ˌkraɪ.əʊˈdʒen.ɪks/ US /ˌkraɪ.əˈdʒen.ɪks/ 低温学 the scientific study of very low temperatures and how to produce them

cryoglobulinemia noun [U] medical specialized UK /ˌkraɪ.əʊ.glɒb.jə.lɪˈniː.mi.ə/ US /ˌkraɪ.oʊˌglɑːb.jə.lɪˈniː.mi.ə/ 冷沉（淀）球蛋白血症 a condition in which the body contains large amounts of a type of protein that does not dissolve when the body temperature drops

cryolite   noun [U] UK /ˈkraɪ.əʊ.laɪt/ US /ˈkraɪ.oʊ.laɪt/ 冰晶石 a white or colourless mineral used in the production of aluminium, glass, and other substances

cryonics   noun [U] UK /ˌkraɪˈɒn.ɪks/ US /ˌkraɪˈɑː.nɪks/ 人体冷冻技术（冷冻保存尸体待来日科学发展使其起死回生） the process of storing a dead body by freezing it until science has advanced to such a degree that it is able to bring that person back to life

cryosurgery   noun [U] medical specialized UK /ˌkraɪ.əʊˈsɜː.dʒər.i/ US /ˌkraɪ.oʊˈsɜː.dʒər.i/ 低温外科，冷冻手术 the use of very cold temperatures to freeze and destroy diseased tissue

cryotherapy   noun [U] medical specialized UK   /ˌkraɪ.əʊˈθe.rə.pi/ US /ˌkraɪ.oʊˈθer.ə.pi/ 低温疗法 the use of liquid nitrogen to create very low temperatures, often to freeze and remove skin cancers

Prefix: crypto- hidden or secret

Meaning in English: hidden or secret

Origin language: Anglo-Saxon/ Latin

English examples:

crypto-   prefix UK   /krɪp.təʊ-/ US   /krɪp.toʊ-/ 隐藏的；秘密的 hidden or secret

cryptography   noun [U] UK   /krɪpˈtɒg.rə.fi/ US   /krɪpˈtɑː.grə.fi/ 密码使用法；密码方式 the practice of creating and understanding codes that keep information secret

cryptocurrency   noun [C] UK   /ˈkrɪp.təʊˌkʌr.ən.si/ US   /ˈkrɪp.toʊˌkɜː.ən.si/ specialized （公共网络的，而非政府发行的）加密电子货币（使用加密法确保付款安全支付及收取） a digital currency produced by a public network, rather than any government, that uses cryptography to make sure payments are sent and received safely

Prefix: custom- "specially designed for a particular person or purpose"

Meaning in English: "specially designed for a particular person or purpose"

Origin language: Anglo-Saxon/ Latin

English examples:

custom-   prefix UK   /kʌs.təm-/ US   /kʌs.təm-/ 按顾客要求专门…的 used before another word to mean "specially designed for a particular person or purpose"

custom-designed   按顾客要求专门设计的

custom-built software   按客户要求专门设计的软件

custom-built   adjective UK /ˌkʌs.təmˈbɪlt/ US /ˌkʌs.təmˈbɪlt/ （汽车、机器等）定制的，定做的 If a car, machine, etc. is custom-built, it is made according to the needs of a particular buyer.

custom-made   adjective UK /ˌkʌs.təmˈmeɪd/ US /ˌkʌs.təmˈmeɪd/ （衣服）定做的，定制的 specially made for a particular person

Prefix (Medical): cut- skin

Meaning in English: skin

Origin language: Latin

English examples:

cutaneous   adjective medical specialized UK /kjuˈteɪ.ni.əs/ US /kjuˈteɪ.ni.əs/ 皮肤的 relating to the skin

机能障碍一般多见于内部器官，但偶尔也会以一处或多处皮肤溃烂的情况反映出来。Lesions are more common in internal organs but may rarely be seen as one or more cutaneous ulcers.

Cutaneous anthrax occurs when anthrax touches a cut or scrape on the skin.

皮肤炭疽病的发生是因为炭疽接触到了皮肤上的割伤或擦伤。

cuticle   noun [C] UK /ˈkjuː.tɪ.kəl/ US /ˈkjuː.t̬ɪ.kəl/ （指甲或趾甲根部的）角质层 the thin skin at the base of the nails on the fingers and toes

cutis   noun [S] MEDICAL specialized /ˈkjuː.tɪs/ /ˈkjuː.t̬ɪs/ 真皮，皮肤（用于作为疾病名称的一部分 the layer of skin under the epidermis (= the thin outer layer of skin), used in the names of some medical conditions）

The ancient anatomists divided the skin into two parts or layers, the inner being called the cutis or dermis, and the outer the cuticle or epidermis.   古代解剖学家将皮肤分为两个部分或两层，内层称为真皮，外层称为表皮。

Leukaemia cutis refers to the infiltration of the skin with leukaemia cells.

皮肤白血病

Prefix (Medical): cutane- skin

Meaning in English: skin

Origin language: Latin cutis

English examples:

cutaneous adjective medical specialized UK /kjuˈteɪ.ni.əs/ US /kjuːˈteɪ.ni.əs/ 皮肤的 relating to the skin

musculocutaneous adjective MEDICAL specialized UK /ˌmʌs.kjə.ləʊ.kjuːˈteɪ.ni.əs/ US /ˌmʌs.kjəˌloʊ.kjuːˈteɪ.ni.əs/ 肌皮的 relating to or supplying the muscles and the skin

肌皮神经 a musculocutaneous nerve

percutaneous adjective MEDICAL specialized UK /ˌpɜːkjuːˈteɪ.ni.əs/ US /ˌpɚː.kjuːˈteɪ.ni.əs/ 经皮的，由皮的 done through the skin

经皮注射是通过皮肤进行注射。 A percutaneous injection is one that is given through the skin.

subcutanea adjective MEDICAL specialized UK /ˌsʌb.kjuːˈteɪ.ni.ə/ US /ˌsʌb.kjuːˈteɪ.ni.ə/ （拉丁语，用于医学术语）皮下的 a Latin word meaning "under the skin", used in medical names and descriptions

subcutaneous adjective MEDICAL specialized UK /ˌsʌb.kjuˈteɪ.ni.əs/ US /ˌsʌb.kjuːˈteɪ.ni.əs/ 皮下的 existing under the skin

皮下脂肪／肌肉 subcutaneous fat/muscle

Meaning in English: Denotes a blue color

Origin language: Latin

English examples: Ancient Greek κύανος, κυάνεος (kýanos, kyáneos), blue

Cyanopsia noun [U] 蓝色视觉; 青视症 Cyanopsia is a medical term for seeing everything tinted with blue. It is also referred to as blue vision. Cyanopsia often occurs for a few days, weeks, or months after removal of a cataract from the eye. Cyanopsia also sometimes occurs as a side effect of taking sildenafil, tadalafil, or vardenafil.

cyan 1 noun [U] UK /ˈsaɪ.ən/ US /ˈsaɪ.ən/ （彩色印刷和摄影的）青色（的），蓝绿色（的） a deep greenish-blue colour, one of the main colours that are used in colour printing and photography 2 adjective UK US 青色的，蓝绿色的 of a deep greenish-blue colour

cyanide noun [U] UK /ˈsaɪə.naɪd/ US /ˈsaɪə.naɪd/ 氰化物 an extremely powerful poison that can kill people

Meaning in English: skull

Origin language: Greek

English examples:

Amphicrania noun [U] 两侧头痛 pain affecting both sides of the head — compare hemicrania.

Hemicrania noun [U] 偏头痛 Hemicrania continua is a headache disorder. It causes constant pain in one side of the face and head. Unlike other headache disorders, environmental or lifestyle factors don't trigger hemicranial headaches. People may also have migraine-like symptoms, such as nausea or sensitivity to light.

Migraine 阵偏头痛 A migraine is a headache that can cause severe throbbing pain or a pulsing sensation, usually on one side of the head. It's often accompanied by nausea, vomiting, and extreme sensitivity to light and sound.

cranial adjective anatomy specialized UK /ˈkreɪ.ni.əl/ US /ˈkreɪ.ni.əl/ 颅的，头盖骨的 of the skull

craniologist Noun 1 [U] 颅骨科医生 The scientific study of the characteristics of the skull, such as size and shape, especially in humans 2 [U] 相颅骨术 someone who claims to be able to read your character from the shape of your skull.

craniofacial implant noun [C] medical specialized UK /kreɪ.ni.əʊ.feɪ.ʃəl ˈɪm.pl ɑ :nt/ US /ˌkreɪ.ni.oʊˈfeɪ.ʃəl ˈɪm.plænt/ （人造眼、耳、鼻等用于整容手术的）颅面植入物 artificial eyes, ears, or noses used in plastic surgery (= medical operations to improve someone's appearance)

craniofacial implant noun [C] medical specialized UK /kreɪ.ni.əʊ.feɪ.ʃəl ˈɪm.pl ɑ :nt/ US /ˌkreɪ.ni.oʊˈfeɪ.ʃəl ˈɪm.plænt/ （人造眼、耳、鼻等用于整容手术的）颅面植入物 artificial eyes, ears, or noses used in plastic surgery (= medical operations to improve someone's appearance)

craniopharyngioma noun [C] medical specialized UK /ˌkreɪ.ni.əʊ.fər.ɪn.dʒiˈəʊ.mə/ US /ˌkreɪ.ni.oʊ.fəˌrɪn.dʒiˈoʊ.mə/颅咽管瘤 a harmless tumour that forms near the pituitary gland in the brain

craniosynostosis noun [U] medical specialized UK /ˌkreɪ.ni.əʊ.sɪn.əˈstəʊ.sɪs/ US /ˌkreɪ.ni.oʊˌsɪn.əˈstoʊ.sɪs/ 颅缝早闭 a medical condition in which one or more of the joins on a baby's head closes earlier than normal；Craniosynostosis is a condition in which one or more of the fibrous sutures in a young infant's skull prematurely fuses by turning into bone (ossification), thereby changing the growth pattern of the skull. Because the skull cannot expand perpendicular to the fused suture, it compensates by growing more in the direction parallel to the closed sutures.

cranium   noun [C] anatomy specialized UK /ˈkreɪ.ni.əm/ US /ˈkreɪ.ni.əm/ plural craniums or crania 颅，头颅；头盖骨 the hard bone case that gives an animal's or a human's head its shape and protects the brain

craniology noun /ˌkreɪniˈɒlədʒi/ 颅骨学 HISTORICAL the scientific study of the shape and size of the skulls of different human races.

intracranial   adjective MEDICAL specialized UK /ˌɪn.trəˈkreɪ.ni.əl/ US /ˌɪn.trəˈkreɪ.ni.əl/ 颅内的 inside the cranium (= the bony part of the skull that holds the brain)

Intracranial pressure can be treated with medication.   颅内压可以用药物治疗。

Prefix: cyber- involving to computers, internet
Meaning in English: involving, using, or relating to computers, especially the internet

Origin language: Anglo-Saxon/ Latin

English examples:

cyber-   prefix UK /saɪ.bər-/ US /saɪ.bɚ-/ 计算机的；与电脑有关的；网络的（尤指因特网） involving, using, or relating to computers, especially the internet

cybercrime   网络犯罪
cyberculture   计算机文化

cyberattack   noun [C] UK /ˈsaɪ.bə.rəˌtæk/ US /ˈsaɪ.bɚ.əˌtæk/（由黑客发起的）网络攻击 an illegal attempt to harm someone's computer system or the information on it, using the internet

cyberbully   noun [C] UK /ˈsaɪ.bəˌbʊl.i/ US /ˈsaɪ.bɚˌbʊl.i/ 网络欺凌 someone who uses the internet to harm or frighten another person, especially by sending them unpleasant messages

cybercafé   noun [C] UK /ˈsaɪ.bəˌkæf.eɪ/ US /ˌsaɪ.bɚ.kæfˈeɪ/ 网吧 a small, informal restaurant where you can pay to use the internet

cybercrime   noun [U] UK /ˈsaɪ.bə.kraɪm/ US /ˈsaɪ.bɚ.kraɪm/ 网络（或计算机）犯罪 crime or illegal activity that is done using the internet

cyberfraud   noun [U] UK /ˈsaɪ.bə.frɔːd/ US /ˈsaɪ.bɚ.frɑːd/ 网上诈骗 the use of the internet to get money, goods, etc. from people illegally by deceiving them

cyberlaw   noun [U or C] UK /ˈsaɪ.bəˌlɔː/ US /ˈsaɪ.bɚˌlɑː/ 网络安全法 laws about how people should use computers, especially the internet, or one of these laws

cyberspace   noun [U] UK /ˈsaɪ.bə.speɪs/ US /ˈsaɪ.bɚ.speɪs/ 网络空间 the internet considered as an imaginary area without limits where you can meet people and discover information about any subject

cybersquatting   noun [U] UK /ˈsaɪ.bəˌskwɒt.ɪŋ/ US /ˈsaɪ.bɚˌskwɑː.t̬ɪŋ/ 域名抢注 the situation in which someone pays for a famous name as an internet address, so that they can later sell it for a high price to the person or organization with that name

cyberterrorism   noun [U] law, internet & telecoms UK /ˈsaɪ.bəˌter.ə.rɪ.zəm/ US /-bɚˌter.ɚ.ɪ-/ 网络恐怖主义 the use of the internet to damage or destroy computer systems for political or other reasons

cyberwarfare   noun [U] UK /ˌsaɪ.bəˈwɔː.feər/ US /ˌsaɪ.bɚˈwɔːr.fer/ 网络战 the use of the internet to attack an enemy, by damaging things such as communication and transport systems or water and electricity supplies

Prefix (Medical): cyph(o)- Denotes something as bent

Meaning in English: Denotes something as bent

Origin language: Ancient Greek κυφός (kȳphós), bent, hunchback

English examples:

Cyphosis   noun [U] 脊柱后凸 Kyphosis (Cyphosis) is curvature of the spine that causes the top of the back to appear more rounded than normal. Everyone has some degree of curvature in their spine. However, a curve of more than 45 degrees is considered excessive.

kyphosis   noun [U] MEDICAL specialized UK /kaɪˈfəʊ.sɪs/ US /kaɪˈfoʊ.sɪs/ 驼背，脊柱后凸 a condition in which someone's spine (= the line of bones down their back) curves outwards too much

Prefix (Medical): cyst(o)-, cyst(i)- Of or pertaining to the urinary bladder

Meaning in English: Of or pertaining to the urinary bladder

Origin language: Ancient Greek κύστις (kýstis); bladder, cyst

English examples:

Cystotomy   noun [U] 膀胱切开术 Cystotomy is a surgical procedure in which an incision is made into the dog's urinary bladder. The procedure can be done for many reasons, the most common being to facilitate removal of bladder and urethral stones.

cystitis   noun [U] mainly uk UK /sɪˈstaɪ.tɪs/ US /sɪˈstaɪ.t̬əs/ （尤指女性患的）膀胱炎 a disease, especially of women, in which the bladder becomes infected and there is pain when urinating

cystocele   noun [C] medical specialized UK /ˈsɪs.te.siːl/ US /ˈsɪs.təˌsiːl/ (also bladder prolapse) 膀胱膨出 a condition in which the bladder (= the organ where urine is stored) pushes through the wall of the vagina

Prefix (Medical): cyt(o)- cell

Meaning in English: cell

Origin language: Greek κύτος

English examples:

cytokine   noun [C] chemistry specialized UK /ˈsaɪ.tə.kaɪn/ US /ˈsaɪ.t̬əˌkaɪn/ 细胞活素，细胞因子 a small protein produced by cells in the nervous and immune systems that affects what happens between cells

cytology   noun [U] UK /saɪˈtɒl.ə.dʒi/ US /saɪˈtɑː.lə.dʒi/ 细胞学 the scientific study of cells from living things

cyton   noun [C] biology specialized UK /ˈsaɪ.tɒn/ US /ˈsaɪ.tɑːn/ 神经元细胞体 the central part of a neuron (= a cell that sends and receives messages within the brain and nerves)

Cytolysis   细胞溶解 Cytolysis, or osmotic lysis, occurs when a cell bursts due to an osmotic imbalance that has caused excess water to diffuse into the cell. Water can enter the cell by diffusion through the cell membrane or through selective membrane channels called aquaporins, which greatly facilitate the flow of water. Wikipedia

cytoplasm   noun [U] biology specialized UK /ˈsaɪ.tə.plæz.əm/ US /ˈsaɪ.tə.plæz.əm/ 细胞质 the substance inside a cell that surrounds the cell's nucleus

cytotoxic   adjective medical specialized UK /ˌsaɪ.təʊˈtɒk.sɪk/ US /ˌsaɪ.toʊˈt ɑ :k.sɪk/ 细胞毒素的 damaging or destroying living cells

细胞毒素药物被用于治疗癌症。   Cytotoxic drugs are used in the treatment of cancer.

cnidocytes 刺细胞 Cnidocytes, also known as stinging cells, are specialized neural cells that typify the phylum Cnidaria (sea anemones, corals, hydroids, and jellyfish). These cells contain an organelle called cnida or cnidocyst, which is the product of extensive Golgi secretions.

DDD

Meaning in English: Of or pertaining to a finger, toe

Origin language: Ancient Greek δάκτυλος (dáktylos), finger, toe

English examples:

dactylology   noun / (ˌdæktɪˈlɒlədʒɪ) / plural -指形学 gies. the method of using manual sign language, as in communicating with deaf people.

zygodactyl   adjective BIOLOGY specialized UK /ˌzaɪ.ɡəˈdæk.tɪl/ US /ˌzaɪ.ɡəˈdæk.tɪl/ （鸟）对趾的，前后各有一双趾的 (of a bird's foot) having two toes pointing forwards and two toes pointing backwards

Meaning in English: reduce down/ away from

Origin language: Latin

English examples:

de- 1 prefix UK /diː-/ /dɪ-/ US /diː-/ /dɪ-/ （用于名词或动词前）表示"相反"、"除去"或"减少" used to add the meaning "opposite", "remove", or "reduce" to a noun or verb

de-escalate verb [I or T] UK /ˌdiːˈes.kə.leɪt/ US /ˌdiːˈes.kə.leɪt/ （使）缓和，（使）缓解 to (cause to) become less dangerous or difficult

debark 1 verb UK /ˌdiˈbɑːk/ US /ˌdiˈbɑːrk/ (GET OFF) [I] （使）下船(飞机、车等);卸(客、货) to leave a ship, aircraft, etc. after a journey: [GRE]

debase verb [T] UK /dɪˈbeɪs/ US /dɪˈbeɪs/ 使堕落；贬低 to reduce the quality or value of something [GRE]

debauch verb [T] UK /dɪˈbɔːtʃ/ US /dɪˈbɑːtʃ/ 使变坏，使败坏 to destroy or damage something so that it is no longer considered good or moral

debauched 1 adjective UK /dɪˈbɔːtʃt/ US /dɪˈbɑːtʃt/ 糜烂的，放荡的；沉湎酒色的；嗜毒的 made weaker or destroyed by bad sexual behaviour, drinking too much alcohol, taking drugs, etc.

debauchery noun [U] UK /dɪˈbɔː.tʃər.i/ US /dɪˈbɑː.tʃɚ.i/ 道德败坏；淫荡；沉湎酒色（或毒品） bad sexual behaviour, drinking too much alcohol, taking drugs, etc.

debilitate verb [T] formal UK /dɪˈbɪl.ɪ.teɪt/ US /dɪˈbɪl.ə.teɪt/ 使虚弱；削弱，使衰弱 to make someone or something physically weak [GRE]

decadence noun [U] UK /ˈdek.ə.dəns/ US /ˈdek.ə.dəns/ 堕落，颓废，腐朽 low moral standards and behaviour [GRE]

decadent adjective UK /ˈdek.ə.dənt/ US /ˈdek.ə.dənt/ （人或组织）腐朽的；颓废的；堕落的 A decadent person or group has low moral standards. [GRE]

decay 1 verb UK /dɪˈkeɪ/ US /dɪˈkeɪ/ B2 腐蚀；（使）衰败，（使）衰弱 [I or T] to become gradually damaged, worse, or less; to cause something to do this

decease noun [U] formal UK /dɪˈsiːs/ US /dɪˈsiːs/ 去世，逝世 a person's death

deceased 1 adjective formal UK /dɪˈsiːst/ US /dɪˈsiːst/ C2 死的，死亡的，去世的 dead

decentralize verb [I or T] (uk usually decentralise) UK /ˌdiːˈsen.trə.laɪz/ US /ˌdiːˈsen.trə.laɪz/ 分散管理，分权管理；将（权力）下放 to move the control of an organization or government from a single place to several smaller ones

decipher verb [T] UK /dɪˈsaɪ.fər/ US /dɪˈsaɪ.fɚ/ 辨认；破解，破译 to discover the meaning of something written badly or in a difficult or hidden way [GRE]

decline 1 verb US UK /dɪˈklaɪn/ (GO DOWN) （逐渐）减少，衰落，降低 B2 [I] to gradually become less, worse, or lower

decode 1 verb UK /diːˈkəʊd/ US /diːˈkoʊd/ 破译，破解；解（码） [T] to discover the meaning of information given in a secret or complicated way [GRE]

decompose　　　1 verb [I or T] UK /ˌdiː.kəmˈpəʊz/ US /ˌdiː.kəmˈpoʊz/ （使）腐化，（使）腐烂 to decay, or to cause something to decay

decrease　　　1 verb [I or T] UK /dɪˈkriːs/ US /ˈdiː.kriːs/ B1 （使）减少；（使）下降；（使）降低 to become less, or to make something become less

decrepit　adjective UK /dɪˈkrep.ɪt/ US /dɪˈkrep.ɪt/ 破旧的，年久失修的；破烂不堪的；老朽的 in very bad condition because of being old, or not having been cared for, or having been used a lot [GRE]

deduce　1 verb [T] UK /dɪˈdʒuːs/ US /dɪˈduːs/ C2 推断，推论 to reach an answer or a decision by thinking carefully about the known facts

deduct　　　1 verb [T] UK /dɪˈdʌkt/ US /dɪˈdʌkt/ 减，减去；扣除 to take away an amount or part from a total

deductable　　1 adjective australian english UK /dɪˈdʌk.tə.bəl/ US /dɪˈdʌk.tə.bəl/ → 可扣除的；可减免的（同 deductible）deductible

deduction　1 noun UK /dɪˈdʌk.ʃən/ US /dɪˈdʌk.ʃən/ (THINKING) （根据已知的事实所作出的）推断，推论；推论所促成的决定 C2 [C or U] the process of reaching a decision or answer by thinking about the known facts, or the decision that is reached

defeat　　　1 verb [T] UK /dɪˈfiːt/ US /dɪˈfiːt/ 击败，打败，战胜 B1 to win against someone in a fight, war, or competition

defect　　　1 noun [C] UK /ˈdiː.fekt/ US /ˈdiː.fekt/ C1 缺点；缺陷；瑕疵 a fault or problem in something or someone that spoils that thing or person or causes it, him, or her not to work correctly 3 verb [I] UK /dɪˈfekt/ US

/dɪˈfekt/ （尤指为加入敌对国家、政党等）脱离，退出，叛逃 to leave a country, political party, etc., especially in order to join an opposing one

defection   noun [C or U] UK /dɪˈfek.ʃən/ US /dɪˈfek.ʃən/ 脱离，退出，叛逃（国家或政党等） the act of leaving a country, political party, etc. to go to another one

defective   adjective UK /dɪˈfek.tɪv/ US /dɪˈfek.tɪv/ C2 有缺陷的，有毛病的，有问题的 Something that is defective has a fault in it and does not work correctly.

defer   verb [T] UK /dɪˈfɜːr/ US /dɪˈfɜː/ -rr- 使延期，使延缓，推迟 to delay something until a later time [GRE]

deference   noun [U] formal UK /ˈdef.ər.əns/ US /ˈdef.ɚ.əns/ 尊重，尊敬 respect and politeness [GRE]

defile   1 verb [T] formal UK /dɪˈfaɪl/ US /dɪˈfaɪl/ 玷污，亵渎 xièdú，糟蹋 to spoil something or someone so that that thing or person is less beautiful or pure 2 noun [C] literary UK /dɪˈfaɪl/ US /dɪˈfaɪl/ （山中）狭径，峡道 a very narrow valley between two mountains [GRE]

deform   1 verb UK /dɪˈfɔːm/ US /dɪˈfɔːrm/ 使变形，使扭曲 [T] to spoil the usual and true shape of something

deforestation   noun [U] UK /diːˌfɒr.ɪˈsteɪ.ʃən/ US /diːˌfɔːr.əˈsteɪ.ʃən/ 大面积砍伐森林；人为毁林 the cutting down of trees in a large area, or the destruction of forests by people

defrost　　verb [I or T] UK　/ˌdiːˈfrɒst/ US　/ˌdiːˈfrɑːst/ 除霜；（使）溶化，（使）解冻 to (cause to) become free of ice, or to (cause to) become no longer frozen

defriend　　verb [T] UK　/ˌdiːˈfrend/ US　/ˌdiːˈfrend/ (also unfriend) 在网络社交平台上将某人从好友名单上去除 to remove someone from your list of friends on a social networking website

degenerate　　　1 verb [I] UK　/dɪˈdʒen.ə.reɪt/ US　/dɪˈdʒen.ə.reɪt/ （质量）下降；退化，衰退 to become worse in quality

degrade　　1 verb UK　/dɪˈɡreɪd/ US　/dɪˈɡreɪd/ (LOSE RESPECT) 贬低；降低…的身份；侮辱…的人格 [T] to cause people to feel that they or other people have no value and do not have the respect or good opinion of others 2 verb (SPOIL) 玷污；损害，危害 [T] to spoil or destroy the beauty or quality of something 4 verb (CHANGE STRUCTURE) 降解，自然分解 [I] chemistry specialized (of a substance) to change into a more simple chemical structure

dehydrate　　　verb [I or T] UK　/ˌdiː.haɪˈdreɪt/ US　/ˌdiː.haɪˈdreɪt/去除（…的）水分，（使）脱水 to lose water, or to cause water to be lost from something, especially from a person's body [GRE]

dejected　　adjective UK　/dɪˈdʒek.tɪd/ US　/dɪˈdʒek.tɪd/ 沮丧的；失意的；失望的 unhappy, disappointed, or without hope [GRE]

delete　　verb [I or T] UK　/dɪˈliːt/ US　/dɪˈliːt/ B1 删除，删去，划掉（尤指文字） to remove or draw a line through something, especially a written word or words

deleterious   adjective formal UK   /ˌdel.ɪˈtɪə.ri.əs/ US   /ˌdel.ɪˈtɪr.i.əs/ 有害的，造成危害的 harmful [GRE]

deleverage   verb [I or T]   FINANCE UK /ˌdiːˈliːvərɪdʒ/ US /ˌdiːˈlevərɪdʒ/ 去杠杆化 to reduce a company's borrowing in relation to its share capital:

demerit   1 noun [C] UK   /ˌdiːˈmer.ɪt/ US   /ˌdiːˈmer.ɪt/ 缺陷；劣势 formal a fault or disadvantage 2 noun （尤指学校给学生的）记过，过失分 a mark given to someone, especially a student in a school, because they have done something wrong or broken a rule

demilitarize   verb [T] (uk usually demilitarise) UK /ˌdiːˈmɪl.ɪ.tər.aɪz/ US /ˌdiːˈmɪl.ə.t̬ə.aɪz/ 从...撤军；使非军事化 to remove military forces from an area

demolish   1 verb [T] UK /dɪˈmɒl.ɪʃ/ US /dɪˈmɑː.lɪʃ/ [T] (DESTROY) B2 （尤指为利用土地而）拆除，拆毁 to completely destroy a building, especially in order to use the land for something else 2 verb C2 推翻（论点），颠覆（理论） to prove that an argument or theory is wrong

demolition   1 noun [C or U] UK /ˌdem.əˈlɪʃ.ən/ US /ˌdem.əˈlɪʃ.ən/ 拆除，拆毁 the act of destroying something such as a building [GRE]

demotivate   verb [T] UK /ˌdiːˈməʊ.tɪ.veɪt/ US /ˌdiːˈmoʊ.t̬ə.veɪt/ 使工作积极性下降，使变得消极 to make someone less enthusiastic about a job

demure   adjective UK /dɪˈmjʊər/ US /dɪˈmjʊr/（尤指女性）端庄的，文静的，安静的 (especially of women) quiet and well behaved

demystify　　　　verb [T] UK　/ˌdiːˈmɪs.tɪ.faɪ/ US　/ˌdiːˈmɪs.tə.faɪ/ 使易懂，(使通俗易懂，使 YAO)通俗化 to make something easier to understand

denigrate　　verb [T] UK　/ˈden.ɪ.greɪt/ US　/ˈden.ə.greɪt/ 贬低，诋毁 to say that someone or something is not good or important [GRE]

denude　　1 verb [T] UK　/dɪˈnjuːd/ US　/dɪˈnuːd/ 使（尤指土地）裸露，使光秃 to remove the covering of something, especially land [GRE]

deplete　　verb [T] UK　/dɪˈpliːt/ US　/dɪˈpliːt/ 消耗；耗费（资源、金钱、精力等） to reduce something in size or amount, especially supplies of energy, money, etc. [GRE]

deport　　verb [T] UK　/dɪˈpɔːt/ US　/dɪˈpɔːrt/ 把…驱逐出境，把…遣送出境 to force someone to leave a country, especially someone who has no legal right to be there or who has broken the law [GRE]

depose　　verb [T] UK　/dɪˈpəʊz/ US　/dɪˈpoʊz/ 罢免，使免职，使下台 to remove someone important from a powerful position [GRE]

deprive　　1 verb [T] UK　/dɪˈpraɪv/ US　/dɪˈpraɪv/ B2 夺走，抢去，剥夺 to take something, especially something necessary or pleasant, away from someone

deprivation　　noun [C or U] UK　/ˌdep.rɪˈveɪ.ʃən/ US　/ˌdep.rəˈveɪ.ʃən/ C2 缺失，缺乏，匮乏 a situation in which you do not have things or conditions that are usually considered necessary for a pleasant life

derail　　1 verb UK　/ˌdiːˈreɪl/ US　/ˌdiːˈreɪl/ (TRAIN) （使）（火车）脱轨 [I or T] If a train derails or is derailed, it comes off the railway tracks.

deracinate   verb /dɪˈrasɪneɪt/ 灭绝；根除；pull out; uproot (someone) from their natural geographical, social, or cultural environment. [GRE]

derelict   1 adjective UK /ˈder.ə.lɪkt/ US /ˈder.ə.lɪkt/ 失修的，破败的；废弃的 Derelict buildings or places are not cared for and are in bad condition. [GRE]

derogate   1 verb [T] formal UK /ˈder.ə.geɪt/ US /ˈder.ə.geɪt/ [T] (CRITICIZE) 贬低；诽谤；损害 to talk about or treat someone or something in a way that shows you do not respect him, her, or it

derogatory   adjective UK /dɪˈrɒg.ə.tər.i/ /dɪˈrɒg.ə.tri/ US /dɪˈrɑː.gə.tɔːr.i/ (also derogative, /dɪˈrɒg.ə.tɪv/ /-ˈrɑː.gə.t̬ɪv/) 诋毁的，贬损的，贬低的 showing strong disapproval and not showing respect

descend   1 verb UK /dɪˈsend/ US /dɪˈsend/ (POSITION) 下降；走下；降下 B2 [I or T] formal to go or come down

descent   1 noun UK /dɪˈsent/ US /dɪˈsent/ (RELATION) 血缘关系，家族关系；祖先；出身 [U] the state or fact of being related to a particular person or group of people who lived in the past

descendant   noun [C] UK /dɪˈsen.dənt/ US /dɪˈsen.dənt/ C2 子孙，后代 a person who is related to you and who lives after you, such as your child or grandchild

deselect   verb [T often passive] politics uk specialized UK /ˌdiː.səˈlekt/ US /ˌdiː.səˈlekt/ 取消…的候选人资格 to choose, as a local political party, not to have the person who now represents your party as your candidate at the next election

desertion   1 noun UK /dɪˈzɜː.ʃən/ US /dɪˈzɝː.ʃən/ 当逃兵 [C or U] the act of leaving the armed forces without permission

desiccated   1 adjective UK /ˈdes.ɪ.keɪ.tɪd/ US /ˈdes.ə.keɪ.t̬ɪd/ 干的；干燥的；脱水的 dried, with the moisture removed [GRE]

detach   verb [T] UK /dɪˈtætʃ/ US /dɪˈtætʃ/使分离，使分开；拆掉 to separate or remove something from something else that it is connected to [GRE]

deter   verb [T] UK /dɪˈtɜːr/ US /dɪˈtɝː/ -rr- 阻挠，阻止；威慑；使不敢 to prevent someone from doing something or to make someone less enthusiastic about doing something by making it difficult for that person to do it or by threatening bad results if they do it [GRE]

deteriorate   verb [I] UK /dɪˈtɪə.ri.ə.reɪt/ US /dɪˈtɪr.i.ə.reɪt/ 恶化，变坏 C1 to become worse

dethrone   1 verb [T] UK /diˈθrəʊn/ US /diˈθroʊn/ 废黜，推翻（国王或女王）；使下台 to remove a king or queen from their position of power

detour   1 noun [C] UK /ˈdiː.tɔːr/ US /ˈdiː.tʊr/ 绕行的路，迂回路 a different or less direct route to a place that is used to avoid a problem or to visit somewhere or do something on the way [GRE]

Prefix: deca- ten; used in forming nouns

Meaning in English: ten

Origin language: Latin/ Greek

English examples:

deca-   prefix UK   /dek.ə-/ US   /dek.ə-/ 十（用以组成名词） ten; used in forming nouns

decathlon   noun [C] UK   /dɪˈkæθ.lɒn/ US   /dɪˈkæθ.lɑːn/男子十项全能（比赛） a competition in which an athlete competes in ten sports events

decagram   In geometry, a decagram is a 10-point star polygon. There is one regular decagram, containing the vertices of a regular decagon, but connected by every third point. Its Schläfli symbol is {10/3}.

decade   noun [C] UK   /ˈdek.eɪd/ /dekˈeɪd/ US   /ˈdek.eɪd/ /dekˈeɪd/ B2 十年；年代 a period of ten years, especially a period such as 2010 to 2019

Prefix: deci- 0.1 or one tenth of the stated unit

Meaning in English: ten

Origin language: Latin/ Greek

English examples:

deci-   prefix science UK   /des.i-/ US   /des.i-/ 表示"十分之一" 0.1 or one tenth of the stated unit

decimetre   noun [C] UK (US decimeter) /ˈdes.ɪˌmiː.tər/ /ˈdes.ɪˌmiː.tɚ/ 分米（十分之一米） (written abbreviation dm) a unit of length equal to 0.1 of a metre

decimal   1 adjective UK   /ˈdes.ɪ.məl/ US   /ˈdes.ə.məl/ 十进位的 relating to or expressed in a system of counting based on the number ten

decimalization   noun [U] (uk usually decimalisation) UK /ˌdes.ɪ.mə.laɪˈzeɪ.ʃən/ US /ˌdes.ə.mə.ləˈzeɪ.ʃən/ 十进制转换 the changing of a system or number to a decimal form

decimate   verb [T usually passive] UK /ˈdes.ɪ.meɪt/ US /ˈdes.ə.meɪt/ 毁灭，大量杀戮；大幅削减 to kill a large number of something, or to reduce something severely

decimation   noun [U] UK /ˌdes.ɪˈmeɪ.ʃən/ US /ˌdes.əˈmeɪ.ʃən/毁灭，大量杀戮；大幅削减 the act of killing a something in large numbers, or reducing something severely

Prefix (Medical): dent- Of or pertaining to teeth

Meaning in English: Of or pertaining to teeth

Origin language: Latin (dens, dentis), tooth

English examples:

dent   1 noun [C] UK /dent/ US /dent/（物体表面上的）坑，凹陷 a small hollow mark in the surface of something, caused by pressure or by being hit 2 verb [T] UK /dent/ US /dent/使产生凹痕，使凹陷 to make a small hollow mark in the surface of something 3 verb 打击，损伤（信心或自豪感） If you dent someone's confidence or pride, you make them feel less confident or proud. [GRE]

dental   1 adjective UK /ˈden.təl/ US /ˈden.t̬əl/牙的，牙齿的 B2 relating to the teeth

dental dam   noun [C] UK /ˈden.təl ˌdæm/ US /ˈden.t̬əl ˌdæm/ 牙科用橡皮布（牙科治疗中使用的胶皮防水布或口交中防止染上艾滋病所使用的

阻隔膜） a piece of rubber that is used to keep the teeth dry during dental treatment, or that is used to protect the mouth during sexual activity

dental floss noun [U] UK /ˈden.təl ˌflɒs/ US /ˈden.t̬əl ˌflɑːs/ 牙线 a type of thread used for cleaning between the teeth

dental hygienist noun [C] UK /ˈden.təl haɪˌdʒiː.nɪst/ US /ˈden.t̬əl haɪˌdʒen.ɪst/ （从事牙齿清洁护理工作的）牙科医师，牙科保健医师 a person who works with a dentist and cleans people's teeth to keep them healthy

dental practitioner/surgeon noun [C] formal UK /ˈden.təl præk̩tɪʃ.ən.ər/ US /ˈden.t̬əl præk̩tɪʃ.ən.ɚ/ 牙科医生 a dentist

dentigerous cyst noun [C] medical specialized UK /denˌtɪdʒ.ə.rəs ˈsɪst/ US /denˌtɪdʒ.ɚ.əs ˈsɪst/ 含牙囊肿 a cyst (= a small growth filled with liquid) that develops around the top of a tooth that has not yet grown through the gum

dentine noun [U] anatomy specialized UK /ˈden.tiːn/ US /ˈden.tiːn/ 象牙质（构成牙齿主体的坚硬含钙物质，表面覆盖白色牙釉质） a hard substance containing calcium that forms the main part of a tooth and has enamel (= a shiny white substance) covering it

dentist noun [C] UK /ˈden.tɪst/ US /ˈden.t̬ɪst/ 牙科医生 A2 a person whose job is treating people's teeth

dentistry noun [U] UK /ˈden.tɪ.stri/ US /ˈden.t̬ɪ.stri/ 牙科医术；牙医的工作 the work of a dentist

dentition noun [U] biology specialized UK /denˈtɪʃ.ən/ US /denˈtɪʃ.ən/ （人或动物）齿系；牙列（牙齿的数量、种类和排列） the number, type, and arrangement of teeth in a person or animal

denture   1 noun [C usually plural] medical UK   /ˈden.tʃər/ US /ˈden.tʃɚ/ (also dentures [plural]) 假牙 a small piece of plastic or similar material, with false teeth attached, that fits inside the mouth of someone who does not have their own teeth

Prefix (Medical): dermat(o)-, derm(o)- Of or pertaining to the skin

Meaning in English: Of or pertaining to the skin

Origin language: Ancient Greek δέρμα, δέρματ- (dérma, démat-), skin, human skin

English examples:

dermatitis   noun [U] medical specialized UK   /ˌdɜː.məˈtaɪ.təs/ US /ˌdɝ.məˈtaɪ.təs/ 皮炎 a disease in which the skin is red and painful   derm- Meaning in English: skin

dermatologist   noun [C] medical UK   /ˌdɜː.məˈtɒl.ə.dʒɪst/ US /ˌdɝ.məˈtɑː.lə.dʒɪst/ 皮肤科医生 a doctor who studies and treats skin diseases   derm- Meaning in English: skin

dermatology   noun [U] UK   /ˌdɜː.məˈtɒl.ə.dʒi/ US /ˌdɝ.məˈtɑː.lə-/ 皮肤学 the scientific study of the skin and its diseases   derm- Meaning in English: skin

dermatographism   noun [U] 皮肤划痕症 Dermatographia is a condition in which lightly scratching your skin causes raised, red lines where you've scratched. Though not serious, it can be uncomfortable. Dermatographia is a condition also known as skin writing.

dermatome   1 noun [C] medical specialized UK   /ˈdɜːm.ə.teʊm/ US /ˈdɝ.m.əˌtoʊm/ [C] (SKIN) 皮区 an area of the skin supplied by a single spinal nerve derm- Meaning in English: skin 2 noun [C] (TOOL) 植皮刀，皮刀 a tool used to take very thin slices of skin from one part of the body to repair skin in another area

dermis   noun [S] medical specialized UK /ˈdɜː.mɪs/ US /ˈdɝː.mɪs/真皮（位于表皮下方，皮层厚，包括血管、汗腺和神经末梢） the thick layer of skin under the epidermis (= thin outer layer) that contains blood vessels, sweat glands and nerve endings

echinoderm   noun [C]   BIOLOGY   specialized UK /ekˈaɪ.nəʊ.dɜːm/ US /ɪˈkaɪ.noʊ.dɝːm/ 棘皮动物（一种海洋生物，表皮有凸起或棘刺，身体呈五辐对称形） a type of sea creature with raised areas or sharp points on its skin and a body made of five equal parts arranged around the centre

ectoderm   noun [C] UK /ˈek.tə.dɜːm/ US /ˈek.tə.dɝːm/ 外胚层 the cells in the embryo of a human or animal that develop into skin, hair, and the nervous system

epidermis   noun [S or U]   ANATOMY   specialized UK /ˌep.ɪˈdɜː.mɪs/ US /ˌep.əˈdɝː.mɪs/ 表皮 the thin outer layer of the skin

hypodermic   adjective   MEDICAL   specialized UK /ˌhaɪ.pəˈdɜː.mɪk/ US /ˌhaɪ.poʊˈdɝː.mɪk/ 皮下注射的 (of medical tools) used to inject drugs (= put them into the body) under a person's skin

pachyderm   noun [C]   old-fashioned UK /ˈpæk.ɪ.dɜːm/ US /ˈpæk.ə.dɝːm/ 厚皮动物（大型哺乳动物，皮厚、有蹄，如大象、犀牛或河马等） a group of large mammals that includes elephants, rhinoceroses, and hippopotamuses

Pachydermata   厚皮動物 Pachydermata is an obsolete order of mammals described by Gottlieb Storr, Georges Cuvier, and others, at one time recognized by many systematists. Because it is polyphyletic, the order is no longer in use, but it is important in the history of systematics. Wikipedia

dermatitis   noun [U] UK /ˌdɜː.məˈtaɪ.təs/ US /ˌdɝː.məˈtaɪ.t̬əs/ specialized 皮炎 a disease in which the skin is red and painful

Scleroderma   硬皮病 Scleroderma is an uncommon condition that results in hard, thickened areas of skin and sometimes problems with internal organs and blood vessels. Scleroderma is caused by the immune system attacking the connective tissue under the skin and around internal organs and blood vessels.

taxidermist   noun [C] UK /ˈtæk.sɪ.dɜː.mɪst/ US /ˈtæk.sɪ.dɝː.mɪst/ （动物标本）剥制师 a person whose job is taxidermy

taxidermy   noun [U] UK /ˈtæk.sɪ.dɜː.mi/ US /ˈtæk.sɪ.dɝː.mi/ （动物标本）剥制术 the activity of cleaning, preserving, and filling the skins of dead animals with special material to make them look as if they are still alive

Prefix (Medical): dextr(o)- right, on the right side

Meaning in English: right, on the right side

Origin language: Latin dexter

English examples:

dextrocardia   noun [U] 右位心 In dextrocardia, the heart is positioned on the right side of the chest instead of its normal position on the left side. Dextrocardia on its own does not usually cause problems, but it tends to occur with other conditions that can have serious effects on the heart, lungs and other vital organs

dexterous   1 adjective (also dextrous) UK /ˈdek.strəs/ UK /ˈdek.stər.əs/ US /ˈdek.strəs/ US /ˈdek.stər.əs/ 纯熟的，娴熟的；灵巧的，敏捷的 having the ability to perform a difficult action quickly and skilfully with the hands 2 头

脑灵活的 having the ability to think quickly and effectively or to do something difficult extremely well:

[GRE]

dexterity noun [U] UK /dek'ster.ə.ti/ US /dek'ster.ə.t̬i/纯熟，娴熟；灵巧，敏捷 the ability to perform a difficult action quickly and skilfully with the hands, or the ability to think quickly and effectively

Dexiarchia The Dexiarchia are a suborder of sea slugs, shell-less marine gastropod molluscs in the order Nudibranchia. This classification is based on the study by Schrödl et al., published in 2001, who recognized within this clade two clades Pseudoeuctenidiacea and Cladobranchia. Wikipedia

ambidextrous adjective UK /ˌæm.bɪˈdek.strəs/ US /ˌæm.bɪˈdek.strəs/双手都很灵巧的；左右开弓的 able to use both hands equally well

Prefix: di-, dia- two/ through/across
Meaning in English: two/ through/across

Origin language: Greek

English examples:

digraph noun [C] LANGUAGE specialized UK /ˈdaɪ.grɑːf/ US /-græf/ 二合字母（两个字母发一个音） two letters written together that make one sound

dialogue 1 noun [C or U] (us also dialog) UK /ˈdaɪ.ə.lɒg/ US /ˈdaɪ.ə.lɑːg/ B2 对话，对白 conversation that is written for a book, play, or film

dialysis noun [U] medical, chemistry specialized UK /daɪˈæl.ə.sɪs/ US /daɪˈæl.ə.sɪs/ 渗析，透析，（尤指对肾病患者做的）血液透析 a process of separating substances from liquid by putting them through a thin piece of skin-like material, especially to make pure the blood of people whose kidneys are not working correctly

diagnose   verb [T] UK   /ˈdaɪ.əg.nəʊz/ US   /ˌdaɪ.əgˈnoʊz/ 诊断（病症）；查出（问题） C2 to recognize and name the exact character of a disease or a problem, by examining it

diagnosis   noun [C or U] UK   /ˌdaɪ.əgˈnəʊ.sɪs/ US   /ˌdaɪ.əgˈnoʊ.sɪs/ plural diagnoses 诊断 C2 a judgment about what a particular illness or problem is, made after examining it

diagnostic   1 adjective UK   /ˌdaɪ.əgˈnɒs.tɪk/ US   /ˌdaɪ.əgˈnɑː.stɪk/ (DISEASE) 诊断的；用于诊断的 medical specialized identifying a particular illness using a combination of signs and symptoms

diagonal   1 adjective UK   /daɪˈæg.ən.əl/ US   /daɪˈæg.ən.əl/ 斜线的，对角线的 A diagonal line is straight and sloping, not horizontal or vertical, for example joining two opposite corners of a square or other flat shape with four sides.

diagram   1 noun [C] UK   /ˈdaɪ.ə.græm/ US   /ˈdaɪ.ə.græm/ B1 图，图解，示意图 a simple plan that represents a machine, system, or idea, etc., often drawn to explain how it works

dialysis   noun [U] medical, chemistry specialized UK   /daɪˈæl.ə.sɪs/ US /daɪˈæl.ə.sɪs/ 渗析，透析，（尤指对肾病患者做的）血液透析 a process of separating substances from liquid by putting them through a thin piece of skin-like material, especially to make pure the blood of people whose kidneys are not working correctly

diameter   noun [C or U] UK   /daɪˈæm.ɪ.tər/ US   /daɪˈæm.ə.t̬ɚ/ 直径 (the length of) a straight line that reaches from one point on the edge of a round shape or object, through its centre, to a point on the opposite edge

diametrically   adverb UK   /ˌdaɪ.əˈmet.rɪ.kəl.i/ US   /ˌdaɪ.əˈmet.rɪ.kəl.i/ 完全地，完整地 completely

Diacetyl   noun [U] 丁二酮 Diacetyl is a chemical that was found to be a prominent volatile constituent in butter flavoring and air at the microwave popcorn plant initially investigated by NIOSH.

diabetes   noun [U] UK   /ˌdaɪ.əˈbiː.tiːz/ US   /ˌdaɪ.əˈbiː.təs/ 糖尿病 a disease in which the body cannot control the level of sugar in the blood

diabetes mellitus   noun [U] medical specialized UK   /daɪ.əˌbiː.tiːz ˈmel.ɪ.təs/ US   /daɪ.əˌbiː.tɪz ˈmel.ɪ.təs/ 糖尿病 a severe form of diabetes in which the body cannot use glucose (= sugar as it is normally used in the body)

diabetic   1 noun [C] UK   /ˌdaɪ.əˈbet.ɪk/ US   /ˌdaɪ.əˈbet̬.ɪk/ 糖尿病患者 a person who has diabetes 2 adjective UK   /ˌdaɪ.əˈbet.ɪk/ US /ˌdaɪ.əˈbet̬.ɪk/ 与糖尿病有关的 relating to diabetes 3 adjective 供糖尿病患者食用的，无糖的 made for diabetic people to eat

diabolical   1 adjective UK   /ˌdaɪ.əˈbɒl.ɪ.kəl/ US   /ˌdaɪ.əˈbɑː.lɪ.kəl/ (us also diabolic) 糟糕透顶的，差得惊人的 informal extremely bad or shocking 2 adjective 邪恶的，恶魔般的 evil, or caused by the Devil [GRE]

diabolic   adjective. (ˌdaɪəˈbɒlɪk) 糟糕透顶的，差得惊人的，恶魔般的；残忍的 of, relating to, or proceeding from the devil; satanic. befitting a devil; extremely cruel or wicked; fiendish. [GRE]

diachronic   adjective UK   /ˌdaɪ.əˈkrɒn.ɪk/ US   /ˌdaɪ.əˈkrɑː.nɪk/ （尤指语言）历经时间长河的，历时的 relating to the changes in something, especially a language, that happen over time

Prefix (Medical): digit- finger, thumb, or toe

Meaning in English: finger, thumb, or toe

Origin language: Latin

English examples:

digit 2 noun [C] (FINGER) 手指；拇指；脚趾 anatomy specialized a finger, thumb, or toe

digitorum adjective anatomy specialized UK /ˌdɪdʒ.ɪˈtɔː.rəm/ US /ˌdɪdʒ.ɪˈtɔːr.əm/ （拉丁语，用于医学术语中）趾的,指的 a Latin word meaning "of the fingers or toes", used in the medical names and descriptions of some muscles

Prefix: dis- not/ opposite of

Meaning in English: not/ opposite of

Origin language: Latin

English examples:

dis- prefix UK /dɪs-/ US /dɪs-/ （加在某些词语前表示相反的意思） added to the front of some words to form their opposites

disability noun [C or U] UK /ˌdɪs.əˈbɪl.ə.ti/ US /ˌdɪs.əˈbɪl.ə.t̬i/ 残疾，缺陷，残障 B2 an illness, injury, or condition that makes it difficult for someone to do the things that other people do

disable 1 verb UK /dɪˈseɪ.bəl/ US /dɪˈseɪ.bəl/ (PERSON) 使伤残，使丧失能力 [T often passive] to cause someone to have an illness, injury, or condition that makes it difficult for them to do the things that other people do

disabuse verb [T] formal UK /ˌdɪs.əˈbjuːz/ US /ˌdɪs.əˈbjuːz/ 使改变想法；使消除误解 to cause someone no longer to have a wrong idea [GRE]

disadvantage　　1 noun [C or U] UK　/ˌdɪs.ədˈvɑːn.tɪdʒ/ US /ˌdɪs.ədˈvæn.t̬ɪdʒ/ 劣势，不利因素 B1 a condition or situation that causes problems, especially one that causes something or someone to be less successful than other things or people

disaffected　　1 adjective UK　/ˌdɪs.əˈfek.tɪd/ US　/ˌdɪs.əˈfek.tɪd/ 失望的，不满的 no longer supporting or being satisfied with an organization or idea　2 adjective （青年人）叛逆的，对社会不满的 Young people who are disaffected are no longer satisfied with society's values. [GRE]

disagree　　verb [I] UK　/ˌdɪs.əˈɡriː/ US　/ˌdɪs.əˈɡriː/ B1 不同意，持异议，反对 to not have the same opinion, idea, etc.

disagreement　　noun [C or U] UK　/ˌdɪs.əˈɡriː.mənt/ US　/ˌdɪs.əˈɡriː.mənt/ B2 分歧，意见不合 an argument or a situation in which people do not have the same opinion

disappear　　1 verb [I] UK　/ˌdɪs.əˈpɪər/ US　/ˌdɪs.əˈpɪr/ B1 消失；失踪 If people or things disappear, they go somewhere where they cannot be seen or found.

disappearance　　noun [C or U] UK　/ˌdɪs.əˈpɪə.rəns/ US　/ˌdɪs.əˈpɪr.əns/ B2 消失；失踪 the fact of someone or something disappearing

disappoint　　verb [I or T] UK　/ˌdɪs.əˈpɔɪnt/ US　/ˌdɪs.əˈpɔɪnt/ B1 （使）失望，（使）沮丧 to fail to satisfy someone or their hopes, wishes, etc., or to make someone feel unhappy

disappointed　　adjective UK　/ˌdɪs.əˈpɔɪn.tɪd/ US　/ˌdɪs.əˈpɔɪn.t̬ɪd/ B1 失望的，沮丧的 unhappy because someone or something was not as good as you hoped or expected, or because something did not happen

disappointing   adjective UK /ˌdɪs.əˈpɔɪn.tɪŋ/ US /ˌdɪs.əˈpɔɪn.t̬ɪŋ/ B1 令人失望的，让人沮丧的 making you feel disappointed

disappointment   1 noun UK /ˌdɪs.əˈpɔɪnt.mənt/ US /ˌdɪs.əˈpɔɪnt.mənt/ 失望，沮丧 B1 [U] the feeling of being disappointed

disapproval   noun [U] UK /ˌdɪs.əˈpruː.vəl/ US /ˌdɪs.əˈpruː.vəl/ 反对，不赞成 C1 the feeling of having a negative opinion of someone or something

disapprove   verb [I] UK /ˌdɪs.əˈpruːv/ US /ˌdɪs.əˈpruːv/ 反对；不赞成 B2 to feel that something or someone is bad, wrong, etc.

disarm   1 verb UK /dɪˈsɑːm/ US /dɪˈsɑːrm/ (REMOVE WEAPONS) 缴…的械,解除…的武装；交出武器,裁军 [I or T] to take weapons away from someone, or to give up weapons or armies [GRE]

disarmament   noun [U] UK /dɪˈsɑː.mə.mənt/ US /dɪˈsɑːr.mə.mənt/ 解除或放弃武器的行为 the act of taking away or giving up weapons [GRE]

disarray   noun [U] formal UK /ˌdɪs.əˈreɪ/ US /ˌdɪs.əˈreɪ/ 凌乱；混乱；杂乱 the state of being confused and having no organization or of being untidy [GRE]

disavow   verb [T] formal UK /ˌdɪs.əˈvaʊ/ US /ˌdɪs.əˈvaʊ/ 声称对…一无所知；否认对…负有任何责任；声称与…毫无关联 to say that you know nothing about something, or that you have no responsibility for or connection with something [GRE]

discern   verb [T] formal UK /dɪˈsɜːn/ US /dɪˈsɜːn/ 看出；辨别出；明白 to see, recognize, or understand something that is not clear [GRE]

discharge   1 verb UK /dɪsˈtʃɑːdʒ/ US /dɪsˈtʃɑːrdʒ/ (ALLOW TO LEAVE) 允许…离开；（尤指）允许…出院；（根据法庭决议）释放 [T] to allow someone officially to leave somewhere, especially a hospital or a law court [GRE]

disclose   verb [I or T] formal UK /dɪˈskləʊz/ US /dɪˈskloʊz/ C2 公开，公布；透露，揭露 to make something known publicly, or to show something that was hidden

discombobulate   verb [T] UK /ˌdɪs.kəmˈbɒb.jə.leɪt/ US /ˌdɪs.kəmˈbɑː.bjə.leɪt/ 使困惑，扰乱，打乱 informal mainly humorous to confuse someone or make someone feel uncomfortable [GRE]

discomfit   verb [T] formal UK /dɪˈskʌm.fɪt/ US /dɪˈskʌm.fɪt/ （尤指在精神上）使感到不舒服，使不安 to make someone feel uncomfortable, especially mentally [GRE]

discommode   verb FORMAL past tense: discommoded; past participle: discommoded; 打扰，使不便 cause (someone) trouble or inconvenience. [GRE]

discompose   verb /dɪskəmˈpəʊz/ 使不安,扰乱或激怒（某人）disturb or agitate (someone).

discomfort   noun [C or U] UK /dɪˈskʌm.fət/ US /dɪˈskʌm.fət/ 不适，不安；令人不适（或不安）的事物 C1 a feeling of being uncomfortable physically or mentally, or something that causes this

disconcert   verb [I or T] UK /ˌdɪs.kənˈsɜːt/ US /ˌdɪs.kənˈsɝːt/ （使）焦虑，（使）不安 to make someone feel suddenly uncertain and worried [GRE]

discontent   noun [U] UK /ˌdɪs.kənˈtent/ US /ˌdɪs.kənˈtent/ (also discontentment,) 不满；不满足 C1 a feeling of wanting better treatment or an improved situation

discord   1 noun UK /ˈdɪs.kɔːd/ US /ˈdɪs.kɔːrd/ (DISAGREEMENT) 看法不一致，缺乏共识 [U] formal the state of not agreeing or sharing opinions [GRE]

discount   1 noun [C] UK /ˈdɪs.kaʊnt/ US /ˈdɪs.kaʊnt/ 减价，打折 A2 a reduction in the usual price

discourage   1 verb [T] UK /dɪˈskʌr.ɪdʒ/ US /dɪˈskɝː.ɪdʒ/ [T] (MAKE LESS CONFIDENT) B2 使泄气，给...泼冷水，使心灰意冷 to make someone feel less confident, enthusiastic, and positive about something, or less willing to do something

discredit   1 verb [T] formal UK /dɪˈskred.ɪt/ US /dɪˈskred.ɪt/ 使名誉受损；使受到怀疑 to cause people to stop respecting someone or believing in an idea or person [GRE]

discreet   adjective UK /dɪˈskriːt/ US /dɪˈskriːt/ 审慎的，谨慎的，小心的 C2 careful not to cause embarrassment or attract too much attention, especially by keeping something secret [GRE]

discrepancy   noun [C or U] formal UK /dɪˈskrep.ən.si/ US /dɪˈskrep.ən.si/ 不一致，出入，差异 a difference between two things that should be the same [GRE]

discrete   adjective UK /dɪˈskriːt/ US /dɪˈskriːt/ 独立的，各自的，单独的 clearly separate or different in shape or form [GRE]

discretion   1 noun [U] UK /dɪˈskreʃ.ən/ US /dɪˈskreʃ.ən/ [U] (CAREFUL BEHAVIOUR) 慎重，谨慎；守口如瓶 C2 the ability to behave without causing embarrassment or attracting too much attention, especially by keeping information secret [GRE]

discriminate   1 verb UK /dɪˈskrɪm.ɪ.neɪt/ US /dɪˈskrɪm.ə.neɪt/ (TREAT DIFFERENTLY) 歧视；区别对待 C1 [I] to treat a person or particular group of people differently, especially in a worse way from the way in which you treat other people, because of their skin colour, sex, sexuality, etc. 2 verb (SEE A DIFFERENCE) 区分，区别；分辨，辨别 C2 [I + adv/prep] formal to be able to see the difference between two things or people [GRE]

disdain   1 noun [U] formal UK /dɪsˈdeɪn/ US /dɪsˈdeɪn/ 轻视，蔑视，鄙视,看不上眼 the feeling of not liking someone or something and thinking that they do not deserve your interest or respect [GRE]

disenchanted   adjective UK /ˌdɪs.ɪnˈtʃɑːn.tɪd/ US /ˌdɪs.ɪnˈtʃæn.t̬ɪd/ 觉醒的；不再着迷的；幻想破灭的 no longer believing in the value of something, especially having learned of the problems with it [GRE]

disengage   verb formal UK /ˌdɪs.ɪŋˈɡeɪdʒ/ US /ˌdɪs.ɪŋˈɡeɪdʒ/ 松开（离合器） [T] If you disengage the clutch of a car, you stop the power produced by the engine being connected to the wheels.

disgorge   1 verb [T] UK /dɪsˈɡɔːdʒ/ US /dɪsˈɡɔːrdʒ/ 大量排放（液体、气体等物质） literary to release large amounts of liquid, gas, or other contents [GRE]

disgrace　　1 noun [U] UK　/dɪsˈɡreɪs/ US　/dɪsˈɡreɪs/ B2 耻辱，丢脸；不光彩的行为 embarrassment and the loss of other people's respect, or behaviour that causes this

disgruntled　　adjective UK　/dɪsˈɡrʌn.təld/ US　/dɪsˈɡrʌn.t̬əld/ 不满的；不悦的 unhappy, annoyed, and disappointed about something

dishearten　　verb [T] UK　/dɪsˈhɑː.tən/ US　/dɪsˈhɑːr.tən/ 使泄气，使绝望，使沮丧 to make a person lose confidence, hope, and energy [GRE]

disinclination　　noun [S or U] UK　/ˌdɪs.ɪŋ.klɪˈneɪ.ʃən/ US /ˌdɪs.ɪŋ.kləˈneɪ.ʃən/ 厌恶，不情愿 a feeling of not wanting to do something [GRE]

disinfect　　verb [T] UK　/ˌdɪs.ɪnˈfekt/ US /ˌdɪs.ɪnˈfekt/ 给…杀菌，为…除菌，替…消毒 to clean something using chemicals that kill bacteria and other very small living things that cause disease [GRE]

disinterest　　1 noun [U] UK　/dɪsˈɪn.tər.est/ US /dɪsˈɪn.t̬ɚ.est/ [U] (NOT INTERESTED) 缺乏兴趣，没有兴趣 lack of interest [GRE]

disjointed　　adjective UK　/dɪsˈdʒɔɪn.tɪd/ US /dɪsˈdʒɔɪn.t̬ɪd/（尤指词语或想法）不连贯的，没有条理的，杂乱无章的 (especially of words or ideas) not well connected or well ordered [GRE]

disjunctive　　adjective UK　/dɪsˈdʒʌŋk.tɪv/ US /dɪsˈdʒʌŋk.tɪv/ disjunctive adjective (DISCONNECTED) 不连贯的，分离的，分裂的 lacking any clear connection [GRE]

dislike　　1 verb [T] UK　/dɪˈslaɪk/ US　/dɪˈslaɪk/ B1 不喜欢，讨厌 to not like someone or something

disloyal   adjective UK /ˌdɪsˈlɔɪ.əl/ US /ˌdɪsˈlɔɪ.əl/ C2 不忠诚的，背叛的 not supporting someone that you should support

dismantle   1 verb UK /dɪˈsmæn.təl/ US /dɪˈsmæn.t̬əl/ 拆开，拆卸 [I or T] to take a machine apart or to come apart into separate pieces [GRE]

dismay   noun [U] UK /dɪˈsmeɪ/ US /dɪˈsmeɪ/ 沮丧，灰心，失望 C2 a feeling of unhappiness and disappointment [GRE]

dismiss   1 verb UK /dɪˈsmɪs/ US /dɪˈsmɪs/ (NOT TAKE SERIOUSLY) 对…不予理会，摒弃，（从头脑中）去除 C1 [T] to decide that something or someone is not important and not worth considering

disorder   1 noun UK /dɪˈsɔː.dər/ US /-ˈsɔːr.dɚ/ (CONFUSION) C2 [U] 混乱，凌乱，杂乱无章 a state of untidiness or lack of organization

disorder   1 noun UK /dɪˈsɔː.dər/ US /-ˈsɔːr.dɚ/ (CONFUSION) C2 [U] 混乱，凌乱，杂乱无章 a state of untidiness or lack of organization

disorganized   1 adjective (uk usually disorganised) UK /dɪˈsɔː.gə.naɪzd/ US /dɪˈsɔːr.gə.naɪzd/ 计划不周的，组织不善的 B2 badly planned and without order

disparage   verb [T] UK /dɪˈspær.ɪdʒ/ US /dɪˈsper.ɪdʒ/ 贬斥，贬低 to criticize someone or something in a way that shows you do not respect or value him, her, or it [GRE]

disparate   adjective formal UK /ˈdɪs.pər.ət/ US /ˈdɪs.pɚ.ət/ 截然不同的，迥然相异的 different in every way [GRE]

dispassionate　adjective UK　/dɪˈspæʃ.ən.ət/ US　/dɪˈspæʃ.ən.ət/ 冷静的，镇静的，沉着的 able to think clearly or make good decisions because of not being influenced by emotions [GRE]

dispatch　1 verb [T] uk also despatch UK　/dɪˈspætʃ/ US　/dɪˈspætʃ/ [T] (SEND) 发送；派遣 to send something, especially goods or a message, somewhere for a particular purpose [GRE]

disperse　verb [I or T] UK　/dɪˈspɜːs/ US　/dɪˈspɝːs/ （使）扩散，（使）散开，（使）分散 to spread across or move away over a large area, or to make something do this

displace　verb [T] UK　/dɪˈspleɪs/ US　/dɪˈspleɪs/ 迫使…离开常居地（或原位） C1 to force something or someone out of its usual or original position

display　1 verb [T] UK　/dɪˈspleɪ/ US　/dɪˈspleɪ/ [T] (ARRANGE) 布置，排列，陈列 B1 to arrange something or a collection of things so that it can be seen by the public

disposal　noun [U] UK　/dɪˈspəʊ.zəl/ US　/dɪˈspoʊ.zəl/ 清除；处理；抛弃 B2 the act of getting rid of something, especially by throwing it away

dispose　verb formal UK　/dɪˈspəʊz/ US　/dɪˈspoʊz/ 使对…产生某种感觉 to make someone feel a particular way towards someone or something [GRE]

disprove　verb [T] UK　/dɪˈspruːv/ US　/dɪˈspruːv/ 证明…是虚假的；驳倒 to prove that something is not true [GRE]

dispute   1 noun [C or U] UK /dɪˈspjuːt/ /ˈdɪs.pjuːt/ US /dɪˈspjuːt/ /ˈdɪs.pjuːt/ C2 （尤指劳资双方或相邻两国之间的）争执，争端，纠纷 an argument or disagreement, especially an official one between, for example, workers and employers or two countries with a common border

disqualify   verb [T] UK /dɪˈskwɒl.ɪ.faɪ/ US /dɪˈskwɑː.lə.faɪ/ 取消…的资格，剥夺…的资格 C2 to stop someone from being in a competition or doing something because they are unsuitable or they have done something wrong

disregard   1 noun [U] UK /ˌdɪs.rɪˈɡɑːd/ US /ˌdɪs.rɪˈɡɑːrd/ 忽视，漠视，无视 the fact of showing no care or respect for something [GRE]

disrespect 1 noun [U] UK /ˌdɪs.rɪˈspekt/ US /ˌdɪs.rɪˈspekt/ C1 不尊敬，无礼，失礼 lack of respect

disrupt   verb [T] UK /dɪsˈrʌpt/ US /dɪsˈrʌpt/ 打断，中断，扰乱 B2 to prevent something, especially a system, process, or event, from continuing as usual or as expected

dissect   1 verb [T] UK /daɪˈsekt/ /dɪˈsekt/ US /daɪˈsekt/ /dɪˈsekt/ 解剖 （尤指尸体或植物） to cut open something, especially a dead body or a plant, and study its structure [GRE]

dissemble verb [I] formal UK /dɪˈsem.bəl/ US /dɪˈsem.bəl/ 掩盖，掩饰 （动机、感情、真相等） to hide your real intentions and feelings or the facts [GRE]

disseminate   verb [T] formal UK /dɪˈsem.ɪ.neɪt/ US /dɪˈsem.ə.neɪt/ 散布，传播，宣传 to spread or give out something, especially news, information, ideas, etc., to a lot of people [GRE]

dissension　noun [U] formal UK　/dɪˈsen.ʃən/ US　/dɪˈsen.ʃən/（尤指组织、团体、政党等内部的）分歧，异议，争议 arguments and disagreement, especially in an organization, group, political party, etc. [GRE]

dissent　1 noun [U] formal UK　/dɪˈsent/ US　/dɪˈsent/（尤指对正式建议、计划或普遍看法的）不同意，异议 a strong difference of opinion on a particular subject, especially about an official suggestion or plan or a popular belief [GRE]

dissipate　verb [I or T] formal UK　/ˈdɪs.ɪ.peɪt/ US　/ˈdɪs.ə.peɪt/（使）逐渐消失；（使）逐渐浪费掉 to (cause to) gradually disappear or waste [GRE]

dissolute　adjective UK　/ˈdɪs.ə.luːt/ US　/ˈdɪs.ə.luːt/ literary 放纵的，放荡的；不道德的 (of a person) living in a way that other people strongly disapprove of [GRE]

dissolve　verb UK　/dɪˈzɒlv/ US　/dɪˈzɑːlv/ (BE ABSORBED)（使）溶解 C2 [I or T] (of a solid) to be absorbed by a liquid, especially when mixed, or (of a liquid) to absorb a solid [GRE]

dissolve　1 verb (END) 解散；解除；终止 C1 [T often passive] to end an official organization or a legal arrangement

dissonance　1 noun [U] UK　/ˈdɪs.ən.əns/ US　/ˈdɪs.ə.nəns/ 不和谐音 music specialized a combination of sounds or musical notes that are not pleasant when heard together [GRE]

dissuade　verb [T] UK　/dɪˈsweɪd/ US　/dɪˈsweɪd/ 劝说…不做某事，劝阻 to persuade someone not to do something [GRE]

distend　　verb [I] UK /dɪˈstend/ US /dɪˈstend/（通常指腹部或身体其他部位）鼓起，隆起，凸起 (usually of the stomach or other part of the body) to swell and become large (as if) by pressure from inside [GRE]

distil　　1 verb mainly uk (us usually distill) UK /dɪˈstɪl/ US /dɪˈstɪl/ -ll- (LIQUID) 蒸馏 [T] to make a liquid stronger or purer by heating it until it changes to a gas and then cooling it so that it changes back into a liquid [GRE]

distinct　　1 adjective UK /dɪˈstɪŋkt/ US /dɪˈstɪŋkt/ (NOTICEABLE) 显著的，明显的；确实的 C1 [before noun] clearly noticeable; that certainly exists

distinctive　　adjective UK /dɪˈstɪŋk.tɪv/ US /dɪˈstɪŋk.tɪv/ 与众不同的，独特的，特别的 C1 Something that is distinctive is easy to recognize because it is different from other things. [GRE]

distort　　verb [T] UK /dɪˈstɔːt/ US /dɪˈstɔːrt/ 扭曲；使变形；歪曲 C1 to change something from its usual, original, natural, or intended meaning, condition, or shape [GRE]

distract　　verb [T] UK /dɪˈstrækt/ US /dɪˈstrækt/ 使分心，使转移注意力，干扰 B2 to make someone stop giving their attention to something [GRE]

distraught　　adjective UK /dɪˈstrɔːt/ US /dɪˈstrɑːt/ 极其不安的，非常焦虑的 extremely worried, nervous, or upset [GRE]

distress　　1 noun [U] UK /dɪˈstres/ US /dɪˈstres/ C1 忧虑；悲伤；痛苦 a feeling of extreme worry, sadness, or pain

distressed   1 adjective UK   /dɪˈstrest/ US /dɪˈstrest/ 烦乱的，焦虑的，忧虑的 C1 upset or worried

distressing   adjective UK   /dɪˈstres.ɪŋ/ US /dɪˈstres.ɪŋ/ (us also distressful) 令人苦恼的,令人担忧的 B2 upsetting or worrying

distribute   verb [T] UK   /dɪˈstrɪb.juːt/ /ˈdɪs.trɪ.bjuːt/ US   /dɪˈstrɪb.juːt/ B2 分发，散发；分配 to give something out to several people, or to spread or supply something

distrust   1 noun [U or S] UK   /dɪˈstrʌst/ US /dɪˈstrʌst/ 不信任，不相信，怀疑 the feeling of not trusting someone or something

disturbed   adjective UK   /dɪˈstɜːbd/ US /dɪˈstɝːbd/ C2 有精神障碍的，精神不正常的，精神受刺激的 not thinking or behaving normally because of mental or emotional problems

disunite   verb [T often passive] UK   /ˌdɪs.juːˈnaɪt/ US   /ˌdɪs.juːˈnaɪt/ 使分裂，使纷争，离间 to cause people to disagree so much that they can no longer work together effectively

disturbed   adjective UK   /dɪˈstɜːbd/ US /dɪˈstɝːbd/ C2 有精神障碍的，精神不正常的，精神受刺激的 not thinking or behaving normally because of mental or emotional problems

Prefix (Medical): dors(o)-, dors(i)- Of or pertaining to the back

Meaning in English:

Origin language: Latin (dorsum), back

English examples:

dorsal   adjective [before noun] biology specialized UK /ˈdɔː.səl/ US /ˈdɔːr.səl/ （动物）背部的，背上的，背侧的 of, on, or near the back of an animal

dorsalis   adjective anatomy specialized UK /dɔːˈseɪ.lɪs/ US /dɔːrˈsæl.ɪs/ （拉丁语）背的，背侧的（用于医学术语中）a Latin word meaning "dorsal" (= relating to the back or top surface of an organ), used in medical names and descriptions

dorsiflexion   noun [U] medical specialized UK /ˌdɔː.sɪˈflek.ʃən/ US /ˌdɔːr.səˈflek.ʃən/ 背屈，向背侧弯曲（如手） the action of bending back part of the body, for example the hand

dorsum   noun [C] anatomy specialized UK /ˈdɔː.səm/ US /ˈdɔːr.səm/ plural dorsa (拉丁语) 背，背部，背面（用于医学术语中）a Latin word meaning "back", used in medical names and descriptions of the back or top surface of an organ

the dorsum of the foot   足背

Dorsocephalad   adv. [dôrˊ sō-sĕfˊ ə-lădˊ] Toward the back of the head.

Prefix: down- at or towards the end or the lower or worse part

Meaning in English: at or towards the end or the lower or worse part

Origin language: Anglo-Saxon/ Latin

English examples:

down-   prefix UK /daʊn-/ US /daʊn-/ 下 at or towards the end or the lower or worse part

down-and-dirty 1 adjective us informal UK /ˌdaʊn.ənˈdɜː.ti/ US /ˌdaʊn.ənˈdɜː.t̬i/ （举止）令人反感的；虚伪的 Down-and-dirty behaviour is not pleasant or honest.

down-and-out 1 adjective UK /ˌdaʊn.əˈnaʊt/ US /ˌdaʊn.əˈnaʊt/ 穷困潦倒的；时运不济的 C2 having no luck, no money, and no opportunities

down-at-heel adjective UK /ˌdaʊn.ətˈhiəl/ US /ˌdaʊn.ətˈhiəl/ (us also down-at-the-heel, down-at-the-heels) 衣衫破旧的；潦倒的；破落的，破败的 wearing old clothes, or in a bad condition, because of not having much money

down-to-earth adjective approving UK /ˌdaʊn.tuːˈɜːθ/ US /ˌdaʊn.tuːˈɜːθ/ 实际的；务实的 C1 practical, reasonable, and friendly

downcast 1 adjective UK /ˈdaʊn.kɑːst/ US /ˈdaʊn.kæst/ (UNHAPPY)垂头丧气的，萎靡不振的；伤心绝望的 formal sad and without hope

downfall noun [S] UK /ˈdaʊn.fɔːl/ US /ˈdaʊn.fɑːl/衰败；倒台，垮台 (something that causes) the usually sudden destruction of a person, organization, or government and their loss of power, money, or health

downgrade verb [T] UK /ˌdaʊnˈɡreɪd/ US /ˌdaʊnˈɡreɪd/ （使）降级；（使）降职；贬低；轻视 to reduce someone or something to a lower rank or position, or to cause something to be considered less important or valuable

downhearted adjective UK /ˌdaʊnˈhɑː.tɪd/ US /ˌdaʊnˈhɑːr.t̬ɪd/ （尤指因失望或失败而）灰心的，丧气的，气馁的 unhappy and having no hope, especially because of a disappointment or failure

downhill adverb, adjective UK /ˌdaʊnˈhɪl/ US /ˌdaʊnˈhɪl/ C2 向山下，朝坡下；下山的，下坡的 (moving) towards the bottom of a hill

download 1 verb [I or T] UK /ˌdaʊnˈləʊd/ /ˈdaʊn.ləʊd/ US /ˈdaʊn.loʊd/ A2 （尤指从因特网或较大型计算机上）下载 to copy or move programs or information into a computer's memory, especially from the internet or a larger computer

downplay verb [T] UK /ˌdaʊnˈpleɪ/ US /ˌdaʊnˈpleɪ/ 对…轻描淡写；贬低；低估 to make something seem less important or less bad than it really is [GRE]

downpour noun [C usually singular] UK /ˈdaʊn.pɔːr/ US /ˈdaʊn.pɔːr/ 暴雨，骤雨 a lot of rain in a short time [GRE]

downright adjective [before noun], adverb informal UK /ˈdaʊn.raɪt/ US /ˈdaʊn.raɪt/ （尤指不好的事情）极端的，极大的，十足的 (especially of something bad) extremely or very great

downward 1 adjective UK /ˈdaʊn.wəd/ US /ˈdaʊn.wɚd/ C1 向下的，朝下的 moving towards a lower position

downwards 1 adverb mainly uk UK /ˈdaʊn.wədz/ US /ˈdaʊn.wɚdz/ (us usually downward) 向下地，朝下地 C1 towards a lower position

downwind adverb, adjective UK /ˌdaʊnˈwɪnd/ US /ˌdaʊnˈwɪnd/ 顺风（地），在下风（地），随风（地） in the direction in which the wind blows; with the wind behind

Prefix (Medical): duodeno- upper part of the small intestine

Meaning in English: duodenum, twelve: upper part of the small intestine (twelve inches long on average), connects to the stomach

Origin language: Latin duodeni

English examples:

Duodenal atresia   noun [U] 十二指肠闭锁 Duodenal atresia is a condition that some babies are born with (congenital disorder). Babies with duodenal atresia have a closure in the first part of their small intestines (duodenum). The closure causes a mechanical blockage that prevents the passage of milk and digestive fluids.

duodecimal   adjective   MATHEMATICS   specialized UK /ˌdʒuː.əʊˈdes.ɪ.məl/ US /ˌduː.oʊˈdes.ə.məl/ 十进位的 relating to or expressed in a system of counting based on the number twelve

duodenal   adjective   MEDICAL   specialized UK /ˌdʒuː.əˈdiː.nəl/ US /ˌduː.əˈdiː.nəl/ 十二指肠的 of the duodenum (= the part of the small bowel the stomach empties into)

duodenal ulcer   十二指肠溃疡

duodenum   noun [C]   ANATOMY   specialized UK /ˌdʒuː.əˈdiː.nəm/ US /ˌduː.əˈdiː.nəm/ plural duodenums or duodena 十二指肠 the first part of the bowels just below the stomach

Prefix (Medical): dys- bad, difficult

Meaning in English: bad, difficult

Origin language: Greek δυσ

English examples:

dyspeptic   1 adjective UK /dɪˈspep.tɪk/ US /dɪˈspep.tɪk/ MEDICAL specialized 消化不良的 having problems with digesting food 2 adjective literary 易怒的，脾气坏的 always angry or easily annoyed

dysphagia   noun [U]   MEDICAL   specialized 吞咽困难 UK /dɪsˈfeɪ.dʒi.ə/ US /dɪsˈfeɪ.dʒi.ə/ difficulty in swallowing

dysphoria   noun [U] UK /dɪsˈfɔː.ri.ə/ /-ˈfɔːr.i.ə/ 烦躁，焦虑 severe unhappiness or mental illness, especially a person's feeling of being very uncomfortable in their body or of being in the wrong body

gender dysphoria   性别焦虑症

dysplasia   noun [U]   MEDICAL   specialized UK /dɪsˈpleɪ.zi.ə/ US /dɪsˈpleɪ.ʒə/ 发育异常，发育不良 development of cells, tissues, or organs that is not normal

dysphasic   adjective /dɪsˈfeɪ.zɪk/ /dɪsˈfeɪ.zɪk/（形容疾病）有语言障碍的 having a brain condition that causes difficulties with producing and sometimes understanding language

dysphasic children   有语言障碍的儿童

dyspnea   noun [U]   MEDICAL   specialized (UK also dyspnoea) UK /dɪspˈniː.ə/ US /dɪspˈniː.ə/ 呼吸困难 difficulty in breathing and the feeling of not getting enough air

dyspraxia   noun [U] /dɪsˈpræk.si.ə/ 运用障碍（进行协调动作的能力部份丧失） difficulties with physical movement and memory, caused by messages from the brain not travelling correctly to the body

dyspraxic   adjective 1 MEDICAL   specialized /dɪsˈpræk.sɪk/ 患有运用障碍的 having dyspraxia 2 noun [C]   MEDICAL   specialized /dɪsˈpræk.sɪk/

a person who has dyspraxia   运用障碍患者

dysthymia   noun [U]   MEDICAL   specialized UK /dɪsˈθaɪ.mi.ə/ US /dɪsˈθaɪ.mi.ə/ 心理沮丧，轻型抑郁症 a form of depression (= a mental illness causing feelings of unhappiness) that lasts for several years and but is less severe than other forms of depression 乏力、注意力难以集中以及无助感都是心理沮丧的常见症状。

Dystocia　难产 Dystocia refers to prolonged or slowly progressing labor. It is common in nulliparous women, as indicated by the number requiring augmentation, operative vaginal delivery, or cesarean section.难产是指产程延长或进展缓慢。 这在未产女性中很常见，如需要增大、阴道手术或剖宫产的数量所示。

dystonia　noun [C or U]　MEDICAL　specialized UK /dɪˈstəʊ.ni.ə/ US /dɪˈstoʊ.ni.ə/ 张力障碍（肌肉张力紊乱） a movement disorder in which the head or an arm or leg is put into an unnatural position

dystopia　noun [U] UK /dɪˈstəʊ.pi.ə/ US /dɪˈstoʊ.pi.ə/ 反乌托邦，反面假想国，敌托邦 (the idea of) a society in which people do not work well with each other and are not happy

dystrophy　noun 1　dys·tro·phy | \ ˈdi-strə-fē \ plural dystrophies: 营养不良 a condition produced by faulty nutrition noun 2: any myogenic atrophy especially 任何肌源性萎缩: MUSCULAR DYSTROPHY

muscular dystrophy　noun [U]　UK /ˌmʌs.kjə.lə ˈdɪs.trə.fi/ US /ˌmʌs.kjə.lɚ ˈdɪs.trə.fi/ 肌肉萎缩 a serious disease in which a person's muscles gradually become weaker until walking is no longer possible

EEE

Prefix: e- abbreviation for electronic

Meaning in English: abbreviation for electronic

Origin language: Anglo-Saxon/ Latin

English examples:

e-   prefix UK /iː-/ US /iː-/ abbreviation for electronic (ELECTRICAL) 电子（electronic 的缩写）

e-bank   noun [C] 网上银行 UK /ˈiː.bæŋk/ US /ˈiː.bæŋk/ a bank that operates over the internet

e-banking   noun [U] UK /ˈiːˌbæŋ.kɪŋ/ US /ˈiːˌbæŋ.kɪŋ/ 网上银行服务 the activity of managing a bank account or operating as a bank over the internet

e-blast   noun [C]   INTERNET & TELECOMS   specialized （为达到营销目的等）群发送电子邮件 an act of sending a copy of the same email to many people at the same time, for example by a company trying to sell something

e-book   noun [C] UK /ˈiː.bʊk/ US /ˈiː.bʊk/ an electronic book （同 electronic book）

e-business   noun [C or U] 电子商务 UK /ˈiːˌbɪz.nɪs/ US /ˈiːˌbɪz.nɪs/ the business of buying and selling goods and services on the internet, or a particular company that does this

e-cash   noun [U] UK /ˈiː.kæʃ/ US /ˈiː.kæʃ/ 电子货币 money from a special bank account that is used to buy goods and services over the internet by sending information from your computer

e-cigarette   noun [C] UK /ˈiːˌsɪg.ər.et/ US /ˈiːˌsɪg.ə.ret/ 电子烟 an electronic device that looks like a cigarette and allows someone to breathe in nicotine (= the drug found in tobacco) using vapour (= gas from heated water) rather than smoke, so there is no tar (= the harmful black substance produced when tobacco burns)

e-commerce   noun [U] UK /ˌiːˈkɒm.ɜːs/ US /ˌiːˈkɑː.mɝːs/ 电子商务 the business of buying and selling goods and services on the internet

e-learning   noun [U] 在线学习 UK /ˈiːˌlɜː.nɪŋ/ US /ˈiːˌlɝː.nɪŋ/ learning done by studying at home using computers and courses provided on the internet

e-reader   noun [C] 电子书阅读器 UK /ˈiː.riː.dər/ US /ˈiː.riː.dɚ/ a small electronic device with a screen that allows you to read books in an electronic form

e-tailer   noun [C] UK /ˈiː.teɪ.lər/ US /ˈiː.teɪ.lɚ/ 网上零售商 a business that uses the internet to sell its products

e-ticket   noun [C] UK /ˈiːˌtɪk.ɪt/ US /ˈiːˌtɪk.ɪt/ 电子机票 a ticket, usually for someone to travel on an aircraft, that is held on a computer and is not printed on paper

Prefix: eco- connected with the environment

Meaning in English: connected with the environment

Origin language: Anglo-Saxon/ Latin

English examples:

eco-   prefix UK /iː.kəʊ-/ US /iː.koʊ-/ 与环境有关的；生态的 connected with the environment

eco-friendly   adjective UK /ˈiː.kəʊˌfrend.li/ US /ˈiː.koʊˌfrend.li/ 环保的；不损害环境的 Eco-friendly products have been designed to do the least possible damage to the environment.

eco-label   noun [C] UK /ˈiː.kəʊˌleɪ.bəl/ US /ˈiː.koʊˌleɪ.bəl/ 环保品牌标识；生态产品标记 an official symbol that shows that a product has been designed to do less harm to the environment than similar products

eco-warrior   noun [C] UK UK /ˈiː.kəʊˌwɒ.r.iər/ US /ˈiː.koʊˌwɔːr.i.ɚ/ （积极投身环保活动的）生态斗士 a person who argues against and tries to stop activities that damage the environment

ecological   adjective UK /ˌiː.kəˈlɒdʒ.ɪ.kəl/ US /ˌiː.kəˈlɑː.dʒɪ.kəl/ B2 生态的；生态学的；环保的 relating to ecology or the environment

Prefix (Medical): ect(o)- outer, outside

Meaning in English: outer, outside

Origin language: Latin

English examples: Greek ἐκτός

ectomorph   noun [C]   ANATOMY   specialized UK /ˈek.tə.mɔːf/ US /-mɔːrf/ 瘦型体型（者） a person with a long body shape and not much fat

Ectomy   切除术 The surgical removal of something.

Entomology   昆虫学 Entomology is the scientific study of insects, a branch of zoology. In the past the term "insect" was less specific, and historically the definition of entomology would also include the study of animals in other arthropod groups, such as arachnids, myriapods, and crustaceans. Wikipedia

ectopia   noun [C or U]   MEDICAL   specialized UK /ekˈtəʊ.pi.ə/ US /ekˈtoʊ.pi.ə/ （先天性或因受伤而）异位 a situation in which an organ or body part is in the wrong position, either from birth or because of an injury

ectopic pregnancy   noun [C] UK /ekˌtɒp.ɪk ˈpreg.nən.si/ US /ekˌtɑː.pɪk ˈpreg.nən.si/（尤指受精卵在输卵管内着床的）宫外孕，异位妊娠 the development of the embryo outside the usual position within the womb, usually inside one of the fallopian tubes

ectoplasm   1 noun [U] UK /ˈek.tə.plæz.əm/ US /ˈek.toʊ.plæz.əm/（细胞外层的）外质 BIOLOGY   specialized

Prefix: en-, em- to cause to be/ to put into or onto/ to go into or onto

Meaning in English: to cause to be/ to put into or onto/ to go into or onto

Origin language: Latin

English examples:

en-   1 prefix UK /ɪn-/ /en-/ US /ɪn-/ /en-/ (before b or p em-)（用于构成动词）放入…中，用…包住 used to form verbs that mean to put into or onto something

embark   verb [I]   formal UK /ɪmˈbɑːk/ US /ɪmˈbɑːrk/ 上船 to go onto a ship [GRE]

employ   1 verb UK /ɪmˈplɔɪ/ US /ɪmˈplɔɪ/ (PROVIDE JOB) B1 [T] 雇用 to have someone work or do a job for you and pay them for it

embed   verb [T] (US also imbed) UK /ɪmˈbed/ US /ɪmˈbed/ -dd- 把…牢牢嵌入（或插入、埋入） to fix something firmly into a substance [GRE]

encase   verb [T] UK /ɪnˈkeɪs/ US /ɪnˈkeɪs/ 把…包住；把…围住 to cover or surround something or someone completely

encapsulate   verb [T] UK /ɪnˈkæp.sjə.leɪt/ US /ɪnˈkæp.sjə.leɪt/ 扼要表述；压缩；概括 to express or show the most important facts about something

encamp   verb [I or T] mainly UK formal UK /ɪnˈkæmp/ US /ɪnˈkæmp/ (US usually camp) （使）扎营；（使）宿营；（使）露营 to make an encampment or put someone in an encampment

encampment   noun [C] UK /ɪnˈkæmp.mənt/ US /ɪnˈkæmp.mənt/ （临时）营地，营帐 a group of tents or temporary shelters put in one place

encircle   verb [T] UK /ɪnˈsɜː.kəl/ US /ɪnˈsɜː.kəl/ 围绕；环绕 to surround something, forming a circle around it

enclave   1 noun [C] UK /ˈeŋ.kleɪv/ US /ˈɑːŋ.kleɪv/ 飞地（被包围在另外一个国家境内，和本国其他领土不接壤）；（在其他人群中聚居的）族群，群体 a part of a country that is surrounded by another country, or a group of people who are different from the people living in the surrounding area

enclose   1 verb [T] UK /ɪnˈkləʊz/ US /ɪnˈkloʊz/(before b or p em-) [T] (SURROUND) C1 把...围起来；围住，包住

embalm   verb [T] UK /ɪmˈbɑːm/ US /ɪmˈbɑːm/ （用药物等）对（尸体）进行防腐处理 to use chemicals to prevent a dead body from decaying [GRE]

embargo   1 noun [C] UK /ɪmˈbɑː.gəʊ/ US /ɪmˈbɑː.goʊ/ plural embargoes （尤指暂时禁止贸易或提供消息的）禁令，禁运；限制 an order to temporarily stop something, especially trading or giving information

embroil   verb [T] UK /ɪmˈbrɔɪl/ US /ɪmˈbrɔɪl/ 使卷入（纠纷）；使陷入（困境） to cause someone to become involved in an argument or a difficult situation

encompass   verb [T]   formal UK /ɪnˈkʌm.pəs/ US /ɪnˈkʌm.pəs/ 包含，包括（尤指很多不同事物） to include different types of things [GRE]

enfold   verb [T]   literary UK /ɪnˈfəʊld/ US /ɪnˈfoʊld/ 拥抱；包住；裹住 to closely hold or completely cover someone or something

enlist   1 verb UK /ɪnˈlɪst/ US /ɪnˈlɪst/ (JOIN) 参军，入伍 [I] to join the armed forces

enmesh   verb [T] UK /enˈmeʃ/ US /enˈmeʃ/ 缠住；使陷入；使卷入 to catch or involve someone in something unpleasant or dangerous from which it is difficult to escape

enshroud   1 verb [T] UK /ɪnˈʃraʊd/ US /ɪnˈʃraʊd/ [T] (COVER) literary 遮蔽；笼罩；掩盖 to cover something so that it cannot be seen clearly

ensnare   verb [T] UK /ɪnˈsneər/ US /ɪnˈsner/ literary 诱捕；使入圈套；使无法脱身 to catch or get control of something or someone

entangle   1 verb [T usually passive] UK /ɪnˈtæŋ.ɡəl/ US /ɪnˈtæŋ.ɡəl/ （用网、绳等）缠住，套住 to cause something to become caught in something such as a net or ropes

entice   verb [T] UK /ɪnˈtaɪs/ US /ɪnˈtaɪs/ 诱惑；诱使；引诱 to persuade someone to do something by offering them something pleasant

entrap   verb [T] UK /ɪnˈtræp/ US /ɪnˈtræp/ -pp- formal 使…陷入圈套；诱捕；诱骗 to cause someone to do something that they would not usually do, by unfair methods [GRE]

entwine   1 verb [T often passive] UK /ɪnˈtwaɪn/ US /ɪnˈtwaɪn/ 缠绕；盘绕；使交错 to twist something together or around something

envelop   verb [T]   literary UK /ɪnˈvel.əp/ US /ɪnˈvel.əp/ 覆盖；包住；围绕；笼罩 to cover or surround something completely

envelope   noun [C] UK /ˈen.və.ləʊp/ US /ˈɑːn.və.loʊp/ A2 信封 a flat, usually square or rectangular, paper container for a letter

Prefix: en-, em- used to form verbs that mean to cause to be something

Meaning in English: used to form verbs that mean to cause to be something

Origin language: Latin

English examples:

en-   2 prefix （用于构成动词）(before b or p em-) 使 used to form verbs that mean to cause to be something

embarrass   1 verb [T] UK /ɪmˈbær.əs/ US /ɪmˈber.əs/ C2 使尴尬，使窘迫；使为难 to cause someone to feel nervous, worried, or uncomfortable [GRE]

embellish   verb [T] UK /ɪmˈbel.ɪʃ/ US /ɪmˈbel.ɪʃ/ 装饰，修饰；给...添枝加叶，渲染 to make something more beautiful or interesting by adding something to it

embezzle   verb [I or T] UK /ɪmˈbez.əl/ US /ɪmˈbez.əl/ 贪污，侵吞；盗用，挪用（钱款）to secretly take money that is in your care or that belongs to an organization or business you work for [GRE]

embitter   verb [T] UK /ɪmˈbɪt.ər/ US /ɪmˈbɪt̬.ɚ/ 使怨恨；使沮丧 to make someone feel embittered

embody   1 verb [T] UK   /ɪmˈbɒd.i/ US   /ɪmˈbɑː.di/ formal 具体表现；体现 C2 to represent a quality or an idea exactly

embolden   verb [T] UK   /ɪmˈbəʊl.dən/ US   /ɪmˈboʊl.dən/ formal 使有胆量 to make someone brave [GRE]

emboss   verb [T] UK   /ɪmˈbɒs/ US   /ɪmˈbɑːs/ 在...表面上用浮雕图案装饰；（尤指）在...上压印浮凸字体 to decorate an object, especially with letters, using special tools that make a raised mark on its surface [GRE]

embrace   1 verb UK   /ɪmˈbreɪs/ US   /ɪmˈbreɪs/ embrace verb (ACCEPT)欣然接受；乐意采纳 C1 [T] formal to accept something enthusiastically [GRE]

embroider   1 verb [I or T] UK   /ɪmˈbrɔɪ.dər/ US   /ɪmˈbrɔɪ.dɚ/ [I or T] (DECORATE CLOTH) 刺绣；绣（花样） to decorate cloth or clothing with patterns or pictures consisting of stitches that are sewn directly onto the material [GRE]

empathize   verb [I] (UK usually empathise) UK   /ˈem.pə.θaɪz/ US /ˈem.pə.θaɪz/ 表示同情；有同感，产生共鸣 to be able to understand how someone else feels

empathy   noun [U] UK   /ˈem.pə.θi/ US   /ˈem.pə.θi/ C2 同情；同感，共鸣 the ability to share someone else's feelings or experiences by imagining what it would be like to be in that person's situation

enable   verb [T] UK   /ɪˈneɪ.bəl/ US   /ɪˈneɪ.bəl/ B2 使能够；使可能 to make someone able to do something, or to make something possible

enabled 1 adjective, suffix UK /ɪˈneɪ.bəld/ US /ɪˈneɪ.bəld/ 配有（某种设备或技术）的；可以使用（某种系统、装置或设计）的 provided with a particular type of equipment or technology, or having the necessary or correct system, device, or arrangement to use it

enact 1 verb UK /ɪˈnækt/ US /ɪˈnækt/ (MAKE LAW) [T often passive] LAW specialized 实行，实施；（尤指）制定（法律）[GRE]

enamoured adjective [after verb] UK formal (US enamored) 喜爱的；迷恋的 UK /ɪˈnæm.əd/ US /ɪˈnæm.ɚd/ 喜爱的；迷恋的 liking something a lot [GRE]

encode 1 verb UK /ɪnˈkəʊd/ US /ɪnˈkoʊd/ [T often passive] 把…译成电码（或密码）；把…编码

encounter 1 noun [C] UK /ɪnˈkaʊn.tər/ US /ɪnˈkaʊn.t̬ɚ/ 偶然相遇，邂逅，不期而遇 a meeting, especially one that happens by chance

encourage 1 verb [T] UK /ɪnˈkʌr.ɪdʒ/ US /ɪnˈkɝː.ɪdʒ/ B1 刺激，激励；促进；助长 to make someone more likely to do something, or to make something more likely to happen

encroachment noun [C or U] UK /ɪnˈkrəʊtʃ.mənt/ US /ɪnˈkroʊtʃ.mənt/ 逐步侵犯（权利）；慢慢侵占（时间）；逐渐干扰（工作）the act of gradually taking away someone else's rights, or taking control of someone's time, work, etc.

encrypt verb [T usually passive] UK /ɪnˈkrɪpt/ US /ɪnˈkrɪpt/ 将…译成密码；把…编码；把…加密 to change electronic information or signals into a secret code (= system of letters, numbers, or symbols) that people cannot understand or use on normal equipment

encumber   verb [T]   formal UK /ɪnˈkʌm.bər/ US /ɪnˈkʌm.bɚ/ 使...负担沉重；妨碍，阻碍；拖累 to weigh someone or something down, or to make it difficult for someone to do something [GRE]

endanger   verb [T] UK /ɪnˈdeɪn.dʒər/ US /ɪnˈdeɪn.dʒɚ/ 使处于险境；危及；危害 to put someone or something at risk or in danger of being harmed, damaged, or destroyed

endow   1 verb [T] UK /ɪnˈdaʊ/ US /ɪnˈdaʊ/ 向（院校、医院等）捐款，捐赠，资助 to give a large amount of money to pay for creating a college, hospital, etc. or to provide an income for it

endear sb to sb   verb UK /ɪnˈdɪər/ US /ɪnˈdɪr/ 使...受...喜爱（或欢迎） to cause someone to be liked by someone

endure   1 verb UK /ɪnˈdʒʊər/ US /ɪnˈdʊr/ endure verb (EXPERIENCE) B2 [T] 忍耐；忍受 to suffer something difficult, unpleasant, or painful

enervate   verb [T]   formal UK /ˈen.ə.veɪt/ US /ˈen.ɚ.veɪt/ 使衰弱；使无力；使丧失活力 to make someone feel weak and without energy

enfeeble   verb [T]   formal UK /ɪnˈfiː.bəl/ US /ɪnˈfiː.bəl/ 使衰弱；使无力 to make someone or something very weak

enforce   1 verb [T] UK /ɪnˈfɔːs/ US /ɪnˈfɔːrs/ C1 使服从（法律）；（强制）实行，执行，把...强加于

enfranchise   verb [T]   formal UK /ɪnˈfræn.tʃaɪz/ US /ɪnˈfræn.tʃaɪz/ 给...选举权 to give a person or group of people the right to vote in elections [GRE]

engender   1 verb [T]   formal UK /ɪnˈdʒen.dər/ US /ɪnˈdʒen.dɚ/ 引起（某种感觉）；导致；产生 to make people have a particular feeling or make a situation start to exist [GRE]

engross   1 verb [T] UK /ɪnˈɡrəʊs/ US /ɪnˈɡroʊs/ 使全神贯注 If something engrosses you, it is so interesting that you give it all your attention. [GRE]

enhance   verb [T] UK /ɪnˈhɑːns/ US /ɪnˈhæns/C1 提高；增加；增强；增进 to improve the quality, amount, or strength of something

enlarge   1 verb UK /ɪnˈlɑːdʒ/ US /ɪnˈlɑːrdʒ/ [I or T] （使）增大；（使）扩大；（使）扩充 to become bigger or to make something bigger

enlighten   verb [I or T] UK /ɪnˈlaɪ.tən/ US /ɪnˈlaɪ.t̬ən/ 启发，启迪；开导；阐明 to provide someone with information and understanding, or to explain the true facts about something to someone [GRE]

ennoble   1 verb [T] UK /ɪˈnəʊ.bəl/ US /ɪˈnoʊ.bəl/ 封...为贵族 to make someone a member of the nobility (= highest social rank) [GRE]

ennui   noun [U]   literary UK /ˌɒnˈwiː/ US /ˌɑːnˈwiː/ （由于无所事事而感到的）无聊，厌倦，倦怠 a feeling of being bored and mentally tired caused by having nothing interesting or exciting to do [GRE]

enrage　　　verb [T often passive] UK /ɪnˈreɪdʒ/ US /ɪnˈreɪdʒ/ 使非常愤怒；激怒；触怒 to cause someone to become very angry

ensemble　　noun [C, + sing/pl verb] UK /ˌɒnˈsɒm.bəl/ US /ˌɑːnˈsɑːm.bəl/ 全体，整体；剧团；（尤指）乐团 a group of things or people acting or taken together as a whole, especially a group of musicians who regularly play together

enslave　　　1 verb [T often passive] UK /ɪnˈsleɪv/ US /ɪnˈsleɪv/ 使遭受；使无法摆脱 to force someone to remain in a bad situation 2 verb 奴役；使成为奴隶 to make a slave of someone

ensure　　　1 verb [T] (US also insure) UK /ɪnˈʃɔːr/ US /ɪnˈʃʊr/ B2 确保；保证 to make something certain to happen

enthral　　　verb [I or T] -ll- mainly uk us usually enthrall UK /ɪnˈθrɔːl/ US /ɪnˈθrɑːl/ 迷住，使着迷；吸引住 to keep someone completely interested [GRE]

enthrone　　1 verb UK /ɪnˈθrəʊn/ US /ɪnˈθroʊn/ 为…举行登基仪式；使登基；立…为王 [T] formal to put a king, queen, etc. through the ceremony of sitting on a throne (= chair used in ceremonies) in order to mark the official beginning of their period in power

entreat　　　verb [T] UK /ɪnˈtriːt/ US /ɪnˈtriːt/ 恳求；乞求；请求 to try very hard to persuade someone to do something [GRE]

entrench　　　　verb [T] UK /ɪnˈtrentʃ/ US /ɪnˈtrentʃ/ mainly disapproving 使处于牢固地位，使根深蒂固，牢固确立（尤指观念、问题） to firmly establish something, especially an idea or a problem, so that it cannot be changed

enumerate verb [T] formal UK /ɪˈnjuː.mə.reɪt/ US /ɪˈnuː.mɚ.eɪt/ 列举，枚举 to name things separately, one by one

enunciate 1 verb formal UK /ɪˈnʌn.si.eɪt/ US /ɪˈnʌn.si.eɪt/ (PRONOUNCE) [I or T] 清楚地念（字）；清晰地发（音） to pronounce words or parts of words clearly [GRE]

envisage 1 verb [T] formal UK /ɪnˈvɪz.ɪdʒ/ US /ɪnˈvɪz.ɪdʒ/ (US also envision) C1 设想；展望，预计 to imagine or expect something in the future, especially something good

Prefix: en-, em- used to form verbs that mean to provide with something

Meaning in English: used to form verbs that mean to cause to be something

Origin language: Latin

English examples:

en- 3 prefix （用于构成动词）(before b or p em-) 使有，使具有 used to form verbs that mean to provide with something

emancipate verb [T] UK /iˈmæn.sɪ.peɪt/ US /iˈmæn.sə.peɪt/ 解放；给予人们政治或社会自由权利 to give people social or political freedom and rights [GRE]

emasculate 1 verb [T] UK /ɪˈmæs.kjə.leɪt/ US /ɪˈmæs.kjə.leɪt/ formal 使衰弱；使效力减弱 to reduce the effectiveness of something

endorse 1 verb [T] UK /ɪnˈdɔːs/ US /ɪnˈdɔːrs/ [T] (SUPPORT) （公开）赞同，认可，支持 C2 to make a public statement of your approval or support for something or someone [GRE]

empower   verb [T] UK /ɪmˈpaʊər/ US /-ˈpaʊr/ 给（某人）做...的权力；授权；使自主 to give someone official authority or the freedom to do something

entrust   verb [T + adv/prep] UK /ɪnˈtrʌst/ US /ɪnˈtrʌst/ 委托；交托；托付 to give someone a thing or a duty for which they are responsible

enrich   1 verb UK /ɪnˈrɪtʃ/ US /ɪnˈrɪtʃ/ enrich verb (IMPROVE) C1 使丰富，使富含；充实 [T] to improve the quality of something by adding something else

enshrine   verb [T usually + adv/prep]   formal UK /ɪnˈʃraɪn/ US /ɪnˈʃraɪn/ 把...奉为神圣；珍藏 to contain or keep something as if in a holy place

Prefix (Medical): encephal(o)- Of or pertaining to the brain.

Meaning in English: Of or pertaining to the brain. Also see Cerebro.

Origin language: Ancient Greek ἐγκέφαλος (enképhalos), the brain

English examples:

electroencephalogram   noun [C]   MEDICAL   specialized UK /iˌlek.trəʊ.enˈsef.ə.lə.græm/ US /iˌlek.troʊ.enˈsef.ə.lə.græm/ (abbreviation EEG) 脑电图 a drawing or image made by an electroencephalograph

electroencephalograph   noun [C]   MEDICAL   (abbreviation EEG) specialized UK /iˌlek.trəʊ.enˈsef.ə.lə.gr ɑ :f / /iˌlek.trəʊ.enˈsef.ə.lə.græf/ US /iˌlek.troʊ.enˈsef.ə.lə.græf/ 脑电图仪 a machine that records the electrical activity of the brain

encephalitis   noun [U]   MEDICAL   specialized UK /ˌen.kef.əˈlaɪ.tɪs/ US /enˌsef.əˈlaɪ.təs/ 脑炎（一种严重疾病，由感染造成的大脑肿胀） a serious illness caused by an infection that makes the brain swell

encephalopathy noun [C or U] MEDICAL specialized UK
/ˌen.kef.əˈlɒp.ə.θi/ US /enˌsef.əˈl ɑ ːp.ə.θi/ 脑病 inflammation affecting the surface of the brain that may be caused by infection or poisonous substances

encephalogram noun en·ceph·a·lo·gram | \ in-ˈse-fə-lə-ˌgram \ an X-ray picture of the brain made by encephalography

myalgic encephalomyelitis noun [U] MEDICAL UK specialized UK
/maɪˌæl.dʒɪk enˌsef.ə.ləʊ.maɪ.əˈlaɪ.tɪs/ US /maɪˌæl.dʒɪk
enˌsef.ə.loʊ.maɪ.əˈlaɪ.tə̣s/ → chronic fatigue syndrome 慢性疲劳综合征（同 chronic fatigue syndrome）(uk also ME); (abbreviation CFS) 慢性疲劳综合征 an illness, sometimes lasting for several years, in which a person's muscles and joints (= places where two bones are connected) hurt and they are generally very tired

Prefix (Medical): endo- Denotes something as 'inside' or 'within'

Meaning in English: Denotes something as 'inside' or 'within'

Origin language: Ancient Greek ἐνδο- (endo-), inside, internal

English examples:

endocarditis noun [U] MEDICAL specialized UK
/ˌen.dəʊ.k ɑ ːdˈaɪ.tɪs/ US /ˌen.doʊ.k ɑ ːrˈdaɪ.tə̣s/ 心内膜炎 inflammation of the lining of the heart

endocrine 1 adjective BIOLOGY specialized UK /ˈen.də.krɪn/ US /ˈen.də.krɪn/ 内分泌；内分泌腺；内分泌物 relating to any of the organs of the body that make hormones (= chemicals that make the body grow and develop) and put them into the blood, or to the hormones that they make

endocrine gland noun [C] BIOLOGY specialized UK /ˈen.də.krɪn ˌglænd/ US /ˈen.də.krɪn ˌglænd/ 内分泌腺 any of the organs of the body, such as the pituitary gland or the ovaries, that produce and release hormones into the blood to be carried around the body

endocrinologist   noun [C]   MEDICAL   specialized UK
/ˌen.dəʊ.krɪˈnɒl.ə.dʒɪst/ US /-doʊ.krɪˈn ɑ ːlə-/ 内分泌学家 a doctor or scientist
who specializes in endocrinology

endocrinology   noun [U]   MEDICAL   specialized UK
/ˌen.dəʊ.krɪˈnɒl.ə.dʒi/ US /-doʊ.krɪˈn ɑ ːlə-/ 内分泌学 the area of science and
medicine that is concerned with the endocrine glands and hormones

endocytosis   内吞作用 Endocytosis is a process in which a cell
internalizes non-particulate materials such as proteins by engulfing them in an
energy-dependent manner.

endogenous   1 adjective   MEDICAL, SOCIAL SCIENCE   specialized
UK /enˈdɒdʒ.ɪ.nəs/ US /enˈd ɑ ːdʒə.nəs/（系统、人体或思维）内生的，内
源的 found or coming from within something, for example a system or a
person's body or mind

endometrial   adjective   MEDICAL   specialized UK /ˌen.dəʊˈmiː.tri.əl/
US /ˌen.doʊˈmiː.tri.əl/ 子宫内膜的 relating to the endometrium (= the lining of
the uterus)

endometriosis   noun [U]   MEDICAL   specialized UK
/ˌen.dəʊ.miː.triˈəu.sɪs/ US /ˌen.doʊ.miː.triˈou.sɪs/ 子宫内膜异位 a condition in
which cells from the lining of the uterus grow outside the uterus

endometrium   noun [S]   MEDICAL   specialized UK /ˌen.dəʊˈmiː.tri.əm/
US /ˌen.doʊˈmiː.tri.əm/ 子宫内膜 the inside surface of the uterus (= the organ
in which a baby develops)

endomorph　　noun [C]　ANATOMY　specialized UK /ˈen.də.mɔːf/ US /-doʊ.mɔːrf/ 体胖型（人）　a person with a round body shape and with a lot of fat

endonuclease　　noun [C]　CHEMISTRY, BIOLOGY　specialized UK /ˌen.doʊˈnjuː.kli.eɪz/ US /ˌen.doʊˈnuː.kli.eɪz/ 核酸内切酶，内切核酸酶 a chemical substance produced in the body that breaks connections in DNA (= the chemical that controls the structure and function of cells)

endoplasmic reticulum　　noun [C]　BIOLOGY　specialized UK /ˌen.dəʊˌplæz.mɪk rəˈtɪk.jə.ləm/ US /ˌen.doʊˌplæz.mɪk rəˈtɪk.jə.ləm/ US plural endoplasmic reticula 内浆网，内质网 a network of tubes within a cell that transports substances inside the cell and is needed for the production of proteins

endorphin　　noun [C] UK /enˈdɔː.fɪn/ US /enˈdɔːr.fɪn/ specialized 内啡呔 a chemical naturally, released in the brain to reduce pain, that in large amounts can make you feel relaxed or full of energy

endospore　noun [C] 内生孢子 An endospore is a dormant, tough, and non-reproductive structure produced by certain bacteria from the Firmicute phylum. Endospore formation is usually triggered by lack of nutrients, and usually occurs in Gram-positive bacteria. In endospore formation, the bacterium divides within its cell wall.

Prefix (Medical): enter(o)- Of or pertaining to the intestine

Meaning in English: Of or pertaining to the intestine

Origin language: Ancient Greek ἔντερον (énteron), intestine

English examples:

enterocele　　noun [C]　MEDICAL　specialized UK /ˈen.tə.rəʊ.siːl/ US /ˈen.t̬ə.roʊˌsiːl/ 肠膨出，肠疝 a place where part of the small bowel pushes into the wall of the vagina at a weak point in the muscle

Gastroenterology 肠胃病学 Gastroenterology is the branch of medicine focused on the digestive system and its disorders. Diseases affecting the gastrointestinal tract, which include the organs from mouth into anus, along the alimentary canal, are the focus of this speciality. Physicians practicing in this field are called gastroenterologists. Wikipedia; Gastroenterology is the study of the normal function and diseases of the esophagus, stomach, small intestine, colon and rectum, pancreas, gallbladder, bile ducts and liver.

gastroenterologists 肠胃病医生 Physicians practicing in Gastroenterology field are called gastroenterologists. Gastroenterology is an area of medicine that focuses on the health of the digestive system, or the gastrointestinal (GI) tract, as well as the liver.

Prefix (Medical): eosin(o)- Red

Meaning in English: Red

Origin language: Eosin comes from Eos, the Greek word for 'dawn' and the name of the Greek Goddess of the Dawn.

English examples:

eosinophil noun [C] BIOLOGY specialized UK /ˌiː.əˈsɪn.ə.fɪl/ US /ˌiː.əˈsɪn.ə.fɪl/ 粒性曙红白细胞 a type of white blood cell

eosinophilia noun [U] MEDICAL specialized UK /iː.əˌsɪn.əˈfɪl.i.ə/ US /iː.əˌsɪn.əˈfɪl.i.ə/ 嗜曙红白细胞增多，嗜酸细胞增多 an abnormal increase in the number of eosinophils (= a type of white blood cells) in the blood

Eosinophil granulocyte 嗜酸性粒细胞 Eosinophil granulocytes, usually called eosinophils or eosinophiles (or, less commonly, acidophils), are white blood cells that are one of the immune system components responsible for combating multicellular parasites and certain infections.

Meaning in English: on, upon

Origin language: Ancient Greek ἐπι- (epi-), before, upon, on, outside, outside of

English examples:

Nosebleeds (Epistaxis) a nosebleed is the loss of blood from the tissue that lines the inside of your nose. Nosebleeds (also called epistaxis) are common. Some 60% of people will have at least one nosebleed in their lifetime.

epicardium noun [U] 心外膜 The epicardium refers to the outermost protective layer of the heart. The epicardium is composed of mesothelium, a cell type that covers and protects most of the internal organs of the body as well as fat and connective tissue.

episclera noun [U] 巩膜外层 The episclera is a fibroelastic structure consisting of two layers loosely joined together. The outer parietal layer, with the vessels of the superficial episcleral capillary plexus, is the more superficial layer. The superficial vessels appear straight and are arranged in a radial fashion.

epidural noun [C] UK /ˌep.ɪˈdʒʊə.rəl/ US /ˌep.əˈdʊr.əl/ 硬膜外麻醉 an anaesthetic (= a substance that stops you feeling pain) that is put into the nerves in a person's lower back with a special needle

They gave my wife an epidural when she was giving birth. 我妻子分娩时，医生给她施行了硬膜外麻醉。

Prefix (Medical): episi(o)- Of or pertaining to the pubic region, the loins

Meaning in English: Of or pertaining to the pubic region, the loins

Origin language: Ancient Greek ἐπίσιον- (epísion), the pubic area, loins; vulva

English examples:

episiotomy noun [C] UK /ɪˌpiːz.iˈɒt.ə.mi/ US /ɪˌpiː.siˈɑː.t̬ə.mi/ 外阴切开术，会阴切开术 a cut made at the opening of the vagina while a woman is giving birth, to make it easier for the baby to come out without causing injury

I didn't have to have a episiotomy, even with a big baby. 我没有做外阴切开术，即使宝宝个头挺大的也不用。

Prefix: equi- equal or equally

Meaning in English: equal or equally

Origin language: Anglo-Saxon/ Latin

English examples:

equi-   prefix UK /ek.wɪ-/ /iː.kwɪ-/ US /iː.kwə-/ /ek.wə-/ 相等的（地）equal or equally

equidistant   adjective UK /ˌek.wɪˈdɪs.tənt/ /ˌiː.kwɪˈdɪs.tənt/ US /ˌiː.kwəˈdɪs.tənt/ /ˌek.wəˈdɪs.tənt/ 等距的 equally far or close

equilibrium   1 noun [S or U] formal UK /ˌek.wɪˈlɪb.ri.əm/ /ˌiː.kwɪˈlɪb.ri.əm/ US /ˌiː.kwəˈlɪb.ri.əm/ /ˌek.wəˈlɪb.ri.əm/ 平衡；均衡 a state of balance [GRE]

equinox   noun [C] UK /ˈek.wɪ.nɒks/ US /ˈek.wə.nɑːks/ 昼夜平分时；春分；秋分 either of the two occasions in the year when day and night are of equal length

equity   1 noun UK /ˈek.wɪ.ti/ US /ˈek.wə.t̬i/ (VALUE) [C or U] FINANCE & ECONOMICS specialized （公司的）股本，股票值；股票 the value of a company, divided into many equal parts owned by the shareholders, or one of the equal parts into which the value of a company is divided [GRE]

equivalent   1 adjective UK /ɪˈkwɪv.əl.ənt/ US /ɪˈkwɪv.əl.ənt/ 等值的；相等的；等同的 C1 having the same amount, value, purpose, qualities, etc. [GRE]

equivocal   adjective UK /ɪˈkwɪv.ə.kəl/ US /ɪˈkwɪv.ə.kəl/ formal 含糊的；模棱两可的；有歧义的 not clear and seeming to have two opposing meanings, or confusing and able to be understood in two different ways

equivocate   verb [I] UK /ɪˈkwɪv.ə.keɪt/ US /ɪˈkwɪv.ə.keɪt/ formal （尤指为隐瞒真相而）说模棱两可的话，含糊其词 to speak in a way that is intentionally not clear and confusing to other people, especially to hide the truth

Prefix (Medical): erythr(o)- Denotes a red color

Meaning in English: a red color

Origin language: Ancient Greek ἐρυθρός (erythros), red

English examples:

erythema   1 noun [U]   MEDICAL   specialized UK /ˌer.ɪˈθiː.mə/ US /ˌer.ɪˈθiː.mə/（皮肤）红斑 redness of the skin

The most commonly reported side effect was mild erythema.

最常见的副作用是皮肤轻微红斑。

erythrocyte   noun [C]   MEDICAL   specialized UK /ɪˈrɪθ.rəʊ.saɪt/ US /erˈɪθ.roʊ.saɪt/ 红细胞；红血球 any of the cells that carry oxygen around the body

erythrophobia   （通常因尴尬而）脸红 Blushing；Blushing is the reddening of a person's face due to psychological reasons. It is normally involuntary and triggered by emotional stress associated with passion, embarrassment, shyness, fear, anger, or romantic stimulation.

Prefix (Medical): esthesio- sensation (AmE)

Meaning in English: sensation (AmE)

Origin language: Greek αἴσθησις

English examples:

anesthesiologist   noun [C] UK /ˌæn.əsˌθiː.ziˈɒl.ə.dʒɪst/ US /ˌæn.əsˌθiː.ziˈɑː.lə.dʒɪst/ us 麻醉师 a doctor who gives anaesthetic to people in hospital

anesthesia   noun [U] UK /ˌæn.əsˈθiː.zi.ə/ /ˌæn.əsˈθiːʒə/ US /ˌæn.əsˈθiː.zi.ə/ /ˌæn.əsˈθiːʒə/ （anaesthesia 的美式拼写 us spelling of anaesthesia （通常指被施用药物后的）麻醉状态

anesthesiology   noun [U] UK /ˌæn.əsˌθiː.ziˈɒl.ə.dʒi/ US /ˌæn.əsˌθiː.ziˈɑː.lə.dʒi/ us spelling of anaesthesiology （anaesthesiology 的美式拼写）麻醉学

anaesthetic   noun [U or C] mainly uk us usually anesthetic UK /ˌæn.əsˈθet.ɪk/ US /ˌæn.əsˈθet̬.ɪk/ 麻醉剂 a substance that makes you unable to feel pain

Prefix: ethno- relating to the study of different societies and cultures

Meaning in English: relating to the study of different societies and cultures

Origin language: Anglo-Saxon/ Latin

English examples:

ethno-   prefix UK /eθ.nəʊ-/ US /eθ.noʊ-/ （与对不同社会和文化的研究有关，常与另一表示研究领域的词语连用） relating to the study of different societies and cultures, combined with another area of study

ethnocentric   adjective UK /ˌeθ.nəʊˈsen.trɪk/ US /ˌeθ.noʊˈsen.trɪk/ 有种族（或民族）优越感的 believing that the people, customs, and traditions of your own race or nationality are better than those of other races

ethnography   noun [C or U] UK /eθˈnɒg.rə.fi/ US /eθˈnɑː.grə.fi/ 人种志，人种论；人种志著作 a scientific description of the culture of a society by someone who has lived in it, or a book containing this

ethos   noun [S] UK /ˈiː.θɒs/ US /ˈiː.θɑːs/ （个人或团体的）精神特质，价值观，信条 the set of beliefs, ideas, etc. about the social behaviour and relationships of a person or group [GRE]

Prefix (Medical): eu- true, good, well, new

Meaning in English: true, good, well, new

Origin language: Greek

English examples:

eugenic   adjective UK /juːˈdʒen.ɪk/ US /juːˈdʒen.ɪk/ 优生学的；人种改良学的 relating to the idea that it is possible to improve humans by allowing only some people to produce children

eugenics   noun [U] UK /juːˈdʒen.ɪks/ US /juːˈdʒen.ɪks/ 优生学；人种改良学 the idea that it is possible to improve humans by allowing only some people to produce children

eukaryote   noun [C] BIOLOGY specialized /juːˈkær.i.əʊt/ /juːˈkær.i.oʊt/ 真核生物 a type of organism that has one or more cells each with a separate nucleus (= central part) containing chromosomes, which includes all animals and plants

eukaryotic   adjective BIOLOGY specialized UK /ˌjuː.kær.iˈɒt.ɪk/ US /juː.ker.iˈɑː.tɪk/ 真核的 (of a cell) containing a nucleus and other structures, each with its own function

eulogize 1 verb [T, I usually + adv/prep] formal (UK usually eulogise) UK /ˈjuː.lə.dʒaɪz/ US /ˈjuː.lə.dʒaɪz/ 歌颂，赞美，称颂 to praise someone or something in a speech or piece of writing [GRE]

eulogy noun [C or U] formal UK /ˈjuː.lə.dʒi/ US /ˈjuː.lə.dʒi/ 悼词，悼文；（为刚刚退休的人所作的）颂词，颂文 a speech, piece of writing, poem, etc. containing great praise, especially for someone who recently died or retired from work

Prefix: Euro- relating to the European Union

Meaning in English: relating to the European Union

Origin language: Anglo-Saxon/ Latin

English examples:

Euro- 3 prefix UK /jʊə.rəʊ-/ US /jʊr.oʊ-/ 欧盟的 relating to the European Union

a Euro-MP (= a Member of the European Parliament) 欧洲议会议员

Europe 1 noun UK /ˈjʊə.rəp/ US /ˈjʊr.əp/ 欧洲 the continent that is to the east of the Atlantic Ocean, to the north of the Mediterranean, and to the west of Asia

Europop noun [U] UK /ˈjʊə.rəʊ.pɒp/ US /ˈjʊr.oʊ.pɑːp/ 欧洲流行音乐（一种于 20 世纪 70 年代起源于欧洲的流行音乐，曲调简单，琅琅上口）a type of pop music that started in Europe in the 1970s. The tunes are easy to remember.

Eurosceptic noun [C] UK UK /ˈjʊə.rəʊˌskep.tɪk/ US /ˈjʊr.oʊˌskep.tɪk/ （反对英国和欧盟建立更密切关系的）欧盟怀疑论者（尤指政客）；反亲

欧派 a person, especially a politician, who opposes closer connections between Britain and the European Union

Prefix: ex- out of/ away from

Meaning in English: out of/ away from

Origin language: Latin/ Greek

English examples:

exacerbate   verb [T] UK /ɪgˈzæs.ə.beɪt/ US /ɪgˈzæs.ɚ.beɪt/ 使恶化；使加重；使加剧 to make something that is already bad even worse [GRE]

exacting   adjective UK /ɪgˈzæk.tɪŋ/ US /ɪgˈzæk.tɪŋ/ 需付出极大努力的；要求小心仔细的；要求严格的 demanding a lot of effort, care, or attention [GRE]

exaggerate   verb [I or T] UK /ɪgˈzædʒ.ə.reɪt/ US /ɪgˈzædʒ.ə.reɪt/ 夸张；夸大；对…言过其实 C1 to make something seem larger, more important, better, or worse than it really is

exceed   verb [T] UK /ɪkˈsiːd/ US /ɪkˈsiːd/ C1 超过，超出（数量）；超越（规定的范围）to be greater than a number or amount, or to go past an allowed limit

except   preposition, conjunction UK /ɪkˈsept/ US /ɪkˈsept/ A2 （表示不包括）除…之外 not including; but not

exceptional   adjective approving UK /ɪkˈsep.ʃən.əl/ US /ɪkˈsep.ʃən.əl/ B2 （尤指在技能、才智、品质等方面）卓越的，杰出的，不同凡响的 much greater than usual, especially in skill, intelligence, quality, etc. [GRE]

excess 1 noun UK /ɪkˈses/ /ˈek.ses/ US /ɪkˈses/ /ˈek.ses/ (TOO MUCH) C1 [S or U] 过分；过量；过度 an amount that is more than acceptable, expected, or reasonable

exclude 1 verb [T] UK /ɪkˈskluːd/ US /ɪkˈskluːd/ C1 阻止...进入；把...排斥在外 to prevent someone or something from entering a place or taking part in an activity

exclusive 1 adjective UK /ɪkˈskluː.sɪv/ US /ɪkˈskluː.sɪv/ (ONLY FOR SOME) C1 专用的，专有的；独有的，独占的 limited to only one person or group of people

excrement noun [U] formal UK /ˈek.skrə.mənt/ US /ˈek.skrə.mənt/ 粪便；排泄物 the solid waste that is released from the bowels of a person or animal [GRE]

excrete 1 verb [I or T] formal UK /ɪkˈskriːt/ US /ɪkˈskriːt/ 排泄 to get rid of material such as solid waste or urine from the body [GRE]

exculpate verb [T] UK /ˈek.skəl.peɪt/ US /ˈek.skəl.peɪt/ formal 证明是清白的，开脱,昭雪,洗脱 to remove blame from someone: [GRE]

excursive 离题的; 混乱的 of the nature of an excursion; ranging widely; digressive. [GRE]

exhale verb [I or T] UK /cksˈheɪl/ US /eksˈheɪl/ formal 呼出, 吐出（肺中的空气），呼气 to send air out of your lungs

exhaust   verb 1 [T] UK /ɪɡˈzɔːst/ US /ɪɡˈzɑːst/ [T] (TIRE)使精疲力竭；使疲惫不堪 C1 to make someone extremely tired verb 2 [T] (USE) 用完；花光；耗尽 to use something completely

exhort   1 verb [T + to infinitive] formal UK /ɪɡˈzɔːt/ US /ɪɡˈzɔːrt/ 激励；规劝；敦促 to strongly encourage or try to persuade someone to do something [GRE]

exhortative adjective formal UK /ɪɡˈzɔː.tə.tɪv/ US /ɪɡˈzɔːr.t̬ə.t̬ɪv/鼓励的 nvolving an attempt to strongly encourage or persuade someone to do something: [GRE]

extort   verb [T] UK /ɪkˈstɔːt/ US /ɪkˈstɔːrt/ 敲诈，勒索；强求 to get something by force or threats, or with difficulty

extortion   noun [U] UK /ɪkˈstɔː.ʃən/ US /ɪkˈstɔːr.ʃən/ 敲诈，勒索；强求 the act of getting something, especially money, by force or threats:

exile   1 noun UK /ˈek.saɪl/ /ˈeɡ.zaɪl/ US /ˈek.saɪl/ /ˈeɡ.zaɪl/ C2 [U] （尤指出于政治原因的）流放，放逐，流亡 the condition of someone being sent or kept away from their own country, village, etc., especially for political reasons

exit   1 noun [C] UK /ˈek.sɪt/ /ˈeɡ.zɪt/ US /ˈek.sɪt/ /ˈeɡ.zɪt/ [C] (DOOR) A2 （建筑物或大型交通工具的）出口，安全门；（尤指演员）退场 the door through which you might leave a building or large vehicle, or the act of leaving something, especially a theatre stage

exodus   1 noun [S] UK /ˈek.sə.dəs/ US /ˈek.sə.dəs/ （大批人的）退出，离开 the movement of a lot of people from a place [GRE]

exogenous   adjective   MEDICAL, SOCIAL SCIENCE   specialized UK /ɪkˈsɒdʒ.ɪ.nəs/ US /ɪkˈsɑː.dʒə.nəs/（系统、人体或人的思想）外源的，外生的 found or coming from outside something, for example a system or a person's body or mind

exotic   adjective UK /ɪɡˈzɒt.ɪk/ US /ɪɡˈzɑː.t̬ɪk/ B2 异国风情的，外国情调的；奇异的 unusual and exciting because of coming (or seeming to come) from far away, especially a tropical country

expand   verb [I or T] UK /ɪkˈspænd/ US /ɪkˈspænd/ B2 （使）（尺寸、数量或重要性）扩大，增加；（使）膨胀 to increase in size, number, or importance, or to make something increase in this way

expanse   noun [C] UK /ɪkˈspæns/ US /ɪkˈspæns/（陆地、水面或天空的）广阔区域 a large, open area of land, water, or sky

expatriate   1 noun [C] UK /ekˈspæt.ri.ət/ US /ekˈspeɪ.tri.ət/ (informal expat,)（旅居国外的）侨民 someone who does not live in their own country

expedition   1 noun UK /ˌek.spəˈdɪʃ.ən/ US /ˌek.spəˈdɪʃ.ən/ (JOURNEY) B1 [C] 远征；探险，考察 an organized journey for a particular purpose

expel   1 verb [T] UK /ɪkˈspel/ US /ɪkˈspel/ -ll- [T] (PERSON) 驱逐；除名；开除 to force someone to leave a school, organization, or country

export   1 verb UK /ɪkˈspɔːt/ US /ˈek.spɔːrt/ B2 [I or T] 出口；输出 to send goods to another country for sale

expose   1 verb [T] UK /ɪkˈspəʊz/ US /ɪkˈspoʊz/ [T] (UNCOVER) 暴露；露出；使曝光 to remove what is covering something so that it can be seen

exposure 1 noun UK /ɪkˈspəʊ.ʒər/ US /ɪkˈspoʊ.ʒɚ/ (EXPERIENCE) C1 [C or U] 接触；面临；遭受 the fact of experiencing something or being affected by it because of being in a particular situation or place

express 1 verb [T] UK /ɪkˈspres/ US /ɪkˈspres/ [T] (SHOW) B2 陈述；表达；表露 to show a feeling, opinion, or fact

extend 1 verb UK /ɪkˈstend/ US /ɪkˈstend/ (INCREASE) B2 扩大；扩展；使增加长度 [T] to add to something in order to make it bigger or longer

exterior 1 adjective UK /ɪkˈstɪə.ri.ər/ US /ɪkˈstɪr.i.ɚ/ 外面的；外表的；外来的 on or from the outside

external adjective UK /ɪkˈstɜː.nəl/ US /ɪkˈstɜː.nəl/ B2 外面的；外表的；来自外部的 of, on, for, or coming from the outside

extinct 1 adjective UK /ɪkˈstɪŋkt/ US /ɪkˈstɪŋkt/ C1 灭绝的；绝种的；消失的 not now existing

extinguish 1 verb [T] UK /ɪkˈstɪŋ.gwɪʃ/ US /ɪkˈstɪŋ.gwɪʃ/ [T] (FIRE/LIGHT) 熄灭，扑灭（火或光） to stop a fire or a light burning 2 verb [T] (FEELING/IDEA) literary 使（想法或感情）破灭；使消亡 to stop or get rid of an idea or feeling [GRE]

extract 1 verb [T] UK /ɪkˈstrækt/ US /ɪkˈstrækt/ B2 取出；拔出；提取 to remove or take out something

Prefix: ex- used to show that someone is no longer what they were

Meaning in English: out of/ away from

Origin language: Latin/ Greek

English examples:

ex-   2 prefix UK /eks-/ US /eks-/ 以前的；前任 used to show that someone is no longer what they were

ex-husband   noun [C] UK /ˌeksˈhʌz.bənd/ US /ˌeksˈhʌz.bənd/ 前夫 Someone's ex-husband is the man they were once married to.

my ex-husband   我的前夫

ex-wife   noun [C] UK /ˌeksˈwaɪf/ US /ˌeksˈwaɪf/ 前妻 Someone's ex-wife is the woman they were once married to.

ex-serviceman   noun [C] UK /ˌeksˈsɜː.vɪs.mən/ US /ˌeksˈsɚ.vɪs.mən/ plural -men UK /-mən/ US 退役男军人，复员男军人 a man who was a member of the armed services in the past

ex-prisoners   刑满释放的人

ex-policemen   从前做过警察的人

my ex-girlfriend   我的前女友

Prefix: exa- 1,000,000,000,000,000,000 times

Meaning in English: 1,000,000,000,000,000,000 times

Origin language: Anglo-Saxon/ Latin

English examples:

exa- prefix SCIENCE specialized /eks.ə/ 1,000,000,000,000,000,000 times the stated unit （计量单位）百亿亿，艾 an exabyte 艾字节

an exabyte 艾字节

Prefix (Medical): exo- Denotes something as 'outside' another

Meaning in English: Denotes something as 'outside' another

Origin language: Ancient Greek ἔξω- (exo-), outside of, external

English examples:

exoskeleton noun [C] BIOLOGY specialized UK /ˌek.səʊˈskel.ɪ.tən/ US /ˌek.soʊˈskel.ətən/ 外骨骼（昆虫和甲壳纲动物裸露在身体表面的用于支撑和保护身体的骨骼） a hard outer layer that covers, supports, and protects the body of an invertebrate animal such as an insect or crustacean

exoteric adjective formal /ek.səˈter.ɪk/ 适于（或打算）传授给公众的 intended or suitable for people generally, not only for some people

esoteric adjective UK /ˌiː.səˈter.ɪk/ US /ˌes.əˈter.ɪk/ 极不寻常的；只有少数人（尤指内行）才懂的；限于小圈子的 very unusual and understood or liked by only a small number of people, especially those with special knowledge

exothermic adjective exo·ther·mic | \ ˌek-sō-ˈthər-mik \ 放热的 characterized by or formed with evolution of heat

exothermic reaction noun [C] CHEMISTRY specialized UK /ˌek.səʊˌθɜː.mɪk riˈæk.ʃən/ US /ˌek.soʊˌθɜː.mɪk riˈæk.ʃən/ 放热反应（放出热量的化学反应） a chemical reaction in which heat is produced

Prefix: extra- outside or in addition to

Meaning in English: outside or in addition to

Origin language: Anglo-Saxon/ Latin

English examples:

extra- prefix UK /ek.strə-/ US /ek.strə-/ 在...之外；超出；越出
outside or in addition to

extraterrestrial beings 外星人 (= imaginary creatures which come
from outside the planet Earth)

an extramarital affair 婚外恋 (= a sexual relationship of a married
person with someone other than their husband or wife)

extracurricular activities 课外活动 (= activities which are not part
of the usual school or college course)

extra-rare adjective UK /ˌek.strəˈreər/ US /ˌek.strəˈrer/ → blue
adjective(MEAT)（肉）未熟的，仍带血色的（同 blue）

extraneous adjective UK /ɪkˈstreɪ.ni.əs/ US /ɪkˈstreɪ.ni.əs/ 无直接关系
的；无关的 not directly connected with or related to something [GRE]

extranet noun [C] UK /ˈeks.trə.net/ US /ˈeks.trə.net/ 外联网 a system of
computers that makes it possible for particular organizations to communicate
with each other and share information

extraordinaire adjective [after noun] usually humorous UK
/ɪkˌstrɔː.dɪˈneər/ US /ɪkˌstrɔːr.dəˈner/ （法语词，用作后置形容词）特别的，
非凡的 used to say that someone is very good at the activity mentioned.
Extraordinaire is French for "extraordinary".

extraordinarily   adverb UK /ɪkˈstrɔː.dɪn.ər.əl.i/ US /ɪkˈstrɔːr.dən.er.əl.i/ 极其，极端；特别地 B2 very; more than usual

extrapolate   verb [I or T] UK /ɪkˈstræp.ə.leɪt/ US /ɪkˈstræp.ə.leɪt/ 推断；推知 to guess or think about what might happen using information that is already known [GRE]

extrasolar   adjective   PHYSICS   specialized UK /ˌek.strəˈsəʊ.lər/ US /-ˈsoʊ.lə/ （存在于）太阳系之外的 outside the solar system (= the area that contains the sun and the planets around it)

extraterrestrial   adjective UK /ˌek.strə.təˈres.tri.əl/ US /ˌek.strə.təˈres.tri.əl/地球外的；天外的 (coming from) outside the planet Earth

extraterritorial   adjective UK /ˌek.strəˌter.ɪˈtɔː.ri.əl/ US /ˌek.strəˌter.ɪˈtɔːr.i.əl/ 境外的；治外法权的 outside (the laws of) a country

extravagance   1 noun UK /ɪkˈstræv.ə.gəns/ US /ɪkˈstræv.ə.gəns/ 奢侈，铺张 [U] behaviour in which you spend more money than you need to 2 奢侈品，奢华物 [C] something expensive that you buy even though you do not need it

extravagant   1 adjective UK /ɪkˈstræv.ə.gənt/ US /ɪkˈstræv.ə.gənt/奢侈的，铺张的；浪费的 C2 spending too much money, or using too much of something [GRE]

extravaganza   noun [C] UK /ɪkˌstræv.əˈgæn.zə/ US /ɪkˌstræv.əˈgæn.zə/ 铺张华丽的娱乐表演 a large, exciting, and expensive event or entertainment

FFF

Prefix (Medical): faci(o)- Of or pertaining to the face

Meaning in English: Of or pertaining to the face

Origin language: Latin (faciēs), the face, countenance

English examples:

Facioplegia noun [U] 面瘫 facioplegia (pathology) paralysis of the muscles of the face.

facial 1 adjective UK /ˈfeɪ.ʃəl/ US /ˈfeɪ.ʃəl/ C2 面部的，脸上的 of or on the face

facies 1 noun [C] MEDICAL specialized UK /ˈfeɪ.ʃiːz/ US /ˈfeɪ.ʃiːz/ plural facies （用于医学术语中）面，面部 the appearance of the face in certain medical conditions

Prefix (Medical): fibr(o)- fiber

Meaning in English: fiber

Origin language: Latin

English examples:

fibre 1 noun UK (US fiber) UK /ˈfaɪ.bər/ US /ˈfaɪ.bɚ/ THREAD) [C] （植物或人造物的）纤维，丝 any of the thread-like parts that form plant or artificial material and can be made into cloth

fibre optics noun [plural] UK (US fiber optics) UK /ˌfaɪ.bər ˈɒp.tɪks/ US /ˌfaɪ.bɚ ˈɑː.p.tɪks/ 光导纤维；光纤 the use of very thin glass or plastic threads through which light can travel to carry information, especially in phone, television, and computer systems

fibrillation   noun [U]   MEDICAL   specialized UK /fɪb.rɪˈleɪ.ʃən/ US /ˌfɪb.rəˈleɪ.ʃən/ （尤指心脏）纤维性颤动 irregular, rapid contractions of muscles, especially the heart

atrial/ventricular fibrillation   心房/心室纤维性颤动

fibrin   noun [U]   MEDICAL   specialized UK /ˈfɪb.rɪn/ US /ˈfaɪ.rɪn/ 纤维蛋白（一种产生于肝脏，帮助伤口凝血的物质）a substance produced in the liver that makes the blood clot (= become solid)

fibrinogen noun [U]   MEDICAL   specialized UK /fɪˈbrɪn.ə.dʒən/ US /faɪˈbrɪn.ə.dʒən/ 纤维蛋白原（产生于肝脏，能转化为纤维蛋白，当人体组织受到损坏时，起凝血作用） a substance produced in the liver that is changed into fibrin to clot the blood when body tissue is damaged

fibroblast   noun [C]   MEDICAL   specialized UK /ˈfaɪ.brə.blæst/ US /ˈfaɪ.brəˌblæst/ 成纤维细胞，纤维母细胞 a cell that produces collagen (= an important protein in the body)

fibrocartilage   noun [C]   MEDICAL   specialized UK /ˌfaɪ.brəʊˈkɑː.tɪ.lɪdʒ/ US /ˌfaɪ.broʊˈkɑːr.t̬əl.ɪdʒ/ 纤维软骨 a type of cartilage that contains groups of collagen fibres (= an important protein found in the body)

fibromyalgia   noun [U]   MEDICAL   specialized UK /ˌfaɪ.brəʊ.maɪˈæl.dʒi.ə/ US /ˌfaɪ.broʊ.maɪˈæl.dʒə/ 纤维肌痛 a medical condition that causes pain in the muscles and surrounding tissue as well as extreme tiredness

fibrosis   noun [U]   MEDICAL   specialized UK /faɪˈbrəʊ.sɪs/ US /faɪˈbroʊ.sɪs/ 纤维变性，纤维化 the formation of too much fibrous tissue as a result of healing, inflammation, or irritation

fibrous   1 adjective UK /ˈfaɪ.brəs/ US /ˈfaɪ.brəs/ (THREAD) 纤维构成的；纤维状的 made of fibres, or like fibre 2 adjective (FOOD) 含纤维素的 Food that is fibrous contains fibre.

Prefix (Medical): flav- yellow

Meaning in English:

Origin language: Latin

English examples:

bioflavonoid   noun [C] UK /ˌbaɪ.əʊˈflæv.ə.nɔɪd/ US /ˌbaɪ.oʊˈflæv.ə.nɔɪd/ 生物类黄酮，维生素 P a flavonoid

flavonoid   noun [C] UK /ˈflæv.ə.nɔɪd/ US /ˈflæv.ə.nɔɪd/ (also bioflavonoid) 类黄酮（水果或蔬菜中的一种物质，可能有助于抵御某些种癌症或心脏病）a substance in fruit and vegetables that may help protect people against some types of cancer or heart disease

riboflavin   noun [U]   CHEMISTRY, BIOLOGY   specialized UK /ˌraɪ.bəʊˈfleɪ.vɪn/ US /ˈraɪ.bə.fleɪ.vɪn/ →   vitamin B2 维生素 B2（同 vitamin B2）

ligamentum flavum   noun [C]   ANATOMY   specialized UK /lɪg.əˌmen.təm ˈfleɪ.vəm/ US /lɪg.əˌmen.t̬əm ˈfleɪ.vəm/ plural ligamenta flava 黄韧带 a ligament (= strong fibre) that helps connect the bones that make up the spine

Prefix: fore- at or towards the front

Meaning in English: before/ earlier

Origin language: Anglo-Saxon

English examples:

fore- prefix UK /fɔːr-/ US /fɔːr-/ 前部的；向前的 at or towards the front

forearm noun [C] UK /ˈfɔː.rɑːm/ US /ˈfɔːr.ɑːrm/ 前臂 the lower part of the arm, between the wrist and the elbow (= the middle of the arm where it bends)

forebear noun [C usually plural] formal (also forbear) UK /ˈfɔː.beər/ US /ˈfɔːr.ber/ 祖先，祖宗 a relative who lived in the past [GRE]

forebode 预示，预兆 (of a situation or occurrence) act as a warning of (something bad). [GRE]

foreboding noun [C or U] literary UK /fɔːˈbəʊ.dɪŋ/ US /fɔːrˈboʊ.dɪŋ/（对不祥之事的）预感 a feeling that something very bad is going to happen soon

forecast 1 noun [C] UK /ˈfɔː.kɑːst/ US /ˈfɔːr.kæst/ B1（尤指对特定形势或天气的）预测，预报 a statement of what is judged likely to happen in the future, especially in connection with a particular situation, or the expected weather conditions

foreclose 1 verb UK /fɔːˈkləʊz/ US /fɔːrˈkloʊz/ (TAKE POSSESSION) [I or T] FINANCE & ECONOMICS, LAW specialized （尤指银行）取消抵押品赎回权 (especially of banks) to take back property that was bought with borrowed money because the money was not being paid back as formally agreed

foreclosure 法院拍卖房屋（俗称法拍屋，法拍房，香港称银主盘）foreclosure (Foreclosure is a legal process that allows lenders to recover the amount owed on a defaulted loan by taking ownership of and selling the mortgaged property.)

forefinger　　noun [C] UK /ˈfɔːˌfɪŋ.gər/ US /ˈfɔːrˌfɪŋ.gɚ/ (also index finger) 食指 the finger next to the thumb

foreground　　　　1 noun [S] UK /ˈfɔː.graʊnd/ US /ˈfɔːr.graʊnd/ the foreground （图片或照片的）前景 the people, objects, countryside, etc. in a picture or photograph that seem nearest to you and form its main part 2 noun 重要位置；瞩目地位 the area that is of most importance and activity, or that people pay attention to 3 verb [T] UK /ˈfɔː.graʊnd/ US /ˈfɔːr.graʊnd/强调，突出（某事物的重要性） to give the most importance to a particular subject, etc. [GRE]

forehand　　noun [C] UK /ˈfɔː.hænd/ US /ˈfɔːr.hænd/（网球等运动中的）正手击球（能力），正手（能力），正拍 (in sports such as tennis) a hit in which the palm of the hand that is holding the racket faces the same direction as the hit itself, or the player's ability to perform this hit

forehead　　noun [C] UK /ˈfɒr.ɪd/ /ˈfɔː.hed/ US /ˈfɑː.rɪd/ 前额，额头 B1 the flat part of the face, above the eyes and below the hair

foremost　　adjective UK /ˈfɔː.məʊst/ US /ˈfɔːr.moʊst/ C2 最重要的；最佳的；领先的 most important or best; leading

forerunner　　noun [C] UK /ˈfɔːˌrʌn.ər/ US /ˈfɔːrˌrʌn.ɚ/先驱，先行者；预兆，前兆 something or someone that acts as an early and less advanced model for what will appear in the future, or a warning or sign of what is to follow

foresight　　　noun [U] UK /ˈfɔː.saɪt/ US /ˈfɔːr.saɪt/ 深谋远虑；先见之明；远见卓识 the ability to judge correctly what is going to happen in the future and plan your actions based on this knowledge

Meaning in English: A hollow or depressed area; trench or channel

Origin language: Latin (fossa), ditch, pit

English examples:

fossa ovalis   noun [C] 卵圆窝 The fossa ovalis is a depression in the right atrium of the heart, at the level of the interatrial septum, the wall between right and left atrium. The fossa ovalis is the remnant of a thin fibrous sheet that covered the foramen ovale during fetal development.

fossa   noun [C]   MEDICAL   specialized UK /ˈfɒs.ə/ US /ˈfɑːs.ə/ plural fossae (拉丁语，用于医学术语中)凹；窝 a natural hollow, especially in a bone

The pituitary gland sits in a bony fossa called the sellar turcica. 脑下垂体位于被称为蝶鞍的骨窝处。

supraspinous fossa   noun [C]   ANATOMY   specialized UK /suː.prəˌspaɪ.nəs ˈfɒs.ə/ US /ˌsuː.prəˈspaɪ.nəs ˈfɑːs.ə/ plural supraspinous fossae 棘上窝 a part of the scapula (= a large, flat bone on each side of the back below the shoulder)

Meaning in English: of or connected with France

Origin language: Anglo-Saxon/ Latin

English examples:

Franco-   prefix UK /fræŋ.kəʊ-/ US /fræŋ.koʊ-/ 法国的；与法国有关的 of or connected with France

Franco-   prefix UK /fræŋ.kəʊ-/ US /fræŋ.koʊ-/ 法国的；与法国有关的 of or connected with France

the Franco-German border　德法边境　(= the border between France and Germany)

a francophile　亲法者　(= someone who loves France)

Prefix: fresh- recently done

Meaning in English: recently done

Origin language: Anglo-Saxon/ Latin

English examples:

fresh-　　11 prefix UK　/freʃ-/ US　/freʃ-/ 新…的 recently done

fresh-baked bread　　新烤的面包

fresh-cut flowers　　新剪下的花朵

fresh-faced　　adjective UK　/ˈfreʃ.feɪst/ US　/ˈfreʃ.feɪst/ 看起来年轻的 looking young

freshen　　1 verb UK /ˈfreʃ.ən/ US /ˈfreʃ.ən/ (AIR) [T] (also freshen up) 使洁净，使凉爽 to make something cleaner and/or cooler

freshen (sb/sth) up　　verb UK /ˈfreʃ.ən/ US /ˈfreʃ.ən/ 梳洗；使干净；使清爽 to make someone or something clean and pleasant

freshen sth up　　verb UK /ˈfreʃ.ən/ US /ˈfreʃ.ən/ 使…焕然一新 to make something different and more interesting or attractive

freshman　　1 noun [C] US UK /ˈfreʃ.mən/ US /ˈfreʃ.mən/ plural -men UK /-mən/ US (informal frosh) （中学或大学的）一年级新生

freshwater   adjective [before noun] UK /ˈfreʃˌwɔː.tər/ US /ˈfreʃˌwɑː.t̬ɚ/ 淡水中生长的；淡水的 living in or containing water that is not salty

Prefix (Medical): front- Of or pertaining to the forehead
Meaning in English: Of or pertaining to the forehead

Origin language: Latin (frōns, front-), the forehead

English examples:

Frontonasal dysplasia   noun [U] 额鼻发育不良 Frontonasal dysplasia is a rare disorder characterized by abnormal development of the head and face before birth. Major physical characteristics may include widely spaced eyes (ocular hypertelorism); a flat broad nose; and/or a vertical groove down the middle of the face.

front-loader   noun [C] UK /ˈfrʌntˌləʊd.ər/ US /ˈfrʌntˌloʊd.ɚ/ 前开式洗衣机（一种门在前部，而非顶部的洗衣机，衣服从前部置入洗衣机） a washing machine with a door at the front, rather than the top, in which you put your clothes

frontal lobotomy   noun [C]   MEDICAL   specialized UK /ˌfrʌn.təl ləˈbɒt.ə.mi/ US /ˌfrʌn.təl ləˈbɑː.t̬ə.mi/ 额叶前部脑白质切断手术（一种大脑前部的医疗手术，以治疗一些精神病） a medical operation on the front part of the brain that is used in treating some mental illnesses

frontalis   adjective   ANATOMY   specialized UK /frʌntˈɑːl.ɪs/ US /frʌnˈtæl.ɪs/ （拉丁语，用于医学术语中）前部的 a Latin word meaning "frontal" (= relating to the forehead), used in medical names and descriptions

confront   1 verb [T] UK /kənˈfrʌnt/ US /kənˈfrʌnt/ 面对，面临；遭遇；直面，正视 C2 to face, meet, or deal with a difficult situation or person

confrontation　　noun [C or U] UK　/ˌkɒn.frʌnˈteɪ.ʃən/ US /ˌkɑːn.frənˈteɪ.ʃən/ C2 对抗；冲突；对峙；争论 a fight or argument

confront sb with sth　　verb [T] UK　/kənˈfrʌnt/ US /kənˈfrʌnt/ 跟…对质，跟…当面对证 C2 to tell someone what they do not want to hear, often because it is about something bad that they have done or because it needs an explanation

effrontery　　noun [U]　formal UK /ɪˈfrʌn.tər.i/ US /efˈrʌn.tər.i/厚颜无耻；放肆 extreme rudeness without any ability to understand that your behaviour is not acceptable to other people [GRE]

在饭桌上他自始至终一言不发，到头来却有脸抱怨我一副百无聊赖的样子。
　　He was silent all through the meal and then had the effrontery to complain that I looked bored!

front-runner　　noun [C] UK /ˌfrʌntˈrʌn.ər/ US /ˌfrʌntˈrʌn.ɚ/ 最有可能获胜者；领先者 the person, animal, or organization that is most likely to win something

她是竞赛中的领先者之一。　　She is one of the front-runners in the contest.

frontage　　noun [C]　formal UK /ˈfrʌn.tɪdʒ/ US /ˈfrʌn.tɪdʒ/ （建筑物的）临街（或河）正面；临街（或河）地界 the front part of a building that faces a road or river, or land near a road or river

frontal　　adjective [before noun]　ANATOMY　formal or specialized UK /ˈfrʌn.təl/ US /ˈfrʌn.təl/ 前面的；前部的 relating to the front of something

大脑前叶/的前部区域　the frontal lobes/regions of the brain

frontal system　　noun [C]　ENVIRONMENT　specialized UK /ˈfrʌn.təl ˌsɪs.təm/ US /ˈfrʌn.təl ˌsɪs.təm/ （由多个锋面组成的）锋系 a combination of weather conditions in which one or more weather fronts can be recognized

有这么多锋系如此接近，我们预计以后几天的天气情况将会多变。

    With so many frontal systems so close together, we can expect the weather to be highly changeable over the next few days.

GGG

Prefix (Medical): galact(o)- milk

Meaning in English: milk

Origin language: Greek γάλα, γαλακτ

English examples:

galactic   adjective UK /ɡəˈlæk.tɪk/ US /ɡəˈlæk.tɪk/ 银河的；星系的 relating to the Galaxy or other galaxies

Galactorrhea   noun [U] 溢乳 Galactorrhea (guh-lack-toe-REE-uh) is a milky nipple discharge unrelated to the normal milk production of breast-feeding. Galactorrhea itself isn't a disease, but it could be a sign of an underlying problem. It usually occurs in women, even those who have never had children or after menopause.

Prefix (Medical): genu- Of or pertaining to the knee

Meaning in English: Of or pertaining to the knee

Origin language: Latin (genū), knee

English examples:

genu noun [C] MEDICAL specialized UK /ˈdʒen.juː/ US /ˈdʒiː.nuː/ （拉丁语，用于医学术语）膝的 a Latin word meaning "of the knee", used in medical names and descriptions of the knee or a knee-like structure in the body

Genu valgum   noun [U] 膝外翻 Genu valgum (knock-knees) is a common lower leg abnormality that is usually seen in the toddler, preschool and early school age child. In genu valgum, the lower extremities turn inward, causing the appearance of the knees to be touching while the ankles remain apart.

Genu varum noun [U] 膝内翻 Bow legs (genu varum) is a condition where one or both of your child's legs curve outward at the knees. This creates a wider space than normal between the knees and lower legs. When your child stands with his or her feet and ankles together, the knees stay wide apart.

genuflect verb [I] UK /ˈdʒen.ju.flekt/ US /ˈdʒen.jə.flekt/ （尤指进出天主教教堂时）下跪，跪拜 to bend one or both knees as a sign of respect to God, especially when entering or leaving a Catholic church

人们跪在圣坛前。 People were genuflecting in front of the altar.

genuflection noun [C or U] UK /ˌdʒen.juˈflek.ʃən/ US /ˌdʒen.jəˈflek.ʃən/ 下跪，跪拜 the act of genuflecting

Prefix (Medical): gastr- stomach

Meaning in English: stomach

Origin language: Latin / Greek

English examples:

gastric adjective MEDICAL specialized UK /ˈgæs.trɪk/ US /ˈgæs.trɪk/ 胃的；胃部的 relating to the stomach

gastric juices 胃液

a gastric ulcer 胃溃疡

gastric band noun [C] UK /ˌgæs.trɪk ˈbænd/ US /ˌgæs.trɪk ˈbænd/ 胃束带，束胃带 a strip of material that can be put around part of someone's stomach in a medical operation so that the person feels less hungry, eats less food, and loses weight

gastritis   noun [U]   MEDICAL   specialized UK /gæsˈtraɪ.tɪs/ US /gæsˈtraɪ.t̬əs/ 胃炎 an illness in which the stomach walls become swollen and painful

gastrocnemius   noun [C]   MEDICAL   specialized UK /ˌgæs.trəʊˈkniː.mi.əs/ US /ˌgæs.troʊˈkniː.mi.əs/ plural gastrocnemii （拉丁语，用于医学术语中）腓肠肌 the outer calf muscle that goes from the back of the knee to the heel

Leg cramps cause shortening of the gastrocnemius muscle in the calf. 腿部痉挛引起小腿腓肠肌收缩。

gastroenteritis   noun [U]   MEDICAL   specialized UK /ˌgæs.trəʊˌen.təˈraɪ.tɪs/ US /-troʊˌen.t̬əˈraɪ.t̬əs/ 胃肠炎 an illness that causes the stomach and bowels to become swollen and painful

gastroesophageal   adjective   MEDICAL   specialized UK /ˌgæs.trəʊ.ɪ.sɒf.əˈdʒi.əl/ US /ˌgæs.troʊ.ɪˌs ɑ ːf.əˈdʒiː.əl/ （拉丁语，用于医学术语）胃食管的 relating to the stomach and oesophagus (= the tube through which food passes to the stomach)

gastroesophageal cancer 胃食管癌

Gastroenterology   肠胃病学 Gastroenterology is the branch of medicine focused on the digestive system and its disorders. Diseases affecting the gastrointestinal tract, which include the organs from mouth into anus, along the alimentary canal, are the focus of this speciality. Physicians practicing in this field are called gastroenterologists. Wikipedia; Gastroenterology is the study of the normal function and diseases of the esophagus, stomach, small intestine, colon and rectum, pancreas, gallbladder, bile ducts and liver.

gastroenterologists   肠胃病医生 Physicians practicing in Gastroenterology field are called gastroenterologists. Gastroenterology is an area of medicine that focuses on the health of the digestive system, or the gastrointestinal (GI) tract, as well as the liver.

gastroesophageal reflux disease   noun [U]   MEDICAL   specialized UK /gæs.trəʊ.ɪ.sɒf.əˌdʒi.əl ˈriː.flʌks dɪˌziːz/ US /ˈgæs.troʊ.ɪˌs ɑ ːf.əˈdʒi.əl ˈriː.flʌks dɪˌziːz/ (US abbreviation GERD); (UK abbreviation GORD) 胃食道逆流 a chronic disease where stomach acid goes up into the oesophagus (= the tube through which food passes to the stomach) causing inflammation and pain

GERD   胃食道逆流

GORD   胃食道逆流

gastrointestinal   adjective   MEDICAL   specialized UK /ˌgæs.trəʊˌɪn.tesˈtaɪ.nəl/ US /ˌgæs.troʊ.ɪnˈtes.tən.əl/ 胃肠（里）的；与肠胃相关的 in or relating to both the stomach and the intestine (= the long tube that food passes through after the stomach)

the gastrointestinal tract 胃肠道

gastrointestinal bleeding 胃肠出血

gastronome   noun [C]   formal UK /ˈgæs.trə.nəʊm/ US /ˈgæs.trə.noʊm/ 美食家，讲究吃喝的人 someone who enjoys and knows about high-quality food and drink

gastronomic   adjective   formal UK /ˌgæs.trəˈnɒm.ɪk/ US /ˌgæs.trəˈn ɑ ːmɪk/ (also gastronomical,) 美食的；烹饪法的 relating to the preparation and consumption (= eating) of good food

gastronomical   adjective 美食的；烹饪法的 relating to the preparation and consumption (= eating) of good food

gastronomy noun [U] formal UK /gæsˈtrɒn.ə.mi/ US /gæsˈtrɑː.nə.mi/ 美食学，美食法；烹饪学 the art and knowledge involved in preparing and eating good food

gastroparesis noun [U] MEDICAL specialized UK /ˌgæs.trəʊ.pəˈriː.sɪs/ US /ˌgæs.troʊ.pəˈriː.sɪs/（拉丁语，用于医学术语）胃轻瘫 a medical condition in which the stomach does not empty properly because of a problem with nerve signals to the stomach rather than a blockage

gastropod noun [C] BIOLOGY specialized UK /ˈgæs.trəʊ.pɒd/ US /ˈgæs.trə.pɑːd/ 软体无脊椎动物（腹部扁平，用于爬行，通常有壳，比如蜗牛或蛞蝓 a type of animal with no spine, a soft body with a flat base used for moving, and often a shell, for example a snail or a slug

gastropub noun [C] UK /ˈgæs.trəʊ.pʌb/ US /ˈgæs.troʊ.pʌb/ 美食吧 a bar where high-quality food is served

an organic gastropub 有机食品美食吧

gastroscope noun [C] MEDICAL specialized /ˈgæs.trə.skəʊp/ /ˈgæs.trə.skoʊp/ 胃镜 a long, thin medical device that is used to examine the inside of the stomach

A special instrument called a gastroscope is put in the mouth and passed down into the stomach. 一个叫做胃镜的特殊工具从口腔置入，下行到胃部。

The gastroscope is fitted with a tiny camera that allows the doctor to see the stomach lining. 胃镜上装有一个微小的摄像机，让医生可以看到胃的内壁。

gastroscopy noun [C or U] MEDICAL specialized /gæsˈtrɒs.kə.pi/ /gæsˈtrɑː.skə.pi/ 胃镜检查 a medical examination of the inside of the stomach and part of the small intestine (= the upper part of the bowels between the stomach and the large intestine) using a gastroscope (= a long, thin medical device with a light and camera)

Gastrostomy   noun [U] 胃造口术 Gastrostomy is the creation of an artificial external opening into the stomach for nutritional support or gastric decompression. Typically this would include an incision in the patient's epigastrium as part of a formal operation. Wikipedia

Prefix: geo- of or relating to the earth

Meaning in English: of or relating to the earth

Origin language: Anglo-Saxon/ Latin

English examples:

geo-   prefix UK /dʒiː.əʊ-/ US /dʒiː.oʊ-/ 地球的 of or relating to the earth

geo-targeted   adjective   BUSINESS UK /ˌdʒiː.əʊˈtɑː.gɪ.tɪd/ US /ˌdʒiː.oʊˈtɑːr.gɪ.t̬ɪd/ 根据用户所在地设计的 designed for customers or users according to where in the world they live

geographer   noun [C] UK /dʒiˈɒg.rə.fər/ US /dʒiˈɑː.grə.fɚ/ 地理学家 a person who studies geography

geographical   adjective mainly UK UK /ˌdʒi.əˈgræf.ɪ.kəl/ US /ˌdʒi.əˈgræf.ɪ.kəl/ (US usually geographic, UK /-ɪk/ US) 地理的；地理学的 relating to geography, or to the geography of a particular area or place

geography   noun [U] UK /dʒiˈɒg.rə.fi/ US /dʒiˈɑː.grə.fi/ A2 地理；地理学 the study of the systems and processes involved in the world's weather, mountains, seas, lakes, etc. and of the ways in which countries and people organize life within an area

geology   noun [U] UK /dʒiˈɒl.ə.dʒi/ US /dʒiˈɑː.lə.dʒi/ C1 地质学 the study of the rocks and similar substances that make up the earth's surface

geometric   adjective UK /ˌdʒiː.əˈmet.rɪk/ US /ˌdʒiː.əˈmet.rɪk/ (also geometrical, UK /-rɪ.kəl/ US) 几何图形的，几何的 A geometric pattern or arrangement is made up of shapes such as squares, triangles, or rectangles.

geometry   noun [U] UK /dʒiˈɒm.ə.tri/ US /dʒiˈɑː.mə.tri/ 几何学 the area of mathematics relating to the study of space and the relationships between points, lines, curves, and surfaces

geothermal   adjective GEOLOGY, ENVIRONMENT specialized UK /ˌdʒiː.əʊˈθɜː.məl/ US /ˌdʒiː.oʊˈθɝː.məl/ 地热的，地温的 of or connected with the heat inside the earth

geotropism   noun [U] BIOLOGY specialized UK /ˌdʒiːəʊˈtrəʊpɪzm/ US /ˌdʒiːoʊˈtroʊpɪzm/ the way plants or plant parts react to gravity 向地性

Prefix: giga- 1,000,000,000 times the stated unit

Meaning in English: 1,000,000,000 times the stated unit

Origin language: Anglo-Saxon/ Latin

English examples:

giga-   prefix UK /gɪg.ə-/ US /gɪg.ə-/ 吉（咖），千兆，十亿 1,000,000,000 times the stated unit

gigavolt   千兆伏特

gigahertz   千兆赫

gigawatt　千兆瓦

gigabit　　noun [C] UK /ˈɡɪɡ.ə.bɪt/ US /ˈɡɪɡ.ə.bɪt/ (abbreviation Gb) 吉（咖）比特 a unit of computer information, consisting of 1,000,000,000 bits, or 125 megabytes c.

gigabyte　　noun [C]　COMPUTING　specialized UK /ˈɡɪɡ.ə.baɪt/ US /ˈɡɪɡ.ə.baɪt/ (written abbreviation GB, Gb); (also gig) 千兆字节，吉字节 a unit of computer information, consisting of 1,024 megabytes

Prefix (Medical): gingiv- Of or pertaining to the gums

Meaning in English: Of or pertaining to the gums

Origin language: Latin (gingīva), gum

English examples:

gingivitis　　noun [U]　MEDICAL　specialized UK /ˌdʒɪn.dʒɪˈvaɪ.tɪs/ US /ˌdʒɪn.dʒɪˈvaɪ.t̬əs/ 牙龈炎 an infection of the gums (= the part of the mouth from which the teeth grow) which causes swelling, pain, and sometimes bleeding

Prefix (Medical): glauc(o)- Denoting a grey or bluish-grey colour

Meaning in English: Denoting a grey or bluish-grey colour

Origin language: Ancient Greek γλαυκός (glaukos), grey, bluish-grey

English examples:

glaucoma　　noun [U] UK /ɡlaʊˈkəʊ.mə/ US /ɡlaʊˈkoʊ.mə/ 青光眼 a disease of the eye that can cause a person to gradually lose their sight

Prefix (Medical): gloss(o)-, glott(o)- Of or pertaining to the tongue

Meaning in English: Of or pertaining to the tongue

Origin language: Ancient Greek γλῶσσα, γλῶττα (glōssa, glōtta), tongue

English examples:

diglossia noun [U] language specialized UK /ˌdaɪˈglɒs.i.ə/ US /ˌdaɪˈglɑ:.si.ə/ 双层语言，双言现象（指在特定语言小区里，一种语言存在两种不同变体，各具特定的社会功能） a situation in which there are two different forms of the same language used by a community, used in different social situations

gloss 3 noun (APPEARANCE) 一种使（嘴唇、头发、皮肤等）显得光亮的物质 [U] a substance used to make your lips, hair, or skin appear shiny

gloss over sth. verb [T] UK /glɒs/ US /glɑ:s/ 搪塞；掩盖 to avoid considering something, such as an embarrassing mistake, to make it seem not important, and to quickly continue talking about something else [GRE]

glossary noun [C] UK /ˈglɒs.ər.i/ US /ˈglɑ:.sɚ.i/ 词汇表；难词汇编 an alphabetical list, with meanings, of the words or phrases in a text that are difficult to understand

glossopharyngeal adjective MEDICAL specialized UK /ˌglɒs.əʊ.fəˈrɪn.dʒi.əl/ US /ˌglɑ:s.oʊ.fəˈrɪn.dʒi.əl/ （拉丁语，用于医学术语）舌咽的 relating to the tongue and the throat

Glossology noun [U] 词汇学；言语学 The science of language; linguistics.

glottal stop noun [C] PHONETICS specialized UK /ˌglɒt.əl ˈstɒp/ US /ˌglɑ:.t̬əl ˈstɑ:p/ 喉塞音，声门闭塞音 a speech sound produced by closing the vocal cords and then opening them quickly so that the air from the lungs is released with force

glottis noun [C usually singular] ANATOMY specialized UK /ˈglɒt.ɪs/ US /ˈglɑː.t̬ɪs/ plural glottises glottides 声门（人喉部声带间的区域） the thin opening between the vocal cords at the top of the larynx (= the organ in the throat), that is closed by the epiglottis when you swallow

heteroglossia noun 2 LANGUAGE （某一个地方的）话语混杂（指在同一个地方存在两种或两种以上的语言或语言类型） the fact of there being two or more languages or types of a language in a place

hypoglossal adjective MEDICAL specialized UK /ˌhaɪ.pəʊˈglɒs.əl/ US /ˌhaɪ.poʊˈglɑː.səl/ 舌下的 relating to the area below the tongue

Glossodynia 舌痛 Glossodynia means pain in the tongue.

epiglottis noun [C] ANATOMY specialized UK /ˌep.ɪˈglɒt.ɪs/ US /ˌep.əˈglɑː.t̬ɪs/ （舌头后部的）会厌 a small flat part at the back of the tongue that closes when you swallow to prevent food from entering the tube that goes to the lungs

Prefix (Medical): gluco- glucose; sweet

Meaning in English: glucose; sweet

Origin language: Greek γλυκός, sweet

English examples:

glucagon noun [U] BIOLOGY specialized UK /ˈgluː.kə.gɒn/ US /ˈgluː.kə.gɑːn/ 高血糖素，增血糖素 a hormone produced in the pancreas that helps glucose (= a type of sugar) to get into the blood

glucose noun [U] UK /ˈgluː.kəʊs/ US /ˈgluː.koʊs/ specialized （植物、尤指水果中的）葡萄糖 a type of sugar that is found in plants, especially fruit, and supplies an important part of the energy that animals need

Glucocorticoid 糖皮质激素，又称葡萄糖皮质素 Glucocorticoids are a class of corticosteroids, which are a class of steroid hormones. Glucocorticoids are corticosteroids that bind to the glucocorticoid receptor that is present in almost every vertebrate animal cell. 糖皮质激素，又称葡萄糖皮质素（英语：Glucocorticoid）是一种肾上腺皮质激素，是由肾上腺皮质中层的束状带分泌的类固醇激素，也可由化学方法人工合成。Wikipedia

Prefix (Medical): glyco- sugar

Meaning in English: sugar

Origin language: Latin

English examples:

glycogen　noun [U]　BIOLOGY, CHEMISTRY　specialized UK /ˈɡlaɪ.kəʊ.dʒən/ US /ˈɡlaɪ.koʊ.dʒən/ 肝糖（存在于动物的肝脏和肌肉中，贮藏碳水化合物，控制血糖浓度）a substance found in the liver and muscles that stores carbohydrate and is important in controlling sugar levels in the blood

glycol　noun [U]　CHEMISTRY　specialized UK /ˈɡlaɪ.kɒl/ US /ˈɡlaɪ.kɑːl/ 乙二醇，甘醇 a poisonous alcohol that is used as an antifreeze (= a liquid that reduces the temperature at which water freezes) and in industry

glycoprotein　noun [C or U]　CHEMISTRY, BIOLOGY　specialized /ˌɡlaɪ.kəʊˈprəʊ.tiːn/ /ˌɡlaɪ.koʊˈproʊ.tiːn/ 糖蛋白 a type of protein molecule that has a carbohydrate group attached to the amino acid chain

Glycolysis　noun [U] 糖酵解, 又称糖解 Glycolysis is the metabolic process that serves as the foundation for both aerobic and anaerobic cellular respiration. In glycolysis, glucose is converted into pyruvate. Glucose is a six- memebered ring molecule found in the blood and is usually a result of the breakdown of carbohydrates into sugars. Wikipedia

Meaning in English: Of or pertaining to the jaw

Origin language: Ancient Greek γνάθος (gnáthos), jaw

English examples:

gnaw verb [I + prep, T] UK /nɔː/ US /n ɑ ː/ (BITE)咬，啮，啃（通常指啃出孔洞或逐渐啃坏） to bite or chew something repeatedly, usually making a hole in it or gradually destroying it

Gnathodynamometer noun [C] 颚测力计 A gnathodynamometer is an instrument for measuring the force exerted in closing the mouth. This device can measure the bite force of humans in the following three measurements: newtons, pounds, or kilograms. The average bite force of a human being is 126 pounds per square inch. Wikipedia

orthognathic adjective MEDICAL specialized UK /ˌɔː.θɒgˈnæθ.ɪk/ US /ˌɔːr.θ ɑ ːgˈnæθ.ɪk/ 正颌学的 relating to moving the position of the jaw (= either of the two bones in your body in which the teeth are held)

Meaning in English: seed, semen; also, reproductive

Origin language: Ancient Greek γόνος

English examples:

gonorrhoea noun [U] UK (US gonorrhea) UK /ˌgɒn.əˈriː.ə/ US /ˌg ɑ ː.nəˈriː.ə/ 淋病 a disease of the sexual organs that can be given from one person to another during sex

Prefix: Greco- (also Graeco-) - of or connected with ancient Greece
Meaning in English: of or connected with ancient Greece

Origin language: Anglo-Saxon/ Latin

English examples:

Graeco- prefix UK /ɡriː.kəʊ-/ /ɡrek.əʊ-/ US /ɡrek.oʊ-/ /ɡriː.koʊ-/ （Greco- 的英式拼法） UK spelling of Greco-

Greco- prefix (also Graeco-) UK /ɡriː.kəʊ-/ /ɡrek.əʊ-/ US /ɡrek.oʊ-/ /ɡriː.koʊ-/ 古希腊的；与古希腊有关的 of or connected with ancient Greece

splendid Greco-Roman ruins 壮观的古希腊罗马建筑遗址

Prefix: great- for a family member to mean one generation away from that member

Meaning in English: for a family member to mean one generation away from that member

Origin language: Anglo-Saxon/ Latin

English examples:

great- 10 prefix UK /ɡreɪt-/ US /ɡreɪt-/ （与表示家庭成员的词连用，表示更高或更低一辈）曾 used with a word for a family member to mean one generation away from that member

your great-grandmother 你的（外）曾祖母 (= the grandmother of one of your parents)

your great-grandson 你的曾（外）孙 (= the grandson of your child)

Prefix (Medical): gyn(aec)o- (BrE), gyn(ec)o- (AmE) woman

Meaning in English: woman

Origin language: Greek γυνή, γυναικ- woman

English examples:

gynaecological 1 adjective UK (US gynecological) UK /ˌɡaɪ.nə.kəˈlɒdʒ.ɪ.kəl/ US /ˌɡaɪ.nə.kəˈl ɑː.dʒɪ.kəl/ MEDICAL specialized 妇科的 relating to gynaecology (= the area of medicine concerned with disorders and functions of women's reproductive organs) 2 adjective 妇科的 relating to gynaecology (= the area of medicine concerned with disorders and functions of women's reproductive organs)

gynaecological surgery　妇科手术

gynaecological problems 妇科问题

gynaecologist　　noun [C]　MEDICAL　UK (US gynecologist) UK /ˌgaɪ.nəˈkɒl.ə.dʒɪst/ US /ˌgaɪ.nəˈkɑː.lə.dʒɪst/ 妇科学家，妇科医生 a doctor skilled in the treatment of women's diseases, especially those of the reproductive organs

gynaecology　　noun [U] UK (US gynecology) UK /ˌgaɪ.nəˈkɒl.ə.dʒi/ US /-ˈkɑː.lə-/ 妇科（学） the area of medicine that involves the treatment of women's diseases, especially those of the reproductive organs

gynaecomastia　　noun [U]　MEDICAL　specialized (US gynecomastia) UK /ˌgaɪ.nɪ.kəʊˈmæst.i.ə/ US /ˌgaɪ.nə.koʊˈmæs.ti.ə/ 男性乳腺发育，男性乳房发育 the development of breast tissue in men

Gynaecomastia is usually harmless but emotionally upsetting.　男性乳房发育一般来说无害，但是令人恼火。

HHH

Prefix (Medical): halluc- to wander in mind

Meaning in English: to wander in mind

Origin language: Classical Latin to wander in mind

English examples:

Hallucinosis   noun [U] 幻觉 Hallucinosis refers to the presence of hallucinations in an otherwise normal mental state, without confusion, disorientation, or psychosis

Alcoholic hallucinosis   noun [U] 酒精性幻觉 Alcoholic hallucinosis is a complication of hazardous recreational alcohol use in people with alcohol use disorder. It can occur during acute intoxication or withdrawal with the potential of having delirium tremens. Alcohol hallucinosis is a rather uncommon alcohol-induced psychotic disorder almost exclusively seen in chronic alcoholics who have many consecutive years of severe and heavy drinking during their lifetime. Alcoholic hallucinosis develops about 12 to 24 hours after the heavy drinking stops suddenly, and can last for days. It involves auditory and visual hallucinations, most commonly accusatory or threatening voices. The risk of developing alcoholic hallucinosis is increased by long-term heavy alcohol use and the use of other substances.

Peduncular hallucinosis   noun [U] 幻觉 Peduncular hallucinosis (PH) is a rare neurological disorder that causes vivid visual hallucinations that typically occur in dark environments and last for several minutes. Unlike some other kinds of hallucinations, the hallucinations that patients with PH experience are very realistic, and often involve people and environments that are familiar to the affected individuals. Because the content of the hallucinations is never exceptionally bizarre, patients can rarely distinguish between the hallucinations and reality.

hallucinate   verb [I] UK /həˈluː.sɪ.neɪt/ US /həˈluː.sə.neɪt/ （因生病或吸毒而）产生幻觉 to seem to see, hear, feel, or smell something that does not exist, usually because you are ill or have taken a drug

Mental disorders, drug use, and hypnosis can all cause people to hallucinate. 精神失常、吸毒和催眠术都可以使人产生幻觉。

hallucination   1 noun [C or U] UK /həˌluː.sɪˈneɪ.ʃən/ US /həˌluː.səˈneɪ.ʃən/ 幻觉 an experience in which you see, hear, feel, or smell something that does not exist, usually because you are ill or have taken a drug [GRE]

auditory/olfactory hallucinations   幻听 / 幻嗅

hallucinatory   adjective UK /həˈluː.sɪ.nə.tər.i/ US /həˈluː.sɪ.nə.tɔːr.i/ 幻觉的；导致幻觉的 relating to or causing hallucinations

hallucinogen   noun [C] UK /ˌhæl.uːˈsɪn.ə.dʒən/ US /həˈluː.sɪ.nə.dʒen/ 致幻药，致幻剂 a drug that makes people hallucinate

hallucinogenic   adjective UK /həˌluː.sɪ.nəˈdʒen.ɪk/ US /həˌluː.sɪ.noʊˈdʒen.ɪk/ 引起幻觉的 causing hallucinations

Prefix: hecto- (also hecta-) 100 个单位的 100 times the stated unit
Meaning in English: 100 times the stated unit

Origin language: Anglo-Saxon/ Latin

English examples:

hecto-   prefix SCIENCE specialized UK /hek.təʊ-/ US /hek.toʊ-/ (also hecta-) 100 个单位的 100 times the stated unit

a hectopascal   百帕 Hectopascal is a 100x multiple of the Pascal which is the SI unit for pressure.

a hectolitre   百升，公石 a metric unit of capacity equal to one hundred litres,

Prefix (Medical): hemat-, haemato- (haem-, hem-) Of or pertaining to blood
Meaning in English: Of or pertaining to blood

Origin language: Latin (hæma) < Ancient Greek αἵμα, αἱματ- (haima, haimat-), blood

English examples:

hematite	noun [C] UK /ˈhiː.mə.taɪt/ US /ˈhiː.mə.taɪt/ （haematite 的美式拼写） (US spelling of haematite) 赤铁矿 a common dark red or grey rock from which iron is obtained

hematology	noun [U] UK /ˌhiː.məˈtɒl.ə.dʒi/ US /ˌhiː.məˈtɑː.lə.dʒi/ US spelling of haematology 血液学（haematology 的美式拼写） the scientific study of blood and the body tissues that make it

hematoma	noun [C] MEDICAL UK /hiː.məˈtəʊ.mə/ US /ˌhiː.məˈtoʊ.mə/ （haematoma 的美式拼写 US spelling of haematoma ） 血肿 a thick mass of blood anywhere in the body resulting from an injury or blood disorder

Hematologic malignancies	noun [U] 血液系统恶性肿瘤 Hematologic malignancies are cancers that begin in blood-forming tissue, such as the bone marrow, or in the cells of the immune system. There are three main types of hematologic malignancies: leukemia, lymphoma and multiple myeloma. 血液系统恶性肿瘤是起源于造血组织（如骨髓）或免疫系统细胞的癌症。 血液系统恶性肿瘤主要分为三种类型：白血病、淋巴瘤和多发性骨髓瘤。

haematite	noun [U] GEOLOGY UK specialized (US hematite) UK /ˈhiː.mə.taɪt/ US /ˈhiː.mə.taɪt/ 赤铁矿（深红或灰色的常见矿石，可提炼出铁） a common dark red or grey rock from which iron is obtained

haematology	noun [U] MEDICAL UK specialized (US hematology) UK /ˌhiː.məˈtɒl.ə.dʒi/ US /ˌhiː.məˈtɑː.lə.dʒi/ 血液学 the scientific study of blood and the body tissues that make it

haematoma	noun [C] MEDICAL UK specialized (US hematoma) UK /hiː.məˈtəʊ.mə/ US /ˌhiː.məˈtoʊ.mə/ 血肿 a thick mass of blood anywhere in the body resulting from an injury or blood disorder

Bruises are haematomas. 瘀伤是血肿

haemifacial spasm noun [C] MEDICAL UK specialized (US hemifacial spasm) UK /hiː.mɪˌfeɪ.ʃəl ˈspæz.əm/ US /ˈhiː.məˌfeɪ.ʃəl ˈspæz.əm/ 半面痉挛 a spasm (= occasion when a muscle suddenly becomes tighter) affecting one side of the face

Haemifacial spasms are caused by a blood vessel pressing on one of the nerves coming from the brain. 半面痉挛是由于血管压迫一股大脑神经造成的。

haemodialysis noun [U] MEDICAL UK specialized (US hemodialysis) UK /ˌhiː.məʊ.daɪˈæl.ə.sɪs/ US /ˌhiː.moʊ.daɪˈæl.ə.sɪs/ 血液透析 a process of removing harmful substances and waste products from the blood by dialysis

haemodynamic adjective MEDICAL UK specialized (US hemodynamic) UK /ˌhiː.məʊ.daɪˈnæm.ɪk/ US /ˌhiː.moʊ.daɪˈnæm.ɪk/ 血液动力的 relating to the forces involved in blood circulation

haemoglobin noun [U] BIOLOGY UK (US hemoglobin) UK /ˌhiː.məˈɡləʊ.bɪn/ US /ˌhiː.məˈɡloʊ.bɪn/ 血红蛋白 a substance in red blood cells that combines with and carries oxygen around the body, and gives blood its red colour

haemolytic adjective MEDICAL specialized (US hemolytic) UK /ˌhiː.məˈlɪt.ɪk/ US /ˌhiː.məˈlɪt̬.ɪk/ 溶血性的 relating to the destruction of blood cells

haemophilia noun [U] UK (US hemophilia) UK /ˌhiː.məˈfɪl.i.ə/ US /ˌhiː.məˈfɪl.i.ə/ 血友病 a rare blood disease in which blood continues to flow after a cut or other injury because one of the substances which causes it to clot does not work correctly

haemophiliac noun [C] UK (US hemophiliac) UK /ˌhiː.məˈfɪl.i.æk/ US /ˌhiː.məˈfɪl.i.æk/ 血友病患者 a person who suffers from haemophilia

haemorrhage   1 noun [C or U] UK (US hemorrhage) UK /ˈhem.ər.ɪdʒ/ US /ˈhem.ɚ.ɪdʒ/ 大出血 a large flow of blood from a damaged blood vessel (= tube carrying blood around the body)

a brain haemorrhage   脑溢血

haemorrhagic   1 adjective MEDICAL   specialized (US hemorrhagic) UK /hem.əˈrædʒ.ɪk/ US /hem.əˈrædʒ.ɪk/ 大出血的；出血的 relating to a haemorrhage (= a large flow of blood from a damaged blood vessel)

haemorrhoids   noun [plural]   MEDICAL   UK specialized (US hemorrhoids) UK /ˈhem.ər.ɔɪdz/ US /ˈhem.ɚ.ɔɪdz/ 痔疮 a medical condition in which the veins at the anus become swollen and painful and sometimes bleed

Prefix (Medical): hemi- one-half

Meaning in English: one-half

Origin language: Ancient Greek ἡμι- (hēmi-), "half"

English examples:

cerebral hemisphere   noun [C] anatomy specialized UK /ˌser.ɪ.brəl ˈhem.ɪ.sfɪər/ US /ˌser.ɪ.brəl ˈhem.ɪ.sfɪr/ 大脑半球（位于脑的前部，左右两边两个大脑半球分别控制对侧部分的身体） one of the two halves of the cerebrum, each of which controls the opposite side of the body

hemifacial spasm   noun [C]   MEDICAL   specialized UK /hiː.mɪˌfeɪ.ʃəl ˈspæz.əm/ US /ˈhiː.məˌfeɪ.ʃəl ˈspæz.əm/ US spelling of haemifacial spasm 半面痉挛（haemifacial spasm 的美式拼写）

hemicycle   noun   hemi·cy·cle | \ ˈhe-mi-ˌsī-kəl \ a curved or semicircular structure or arrangement

hemisphere 1 noun [C] UK /ˈhem.ɪ.sfɪər/ US /ˈhem.ə.sfɪr/ （尤指地球的）半球 one of two halves of the earth, especially above or below the equator

Prefix (Medical): hepat- (hepatic-) Of or pertaining to the liver

Meaning in English: Of or pertaining to the liver

Origin language: Ancient Greek ἧπαρ, ἥπατο- (hēpar, hēpato-), the liver

English examples:

heparin noun [U] MEDICAL specialized UK /ˈhep.ə.rɪn/ US /ˈhep.ə.rɪn/ 肝素 a drug that stops the blood from getting too thick

hepatic adjective MEDICAL specialized UK /hepˈæt.ɪk/ US /hepˈæt̬.ɪk/ 肝的 relating to the liver

hepatic portal vein noun [C usually singular] ANATOMY specialized UK /hepˌæt.ɪk ˈpɔː.təl ˌveɪn/ US /hepˌæt̬.ɪk ˈpɔːr.t̬əl ˌveɪn/ (also portal vein) 肝门静脉 the vein that carries blood, containing substances obtained from food, from the intestines to the liver

portal vein 肝门静脉

hepatitis noun [U] UK /ˌhep.əˈtaɪ.tɪs/ US /ˌhep.əˈtaɪ.t̬əs/ 肝炎（主要包括甲型、乙型和丙型三种类型） a serious disease of the liver. There are three main types of hepatitis: hepatitis A, B, and C.

hepatocellular adjective MEDICAL specialized UK /ˌhep.ə.təʊˈsel.jə.lər/ US /ˌhep.ə.toʊˈsel.jə.lɚ/ 肝细胞的 relating to liver cells

肝癌 / 黄疸 hepatocellular carcinoma/jaundice

hepatopulmonary syndrome noun [U] MEDICAL specialized UK /hep.əˌtəʊˈpʌl.mə.nər.i ˌsɪn.drəʊm/ US /ˌhep.ə.toʊˈpʊl.məˌner.i ˌsɪn.droʊm/ 肝肺综合症 a medical condition in which someone finds it difficult to breathe and has low oxygen levels in the blood because of problems in the blood vessels of the lungs due to liver disease

hepatology   noun [U]   MEDICAL   specialized UK/ˌhep.əˈtɒl.ə.dʒi/ US/ˌhep.əˈtɑː.lə.dʒi/ 肝病学 the treatment of diseases of the liver (= a large organ that cleans the blood and produces bile):

Prefix (Medical): hist(o)-, histio- tissue

Meaning in English: tissue

Origin language: Greek ἱστός

English examples:

histological adjective   BIOLOGY   specialized UK /ˌhɪs.təˈlɒdʒ.ɪ.kəl/ US /ˌhɪs.təˈlɑː.dʒɪ.kəl/ (also histologic,) 组织学的，显微解剖学的 relating to the study of the structure of cells and tissue seen under a microscope (= a device for looking at very small objects)

histologically   adverb   BIOLOGY   specialized UK /ˌhɪs.təˈlɒdʒ.ɪ.kə.li/ US /ˌhɪs.təˈlɑː.dʒɪ.kəl.i/ 组织学地，显微解剖学地 relating to the science that is concerned with the structure of cells and tissue at the microscopic level

histology   noun [U]   BIOLOGY   specialized UK /hɪˈstɒl.ə.dʒi/ US /hɪˈstɑː.lə.dʒi/ 组织学，显微解剖学 the scientific study of the structure of tissue from plants, animals, and other living things

Prefix: hetero- different/ other

Meaning in English: different/ other

Origin language: Greek

English examples:

heterodox   1 adjective   formal UK /ˈhet.ər.ə.dɒks/ US /ˈhet̬.ɚ.ə.dɑːks/（信仰、想法或活动）非正统的，异端的 (of beliefs, ideas, or activities) different to and opposing generally accepted beliefs or standards

heterogeneous adjective formal UK /ˌhet.ər.əˈdʒiː.ni.əs/ US /ˌheṭ.ə.roʊˈdʒiː.ni.əs/ 各种各样的；混杂的 consisting of parts or things that are very different from each other

heteroglossia noun 1 [U] specialized /ˌhet.ər.əʊˈglɒs.i.ə/ US /ˌheṭ.ə.roʊˈgl ɑ ː.si.ə/ LITERATURE （文章中的）话语混杂（指在同一篇文章中存在两种或两种以上不同的语言或观点） the fact of there being two or more different types of language or opinions in a text

heteronormative adjective formal usually disapproving UK /ˌhet.ər.əˈnɔː.mə.tɪv/ US /ˌheṭ.ə.roʊˈnɔːr.mə.ṭɪv/ 异性恋常态化的，异性恋霸权的，异性规范性的 suggesting or believing that only heterosexual relationships are normal or right and that men and women have naturally different roles

heterosexual noun [C] UK /ˌhet.ər.əˈsek.ʃu.əl/ US /ˌheṭ.ə.roʊˈsek.ʃu.əl/ (informal hetero) 异性恋者 a person who is sexually attracted to people of the opposite sex

heterotroph noun [C] BIOLOGY specialized UK /ˈhet.ər.əˌtrəʊf/ US /ˈheṭ.ɚ.əˌtroʊf/ 异养生物 a living thing that gets its food from other plants or animals

Prefix (Medical): home(o)- similar

Meaning in English: similar

Origin language: Ancient Greek ὅμοιος (homoios)

English examples:

Homeomorphism 同胚 In the mathematical field of topology, a homeomorphism, topological isomorphism, or bicontinuous function is a continuous function between topological spaces that has a continuous inverse function. Wikipedia

homeopath noun [C] (UK also homoeopath) UK /ˈhəʊ.mi.ə.pæθ/ US /ˈhoʊ.mi.oʊ.pæθ/ 顺势疗法医师 a person who treats ill people by homeopathy

homeopathy noun [U] (UK also homoeopathy) UK /ˌhəʊ.miˈɒp.ə.θi/ US /ˌhoʊ.miˈɑː.pə.θi/ 顺势疗法 a system of treating diseases in which sick people are given very small amounts of natural substances that, in healthy people, would produce the same effects as the diseases produce; Homeopathy or homoeopathy is a pseudoscientific system of alternative medicine. Its practitioners, called homeopaths, believe that a substance that causes symptoms of a disease in healthy people can cure similar symptoms in sick people; this doctrine is called similia similibus curentur, or "like cures like". Wikipedia

homeostasis noun [U] BIOLOGY specialized UK /ˌhəʊ.mi.əʊˈsteɪ.sɪs/ US /ˌhoʊ.mi.oʊˈsteɪ.sɪs/ 体内动态平衡（机体、活细胞、组织等，在其外部环境变化的情况下，保持内部不变或平衡状态的能力或趋向） the ability or tendency of a living organism, cell, or group to keep the conditions inside it the same despite any changes in the conditions around it, or this state of internal balance

homeothermic adjective BIOLOGY specialized UK /ˌhəʊ.mi.əʊˈθɜː.mɪk/ US /ˌhoʊ.mi.oʊˈθɜː.mɪk/ 恒温的，温血的（有机体在外部温度变化的情况下保持体温的能力） If a living organism is homeothermic, it is able to keep its body temperature at the same level despite any change in the temperature around it.

homeotherm noun [C] BIOLOGY specialized UK /ˈhəʊ.mi.əʊˌθɜː.m/ US /ˈhoʊ.mi.oʊˌθɜː.m/ 热血动物 a homeothermic animal

Homeothermy   Homeothermy, homothermy or homoiothermy is thermoregulation that maintains a stable internal body temperature regardless of external influence. This internal body temperature is often, though not necessarily, higher than the immediate environment (from Greek ὅμοιος homoios "similar" and θέρμη thermē "heat").

Prefix (Medical): hom(o)- the same
Meaning in English: Denotes something as 'the same' as another or common

Origin language: Ancient Greek όμο- (homo-), the same, common

English examples:

homogeneous   adjective UK /ˌhɒm.əˈdʒiː.ni.əs/ /ˌhəʊ.məˈdʒiː.ni.əs/ US /ˌhoʊ.moʊˈdʒiː.ni.əs/ /ˌhɑː.məˈdʒiː.ni.əs/ 由同类事物（或人）组成的；同类的；相似的 consisting of parts or people that are similar to each other or are of the same type

homogenized   1 adjective (UK usually homogenised) UK /həˈmɒdʒ.ɪ.naɪzd/ US /həˈmɑː.dʒə.naɪzd/ FOOD & DRINK   specialized （牛奶）经过均质处理的 Homogenized milk has been treated so that the cream is mixed into the other parts of the liquid. [GRE]

homograph   noun [C] LANGUAGE   specialized UK /ˈhɒm.ə.grɑːf/ US /ˈhɑː.mə.græf/ 同形异义词（读音可能相同或不同）   a word that is spelled the same as another word but has a different meaning

homologous   1 adjective UK /həˈmɒl.ə.gəs/ US /hoʊˈmɑː.lə.gəs/ BIOLOGY   formal （位置、结构、价值或目的等）相似的，相应的 having a similar position, structure, value, or purpose 2 specialized 同源的（生物学术语，指经过了数百万年的进化演变，尽管形态、用途已不尽相同，但拥有相同的起源）

homologous chromosomes   noun [plural]   BIOLOGY   specialized UK /həˌmɒl.ə.gəs ˈkrəʊ.mə.səʊmz/ US /hoʊˌm ɑ ː.lə.gəs ˈkroʊ.mə.soʊmz/ 同源染色体 two chromosomes (= cell parts that control what an animal or plant is like), one from the father and one from the mother, that come together during meiosis (= cell division that happens as part of reproduction)

homologous series   noun [C]   CHEMISTRY   specialized UK /həˌmɒl.ə.gəs ˈsɪə.riːz/ US /hoʊˌm ɑ ː.lə.gəs ˈsɪr.iːz/

homonym   noun [C]   LANGUAGE   specialized UK /ˈhɒm.ə.nɪm/ US /ˈh ɑ ː.mə.nɪm/ 同形（或同音）异义词 a word that sounds the same or is spelled the same as another word but has a different meaning

homophobia   noun [U] UK /ˌhəʊ.məˈfəʊ.bi.ə/ US /ˌhoʊ.məˈfoʊ.bi.ə/ 对同性恋的恐惧（或厌恶） a fear or dislike of gay people

homosexual   noun [C] UK /ˌhəʊ.məˈsek.ʃu.əl/ US /ˌhoʊ.moʊˈsek.ʃu.əl/ （尤指男性）同性恋者 a person who is sexually attracted to people of the same sex and not to people of the opposite sex

homosexuality   noun [U] UK /ˌhəʊ.mə.sek.ʃuˈæl.ə.ti/ US /ˌhoʊ.moʊ.sek.ʃuˈæl.ə.ti/ 同性恋 the quality or fact of being sexually attracted to people of the same sex as you

homozygote   noun [C]   BIOLOGY   specialized UK /ˌhɒm.əˈzaɪ.gəʊt/ US /ˌhoʊ.məˈzaɪ.goʊt/ 纯合子 a homozygous person, animal, or organism (= having two of the same form of cell material that controls a particular characteristic and so able to pass on only that form to his, her, or its young)

homozygous   adjective BIOLOGY   specialized UK /ˌhɒm.əˈzaɪ.gəs/ US /ˌhoʊ.məˈzaɪ.gəs/ 纯合子的，同型合子的（带有两种同型基因的，基因中

包含控制细胞某种特性的 DNA 信息，因此只可遗传同型基因的特性）
having two of the same form of gene (= part of a cell containing DNA
information) that controls a particular characteristic and is therefore able to pass
on that form only

Meaning in English: Of or pertaining to the shoulder (or [rarely] the upper arm)

Origin language: Latin (umerus), shoulder

English examples:

humeral　　adjective　MEDICAL　specialized UK　/ˈhjuː.mər.əl/ US
/ˈhjuː.mɚ.əl/ 肱骨的 relating to the humerus (= the long bone in the upper arm)

humerus　　noun [C]　ANATOMY　specialized UK　/ˈhjuː.mə.rəs/ US
/ˈhjuː.mə.rəs/ plural humeri （人体大臂的）肱骨 the long bone in the upper
half of your arm, between your shoulder and your elbow (= the middle part of
the arm where it bends)

glenohumeral　　adjective　MEDICAL　specialized UK
/ˌglen.əʊˈhjuː.mə.rəl/ US /ˌglen.oʊˈhjuː.mɚ.əl/ （拉丁语，用于医学术语）盂
肱的 relating to the shoulder joint

the glenohumeral joint　　盂肱关节

Meaning in English: water

Origin language: Greek ὕδωρ

English examples:

hydrant　　noun [C] UK / ˈhaɪ.drənt/ US / ˈhaɪ.drənt/ 消防栓 a vertical pipe,
usually at the side of the road, that is connected to the main water system of a
town and can supply water, especially for dealing with fires

hydrate   1 verb [I or T] UK /haɪˈdreɪt/ US /ˈhaɪ.dreɪt/ （身体）补充水分 to make your body absorb water or other liquid

hydration   noun [U] UK /haɪˈdreɪ.ʃən/ US /haɪˈdreɪ.ʃən/ （身体）补水过程 the process of making your body absorb water or other liquid

hydrocephalus   noun [U]   MEDICAL   specialized UK /ˌhaɪ.drəˈsef.ə.ləs/ US /ˌhaɪ.drəˈsef.ə.ləs/ (also water on the brain) 脑积水 an abnormal increase in the amount of fluid in the skull that results in an increase in pressure inside the skull and an increase in the size of the head

water on the brain 脑积水

hydrolyse   verb [T or I]   CHEMISTRY   specialized UK (US hydrolyze) UK /ˈhaɪ.drəl.aɪz/ US /ˈhaɪ.drəl.aɪz/ 水解 to have or to make something have a chemical reaction with water to produce another substance

hydrophilic   adjective   CHEMISTRY   specialized UK /ˌhaɪdrəʊˈfɪlɪk/ US /ˌhaɪdroʊˈfɪlɪk/ （物质）亲水的 Hydrophilic substances can be mixed with or dissolved in water.

hydrophily   noun hy·droph·i·ly | \ -lē \ plural -es : 亲水性 the quality or state of being hydrophilous

hydrophilous   adjective hy·droph·i·lous | \ hī'dräfələs \ 1: 亲水的 pollinated by the agency of water

hydrophobia   1 noun [U] UK /ˌhaɪ.drəˈfəʊ.bi.ə/ US /ˌhaɪ.droʊˈfoʊ.bi.ə/ MEDICAL   specialized （作为狂犬病特征的）恐水症 a great fear of drinking and water, often a sign of rabies 2 noun old-fashioned 狂犬病 the disease of rabies

hydrophobiac   noun [C] One who is affected with hydrophobia. 恐水的人

hydrophobic   1 adjective specialized UK /ˌhaɪdrəʊˈfəʊbɪk/ US /ˌhaɪdroʊˈfoʊbɪk/ CHEMISTRY （物质）疏水的 Hydrophobic substances cannot be mixed with or dissolved in water. 2 adjective MEDICAL 恐水的 suffering from hydrophobia

hydrotherapy   noun [U] UK /ˌhaɪ.drəʊˈθer.ə.pi/ US /ˌhaɪ.droʊˈθer.ə.pi/ 水疗法 a method of treating people with particular diseases or injuries by making them exercise in water

Prefix: hydro- connected with or using the power of water

Meaning in English: connected with or using the power of water

Origin language: Anglo-Saxon/ Latin

English examples:

hydro-   prefix UK /haɪ.drəʊ-/ US /haɪ.droʊ-/ (WATER) 水力的；利用水力的 connected with or using the power of water

hydroponic   溶液培养（一种在溶液中培养植物的方式） (= a method of growing plants in water)

hydrocephalus   noun [U] MEDICAL specialized UK /ˌhaɪ.drəˈsef.ə.ləs/ US /ˌhaɪ.drəˈsef.ə.ləs/ (also water on the brain) 脑积水 an abnormal increase in the amount of fluid in the skull that results in an increase in pressure inside the skull and an increase in the size of the head

hydroelectric   adjective UK /ˌhaɪ.drəʊ.ɪˈlek.trɪk/ US /ˌhaɪ.droʊ.ɪˈlek.trɪk/ 水力发电的，水电的 producing electricity by the force of fast moving water such as rivers or waterfalls

a hydroelectric power station   水电站

hydrofoil   noun [C] UK /ˈhaɪ.drə.fɔɪl/ US /ˈhaɪ.droʊ.fɔɪl/ 水翼船 a large boat that is able to travel quickly above the surface of the water on wing-like structures

hydrograph   noun [C] UK /ˈhaɪ.drəʊ.grɑ:f/ US /ˈhaɪ.droʊ.græf/ 水文图，水位曲线 a graph showing the amount of water in a place at different times, for example in a lake

hydrological   adjective UK /ˌhaɪ.drəˈlɒdʒ.ɪ.kəl/ US /ˌhaɪ.drəˈlɑ:.dʒɪ.kəl/ (also hydrologic, /ˌhaɪ.drəˈlɒdʒ.ɪk/ US /ˌhaɪ.drəˈlɑ:.dʒɪk/) 水文学的 GEOLOGY   specialized

hydrologist   noun [C]   GEOLOGY   specialized UK /haɪˈdrɒl.ə.dʒɪst/ US /haɪˈdrɑ:.lə.dʒɪst/ 水文学家 a person who studies water on the earth, for example, where it is and how it is used

hydrology   noun [U] UK /haɪˈdrɒl.ə.dʒi/ US /haɪˈdrɑ:.lə.dʒi/ 水文学 the study of water on the earth, for example, where it is and how it is used

hydrolyse   verb [T or I]   CHEMISTRY   specialized UK (US hydrolyze) UK /ˈhaɪ.drəl.aɪz/ US /ˈhaɪ.drəl.aɪz/ 水解 to have or to make something have a chemical reaction with water to produce another substance

hydrolysis   noun [U]   CHEMISTRY   specialized UK /haɪˈdrɒl.ə.sɪs/ US /haɪˈdrɑ:.lə.sɪs/ 水解 a chemical reaction in which one substance reacts with water to produce another

hydrometer   noun [C]   CHEMISTRY   specialized UK /haɪˈdrɒm.ɪ.tər/ US /haɪˈdrɑ:.mə.t̬ɚ/ 液体比重计，浮秤（用于测量溶液密度的仪器，尤指封闭的长试管，一端有砝码，可使液体竖直流动）a piece of equipment used to measure the density (= amount of matter in a particular quantity) of liquids, especially a long glass tube, closed and with a weight at one end so that it floats vertically

hydrophilic   adjective   CHEMISTRY   specialized UK /ˌhaɪdrəʊˈfɪlɪk/ US /ˌhaɪdroʊˈfɪlɪk/ （物质）亲水的 Hydrophilic substances can be mixed with or dissolved in water.

hydrophily noun hy·droph·i·ly | \ -lē \ plural -es : 亲水性 the quality or state of being hydrophilous

hydrophobia   1 noun [U] UK /ˌhaɪ.drəˈfəʊ.bi.ə/ US /ˌhaɪ.droʊˈfoʊ.bi.ə/ MEDICAL   specialized （作为狂犬病特征的）恐水症 a great fear of drinking and water, often a sign of rabies

hydrophobic   1 adjective   specialized UK /ˌhaɪdrəʊˈfəʊbɪk/ US /ˌhaɪdroʊˈfoʊbɪk/ CHEMISTRY （物质）疏水的 Hydrophobic substances cannot be mixed with or dissolved in water. 2 adjective MEDICAL 恐水的 suffering from hydrophobia

hydroplane   verb [I] US UK /ˈhaɪ.drə.pleɪn/ US /ˈhaɪ.droʊ.pleɪn/ (UK aquaplane) （汽车）在潮湿的路面上失控打滑 If a motor vehicle hydroplanes, it slides out of control on a wet road.

hydroplaning   noun [U] US UK /ˈhaɪ.drə.pleɪn.ɪŋ/ US /ˈhaɪ.droʊ.pleɪn.ɪŋ/ (UK aquaplaning) （汽车）在潮湿的路面上失控打滑 a situation in which a vehicle slides out of control on a wet road

hydroponics   noun [U]   BIOLOGY   specialized UK /ˌhaɪ.drəˈpɒn.ɪks/ US /ˌhaɪ.droʊˈpɑː.nɪks/ （植物的）无土栽培法，水栽法 the method of growing plants in water to which special chemicals are added, rather than growing them in earth

hydropower   noun [U] UK /ˈhaɪd.rəʊ.paʊər/ US /ˈhaɪd.roʊ.paʊ.ɚ/ 水力发电 hydroelectric power (= the production of electricity by the force of fast moving water)

hydrostatic   adjective PHYSICS specialized UK /ˌhaɪ.drəʊˈstæt.ɪk/ US /ˌhaɪ.droʊˈstæt̬.ɪk/ 流体静力的，水静力的 relating to fluids (= liquids or gases) that are not in motion

hydrostatics   noun [U] PHYSICS specialized UK /ˌhaɪ.drəʊˈstæt.ɪks/ US /ˌhaɪ.droʊˈstæt̬.ɪks/ 流体静力学 the scientific study of the behaviour of fluids (= liquids or gases) that are not in motion

hydrotherapy   noun [U] UK /ˌhaɪ.drəʊˈθer.ə.pi/ US /ˌhaɪ.droʊˈθer.ə.pi/ 水疗法 a method of treating people with particular diseases or injuries by making them exercise in water

Prefix: hydro- showing that hydrogen is present

Meaning in English: showing that hydrogen is present

Origin language: Anglo-Saxon/ Latin

English examples:

hydro-   prefix (GAS) 含氢的；氢化的 showing that hydrogen is present

hydrogen   noun [U] UK /ˈhaɪ.drə.dʒən/ US /ˈhaɪ.drə.dʒən/ (symbol H) 氢，氢气 a chemical element that is the lightest gas, has no colour, taste, or smell, and combines with oxygen to form water

hydrogen bomb   noun [C usually singular] UK /ˈhaɪ.drɪ.dʒən ˌbɒm/ US /ˈhaɪ.drɪ.dʒən ˌbɑ ːm/ (abbreviation H-bomb) 氢弹 a nuclear bomb that explodes when the central parts of its hydrogen atoms join together

hydrogenated   adjective UK /haɪˈdrɒd.ɪ.neɪ.tɪd/ US /haɪˈdr ɑ ːdʒə.neɪ.t̬ɪd/ 氢化的（食物中的脂肪中加入氢，有害健康）Hydrogenated fat is fat in foods that has had hydrogen added to it. Hydrogenated fats are bad for your health.

hydrogenation   noun [U] UK /ˌhaɪ.drə.dʒəˈneɪ.ʃən/ US /haɪˌdr ɑ ːdʒəˈneɪ.ʃən/ 氢化作用（产生氢化油脂的过程）the process of producing hydrogenated fats

hydrocarbon   noun [C] UK /ˌhaɪ.drəʊˈk ɑ ː.bən/ US /ˌhaɪ.droʊˈk ɑ ːr.bən/ 烃，碳氢化合物 a chemical combination of hydrogen and carbon, such as in oil or petrol

hydrocarbon emissions   碳氢化合物的排放

hydrochloric acid   noun [U] UK /ˌhaɪ.drə.klɔː.rɪk ˈæs.ɪd/ US /ˌhaɪ.drə.klɔːr.ɪk ˈæs.ɪd/ 盐酸 an acid containing hydrogen and chlorine

hydrochloride   noun [C]   CHEMISTRY   specialized UK /ˌhaɪ.drəˈklɔː.raɪd/ US /ˌhaɪ.drəˈklɔːr.aɪd/ 氢氯化合物 a chemical substance that is a combination of a metal or base with hydrochloric acid

hydrochlorofluorocarbon   noun [U or C]   CHEMISTRY   specialized UK /ˈhaɪ.drəʊˌklɔː.rəʊˌflɔː.rəʊˌk ɑ ː.bən/ US /ˈhaɪ.droʊˌklɔːr.oʊˌflɔːr.oʊˌk ɑ ːr.bən/ (abbreviation HCFC) 氢氯氟碳化合物，氟氯烃化合物 a type of gas used especially in aerosols (= containers that force out liquids in very small drops)

hydroxide   noun [C]   CHEMISTRY   specialized UK /haɪˈdrɒk.saɪd/ US /haɪˈdr ɑ ːk.saɪd/ 氢氧化物（含有氢氧离子的复合物，或氧化物的水合

物）a chemical compound that contains the hydroxyl ion, or a compound of an oxide with water

calcium hydroxide   氢氧化钙

hydroxyl ion   noun [C]   CHEMISTRY   specialized UK /haɪˌdrɒk.sɪl ˈaɪən/ US /haɪˌdrɑ:k.sɪl ˈaɪ.ən/ 氢氧离子；羟离子（有一个氧原子和一个氢原子组成的带有负电荷的离子） an ion with a negative charge, consisting of an oxygen atom and a hydrogen atom

Prefix: hyper- having too much of a quality

Meaning in English: over/ above/ excessive over/ above/ excessive

Origin language: Ancient Greek ὑπέρ (hyper), over, above; beyond, to the extreme

English examples:

hyper-   prefix UK /haɪ.pər-/ US /haɪ.pɚ-/ 超出，过度 having too much of a quality

hyperactive   adjective UK /ˌhaɪ.pərˈæk.tɪv/ US /ˌhaɪ.pɚˈæk.tɪv/ 多动亢奋的，过分活跃的 Someone who is hyperactive has more energy than is normal, gets excited easily, and cannot stay still or think about work.

Hyperactive children often have poor concentration and require very little sleep. 多动的孩子经常注意力不够集中而且睡觉很少。

hyperbola   noun [C]   MATHEMATICS   specialized UK /haɪˈpɜː.bəl.ə/ US /haɪˈpɝː.bəl.ə/ 双曲线 a curve whose ends continue to move apart from each other

hyperbole   noun [U]   formal UK /haɪˈpɜː.bəl.i/ US /haɪˈpɝː.bəl.i/ 夸张法 a way of speaking or writing that makes someone or something sound bigger, better, more, etc. than they are

hypercritical   adjective UK /ˌhaɪ.pəˈkrɪt.ɪ.kəl/ US /ˌhaɪ.pɚˈkrɪt̬.ɪ.kəl/ 吹毛求疵的，过分挑剔的 extremely critical (= too eager to find mistakes in everything)

hyperglycaemia   noun [U]   MEDICAL   specialized (US hyperglycemia) UK /ˌhaɪ.pə.glaɪˈsiː.mi.ə/ US /ˌhaɪ.pɚ.glaɪˈsiː.mi.ə/ 高血糖症 a condition in which there is too much glucose in the blood

hyperhidrosis   noun [U]   MEDICAL   specialized UK /ˌhaɪ.pə.hɪˈdrəʊ.sɪs/ US /ˌhaɪ.pɚ.hɪˈdroʊ.sɪs/ 多汗症 a condition in which a person produces much more sweat (= a salty liquid passed through the skin) than normal

hyperinflation   noun [U] UK /ˌhaɪ.pə.rɪnˈfleɪʃ.ən/ US /ˌhaɪ.pɚ.ɪnˈfleɪ.ʃən/ 极度通货膨胀，恶性通货膨胀 a condition where the price of everything in a national economy goes out of control and increases very quickly

hyperkalaemia   noun [U]   MEDICAL   specialized (US hyperkalemia) UK /ˌhaɪ.pə.kəˈliː.mi.ə/ US /ˌhaɪ.pɚ.kəˈliː.mi.ə/ 高钾血症 a condition in which there is too much potassium in the blood, which may be caused by diuretics (= substances that increase the production of urine) having been used too often or kidney failure

hypermarket   noun [C] mainly UK UK /ˈhaɪ.pəˌmɑː.kɪt/ US /ˈhaɪ.pɚˌmɑːr.kɪt/ （通常位于城郊的）超大型自选超市 a very large shop, usually outside the centre of town

hyperplasia   noun [U] MEDICAL   specialized UK /ˌhaɪ.pəˈpleɪ.ʒə/
US /ˌhaɪ.pɚˈpleɪ.ʒə/ 过度增生 an abnormal increase in the number of cells in a
body tissue or organ

hypersensitive   1 adjective UK /ˌhaɪ.pəˈsen.sɪ.tɪv/ US /ˌhaɪ.pɚˈsen.sə.t̬ɪv/
过于敏感的 too easily upset by criticism

hypersensitivity   noun [U] MEDICAL   specialized UK
/ˌhaɪ.pə.sens.əˈtɪv.ə.ti/ US /ˌhaɪ.pɚˌsen.sə.ˈtɪv.ə.t̬i/ 过敏 a condition in which the
immune system reacts in an extreme way to a substance in the body

hypersomnia   noun [U] MEDICAL   specialized UK /ˌhaɪ.pəˈsɒm.ni.ə/
US /ˌhaɪ.pɚˈs ɑ ːm.ni.ə/嗜睡症 a sleep disorder in which someone sleeps for
very long periods and is always very tired during the day

hypertensive   adjective MEDICAL   specialized UK /ˌhaɪ.pəˈten.sɪv/ US
/ˌhaɪ.pɚˈten.sɪv/ 高血压的 having or relating to increased pressure, for example
high blood pressure

hyperthyroidism   noun [U] MEDICAL   specialized UK
/ˌhaɪ.pəˈθaɪ.rɔɪd.ɪzəm/ US /ˌhaɪ.pɚˈθaɪ.rɔɪˌdɪz.əm/ 甲状腺亢进 a condition in
which the thyroid gland produces large amounts of hormones

Prefix (Medical): hypo-, hyp- below/ less than normal

Meaning in English: below/ less than normal

Origin language: Ancient Greek ὑπ(ο)- (hypo-), below, under

English examples:

hypoallergenic   adjective UK /ˌhaɪ.pəʊˌæl.əˈdʒen.ɪk/ US
/ˌæl.ɚˌæl.əˈdʒen.ɪk/ 低过敏原的（产品） designed to be less likely to cause
allergic reactions (= physical problems caused by particular substances) in
people who use a product

hypoallergenic cosmetics/earrings 低过敏原化妆品／耳环

hypochondria noun [U] UK /ˌhaɪ.pəˈkɒn.dri.ə/ US /ˌhaɪ.poʊˈkɑːn.dri.ə/ 疑病症 a state in which a person continuously worries about their health without having any reason to do so

hypocrisy noun [U] disapproving UK /hɪˈpɒk.rɪ.si/ US /hɪˈpɑː.krə.si/ C2 虚伪，伪善 a situation in which someone pretends to believe something that they do not really believe, or that is the opposite of what they do or say at another time

hypocrite noun [C] disapproving UK /ˈhɪp.ə.krɪt/ US /ˈhɪp.ə.krɪt/ 伪君子，伪善者 someone who says they have particular moral beliefs but behaves in way that shows these are not sincere

hypocritical adjective disapproving UK /ˌhɪp.əˈkrɪt.ɪ.kəl/ US /ˌhɪp.əˈkrɪt̬.ɪ.kəl/ C2 虚伪的；伪善的 saying that you have particular moral beliefs but behaving in a way that shows these are not sincere

hypodermic adjective MEDICAL specialized UK /ˌhaɪ.pəˈdɜː.mɪk/ US /ˌhaɪ.poʊˈdɚ.mɪk/ 皮下注射的 (of medical tools) used to inject drugs (= put them into the body) under a person's skin

hypogastric adjective MEDICAL specialized UK /ˌhaɪ.poʊˈgæs.trɪk/ US /ˌhaɪ.poʊˈgæs.trɪk/ 下腹的，腹下方的 relating to the hypogastrium (= the lower part of the abdomen)

a hypogastric nerve 腹下神经

hypoglossal　　adjective　MEDICAL　specialized UK /ˌhaɪ.pəʊˈglɒs.əl/ US /ˌhaɪ.poʊˈglɑ ː.səl/ 舌下的 relating to the area below the tongue

舌下神经　 a hypoglossal nerve

hypoglycaemia　noun [U]　MEDICAL　specialized (US hypoglycemia) UK /ˌhaɪ.pəʊ.glaɪˈsiː.mi.ə/ US /ˌhaɪ.poʊ.glaɪˈsiː.mi.ə/ 低血糖 a medical condition resulting from dangerously low levels of sugar in the blood

hypoglycaemic　　adjective　MEDICAL　UK specialized (US hypoglycemic) UK /ˌhaɪ.pəʊ.glaɪˈsiː.mɪk/ US /ˌhaɪ.poʊ.glaɪˈsiː.mɪk/ 低血糖的 related to or suffering from a medical condition resulting from dangerously low levels of sugar in the blood

hypospadias　　noun [U]　MEDICAL　specialized UK /ˌhaɪ.pəʊˈspeɪ.di.əs/ US /ˌhaɪ.poʊˈspeɪ.di.əs/ （男性疾病）尿道下裂 a physical problem present from birth in which the opening of the urethra (= the tube that carries urine out of the body) is on the underside of the penis

hypotension　　noun [U]　MEDICAL　specialized UK /ˌhaɪ.pəʊˈten.ʃən/ US /ˌhaɪ.poʊˈten.ʃən/ 低血压 a condition in which the blood pressure in the arteries is too low

hypothalamus　　noun [S]　ANATOMY　specialized UK /ˌhaɪ.pəʊˈθæl.ə.məs/ US /ˌhaɪ.poʊˈθæl.ə.məs/ 下丘脑 （大脑的一个小部分, 位于丘脑下面, 控制体温、荷尔蒙分泌等） a small part in the brain that controls things such as body temperature and the release of hormones, that is below the thalamus

hypothermia　　noun [U] UK /ˌhaɪ.pəˈθɜː.mi.ə/ US /ˌhaɪ.poʊˈθɜː.mi.ə/ （因持续寒冷而）体温过低 a serious medical condition in which a person's body temperature falls below the usual level as a result of being in severe cold for a long time

hypothesis noun [C] UK /haɪˈpɒθ.ə.sɪs/ US /haɪˈp ɑ ː.θə.sɪs/ plural hypotheses C2 假设，假说 an idea or explanation for something that is based on known facts but has not yet been proved

hypothesize verb [I or T] formal UK /haɪˈpɒθ.ə.saɪz/ US /haɪˈp ɑ ː.θə.saɪz/ 假设，假定 to give a possible but not yet proved explanation for something [GRE]

hypothetical adjective UK /ˌhaɪ.pəˈθet.ɪ.kəl/ US /ˌhaɪ.pəˈθet̬.ɪ.kəl/ 假定的，假设的 imagined or suggested but not necessarily real or true

hypothyroidism noun [U] MEDICAL specialized UK /ˌhaɪ.pəʊˈθaɪ.rɔɪd.ɪzəm/ US /ˌhaɪ.pəˈθaɪ.rɔɪˌdɪz.əm/ 甲状腺机能减退 a condition in which the thyroid gland does not produce enough thyroid hormone, leading to heart problems, problems with nerve function in the hands and feet, and mental health issues such as depression

Hypovolemia noun [U] 血容量减少; 低血容量; 血容量不足 Hypovolemia is a condition that occurs when your body loses fluid, like blood or water. Fluids are essential to keep your organs functioning. Symptoms of hypovolemia include weakness, fatigue and dizziness. Treatment with IV fluids rehydrates and replenishes the fluid your body lost.

hypoxia noun [U] MEDICAL specialized UK /haɪˈpɒk.si.ə/ US /haɪˈp ɑ ːk.si.ə/ 缺氧 a condition in which there is not enough oxygen available to the blood and body tissues

Prefix (Medical): hyster(o)- Of or pertaining to the womb, the uterus
Meaning in English: Of or pertaining to the womb, the uterus

Origin language: Ancient Greek ὑστέρα (hystéra), womb

English examples:

hysterectomy   noun [C] UK /ˌhɪs.tərˈek.tə.mi/ US /ˌhɪs.təˈrek.tə.mi/ 子宫切除术 a medical operation to remove part or all of a woman's womb

hysteria   noun [U] UK /hɪˈstɪə.ri.ə/ US /hɪˈstɪr.i.ə/ 歇斯底里 extreme fear, excitement, anger, etc. that cannot be controlled

hysterical   1 adjective UK /hɪˈster.ɪ.kəl/ US /hɪˈster.ɪ.kəl/ C1 歇斯底里的，情绪过分激动的 unable to control your feelings or behaviour because you are extremely frightened, angry, excited, etc.

hysterics   1 noun [plural] UK /hɪˈster.ɪks/ US /hɪˈster.ɪks/ 歇斯底里发作 uncontrolled behaviour or crying, usually caused by extreme fear or sadness

have hysterics   informal 暴怒，暴跳如雷；极度心烦 to get extremely angry or upset

Hysterosalpingography 子宫输卵管造影检查 Hysterosalpingography (HSG), also known as uterosalpingography, is a radiologic procedure to investigate the shape of the uterine cavity and the shape and patency of the Fallopian tubes. It is a special x-ray using dye to look at the womb (uterus) and Fallopian tubes It injects a radio-opaque material into the cervical canal and usually fluoroscopy with image intensification.

III

Prefix (Medical): iatr(o)- Of or pertaining to medicine, or a physician

Meaning in English: Of or pertaining to medicine, or a physician [uncommon as a prefix; common as as suffix, see -iatry]

Origin language: Ancient Greek ἰᾱτρός (iātrós), healer, physician

English examples:

Iatrochemistry   noun [U] 医疗化学 Iatrochemistry is a branch of both chemistry and medicine. Having its roots in alchemy, iatrochemistry seeks to provide chemical solutions to diseases and medical ailments. This area of science has fallen out of use in Europe since the rise of modern establishment medicine. Wikipedia

iatrogenic   adjective   MEDICAL   specialized /aɪˌæt.rəˈdʒen.ɪk/ /aɪˌæt.roʊˈdʒen.ɪk/ 医原性的，由于医师活动所引起的 (of a disease or problem) caused by medical treatment or by a doctor

Prefix (Medical): idio- self, one's own

Meaning in English: self, one's own

Origin language: Greek ἴδιος, idios, "one's own"

English examples:

idiomatic   1 adjective UK /ˌɪd.i.əˈmæt.ɪk/ US /ˌɪd.i.əˈmæt̬.ɪk/ 习语的；成语的；合乎语言习惯的 containing or consisting of an idiom

idiopathic   adjective   MEDICAL   specialized UK /ˌɪd.i.əˈpæθ.ɪk/ US /ˌɪd.i.əˈpæθ.ɪk/ 特发的，自发的，原因不明的（疾病） an idiopathic disease or medical condition has no known cause

Idiopathic pulmonary fibrosis is a lung condition which causes scarring of the lungs. 特发性肺纤维化是一种造成肺部形成瘢疤的疾病。

idiosyncrasy   noun [C usually plural] UK /ˌɪd.i.əˈsɪŋ.krə.si/ US /ˌɪd.i.əˈsɪŋ.krə.si/ 癖好，怪癖；特征 a strange or unusual habit, way of behaving, or feature that someone or something has [GRE]

idiosyncratic   adjective UK /ˌɪd.i.ə.sɪŋˈkræt.ɪk/ US /ˌɪd.i.ə.sɪŋˈkræt̬.ɪk/ having strange or unusual habits, ways of behaving, or features:

idiotic   adjective UK /ˌɪd.iˈɒt.ɪk/ US /ˌɪd.iˈɑ:.t̬ɪk/ 白痴似的，愚蠢的 stupid

idiot   noun [C] UK /ˈɪd.i.ət/ US /ˈɪd.i.ət/ B2 白痴，笨蛋 a stupid person or someone who is behaving in a stupid way

Prefix (Medical): ileo- ileum
Meaning in English:

Origin language: Greek ἰλεός

English examples:

ileocecal valve   noun [U] 回盲瓣 The ileocecal valve is a sphincter muscle situated at the junction of the ileum (last portion of your small intestine) and the colon (first portion of your large intestine). Its function is to allow digested food materials to pass from the small intestine into your large intestine.

ileum   noun [C usually singular]   ANATOMY   specialized UK /ˈɪl.i.əm/ US /ˈɪl.i.əm/ plural ilea UK /ˈɪl.i.ə/ US 回肠（胃部下方，小肠末端和最窄的一段，负责从食物中吸收营养物质） the last and narrowest part of the small intestine (= part of bowels after the stomach), where substances from food are absorbed

ileitis   noun [U]   MEDICAL   specialized UK /ˌɪl.iˈaɪ.tɪs/ US /ˌɪl.iˈaɪ.t̬əs/ 回肠炎 inflammation of the ileum (= small intestine)

Prefix: ill- in a way that is bad or not suitable
Meaning in English: in a way that is bad or not suitable

Origin language: Anglo-Saxon/ Latin

English examples:

ill-   6 prefix UK /ɪl-/ US /ɪl-/ 不好的；不合适的 in a way that is bad or not suitable

ill-prepared   准备得不好的

an ill-judged remark   判断不当的评论

ill-advised   adjective UK /ˌɪl.ədˈvaɪzd/ US /ˌɪl.ədˈvaɪzd/ 不明智的 not wise, and likely to cause problems in the future

ill-assorted   adjective mainly UK UK /ˌɪl.əˈsɔː.tɪd/ US /ˌɪlˈsɔːr.t̬ɪd/ 不相称的，不相配的 looking strange together and not seeming to be a good match

ill-bred   adjective   old-fashioned UK /ˌɪlˈbred/ US /ˌɪlˈbred/ 粗鲁的，没教养的 rude and behaving badly [GRE]

ill-conceived   adjective UK /ˌɪl.kənˈsiːvd/ US /ˌɪl.kənˈsiːvd/ 计划不周的；不明智的 badly planned and unwise

ill-disposed   adjective   formal UK /ˌɪl.dɪˈspəʊsd/ US /ˌɪl.dɪˈspoʊzd/ 对（某人）不友好；不支持（某人） be ill-disposed towards sb to not be friendly to someone or not support them

ill-equipped   1 adjective UK /ˌɪl.ɪˈkwɪpt/ US /ˌɪl.ɪˈkwɪpt/ 能力不足的；装备不良的 without the ability, qualities, or equipment to do something

ill-fated   adjective [before noun] UK /ˌɪlˈfeɪ.tɪd/ US /ˌɪlˈfeɪ.t̬ɪd/ 命不好的，倒霉的；（常指）致人送命的 unlucky and unsuccessful, often resulting in death

ill-fitting   adjective UK /ˌɪlˈfɪt.ɪŋ/ US /ˌɪlˈfɪt̬.ɪŋ/ （衣服等）不合身的 Ill-fitting clothes do not fit well.

ill-gotten   adjective [before noun]   mainly humorous UK /ˌɪlˈɡɒt.ən/ US /ˌɪlˈɡɑː.tən/ 非法获得的，来路不正的 dishonestly obtained

ill-informed   adjective UK /ˌɪl.ɪnˈfɔːmd/ US /ˌɪl.ɪnˈfɔːrmd/ 消息闭塞的；了解不够的 knowing less than you should about a particular subject

ill-mannered   adjective UK /ˌɪlˈmæn.əd/ US /ˌɪlˈmæn.ɚd/ 无礼的，粗鲁的 rude and unpleasant

ill-starred   adjective [before noun]   literary UK /ˌɪlˈstɑːd/ US /ˌɪlˈstɑːrd/ (also ill-omened) → ill-fated （同 ill-fated）命不好的，倒霉的；（常指）致人送命的 unlucky and unsuccessful, often resulting in death

ill-tempered   1 adjective UK /ˌɪlˈtem.pəd/ US /ˌɪlˈtem.pɚd/   formal 脾气坏的，易怒的 easily annoyed 2 adjective （比赛等）火药味浓的 If an occasion, such as a game, is ill-tempered, people get angry during it.

ill-timed   adjective UK /ˌɪlˈtaɪmd/ US /ˌɪlˈtaɪmd/ 不适时的，不合时宜的 done or made at a wrong or unsuitable time

ill-treat   verb [T] UK /ˌɪlˈtriːt/ US /ˌɪlˈtriːt/ 虐待 to treat someone badly, especially by being violent or by not taking care of them

ill-used   adjective   literary 虐待的；不公平对待的 treated badly

Prefix: in- (il-, im-, ir-) – not
Meaning in English: not (il- used before roots beginning with l, illegible; im- used before roots beginning with b, m, p, immature, imbalance, impatient, ir- used before roots beginning with r irregular)

Origin language: Latin

English examples:

in- 27 prefix (before l il-); (before b, m or p im-); (before r ir-) UK /ɪn-/ US /ɪn-/ （加在形容词及由形容词转化而来的词前）不，无，非 used to add the meaning "not", "lacking", or "the opposite of" to adjectives and to words formed from adjectives

illegal 1 adjective UK /ɪˈliː.ɡəl/ US /ɪˈliː.ɡəl/ B2 非法的，违法的 not allowed by law

illegible adjective UK /ɪˈledʒ.ə.bəl/ US /ɪˈledʒ.ə.bəl/ （字迹或印刷）模糊的，难以辨认的 (of writing or print) impossible or almost impossible to read because of being very untidy or not clear

illegitimate 1 adjective UK /ˌɪl.ɪˈdʒɪt.ə.mət/ US /ˌɪl.ɪˈdʒɪt̬.ə.mət/ 非婚生的，私生的 born of parents not married to each other

illiberal adjective UK /ɪˈlɪb.ər.əl/ US /ɪˈlɪb.ɚ.əl/ formal （言论、思想、行为等）不自由的，不开明的，狭隘的 limiting freedom of expression, thought, behaviour, etc.

illicit adjective UK /ɪˈlɪs.ɪt/ US /ɪˈlɪs.ɪt/ 非法的；违禁的；社会不容许的 illegal or disapproved of by society

illiterate 1 adjective UK /ɪˈlɪt.ər.ət/ US /ɪˈlɪt̬.ɚ.ət/ C2 文盲的，不会读写的 unable to read and write

illiteracy 1 noun [U] UK /ɪˈlɪt.ər.ə.si/ US /ɪˈlɪt̬.ɚ.ə.si/ 文盲的，不会读写的 a lack of the ability to read and write:

illogical   adjective UK /ɪˈlɒdʒ.ɪ.kəl/ US /ɪˈlɑː.dʒɪ.kəl/ 不合逻辑的，无缘由的；不明智的 not reasonable, wise, or practical, usually because directed by the emotions rather than by careful thought

impossible   1 adjective UK /ɪmˈpɒs.ə.bəl/ US /ɪmˈpɑː.sə.bəl/ B1 （行动或事件）不可能的，办不到的 If an action or event is impossible, it cannot happen or be achieved.

imbalance   noun [C] UK /ˌɪmˈbæl.əns/ US /ˌɪmˈbæl.əns/ 不平衡，不均衡，失调 a situation in which two things that should be equal or that are normally equal are not

immaterial   adjective UK /ˌɪm.əˈtɪə.ri.əl/ US /ˌɪm.əˈtɪr.i.əl/ 不重要的，无关紧要的 not important, or not relating to the subject you are thinking about [GRE]

immature   1 adjective UK /ˌɪm.əˈtʃʊər/ US /ˌɪm.əˈtʊr/ C2 disapproving 不成熟的 not behaving in a way that is as calm and wise as people expect from someone of your age [GRE]

immeasurable   adjective UK /ɪˈmeʒ.ər.ə.bəl/ US /ɪˈmeʒ.ɚ.ə.bəl/ 不可计量的，无限的 so large or great that it cannot be measured or known exactly

impatient   1 adjective UK /ɪmˈpeɪ.ʃənt/ US /ɪmˈpeɪ.ʃənt/ B2 不耐烦的，无耐心的 easily annoyed by someone's mistakes or because you have to wait 2 B2 切望的；焦急的 wanting something to happen as soon as possible

impeccable   adjective UK /ɪmˈpek.ə.bəl/ US /ɪmˈpek.ə.bəl/ 完美的，无可挑剔的 perfect, with no problems or bad parts [GRE]

impotence   1 noun [U] UK /ˈɪm.pə.təns/ US /ˈɪm.pə.t̬əns/ impotence noun [U] (LACK OF POWER) 无力量；无能力 lack of power to change or improve a situation

impracticable   adjective UK /ɪmˈpræk.tɪ.kə.bəl/ US /ɪmˈpræk.tɪ.kə.bəl/（行动方案、计划等）行不通的，不可行的 If a course of action, plan, etc. is impracticable, it is impossible to do in an effective way.

imprecise   adjective UK /ˌɪm.prɪˈsaɪs/ US /ˌɪm.prɪˈsaɪs/ 不精确的；不确切的 not accurate or exact [GRE]

impromptu   adjective UK /ɪmˈprɒmp.tʃuː/ US /ɪmˈprɑːmp.tuː/ 无准备的，即兴的 done or said without earlier planning or preparation [GRE]

improper   1 adjective UK /ɪmˈprɒp.ər/ US /ɪmˈprɑː.pɚ/ (DISHONEST) formal 违法的，违规的，不正当的 dishonest and against a law or a rule

inhospitable   1 adjective UK /ˌɪn.hɒsˈpɪt.ə.bəl/ US /ˌɪn.hɑːˈspɪt̬.ə.bəl/ (PERSON) 不好客的；不殷勤待客的 not welcoming or generous to people who visit you

inhuman   1 adjective UK /ɪnˈhjuː.mən/ US /ɪnˈhjuː.mən/ C2 残暴的；无人性的；非人的 extremely cruel

inimical   adjective formal UK /ɪˈnɪm.ɪ.kəl/ US /ɪˈnɪm.ɪ.kəl/ 有害的；不利的；限制性的 harmful or limiting [GRE]

irrational   adjective UK /ɪˈræʃ.ən.əl/ US /ɪˈræʃ.ən.əl/ C2 不理智的，没有理性的 not using reason or clear thinking

irreconcilable   adjective UK /ˌɪr.ek.ənˈsaɪ.lə.bəl/ US /ˌɪr.ek.ənˈsaɪ.lə.bəl/ 不可调和的；难以应付的 impossible to find agreement between or with, or impossible to deal with

ineradicable   adjective formal UK /ˌɪn.ɪˈræd.ɪ.kə.bəl/ US /ˌɪn.ɪˈræd.ɪ.kə.bəl/ 不能根除的 not able to be removed: [GRE]

irreducible   adjective formal UK /ˌɪr.ɪˈdʒuː.sə.bəl/ US /ˌɪr.əˈduː.sə.bəl/ 不能减缩的；不可简化的 impossible to make smaller or simpler [GRE]

irrefutable   adjective formal UK /ˌɪr.ɪˈfjuː.tə.bəl/ US /ˌɪr.əˈfjuː.t̬ə.bəl/ 无可辩驳的，驳不倒的 impossible to prove wrong

irregular   1 adjective UK /ɪˈreg.jə.lər/ US /ɪˈreg.jə.lɚ/ (RULE) formal （行为）不合常规的，不正常的 (of behaviour or actions) not according to usual rules or what is expected

irregularity   1 noun UK /ɪˌreg.jəˈlær.ə.ti/ US /ɪˌreg.jəˈler.ə.t̬i/ (SHAPE) [C or U] 不规则；不整齐 the quality of not being regular in shape or form, or an example of this

irrelevance   noun [C or U] UK /ɪˈrel.ə.vəns/ US /ɪˈrel.ə.vəns/ (formal irrelevancy, UK /-vən.si/ US) 不相关，不切题 the fact that something is not related to what is being discussed or considered and therefore not important, or an example of this

irrelevant   adjective UK /ɪˈrel.ə.vənt/ US /ɪˈrel.ə.vənt/ 不相关的，不切题的 not related to what is being discussed or considered and therefore not important

irreligious   adjective   formal disapproving UK /ˌɪr.ɪˈlɪdʒ.əs/ US /ˌɪr.əˈlɪdʒ.əs/ 无宗教信仰的；反对宗教的 having no interest in religion, or generally opposed to religion

irremediable   adjective   formal UK /ˌɪr.ɪˈmiː.di.ə.bəl/ US /ˌɪr.əˈmiː.di.ə.bəl/ 不能改正的，无可救药的 impossible to correct or cure

irreparable adjective UK /ɪˈrep.ər.ə.bəl/ US /ɪˈrep.ər.ə.bəl/ 不能修复的，无可挽救的 impossible to repair or make right again

irreplaceable   adjective UK /ˌɪr.ɪˈpleɪ.sə.bəl/ US /ˌɪr.əˈpleɪ.sə.bəl/ 不可替代的，独一无二的 too special, unusual, or valuable to replace with something or someone else

irrepressible   adjective UK /ˌɪr.ɪˈpres.ə.bəl/ US /ˌɪr.əˈpres.ə.bəl/ 狂热的；抑制不住的 full of energy and enthusiasm; impossible to stop

irreproachable   adjective   formal approving UK /ˌɪr.ɪˈprəʊ.tʃə.bəl/ US /ˌɪr.əˈproʊ.tʃə.bəl/ 无可指责的，无瑕疵的 without fault and therefore impossible to criticize

irresistible   adjective UK /ˌɪr.ɪˈzɪs.tə.bəl/ US /ˌɪr.əˈzɪs.tə.bəl/ C2 不可抗拒的，无法抵挡的 impossible to refuse, oppose, or avoid because it is too pleasant, attractive, or strong

irresolute   adjective   formal disapproving UK /ɪˈrez.əl.uːt/ US /ɪˈrez.əl.uːt/ 犹豫不决的，优柔寡断的 not able or willing to take decisions or actions

irrespective   adverb UK /ˌɪr.ɪˈspek.tɪv/ US /ˌɪr.əˈspek.tɪv/ C2 不考虑地，不顾地 without considering; not needing to allow for

irresponsible   adjective   disapproving UK /ˌɪr.ɪˈspɒn.sə.bəl/ US /ˌɪr.əˈspɑːn.sə.bəl/ B2 不负责任的，无责任感的 not thinking enough or not worrying about the possible results of what you do

inability   noun [S or U] UK /ˌɪn.əˈbɪl.ə.ti/ US /ˌɪn.əˈbɪl.ə.t̬i/ C1 无能，无力 lack of ability to do something

inaccessible   1 adjective UK /ˌɪn.əkˈses.ə.bəl/ US /ˌɪn.əkˈses.ə.bəl/ (PLACE) 难到达的，无法去的 very difficult or impossible to travel to

inaccuracy   noun [C or U] UK /ɪnˈæk.jə.rə.si/ US /ɪnˈæk.jɚ.ə.si/ C1 不准确性；不精确性 a situation in which a fact or measurement is not completely correct or exact

inaccurate   adjective UK /ɪnˈæk.jə.rət/ US /ɪnˈæk.jɚ.ət/ B2 不准确的；不精确的 not completely correct or exact, or not able to do something correctly or exactly

inaction   noun [U]   formal UK /ɪnˈæk.ʃən/ US /ɪnˈæk.ʃən/ 无行动，不作为 failure to do anything that might provide a solution to a problem

inactive   adjective UK /ɪnˈæk.tɪv/ US /ɪnˈæk.tɪv/ 无行动的，不活动的，不活跃的 doing nothing

inadequacy   1 noun UK /ɪˈnæd.ɪ.kwə.si/ US /ɪˈnæd.ə.kwə.si/ 不够好，劣质 [C or U] the fact that something is not good enough or is too small in amount

inadequate   1 adjective UK /ɪˈnæd.ɪ.kwət/ US /ɪˈnæd.ə.kwət/ C1 不够好的，劣质的 not good enough or too low in quality

inadmissible   adjective UK /ˌɪn.ədˈmɪs.ə.bəl/ US /ˌɪn.ədˈmɪs.ə.bəl/ formal （在法庭上）不可接受的，不能采信的 unable to be accepted in a law court

inadvertent   adjective UK /ˌɪn.ədˈvɜː.tənt/ US /ˌɪn.ədˈvɜː.t̬ənt/ 非故意的，无意的 not intentional [GRE]

inadvisable   adjective UK /ˌɪn.ədˈvaɪ.zə.bəl/ US /ˌɪn.ədˈvaɪ.zə.bəl/ 不可取的，不明智的 unwise and likely to have unwanted results, and therefore worth avoiding

inalienable   adjective formal UK /ɪˈneɪ.li.ə.nə.bəl/ US /ɪˈneɪ.li.ə.nə.bəl/ 不可剥夺的；不可分割的 unable to be removed [GRE]

inanimate   adjective UK /ɪˈnæn.ɪ.mət/ US /ɪˈnæn.ə.mət/ 无生命的 having none of the characteristics of life that an animal or plant has [GRE]

inapplicable   adjective UK /ˌɪn.əˈplɪk.ə.bəl/ US /ˌɪn.əˈplɪk.ə.bəl/ 不适用的，不适宜的 not directed at, intended for, or suitable for someone or something

inappropriate   adjective UK /ˌɪn.əˈprəʊ.pri.ət/ US /ˌɪn.əˈproʊ.pri.ət/ C1 不适合的；不恰当的 unsuitable

inattention   noun [U] UK /ˌɪn.əˈten.ʃən/ US /ˌɪn.əˈten.ʃən/ 漫不经心，不注意 failure to give attention

inattentive　　　　adjective　disapproving UK /ˌɪn.əˈten.tɪv/ US /ˌɪn.əˈten.t̬ɪv/ 漫不经心的，不注意的 not giving attention to someone or something

inaudible　　　　adjective UK /ɪˈnɔː.də.bəl/ US /ɪˈnɑː.də.bəl/ 听不见的 unable to be heard

incapable　adjective UK /ɪnˈkeɪ.pə.bəl/ US /ɪnˈkeɪ.pə.bəl/ C1 不能的，不胜任的 unable to do something

incapacitate　　　　verb [T often passive] UK /ˌɪn.kəˈpæs.ɪ.teɪt/ US /ˌɪn.kəˈpæs.ə.teɪt/ 使无能力（正常工作或做事）；使无法（做想做之事）to make someone unable to work or do things normally, or unable to do what they intended to do

incurable　　　　1 adjective UK /ɪnˈkjʊə.rə.bəl/ US /ɪnˈkjʊr.ə.bəl/ (DISEASE) C2 无法治愈的 not able to be cured

incurious　　　　adjective　formal UK /ɪnˈkjʊə.ri.əs/ US /ɪnˈkjʊr.i.əs/ 不感兴趣的；不好奇的 not interested in knowing what is happening, or not wanting to discover anything new

indecipherable　adjective UK /ˌɪn.dɪˈsaɪ.fər.ə.bəl/ US /ˌɪn.dɪˈsaɪ.fɚ.ə.bəl/ 难辨认的；难懂的 unable to be read or understood

indecision　　　　noun [U] UK /ˌɪn.dɪˈsɪʒ.ən/ US /ˌɪn.dɪˈsɪʒ.ən/ (also indecisiveness,) 优柔寡断，无决断力 the state of being unable to make a choice

indecisive　　　　1 adjective UK /ˌɪn.dɪˈsaɪ.sɪv/ US /ˌɪn.dɪˈsaɪ.sɪv/ 优柔寡断的，犹豫不决的 not good at making decisions

indecorous   adjective   formal UK /ɪnˈdek.ər.əs/ US /ɪnˈdek.ɚ.əs/ 不得体的；不雅的；粗鲁的 behaving badly or rudely

indefatigable   adjective   formal UK /ˌɪn.dɪˈfæt.ɪ.gə.bəl/ US /ˌɪn.dɪˈfæt̬.ɪ.gə.bəl/ 不倦的；不屈不挠的 always determined and energetic in trying to achieve something and never willing to admit defeat

indefensible   1 adjective UK /ˌɪn.dɪˈfen.sə.bəl/ US /ˌɪn.dɪˈfen.sə.bəl/ 无可辩解的；站不住脚的 too bad to be protected from criticism

indefinable   adjective UK /ˌɪn.dɪˈfaɪ.nə.bəl/ US /ˌɪn.dɪˈfaɪ.nə.bəl/ (also undefinable) 难下定义的；难以确切描述（或解释）的 impossible to clearly describe or explain

indelible   1 adjective UK /ɪnˈdel.ə.bəl/ US /ɪnˈdel.ə.bəl/ 洗不掉的；无法去除的 An indelible mark or substance is impossible to remove by washing or in any other way. [GRE]

indelicate   adjective UK /ɪnˈdel.ɪ.kət/ US /ɪnˈdel.ə.kət/ （言语或行为）不适当的，无礼的 Indelicate words or actions are not suitable for a situation and are likely to be offensive.

independence   1 noun [U] UK /ˌɪn.dɪˈpen.dəns/ US /ˌɪn.dɪˈpen.dəns/ B2 （国家的）独立 freedom from being governed or ruled by another country

independent   1 adjective UK /ˌɪn.dɪˈpen.dənt/ US /ˌɪn.dɪˈpen.dənt/ (NOT INFLUENCED) B2 独立的

indescribable   adjective UK /ˌɪn.dɪˈskraɪ.bə.bəl/ US /ˌɪn.dɪˈskraɪ.bə.bəl/ 难以形容的；不可名状的 impossible to describe, especially because of being extremely good or bad

indestructible   adjective UK /ˌɪn.dɪˈstrʌk.tə.bəl/ US /ˌɪn.dɪˈstrʌk.tə.bəl/ 不可毁灭的；破坏不了的 impossible to destroy or break

indeterminate   adjective UK /ˌɪn.dɪˈtɜː.mɪ.nət/ US /ˌɪn.dɪˈtɜː.mɪ.nət/ 不确定的；不明确的 not measured, counted, or clearly known

indifference   noun [U] UK /ɪnˈdɪf.ər.əns/ US /ɪnˈdɪf.ɚ.əns/ C2 不感兴趣的；不关心的，冷淡的 lack of interest in someone or something

indifferent   1 adjective UK /ɪnˈdɪf.ər.ənt/ US /ɪnˈdɪf.ɚ.ənt/ (NOT INTERESTED) C2 不感兴趣；不关心，冷淡 not thinking about or interested in someone or something

indigestible   1 adjective UK /ˌɪn.dɪˈdʒes.tə.bəl/ US /ˌɪn.dɪˈdʒes.tə.bəl/ (FOOD) 难消化的；不能消化的 Ingestible food is difficult or impossible for the stomach to break down.

indirect   1 adjective UK /ˌɪn.daɪˈrekt/ /ˌɪn.dɪˈrekt/ US /ˌɪn.daɪˈrekt/ /ˌɪn.dɪˈrekt/ indirect adjective (NOT OBVIOUS) C2 间接的 happening in addition to an intended result, often in a way that is complicated or not obvious

indiscernible   adjective UK /ˌɪn.dɪˈsɜː.nə.bəl/ US /ˌɪn.dɪˈsɜː.nə.bəl/ 不可识别的；难以辨认的；无法理解的 impossible to see, see clearly, or understand

indiscipline   noun [U]   formal UK /ɪnˈdɪs.ə.plɪn/ US /ɪnˈdɪs.ə.plɪn/ 无纪律；缺乏管教 a situation in which people do not control their behaviour or obey rules

indiscreet   adjective UK /ˌɪn.dɪˈskriːt/ US /ˌɪn.dɪˈskriːt/ 轻率的，不慎重的；言行失检的 saying or doing things that tell people things that should be secret or that embarrass people

indiscretion   1 noun UK /ˌɪn.dɪˈskreʃ.ən/ US /ˌɪn.dɪˈskreʃ.ən/ 轻率，不慎重 [U] the quality of being indiscreet 2 noun [C] （尤指性关系上的）不检点 something, especially a sexual relationship, that is considered embarrassing or morally wrong

indiscriminate   adjective UK /ˌɪn.dɪˈskrɪm.ɪ.nət/ US /ˌɪn.dɪˈskrɪm.ə.nət/ 不加思考的，未加计划的，任意的（尤指带来不良后果） not showing careful thought or planning, especially so that harm results

indispensable   adjective UK /ˌɪn.dɪˈspen.sə.bəl/ US /ˌɪn.dɪˈspen.sə.bəl/ C2 必不可少的，必需的 Something or someone that is indispensable is so good or important that you could not manage without it, him, or her.

indisputable   adjective UK /ˌɪn.dɪˈspjuː.tə.bəl/ US /ˌɪn.dɪˈspjuː.t̬ə.bəl/ C2 不容置疑的，无可争辩的 true, and impossible to doubt

indissoluble   adjective UK /ˌɪn.dɪˈsɒl.jə.bəl/ US /ˌɪn.dɪˈsɑːl.jə.bəl/ 牢不可破的；稳定持久的 impossible to take apart or bring to an end, or existing for a very long time

indistinct   adjective UK /ˌɪn.dɪˈstɪŋkt/ US /ˌɪn.dɪˈstɪŋkt/ 不清楚的，模糊的 not clear

indomitable   adjective UK /ɪnˈdɒm.ɪ.tə.bəl/ US /ɪnˈdɑː.mə.t̬ə.bəl/ 不屈不挠的；勇敢坚定的 used to say that someone is strong, brave, determined, and difficult to defeat or frighten

indubitable   adjective formal UK /ɪnˈdʒuː.bɪ.tə.bəl/ US /ɪnˈduː.bɪ.t̬ə.bəl/ 不容置疑的 that cannot be doubted

inedible   adjective UK /ɪˈned.ə.bəl/ US /ˌɪnˈed.ə.bəl/ C1 不可食用的，不适合食用的 not suitable as food

ineffable   adjective formal UK /ɪˈnef.ə.bəl/ US /ˌɪnˈef.ə.bəl/ （尤指喜悦）言语难以表达的，不可言喻的 causing so much emotion, especially pleasure, that it cannot be described [GRE]

ineffective   adjective UK /ˌɪn.ɪˈfek.tɪv/ US /ˌɪn.ɪˈfek.tɪv/ 不起作用的，无效果的，不奏效的 not producing the effects or results that are wanted

ineffectual   adjective formal UK /ˌɪn.ɪˈfek.tʃu.əl/ US /ˌɪn.ɪˈfek.tʃu.əl/ 无能力的；不起作用的，无效果的 not skilled at achieving, or not able to produce, good results

inefficient   adjective UK /ˌɪn.ɪˈfɪʃ.ənt/ US /ˌɪn.ɪˈfɪʃ.ənt/ C1 低效率的；能力差的 not organized, skilled, or able to work in a satisfactory way

inelastic   adjective UK /ˌɪn.ɪˈlæs.tɪk/ US /ˌɪn.ɪˈlæs.t̬ɪk/ 无变化的，不容许变化的，没有弹性的 not changing much, or not allowing much change

inelegant   adjective UK /ɪˈnel.ɪ.gənt/ US /ˌɪnˈel.ə.gənt/ 不雅的；粗俗的 not attractive

ineligible adjective UK /ɪˈnel.ɪ.dʒə.bəl/ US /ˌɪnˈel.ɪ.dʒə.bəl/ 无资格的；不合格的 not allowed to do or have something, according to particular rules

ineluctable adjective formal UK /ˌɪn.ɪˈlʌk.tə.bəl/ US /ˌɪn.ɪˈlʌk.tə.bəl/ 无法躲避的，无法避免的 impossible to avoid [GRE]

inept adjective UK /ɪˈnept/ US /ˌɪnˈept/ 无能的；笨拙的；无效的 not skilled or effective [GRE]

inequality noun [C or U] UK /ˌɪn.ɪˈkwɒl.ə.ti/ US /ˌɪn.ɪˈkwɑ:.lə.t̬i/ C2 不平等，不均等 the unfair situation in society when some people have more opportunities, money, etc. than other people

inequitable adjective formal UK /ɪˈnek.wɪ.tə.bəl/ US /ˌɪnˈek.wə.t̬ə.bəl/ 不公正的，不公平的 not fair

inequity noun [C or U] UK /ɪˈnek.wɪ.ti/ US /-t̬i/ 不公正，不公平 the fact that a situation is not fair, or something that is not fair in a situation

ineradicable adjective formal UK /ˌɪn.ɪˈræd.ɪ.kə.bəl/ US /ˌɪn.ɪˈræd.ɪ.kə.bəl/ 不能根除的；根深蒂固的 not able to be removed

inescapable adjective UK /ˌɪn.ɪˈskeɪ.pə.bəl/ US /ˌɪn.ɪˈskeɪ.pə.bəl/ 不可忽视的；不可避免的 If a fact or a situation is inescapable, it cannot be ignored or avoided.

inessential 1 adjective UK /ˌɪn.ɪˈsen.ʃəl/ US /ˌɪn.ɪˈsen.ʃəl/ 非必要的，无关紧要的 not necessary

inestimable adjective formal UK /ɪˈnes.tɪ.mə.bəl/ US /ˌɪnˈes.tə.mə.bəl/ 无法估价的，极大的，无价的 extremely great, or too great to be described or expressed exactly

inevitable adjective UK /ɪˈnev.ɪ.tə.bəl/ US /ˌɪnˈev.ə.t̬ə.bəl/ C1 不可避免的；必然发生的 certain to happen and unable to be avoided or prevented [GRE]

inevitable adjective UK /ɪˈnev.ɪ.tə.bəl/ US /ˌɪnˈev.ə.t̬ə.bəl/ C1 不可避免的；必然发生的 certain to happen and unable to be avoided or prevented [GRE]

inexact adjective UK /ˌɪn.ɪɡˈzækt/ US /ˌɪn.ɪɡˈzækt/ 不精确的，不准确的 not exact or not known in detail

inexcusable adjective UK /ˌɪn.ɪkˈskjuː.zə.bəl/ US /ˌɪn.ɪkˈskjuː.zə.bəl/ （行为）不可原谅的，不可宽恕的 (of behaviour) too bad to be accepted

inexhaustible adjective UK /ˌɪn.ɪɡˈzɔː.stə.bəl/ US /ˌɪn.ɪɡˈzɑː.stə.bəl/ 用不完的，无穷无尽的 existing in very great amounts that will never be finished

inexorable adjective formal UK /ɪˈnek.sər.ə.bəl/ US /ˌɪnˈek.sər.ə.bəl/ 不可阻拦的 continuing without any possibility of being stopped [GRE]

inexpedient adjective [+ to infinitive] formal UK /ˌɪn.ɪkˈspiː.di.ənt/ US /ˌɪn.ɪkˈspiː.di.ənt/ 不适当的；不方便的 not suitable or convenient

inexpensive adjective UK /ˌɪn.ɪkˈspen.sɪv/ US /ˌɪn.ɪkˈspen.sɪv/ B1 花费不多的，价钱不贵的 not costing a lot of money

inexperience   noun [U] UK /ˌɪn.ɪkˈspɪə.ri.əns/ US /ˌɪn.ɪkˈspɪr.i.əns/ 缺乏经验，不熟练 lack of knowledge or experience

inexperienced   adjective UK /ˌɪn.ɪkˈspɪə.ri.ənst/ US /ˌɪn.ɪkˈspɪr.i.ənst/ B2 缺乏经验的，不熟练的 having little knowledge or experience

inexplicable   adjective UK /ˌɪn.ɪkˈsplɪk.ə.bəl/ US /ˌɪn.ɪkˈsplɪk.ə.bəl/ C2 无法说明的；费解的 unable to be explained or understood

infallibility   noun [U] UK /ɪnˌfæl.əˈbɪl.ə.ti/ US /ɪnˌfæl.əˈbɪl.ə.t̬i/ 永无过失 the fact of never being wrong, failing, or making a mistake:

infallible   adjective UK /ɪnˈfæl.ə.bəl/ US /ɪnˈfæl.ə.bəl/ 不可能错误的；永无过失的；不会犯错误的 never wrong, failing, or making a mistake

infamous   adjective UK /ˈɪn.fə.məs/ US /ˈɪn.fə.məs/ 臭名昭著的，声名狼藉的 famous for something considered bad [GRE]

infertile   1 adjective UK /ɪnˈfɜː.taɪl/ US /ɪnˈfɜː.t̬əl/ 不能生育的；不结果实的 An infertile person, animal, or plant cannot have babies, produce young, or produce new plants.

infidelity   noun [C or U] UK /ˌɪn.fɪˈdel.ə.ti/ US /ˌɪn.fəˈdel.ə.t̬i/ （夫妇间的）不忠实，不贞行为 (an act of) having sex with someone who is not your husband, wife, or regular sexual partner

infinite   1 adjective UK /ˈɪn.fɪ.nət/ US /ˈɪn.fə.nət/ C2 无限的，无边的；极大的 without limits; extremely large or great

inflexible   adjective   usually disapproving UK /ɪnˈflek.sə.bəl/ US /ɪnˈflek.sə.bəl/ (especially of opinions and rules)（尤指意见和规则）不可改变的，不愿变更的 fixed and unable or unwilling to change

inhuman   1 adjective UK /ɪnˈhjuː.mən/ US /ɪnˈhjuː.mən/ C2 残暴的；无人性的；非人的 extremely cruel

inimical   adjective   formal UK /ɪˈnɪm.ɪ.kəl/ US /ɪˈnɪm.ɪ.kəl/ 有害的；不利的；限制性的 harmful or limiting [GRE]

inimitable   adjective UK /ɪˈnɪm.ɪ.tə.bəl/ US /ɪˈnɪm.ə.tə.bəl/ 无双的，无与伦比的；无法模仿的 very unusual or of very high quality and therefore impossible to copy [GRE]

iniquity   noun [C or U]   formal UK /ɪˈnɪk.wə.ti/ US /ɪˈnɪk.wə.t̬i/ 极其错误；极不公正 a very wrong and unfair action or situation [GRE]

injustice   noun [C or U] UK /ɪnˈdʒʌs.tɪs/ US /ɪnˈdʒʌs.tɪs/不公正；非正义 C1 (an example of) a situation in which there is no fairness and justice

innocence   1 noun [U] UK /ˈɪn.ə.səns/ US /ˈɪn.ə.səns/ C1 无罪 the fact that someone is not guilty of a crime

innocent   1 adjective UK /ˈɪn.ə.sənt/ US /ˈɪn.ə.sənt/ (NOT GUILTY) B2 （人）无罪的 (of a person) not guilty of a particular crime

innocuous   1 adjective UK /ɪˈnɒk.ju.əs/ US /ɪˈnɑː.kju.əs/ 无害的 completely harmless (= causing no harm) [GRE]

innominate   1 adjective   MEDICAL   specialized UK /ɪˈnɒm.ɪ.nət/ US /ɪˈnɑːm.ə.nət/ 未命名的；无名的 without a name

innumerable   adjective UK /ɪˈnjuː.mər.ə.bəl/ US /ɪˈnuː.mɚ.ə.bəl/ C2 无数的，数不清的 too many to be counted

innumerate   adjective UK /ɪˈnjuː.mər.ət/ US /ɪˈnuː.mɚ.ət/ 不会算术的 unable to understand and use numbers in calculations

inoffensive   adjective UK /ˌɪn.əˈfen.sɪv/ US /ˌɪn.əˈfen.sɪv/ （尤指人或其行为）无害的，不冒犯人的 not causing any harm or offence

inoperable   1 adjective UK /ɪˈnɒp.ər.ə.bəl/ US /ˌɪnˈɑː.pɚ.ə.bəl/ (DISEASE) （肿瘤等）不宜动手术的，手术不能治愈的 If a tumour (= a growth) or other medical condition is inoperable, doctors are unable to remove or treat it with an operation.

inopportune   adjective   formal UK /ɪˈnɒp.ə.tʃuːn/ US /ˌɪnˌɑː.pɚˈtuːn/ 不合时宜的；不合适的 happening or done at a time that is not suitable or convenient

inordinate   adjective   formal UK /ɪˈnɔː.dɪ.nət/ US /ˌɪnˈɔːr.dən.ət/ 过度的 much more than usual or expected

insane   1 adjective UK /ɪnˈseɪn/ US /ɪnˈseɪn/ 疯癫的，精神失常的 C2 mentally ill

insanely   adverb UK /ɪnˈseɪn.li/ US /ɪnˈseɪn.li/ 疯狂地 extremely and unreasonably

insanity   1 noun [U] UK /ɪnˈsæn.ə.ti/ US /ɪnˈsæn.ə.t̬i/精神错乱，精神失常 the condition of being seriously mentally ill

inscrutable   adjective UK /ɪnˈskruː.tə.bəl/ US /ɪnˈskruː.t̬ə.bəl/ （尤指人或其表情）高深莫测的，不可测知的 not showing emotions or thoughts and therefore very difficult to understand or get to know [GRE]

insecure   1 adjective UK /ˌɪn.sɪˈkjʊər/ US /ˌɪn.səˈkjʊr/ (NOT CONFIDENT) C1 无把握的；不自信的 Insecure people have little confidence and are uncertain about their own abilities or if other people really like them.

insensible   adjective formal UK /ɪnˈsen.sə.bəl/ US /ɪnˈsen.sə.bəl/ 失去知觉的 unconscious [GRE]

insensitive   1 adjective UK /ɪnˈsen.sɪ.tɪv/ US /ɪnˈsen.sə.t̬ɪv/ C1 disapproving （人或其行为）未意识到（他人感受）的；漠不关心的 not feeling or showing sympathy for other people's feelings, or refusing to give importance to something

insentient   无感觉的，无知觉的：lacking perception;一知半解的，略懂的：not having a deep understanding [GRE]

insignificant   adjective UK /ˌɪn.sɪɡˈnɪf.ɪ.kənt/ US /ˌɪn.sɪɡˈnɪf.ə.kənt/不重要的，无足轻重的 C1 small or not noticeable, and therefore not considered important

insipid   adjective disapproving UK /ɪnˈsɪp.ɪd/ US /ɪnˈsɪp.ɪd/ 无味的；无特色的；无生气；乏味的 not having a strong taste or character, or having no interest or energy [GRE]

insistence   1 noun [U] UK /ɪnˈsɪs.təns/ US /ɪnˈsɪs.təns/ 坚决要求；坚持主张；坚持 an occasion when you demand something and refuse to accept opposition, or when you say firmly that something is true

insolvable   1 adjective UK /ɪnˈsɒl.jə.bəl/ US /ɪnˈsɑːl.jə.bəl/ (PROBLEM) (US also insolvable) （问题）无法解决的 (of a problem) so difficult that it is impossible to solve [GRE]

insouciant   1 adjective   literary UK /ɪnˈsuː.si.ənt/ US /ɪnˈsuː.si.ənt/ 无忧虑的，不在乎的 relaxed and happy, with no feelings of worry or guilt: [GRE]

insubordinate   adjective   formal disapproving UK /ˌɪn.səˈbɔː.dɪ.nət/ US /ˌɪn.səˈbɔːr.dən.ət/ （人）不服从的，不顺从的；（言行）违抗命令的 (of a person) not willing to obey orders from people in authority, or (of actions and speech, etc.) showing that you are not willing to obey orders

insufferable   adjective UK /ɪnˈsʌf.ər.ə.bəl/ US /ɪnˈsʌf.ɚ.ə.bəl/ 难以忍受的，不能容忍的 very annoying, unpleasant, or uncomfortable, and therefore extremely difficult to bear

insufficiency   1 noun [C or U] UK /ˌɪn.səˈfɪʃ.ən.si/ US /ˌɪn.səˈfɪʃ.ən.si/ 不够，不足；不充分 the fact of not being enough

insufficient   adjective UK /ˌɪn.səˈfɪʃ.ənt/ US /ˌɪn.səˈfɪʃ.ənt/ C1 不够的，不足的；不充分的 not enough

intangible   adjective UK /ɪnˈtæn.dʒə.bəl/ US /ɪnˈtæn.dʒə.bəl/ （感觉或性质）难以捉摸的，无法形容的，难以确定的 An intangible feeling or quality exists but you cannot describe it exactly or prove it. [GRE]

intemperate adjective formal UK /ɪnˈtem.pər.ət/ US /ɪnˈtem.pɚ.ət/ （人或其言行）无节制的，过激的，放纵的 showing anger or violence that is too extreme and not well controlled [GRE]

intolerable adjective UK /ɪnˈtɒl.ər.ə.bəl/ US /ɪnˈtɑː.lɚ.ə.bəl/ C2 无法容忍的，不能接受的 too bad or unpleasant to deal with or accept

intolerance noun UK /ɪnˈtɒl.ər.əns/ US /ɪnˈtɑː.lɚ.əns/ C2 [U] 不宽容，偏狭 the fact of refusing to accept ideas, beliefs, or behaviour that are different from your own

intolerant 1 adjective disapproving UK /ɪnˈtɒl.ər.ənt/ US /ɪnˈtɑː.lɚ.ənt/ C2 不容异说的；不包容的；心胸狭隘的 disapproving of or refusing to accept ideas or ways of behaving that are different from your own

invariable adjective formal UK /ɪnˈveə.ri.ə.bəl/ US /ɪnˈver.i.ə.bəl/ 不变的，始终如一的 staying the same and never changing

invincible adjective UK /ɪnˈvɪn.sə.bəl/ US /ɪnˈvɪn.sə.bəl/ 不可战胜的；无法阻挡的 impossible to defeat or prevent from doing what is intended [GRE]

invincibility noun [U] UK /ɪnˌvɪn.sɪˈbɪl.ə.ti/ US /ɪnˌvɪn.səˈbɪl.ə.t̬i/ 无敌 (Google); 不可战胜的；无法阻挡的 the quality of being impossible to defeat or prevent from doing what is intended: [GRE]

invisible 1 adjective UK /ɪnˈvɪz.ə.bəl/ US /ɪnˈvɪz.ə.bəl/ B2 看不见的，隐形的 impossible to see

invulnerable adjective UK /ɪnˈvʌl.nər.ə.bəl/ US /ɪnˈvʌl.nɚ.ə.bəl/ 无法伤害的；无法损坏的 impossible to damage or hurt in any way

Prefix: in- (il-, im-, ir-) - in/ on/ toward

Meaning in English: in/ on/ toward (il- used before roots beginning with l, illegible; im- used before roots beginning with b, m, p, immature, imbalance, impatient, ir- used before roots beginning with r irregular)

Origin language:

English examples:

illuminate   1 verb [T]   formal UK /ɪˈluː.mɪ.neɪt/ US /ɪˈluː.mə.neɪt/ 为…照明，照亮 to light something and make it brighter [GRE]

illuminati   智者：enlightened;精英：best of a class [GRE]

illusion   1 noun UK /ɪˈluː.ʒən/ US /ɪˈluː.ʒən/ C2 [C or U] 幻觉，幻想 an idea or belief that is not true

illusory   adjective   formal UK /ɪˈluː.sər.i/ US /ɪˈluː.sɚ.i/ (also illusive,) 虚假的，幻觉的，不实际的 not real and based on illusion [GRE]

illustrate   1 verb [T] UK /ˈɪl.ə.streɪt/ US /ˈɪl.ə.streɪt/ [T] (DRAW PICTURES) B2 给（书籍、杂志等）画插图 to draw pictures for a book, magazine, etc.

illustrious   adjective   formal UK /ɪˈlʌs.tri.əs/ US /ɪˈlʌs.tri.əs/ 著名的；卓越的; 显赫; famous, well respected, and admired [GRE]

immaculate   1 adjective   approving UK /ɪˈmæk.jə.lət/ US /ɪˈmæk.jə.lət/ 洁净的，整洁的 perfectly clean or tidy

immerse   1 verb UK /ɪˈmɜːs/ US /ɪˈmɜːs/ 埋头做… to become completely involved in something

immigrant   noun [C] UK /ˈɪm.ɪ.grənt/ US /ˈɪm.ə.grənt/ B2 （外来的）移民 a person who has come to a different country in order to live there permanently

immigrate   verb [I] UK /ˈɪm.ɪ.greɪt/ US /ˈɪm.ə.greɪt/ （外来的）移民 to come to live in a different country

imminent   adjective UK /ˈɪm.ɪ.nənt/ US /ˈɪm.ə.nənt/ 临近的，即将发生的 C2 coming or likely to happen very soon (Root: min- Meaning in English: jut)

immune   1 adjective UK /ɪˈmjuːn/ US /ɪˈmjuːn/ 免疫的 protected against a particular disease by particular substances in the blood [GRE]

immunize   verb [T] (UK usually immunise) UK /ˈɪm.jə.naɪz/ US /ˈɪm.jə.naɪz/ MEDICAL   specialized （通常指通过注射）使免疫 to protect a person or animal against a disease by putting a substance into the body to make it produce antibodies (= proteins in the blood that fight disease)

immure   verb 2 限制（发展），桎梏 to keep someone or something within certain limits and prevent them or it from developing freely [GRE]

immured   adjective   literary UK /ɪˈmjʊəd/ US /ɪˈmjʊrd/ 监禁的，禁闭的 kept as a prisoner or closed away and out of sight [GRE]

impart   1 verb [T]   formal UK /ɪmˈpɑːt/ US /ɪmˈpɑːrt/ 传授；告知 to communicate information to someone 2 verb 赋予，给予 to give something a particular feeling, quality, or taste

impassive adjective UK /ɪmˈpæs.ɪv/ US /ɪmˈpæs.ɪv/ 神情冷漠的，木然的 If someone's face is impassive, it expresses no emotion, because the person seems not to be affected by the situation they are experiencing. [GRE]

impeach verb [T] UK /ɪmˈpiːtʃ/ US /ɪmˈpiːtʃ/ （尤指在美国）控告，弹劾（公职人员） to make a formal statement saying that a public official is guilty of a serious offence in connection with their job, especially in the US

impede verb [T] formal UK /ɪmˈpiːd/ US /ɪmˈpiːd/ 妨碍，阻碍；阻止 to make it more difficult for something to happen or more difficult for someone to do something [GRE]

impediment noun [C] formal UK /ɪmˈped.ɪ.mənt/ US /ɪmˈped.ə.mənt/ 妨碍，阻碍；阻止 something that makes progress, movement, or achieving something difficult or impossible [GRE]

impel verb [T] UK /ɪmˈpel/ US /ɪmˈpel/ -ll- 促使，驱使 to make someone feel that they must do something

impending adjective [before noun] UK /ɪmˈpen.dɪŋ/ US /ɪmˈpen.dɪŋ/ （通常指不愉快或不受欢迎的事件）即将发生的，逼近的 used to refer to an event, usually something unpleasant or unwanted, that is going to happen soon [GRE]

impenetrable adjective UK /ɪmˈpen.ɪ.trə.bəl/ US /ɪmˈpen.ə.trə.bəl/ 不能看透的；不能穿过的 impossible to see through or go through [GRE]

impenitent adjective formal UK /ɪmˈpen.ɪ.tənt/ US /ɪmˈpen.ə.tənt/ 不知悔悟的；不觉羞耻的 not sorry or ashamed about something bad you have done [GRE]

imperil   verb [T] UK   /ɪmˈper.əl/ US   /ɪmˈper.əl/ -ll- or us usually -l- formal 危及，使陷入危险 to put something or someone at risk or in danger of being harmed or destroyed

imperious   adjective UK   /ɪmˈpɪə.ri.əs/ US   /ɪmˈpɪr.i.əs/专横的，跋扈的 unpleasantly proud and expecting to be obeyed [GRE]

imperishable   adjective UK   /ɪmˈper.ɪ.ʃə.bəl/ US   /ɪmˈper.ɪ.ʃə.bəl/ literary 永存的，不朽的 lasting for ever, or never becoming weaker with age [GRE]

impious   adjective formal UK   /ˈɪm.pi.əs/ US   /ˈɪm.pi.əs/ （尤指对上帝或宗教）不敬的；不恭的 showing no respect, especially for God or religion [GRE]

implant   1 verb [T] UK   /ɪmˈplɑ ːnt/ US   /ɪmˈplænt/ [T] (OBJECT) （手术中）植入，移植 to put an organ, group of cells, or device into the body in a medical operation 2 verb [T] (IDEA) 灌输 to fix ideas, feelings, or opinions in someone else's mind

implicate   verb [T] UK   /ˈɪm.plɪ.keɪt/ US   /ˈɪm.plə.keɪt/ 牵连，涉及 to show that someone is involved in a crime or partly responsible for something bad that has happened

implode   1 verb [I] UK   /ɪmˈpləʊd/ US   /ɪmˈploʊd/ 向心压挤；内爆 PHYSICS   specialized to fall towards the inside with force [GRE]

implore   1 verb UK   /ɪmˈplɔːr/ US   /ɪmˈplɔːr/ [T + to infinitive] 恳求（某人）（不）做…，哀求（某人）（不）做… to ask someone to do or not do something in a very sincere, emotional, and determined way

imply   1 verb [T] UK /ɪmˈplaɪ/ US /ɪmˈplaɪ/ C2 暗指，暗示 to communicate an idea or feeling without saying it directly

importune   1 verb [T]   formal UK /ˌɪm.pɔːˈtʃuːn/ US /ˌɪm.pɔːrˈtuːn/ 没完没了地强求，纠缠 to make repeated, forceful requests for something, usually in a way that is annoying or causing slight problems [GRE]

impose   1 verb UK /ɪmˈpəʊz/ US /ɪmˈpoʊz/ (FORCE) C1 [T] 推行；强制实行 to officially force a rule, tax, punishment, etc. to be obeyed or received

impress   verb [I or T, not continuous] UK /ɪmˈpres/ US /ɪmˈpres/ B2 给…留下深刻印象；使钦佩 to cause someone to admire or respect you

imprison   verb [T usually passive] UK /ɪmˈprɪz.ən/ US /ɪmˈprɪz.ən/ C1 关押，囚禁 to put someone in prison

improve   1 verb [I or T] UK /ɪmˈpruːv/ US /ɪmˈpruːv/ A2 改进，改善 to (cause something to) get better

improvise   1 verb [I or T] UK /ˈɪm.prə.vaɪz/ US /ˈɪm.prə.vaɪz/ 临时做；即兴做 to invent or make something, such as a speech or a device, at the time when it is needed without already having planned it [GRE]

inaugurate   1 verb [T] UK /ɪˈnɔː.gjə.reɪt/ US /ɪˈnɑː.gjə.reɪt/ 使正式就职，为…举行就职典礼 to put someone into an official position with a ceremony [GRE]

incarcerate   1 verb [T] UK /ɪnˈkɑː.sər.eɪt/ US /ɪnˈkɑːr.sə.reɪt/ formal 监禁；禁闭 to put or keep someone in prison or in a place used as a prison

incarnate   adjective [after noun] UK /ɪnˈkɑː.nət/ US /ɪnˈkɑːr.nət/ 人体化的，化身的 in human form [GRE]

incarnation   1 noun UK /ˌɪn.kɑːˈneɪ.ʃən/ US /ˌɪn.kɑːrˈneɪ.ʃən/ [C]（宗教观念中人的）化身 a particular life, in religions that believe that we have many lives

reincarnation   1 noun UK /ˌriː.ɪn.kɑːˈneɪ.ʃən/ US /ˌriː.ɪn.kɑːrˈneɪ.ʃən/ 轮回转世说 [U] the belief that a dead person's spirit returns to life in another body

incense   2 verb [T usually passive] UK /ɪnˈsens/ US /ɪnˈsens/ 激怒，使大怒 to cause someone to be extremely angry [GRE]

incinerate   verb [T] UK /ɪnˈsɪn.ər.eɪt/ US /ɪnˈsɪn.ə.reɪt/ 把…烧成灰烬，焚毁 to burn something completely [GRE]

incite   verb [T] UK /ɪnˈsaɪt/ US /ɪnˈsaɪt/ 鼓动，煽动 to encourage someone to do or feel something unpleasant or violent [GRE]

incline   1 verb   formal UK /ɪnˈklaɪn/ US /ɪnˈklaɪn/ verb (FEEL) [I or T, usually + adv/prep]（使）倾向于 to (make someone) feel something or want to do something

incorporate   verb [T] UK /ɪnˈkɔː.pər.eɪt/ US /ɪnˈkɔːr.pɚ.eɪt/ C2 包含；将…包括在内 to include something as part of something larger

increase   1 verb [I or T] UK /ɪnˈkriːs/ US /ɪnˈkriːs/ B1 增大；增加；增强 to (make something) become larger in amount or size

incriminate　　　verb [T] UK /ɪnˈkrɪm.ɪ.neɪt/ US /ɪnˈkrɪm.ə.neɪt/ 使（某人）看似有罪；连累，牵连 to make someone seem guilty, especially of a crime [GRE]

incubate　　1 verb [I or T] UK /ˈɪŋ.kjə.beɪt/ US /ˈɪŋ.kjə.beɪt/ [I or T] (EGG) 孵（卵），孵化 When a bird, etc. incubates its eggs, it keeps them warm until the young come out, and when eggs incubate, they develop to the stage at which the young come out. [GRE]

inculcate　　verb [T]　formal UK /ˈɪŋ.kʌl.keɪt/ US /ˈɪŋ.kʌl.keɪt/ 反复灌输；谆谆教诲 to fix beliefs or ideas in someone's mind, especially by repeating them often

incur　　verb [T]　formal UK /ɪnˈkɜːr/ US /ɪnˈkɝː/ -rr- C2 招致；遭受 to experience something, usually something unpleasant, as a result of actions you have taken

indicate　　1 verb UK /ˈɪn.dɪ.keɪt/ US /ˈɪn.də.keɪt/ (SHOW) B2 [T] 标示；表明；显示；暗示 to show, point, or make clear in another way

indict　　verb [T]　LAW　specialized UK /ɪnˈdaɪt/ US /ɪnˈdaɪt/ 控告，告发；起诉 If a law court or a grand jury indicts someone, it accuses them officially of a crime. [GRE]

indictment　　1 noun UK /ɪnˈdaɪt.mənt/ US /ɪnˈdaɪt.mənt/ [C usually singular] 控诉；谴责 a sign that a policy, system, society, etc. is bad or wrong [GRE]

indoctrinate　　　verb [T]　disapproving UK /ɪnˈdɒk.trɪ.neɪt/ US /ɪnˈdɑ ːk.trə.neɪt/ 向…灌输 to often repeat an idea or belief to someone in order to persuade them to accept it [GRE]

induce　　　1 verb UK /ɪnˈdʒuːs/ US /ɪnˈduːs/ formal (PERSUADE) 诱使；劝说 [T + obj + to infinitive] to persuade someone to do something

inducement　　　noun [C or U] UK /ɪnˈdʒuːs.mənt/ US /ɪnˈduːs.mənt/ 引诱；引诱物；诱因 an act or thing that is intended to persuade someone or something [GRE]

indulge　　　verb UK /ɪnˈdʌldʒ/ US /ɪnˈdʌldʒ/ C2 [I or T] （使）沉溺于；（尤指）放纵 to allow yourself or another person to have something enjoyable, especially more than is good for you

indulgent　　　adjective UK /ɪnˈdʌl.dʒənt/ US /ɪnˈdʌl.dʒənt/ 迁就的；纵容的；宽容的 allowing someone to have or do what they want, especially when this is not good for them [GRE]

inebriated　adjective　formal UK /ɪˈniː.bri.eɪ.tɪd/ US /ɪˈniː.bri.eɪ.t̬ɪd/ 喝醉的 having drunk too much alcohol

inedible　　　adjective UK /ɪˈned.ə.bəl/ US /ˌɪnˈed.ə.bəl/ C1 不可食用的，不适合食用的 not suitable as food

inert　　　1 adjective UK /ɪˈnɜːt/ US /ˌɪnˈɜ·t/ (NOT MOVING) 不动的；不能动的 not moving or not able to move 2 无生气的；无趣的 not energetic or interesting [GRE]

infect   1 verb [T] UK /ɪnˈfekt/ US /ɪnˈfekt/ [T] (DISEASE) C1 （疾病）传染，感染 to pass a disease to a person, animal, or plant

infer   verb [T] formal UK /ɪnˈfɜːr/ US /-ˈfɝː/ -rr- C2 推断，推论，推理 to form an opinion or guess that something is true because of the information that you have

infiltrate   1 verb [I + adv/prep, T] UK /ˈɪn.fɪl.treɪt/ US /ˈɪn.fɪl.treɪt/ （使）潜入；（使）渗透 to secretly become part of a group in order to get information or to influence the way that group thinks or behaves [GRE]

inflate   1 verb UK /ɪnˈfleɪt/ US /ɪnˈfleɪt/ inflate verb (FILL WITH AIR) [I or T] （使）充气；（使）膨胀 to make something increase in size by filling it with air

inflow   noun [C or U] UK /ˈɪn.fləʊ/ US /ˈɪn.floʊ/ 流入，涌入 the action of people or things arriving somewhere

influence   2 verb [T] UK /ˈɪn.flu.əns/ US /ˈɪn.flu.əns/ B2 影响 to affect or change how someone or something develops, behaves, or thinks

influx   noun [C usually singular] UK /ˈɪn.flʌks/ US /ˈɪn.flʌks/ C2 涌进；汇集 the fact of a large number of people or things arriving at the same time [GRE]

inform   verb [T] UK /ɪnˈfɔːm/ US /ɪnˈfɔːrm/ B1 通知，告知 to tell someone about particular facts

infringe   verb [T] formal UK /ɪnˈfrɪndʒ/ US /ɪnˈfrɪndʒ/ 违反，违背（规定、法律等）to break a rule, law, etc.

infuriate   verb [T] UK /ɪnˈfjʊə.ri.eɪt/ US /ɪnˈfjʊr.i.eɪt/ 使大怒，激怒 to make someone extremely angry [GRE]

infuse   1 verb UK /ɪnˈfjuːz/ US /ɪnˈfjuːz/ (EMOTION) [T + prep] 使（某人）充满（某种感情）；将（某特性）注入（某物） to fill someone or something with an emotion or quality [GRE]

ingest   verb [T] MEDICAL specialized UK /ɪnˈdʒest/ US /ɪnˈdʒest/ 摄取，咽下（食物） to eat or drink something [GRE]

ingratiate   verb disapproving UK /ɪŋˈɡreɪ.ʃiː.eɪt/ US /ɪŋˈɡreɪ.ʃiː.eɪt/ 讨好，奉承 to make someone like you by praising or trying to please them [GRE]

inhabit   1 verb [T often passive] UK /ɪnˈhæb.ɪt/ US /ɪnˈhæb.ɪt/ C2 居住于 to live in a place

inherit   1 verb UK /ɪnˈher.ɪt/ US /ɪnˈher.ɪt/ (FROM DEAD PERSON) C2 [I or T] 继承 to receive money, a house, etc. from someone after they have died

inhibit   1 verb [T] UK /ɪnˈhɪb.ɪt/ US /ɪnˈhɪb.ɪt/ 使…拘谨；使…有顾忌 to prevent someone from doing something by making them feel nervous or embarrassed

initiate   1 verb [T] UK /ɪˈnɪʃ.i.eɪt/ US /ɪˈnɪʃ.i.eɪt/ [T] (START) C2 formal 开始，创始 to cause something to begin

inject   1 verb [T] UK /ɪnˈdʒekt/ US /ɪnˈdʒekt/ [T] (DRUG)注射；给…注射 to use a needle and syringe (= small tube) to put a liquid such as a drug into a person's body

injure   1 verb [T] UK /ˈɪn.dʒər/ US /ˈɪn.dʒɚ/ B1 伤害，损害 to hurt or cause physical harm to a person or animal

innovate   verb [I] UK /ˈɪn.ə.veɪt/ US /ˈɪn.ə.veɪt/ 改革；创新 to introduce changes and new ideas

inoculate   verb [T] UK /ɪˈnɒk.jə.leɪt/ US /ɪˈnɑ:.kjə.leɪt/ 给…接种，给…作预防注射 to give a weak form of a disease to a person or animal, usually by injection, as a protection against that disease

input   1 noun UK /ˈɪn.pʊt/ US /ˈɪn.pʊt/ B2 [C or U] （能源、资金或信息的）投入，输入 something such as energy, money, or information that is put into a system, organization, or machine so that it can operate

inquire   1 verb [I or T] (UK also enquire) UK /ɪnˈkwaɪər/ US /ɪnˈkwaɪr/ B2 询问，打听 to ask for information

insert   1 verb [T] UK /ɪnˈsɜːt/ US /ɪnˈsɜ:t/ C1 插入 to put something inside something else

insinuate   verb [T] UK /ɪnˈsɪn.ju.eɪt/ US /ɪnˈsɪn.ju.eɪt/ 含沙射影地说，影射 to suggest, without being direct, that something unpleasant is true

insist   verb [I] UK /ɪnˈsɪst/ US /ɪnˈsɪst/ B1 坚持说，强调；坚决要求 to say firmly or demand forcefully, especially when others disagree with or oppose what you say

inspect   1 verb [T] UK /ɪnˈspekt/ US /ɪnˈspekt/ C1 检查；审视 to look at something or someone carefully in order to discover information, especially about their quality or condition

inspire   1 verb [T] UK /ɪnˈspaɪər/ US /ɪnˈspaɪr/ B2 激励，鼓舞 to make someone feel that they want to do something and can do it

install   1 verb [T] UK /ɪnˈstɔːl/ US /ɪnˈstɑːl/ [T] (READY TO USE) B1 安装 to put furniture, a machine, or a piece of equipment into position and make it ready to use

instate   verb [T]   formal UK /ɪnˈsteɪt/ US /ɪnˈsteɪt/ 设立；建立 to establish something [GRE]

instigate   verb [T]   formal UK /ˈɪn.stɪ.geɪt/ US /ˈɪn.stə.geɪt/ 促使发生；发起 to cause an event or situation to happen by making a set of actions or a formal process begin [GRE]

instil   verb [T] UK (US instill) UK /ɪnˈstɪl/ US /ɪnˈstɪl/ -ll- 逐渐灌输 to put a feeling, idea, or principle gradually into someone's mind, so that it has a strong influence on the way that person thinks or behaves [GRE]

institute   2 verb [T]   formal UK /ˈɪn.stɪ.tʃuːt/ US /ˈɪn.stə.tuːt/ 建立；制定；开始 to start or cause a system, rule, legal action, etc. to exist [GRE]

instruct   1 verb UK /ɪnˈstrʌkt/ US /ɪnˈstrʌkt/ (ORDER) C1 [T + to infinitive] （尤指正式地）指示，命令，吩咐 to order or tell someone to do something, especially in a formal way

insulate　　1 verb [T] UK /ˈɪn.sjə.leɪt/ US /ˈɪn.sə.leɪt/ [T] (COVER) 使隔热；使隔音；使绝缘 to cover and surround something with a material or substance in order to stop heat, sound, or electricity from escaping or entering [GRE]

insure　　1 verb UK /ɪnˈʃɔːr/ US /ɪnˈʃʊr/ [I or T, usually + adv/prep] （给…上）保险，（为…）投保 to protect yourself against risk by regularly paying a special company that will provide a fixed amount of money if you are killed or injured or if your home or possessions are damaged, destroyed, or stolen

integrate　　1 verb UK /ˈɪn.tɪ.ɡreɪt/ US /ˈɪn.tə.ɡreɪt/ C1 [I or T] （使）融入（某社会或群体）；（使）成为一体 to mix with and join society or a group of people, often changing to suit their way of life, habits, and customs

intend　　1 verb [T] UK /ɪnˈtend/ US /ɪnˈtend/ B1 打算，计划 to have as a plan or purpose

intensify　　verb [I or T] UK /ɪnˈten.sɪ.faɪ/ US /ɪnˈten.sə.faɪ/ C2 加强，增强；强化 to become greater, more serious, or more extreme, or to make something do this

inter　　1 verb [T]　formal UK /ɪnˈtɜːr/ US /ɪnˈtɜː/ -rr- 埋葬 to bury a dead body [GRE]

intimidate　　verb [T] UK /ɪnˈtɪm.ɪ.deɪt/ US /ɪnˈtɪm.ə.deɪt/ 恫吓，恐吓 to frighten or threaten someone, usually in order to persuade them to do something that you want them to do [GRE]

intoxicate　　1 verb [I or T]　formal UK /ɪnˈtɒk.sɪ.keɪt/ US /ɪnˈtɑːk.sɪ.keɪt/ 使（某人）喝醉 to make someone drunk 2 verb 使（某人）陶醉，兴奋，略微失去控制 to make someone excited, happy, and slightly out of control

intrigue   1 verb [T] UK /ɪnˈtriːg/ US /ɪnˈtriːg/（尤指因奇怪、不寻常或神秘而）使很感兴趣，迷住 to interest someone a lot, especially by being strange, unusual, or mysterious 2 noun [C or U] UK /ˈɪn.triːg/ US /ˈɪn.triːg/（尤指伤害他人的）密谋；阴谋，诡计 (the making of) a secret plan to do something, especially something that will harm another person [GRE]

intrude   1 verb [I] UK /ɪnˈtruːd/ US /ɪnˈtruːd/ C2 闯入，侵扰 to go into a place or situation in which you are not wanted or not expected to be

inundate   1 verb [T] UK /ˈɪn.ʌn.deɪt/ US /ˈɪn.ʌn.deɪt/ [T] (TOO MUCH) 使应接不暇 to give someone so much work or so many things that they cannot deal with it all [GRE]

invade   1 verb UK /ɪnˈveɪd/ US /ɪnˈveɪd/ B2 [I or T] 入侵，侵略 to enter a country by force with large numbers of soldiers in order to take possession of it

inveigh   激烈抗议，表示强烈不满：protest vehemently

inveigh against sb/sth   verb UK /ɪnˈveɪ/ US /ɪnˈveɪ/ formal 猛烈抨击；痛骂 to strongly criticize something or someone [GRE]

invent   1 verb [T] UK /ɪnˈvent/ US /ɪnˈvent/ [T] (NEW DESIGN) B1 发明，创造 to design and/or create something that has never been made before

invest   verb [I or T] UK /ɪnˈvest/ US /ɪnˈvest/ B2 投（资），投入 to put money, effort, time, etc. into something to make a profit or get an advantage

investigate verb [T] UK /ɪnˈves.tɪ.ɡeɪt/ US /ɪnˈves.tə.ɡeɪt/ B2 （尤指为揭开真相）调查，审查 to examine a crime, problem, statement, etc. carefully, especially to discover the truth

invigilate verb [I or T] UK /ɪnˈvɪdʒ.ə.leɪt/ US /ɪnˈvɪdʒ.ə.leɪt/ uk us proctor 监考 to watch people taking an exam in order to check that they do not cheat

invigorate verb [T] UK /ɪnˈvɪɡ.ər.eɪt/ US /ɪnˈvɪɡ.ɚ.eɪt/ 使精力充沛，使活跃使精力充沛，使活跃 to make someone feel fresher, healthier, and more energetic [GRE]

invite 1 verb [T] UK /ɪnˈvaɪt/ US /ɪnˈvaɪt/ [T] (ASK TO AN EVENT) A1 邀请，约请 to ask or request someone to go to an event

invoke 1 verb [T] formal UK /ɪnˈvəʊk/ US /ɪnˈvoʊk/ 援引，借助（法律） to use a law in order to achieve something, or to mention something in order to explain something or to support your opinion or action 2 verb 求助于，借助于（尤指神灵） to request help from someone, especially a god, when you want to improve a situation 3 verb 唤起，引起，使记起 to make someone have a particular feeling or remember something [GRE]

involve 1 verb [T not continuous] UK /ɪnˈvɒlv/ US /ɪnˈvɑ:lv/ B1 包括，包含 If an activity, situation, etc. involves something, that thing is a part of the activity, etc.

irrigate 1 verb [T] UK /ˈɪr.ɪ.ɡeɪt/ US /ˈɪr.ə.ɡeɪt/ [T] (SUPPLY WATER) 灌溉 to supply land with water so that crops and plants will grow [GRE]

irritate   1 verb [T] UK /ˈɪr.ɪ.teɪt/ US /ˈɪr.ə.teɪt/ [T] (MAKE ANGRY) C1
激怒，使恼火 to make someone angry or annoyed [GRE]

Prefix: Indo- of or connected with India

Indo- prefix UK /ɪn.dəʊ-/ US /ɪn.doʊ-/ of or connected with India 印度的；与
印度有关的

Indo-European languages   印欧语系

the Indo-Chinese border   印中边界

Indo-European   adjective UK /ˌɪn.dəʊ.jʊə.rəˈpiː.ən/ US
/ˌɪn.doʊ.jʊr.əˈpiː.ən/ 印欧（语系）的 related to the group of European and
Asian languages that are spoken in most of Europe and in parts of Asia and that
include English, French, Greek, Russian, and Hindi

Prefix (Medical): infra- below

Meaning in English:

Origin language: Latin

English examples:

infraglenoid   adjective MEDICAL specialized UK /ˌɪn.frəˈgliː.nɔɪd/ US
/ˌɪn.frəˈgliː.nɔɪd/ 关节盂下的 below the glenoid cavity (= a shallow, hollow part
of the shoulder blade)

Infrahyoid muscles   noun [U] 舌骨下肌 Infrahyoid muscles are also
known as "strap muscles" which connect hyoid, sternum, clavicle and
scapula. They are located below the hyoid bone on the anterolateral surface of
the thyroid gland and are involved in movements of the hyoid bone and thyroid
cartilage during vocalization, swallowing and mastication.; The infrahyoid
muscles, or strap muscles, are a group of four pairs of muscles in the anterior

(frontal) part of the neck.[1] The four infrahyoid muscles are the sternohyoid, sternothyroid, thyrohyoid and omohyoid muscles. Wikipedia

infraorbital adjective MEDICAL specialized UK /ˌɪn.frəˈɔː.bɪ.təl/ US /ˌɪn.frəˈɔːr.bɪ.t̬əl/ 眶下的 below the orbit (= the eye socket)

infrapatellar adjective MEDICAL specialized UK /ˌɪn.frə.pəˈtel.ər/ US /ˌɪn.frə.pəˈtel.ɚ/ 髌骨下的 below the patella (= the bone at the front of the knee)

infraspinatous adjective MEDICAL specialized UK /ˌɪn.frə.spiːˈnɑː.təs/ US /ˌɪn.frə.spaɪˈneɪ.t̬əs/ 冈下肌的 used to refer to the infraspinatus muscle (= a muscle in the middle of the shoulder blade)

infraspinatus noun [C] MEDICAL specialized UK /ˌɪn.frə.spiːˈnɑː.təs/ US /ˌɪn.frə.spaɪˈneɪ.t̬əs/ plural infraspinati 冈下肌 a muscle in the middle of the shoulder blade

Prefix: inter- between or among the people, things, or places mentioned
Meaning in English: between

Origin language: Latin

English examples:

inter- 2 prefix UK /ɪn.tər-/ US /ɪn.tɚ-/ 互相；在…之间，在…中间 used to form adjectives meaning "between or among the people, things, or places mentioned"

interactive 1 adjective UK /ˌɪn.təˈræk.tɪv/ US /ˌɪn.t̬ɚˈræk.tɪv/ B2 交互的，人机对话的 An interactive system or computer program is designed to involve the user in the exchange of information.

intercept   verb [T] UK /ˌɪn.təˈsept/ US /ˌɪn.t̬ɚˈsept/ 拦截，截住 to stop and catch something or someone before that thing or person is able to reach a particular place

interdict   1 noun [C]   specialized UK /ˈɪn.tə.dɪkt/ US /ˈɪn.t̬ɚ.dɪkt/ LAW （法庭发出的）强制令；禁令 an official instruction from a law court telling someone that they are not allowed to do something 2 noun RELIGION （罗马天主教发出的）禁止令 an instruction from the Roman Catholic Church telling someone they are not allowed to take part in official Church activities [GRE]

interfere   verb [I] UK /ˌɪn.təˈfɪər/ US /ˌɪn.t̬ɚˈfɪr/ B2 干涉，干预 to involve yourself in a situation when your involvement is not wanted or is not helpful

interject   verb [I or T]   formal UK /ˌɪn.təˈdʒekt/ US /ˌɪn.t̬ɚˈdʒekt/ 插（话）to say something while another person is speaking

interlace   verb [T] UK /ˌɪn.təˈleɪs/ US /ˌɪn.t̬ɚˈleɪs/ 使结合；（尤指）使交织，使交错 to join different parts together to make a whole, especially by crossing one thing over another or fitting one part into another

interlink   verb [I or T] UK /ˌɪn.təˈlɪŋk/ US /ˌɪn.t̬ɚˈlɪŋk/ 连接；（使）互相关联 to cause to join or connect together, with the parts joined often having an effect on each other

interlock   verb [I or T] UK /ˌɪn.təˈlɒk/ US /ˌɪn.t̬ɚˈlɑːk/ （使）紧密连接，（使）互相锁扣 to fit together firmly [GRE]

interpolate   1 verb [T]   formal UK /ɪnˈtɜː.pə.leɪt/ US /ɪnˈtɜː.pə.leɪt/ 插入（文字）to add words to a text

interpose   1 verb [T]   formal UK /ˌɪn.təˈpəʊz/ US /ˌɪn.t̬əˈpoʊz/ [T] (PUT BETWEEN) （尤指为阻止双方做某事而）插入，介入，干预 to put yourself or something between two things, people, or groups, especially in order to stop them doing something

interpose   1 verb [T]   formal UK /ˌɪn.təˈpəʊz/ US /ˌɪn.t̬əˈpoʊz/ [T] (PUT BETWEEN) （尤指为阻止双方做某事而）插入，介入，干预 to put yourself or something between two things, people, or groups, especially in order to stop them doing something

interpret   1 verb UK /ɪnˈtɜː.prɪt/ US /-ˈtɝː-/ (FIND MEANING) C1 [T] 理解，解释，阐释 to decide what the intended meaning of something is

interrelate   verb [I] UK /ˌɪn.tə.rɪˈleɪt/ US /ˌɪn.t̬ə.rɪˈleɪt/ 相互关联 to be connected in such a way that each thing has an effect on or depends on the other

interrogate   1 verb [T] UK /ɪnˈter.ə.geɪt/ US /ɪnˈter.ə.geɪt/ 讯问，审问，盘问 to ask someone a lot of questions for a long time in order to get information, sometimes using threats or violence

interrupt   1 verb UK /ˌɪn.təˈrʌpt/ US /ˌɪn.t̬əˈrʌpt/ (STOP SPEAKING) B1 [I or T] 打断（其他人说话）to stop a person from speaking for a short period by something you say or do

intersect   1 verb UK /ˌɪn.təˈsekt/ US /ˌɪn.t̬əˈsekt/ [I or T] （线条、道路等）（和…）相交，（和…）交叉 (of lines, roads, etc.) to cross one another

intersperse   verb [T] UK /ˌɪn.təˈspɜːs/ US /ˌɪn.t̬əˈspɝːs/ 无规律地混入；散布；点缀 to mix one thing in with another in a way that is not regular

interstate 1 adjective [before noun] UK /ˌɪn.təˈsteɪt/ US /ˈɪn.tɚ.steɪt/ 州际的，州与州之间的 involving two or more of the states into which some countries such as the US are divided

intervene 1 verb [I] UK /ˌɪn.təˈviːn/ US /ˌɪn.tɚˈviːn/ [I] (GET INVOLVED) C2 干涉，干预；调停 to intentionally become involved in a difficult situation in order to improve it or prevent it from getting worse

interview 4 verb UK /ˈɪn.tə.vjuː/ US /ˈɪn.tɚ.vjuː/ B1 [T] 采访；对…进行面试；讯问 to ask someone questions in an interview

Prefix (Medical): inter- between, among

Meaning in English: between, among

Origin language: Latin

English examples:

Interarticular ligament 肋骨头的关节内韧带 The intra-articular ligament of head of rib (interarticular in older texts; ligamentum capitis costae intraarticulare) is situated in the interior of the articulation of head of rib between the superior costal facet and the inferior costal facet. 肋骨头的关节内韧带（旧文献中的关节间韧带；关节内的头状韧带）位于上肋小面和下肋小面之间的肋小头关节的内部。

The costovertebral joints 肋椎关节 The costovertebral joints are the joints that connect the ribs to the vertebral column. The articulation of the head of the rib connects the head of the rib to the bodies of the thoracic vertebrae.

interbreed verb [I or T] UK /ˌɪn.təˈbriːd/ US /ˌɪn.tɚˈbriːd/ interbred | interbred （使）杂交繁殖 to breed or cause to breed with members of another breed or group

其中有些狼与驯养的狗杂交过。　　Some of the wolves had interbred with domestic dogs.

intercarpal　　adjective　MEDICAL　specialized UK /ɪn.təˈkɑː.pəl/ US /ˌɪn.t̬ɚˈkɑːr.pəl/ 腕骨间的 between the carpal bones (= small bones in the wrist)

an intercarpal ligament　腕骨间的韧带

intercondylar　　adjective　MEDICAL　specialized UK /ɪn.təˈkɒn.dɪ.lər/ US /ˌɪn.t̬ɚˈkɑːn.də.lɚ/ 髁间的 between condyles (= the round part at the end of a bone where it fits into another bone)

an intercondylar fracture 髁间的骨折

intercostal　　1 adjective　MEDICAL　specialized UK /ˌɪn.təˈkɒs.təl/ US /ˌɪn.t̬ɚˈkɑː.stəl/ 肋间的 between the ribs (= bones around the chest)

intercostal muscles　　肋间肌肉

intercostal pain　肋间疼痛

intercostal　　2 noun　MEDICAL　specialized UK /ˌɪn.təˈkɒs.təl/ US /ˌɪn.t̬ɚˈkɑː.stəl/ 肋间肌肉 one of the muscles between the ribs (= bones around the chest)

interferon　　noun [C or U]　BIOLOGY　specialized UK /ˌɪn.təˈfɪə.rɒn/ US /ˌɪn.t̬ɚˈfɪr.ɑːn/ 干扰素（任何一种由细胞产生的体内抗病毒蛋白质）one of several proteins in the body that are produced by cells as a reaction to infection by a virus

intermolecular　　adjective　PHYSICS　specialized UK /ˌɪn.tə.məˈlek.jə.lər/ US /ˌɪn.t̬ɚ.məˈlek.jə.lɚ/ 分子间的 happening among or between molecules

intermuscular   adjective   MEDICAL   specialized UK /ˌɪn.təˈmʌsk.jə.lər/ US /ˌɪn.təˈmʌs.kjə.lə/ 肌间的 between muscles

intermuscular tendons   肌间腱

internal medicine   noun [U] US UK /ɪnˌtɜː.nəl ˈmed.ɪ.sən/ US /ɪnˌtɜː.nəl ˈmed.ɪ.sən/ 内科（学） the part of medical science that is involved in the discovery of diseases inside the body and the treatment of them without cutting the body open

internist   noun [C]   MEDICAL   US UK /ˈɪn.tɜː.nɪst/ US /ˈɪn.tɜː.nɪst/ 内科医生 a doctor who specializes in identifying and treating diseases that do not need surgery (= cutting into the body)

internus   adjective   MEDICAL   specialized UK /ɪnˈtɜː.n.əs/ US /ɪnˈtɜː.nəs/ （拉丁语，用于医学术语）内的 a Latin word meaning "inside", used in medical names and descriptions

interosseous   adjective   MEDICAL   specialized UK /ɪn.təˈrɒs.i.əs/ US /ˌɪn.təˈɑːs.i.əs/ 骨间的 between bones or connecting bones

an interosseus ligament   骨间韧带

interosseus   noun [C]   ANATOMY   specialized UK /ɪn.təˈrɒs.i.əs/ US /ˌɪn.təˈɑːs.i.əs/ plural interossei 骨间肌 one of the muscles between bones of the hands and feet

interphalangeal   adjective   MEDICAL   specialized UK /ˌɪn.tə.fəˈlæn.dʒi.əl/ US /ˌɪn.tə.fəˈlæn.dʒi.əl/ 指节间的；趾节间的 relating to an area between two phalanges (= bones of the fingers and toes)

interstitial 1 adjective UK /ˌɪn.təˈstɪʃ.əl/ US /ˌɪn.təˈstɪʃ.əl/ (MEDICAL) MEDICAL specialized （细胞、组织、器官间的）间隙的 relating to spaces between cells, tissues, or organs in the body

Deficiencies of sodium and water can cause shrinkage of the interstitial space. 钠和水缺乏会导致细胞间空间缩小。

interstitial 2 adjective MEDICAL specialized （器官间的）间质的 relating to connective tissue that supports the working parts of an organ in the body

interstitial 3 adjective (BETWEEN) formal （两者之间）间隙的 relating to the space or time between things

intertarsal adjective MEDICAL specialized UK /ˌɪn.təˈtɑː.səl/ US /ˌɪn.təˈtɑːr.səl/ 跗骨间的 between the tarsus (= the bones of the ankle and heel)

the intertarsal joint 跗骨关节

intertrochanteric adjective MEDICAL specialized UK /ˌɪn.tə.trəʊ.kənˈte.rɪk/ US /ˌɪn.tə.troʊ.kənˈter.ɪk/ （股骨）粗隆间的 relating to the bones of the thigh

interventricular adjective MEDICAL specialized UK /ˌɪn.tə.venˈtrɪk.jə.lər/ US /ˌɪn.tə.venˈtrɪk.jə.lə/ （心）室间的 between the ventricles (= hollow spaces in the heart that pump blood)

intervertebral adjective MEDICAL specialized UK /ˌɪn.təˈvɜː.tɪ.brəl/ US /ˌɪn.təˈvɜː.tə.brəl/ 椎间的 between the vertebrae (= the small bones that form the spine)

Prefix: intra- "within" (the stated place or group)
Meaning in English: within

Origin language: Latin

English examples:

intra- prefix UK /ɪn.trə-/ US /ɪn.trə-/ （构成形容词）在内，内部 used to form adjectives meaning "within" (the stated place or group)

intranet noun [C] UK /ˈɪn.trə.net/ US /ˈɪn.trə.net/ 局域网，内联网，内部网 a system of connected computers that works like the internet and allows people within an organization to communicate with each other and share information

intransigent adjective formal disapproving UK /ɪnˈtræn.sɪ.dʒənt/ /ɪnˈtrɑ:n.sɪ.dʒənt/ US /ɪnˈtræn.sə.dʒənt/ 固执的，不妥协的，不让步的 refusing to change your opinions or behaviour [GRE]

intramural adjective UK /ˌɪn.trəˈmjʊə.rəl/ US /ˌɪn.trəˈmjʊr.əl/ 学校内的 happening within or involving the members of one school, college, or university

Prefix (Medical): intra- within

Meaning in English:

Origin language: Latin

English examples:

intracapsular adjective ANATOMY specialized UK /ˌɪn.trəˈkæp.sjəl.ər/ US /ˌɪn.trəˈkæp.sə.lə/ 囊内的 inside a capsule (= a flexible structure around an organ, joint, or other body structure)

intracapsular pressure 囊内压力

intracellular adjective BIOLOGY specialized UK /ˌɪn.trəˈsel.jə.lər/ US /ˌɪn.trəˈsel.jə.lə/ 细胞内的 happening inside a cell or cells

intracranial　adjective　MEDICAL　specialized UK /ˌɪn.trəˈkreɪ.ni.əl/ US /ˌɪn.trəˈkreɪ.ni.əl/ 颅内的　inside the cranium (= the bony part of the skull that holds the brain)

颅内压可以用药物治疗。　　Intracranial pressure can be treated with medication.

intraluminal　adjective　MEDICAL　specialized /ˌɪn.trəˈluː.mɪ.nəl/ /ˌɪn.trəˈluː.mɪ.nəl/ 食道内的 existing, happening, or placed inside the oesophagus (= the tube in the body that takes food from the mouth to the stomach)

intraluminal cancer cells 食道内癌细胞

intraluminal digestion of gluten 谷蛋白在食道内的消化

an intraluminal catheter　食道置管

Intracranial hemorrhage　　脑溢血; 脑出血 Intracerebral hemorrhage (ICH) is when blood suddenly bursts into brain tissue, causing damage to your brain. Symptoms usually appear suddenly during ICH. They include headache, weakness, confusion, and paralysis, particularly on one side of your body.

intramolecular　adjective　CHEMISTRY　specialized UK /ˌɪn.trə.məˈlek.jə.lər/ US /ˌɪn.trə.məˈlek.jə.lɚ/ 分子内的 happening inside a molecule or molecules

intramuscular　adjective　MEDICAL　specialized UK /ˌɪn.trəˈmʌs.kjə.lər/ US /ˌɪn.trəˈmʌs.kjə.lɚ/ 肌内的 inside a muscle, or put into a muscle

intramuscular fat　肌内脂肪

an intramuscular injection　　肌肉注射

intraoperative　　adjective　MEDICAL　specialized UK /ˌɪn.trəˈɒp.ər.ə.tɪv/ US /ˌɪn.trəˈɑ:.p.ɚ.ə.t̬ɪv/ 手术（期）中的　during a medical operation

intraoperative complications　　手术间并发症

intrathecal adjective　MEDICAL　specialized UK /ˌɪn.trəˈθi:.kəl/ US /ˌɪn.trəˈθi:.kəl/ 鞘内的 in the fluid-filled space under the lining of the brain or spinal cord

an intrathecal injection　鞘内注射

intrauterine　　adjective　MEDICAL　specialized UK /ˌɪn.trəˈju:.tər.aɪn/ US /ˌɪn.trəˈju:.t̬ɚ.ɪn/ 子宫内的 inside the uterus (= the organ in a woman's body where a baby develops)

IUD　　noun [C] UK /ˌaɪ.ju:ˈdi:/ US /ˌaɪ.ju:ˈdi:/ 宫内避孕器（intra-uterine device 的缩写） abbreviation for intra-uterine device: a small object put by a doctor into the womb of a woman who wants to avoid becoming pregnant

intravascular　　adjective　MEDICAL　specialized UK /ˌɪn.trəˈvæs.kjə.lər/ US /ˌɪn.trəˈvæs.kjə.lɚ/ 血管内的 in blood vessels

intravascular coagulation 血管内凝血

intravenous　　adjective UK /ˌɪn.trəˈvi:.nəs/ US /ˌɪn.trəˈvi:.nəs/ (abbreviation IV) Medical Specialized 进入静脉的；静脉的 into or connected to a vein

intravenous feeding/fluids　　静脉进食 / 输液

an intravenous drip/injection　　静脉滴注 / 注射

Intravenous drug users are at particular risk of contracting the disease.

静脉注射毒品的人特别容易感染这种病。

Meaning in English: iris

Origin language: Greek ἶρις

English examples:

iris　　2 noun [C] (EYE) 虹膜 the coloured circular part of that eye that surrounds the black pupil (= central part)

Iridectomy　　　　　noun [U] 虹膜切除术 （Hóngmó qiēchú shù） An iridectomy, also known as a surgical iridectomy or corectomy, is the surgical removal of part of the iris. These procedures are most frequently performed in the treatment of closed-angle glaucoma and iris melanoma. Wikipedia

Meaning in English: same

Origin language: Latin

English examples:

ipsilateral　　　　adjective　MEDICAL　specialized UK /ɪp.sɪˈlæt.ər.əl/ US /ˌɪp.səˈlæt̬.ɚ.əl/ （身体）同侧的 on, affecting, or referring to the same side of the body

an ipsilateral stroke　　同侧中风

Ipsilateral hemiparesis　　　　noun [U] 同侧偏瘫 Paralysis occurring on the side of the body opposite to the side of the brain in which the causal lesion occurs.

solipsism　　noun [U]　SOCIAL SCIENCE, PSYCHOLOGY　specialized UK /ˈsɒl.ɪp.sɪ.zəm/ US /ˈsɑː.lɪp.sɪ.zəm/ 唯我论 the belief that only your own experiences and existence can be known

Meaning in English: restriction

Origin language: Greek ἴσχω

English examples:

ischaemia noun [U] MEDICAL specialized UK (US ischemia) UK /ɪˈskiː.mi.ə/ US /ɪˈskiː.mi.ə/ 局部缺血 a medical problem in which there is not enough blood flowing to a part of the body, usually because the arteries have become too narrow. It can lead to very serious health conditions

cerebral/myocardial ischaemia   大脑／心肌局部缺血

ischaemic adjective MEDICAL specialized UK (US ischemic) UK /ɪˈskiː.mɪk/ US /ɪˈskiː.mɪk/ 局部缺血的 relating to ischaemia (= a medical problem in which there is not enough blood flowing to a part of the body)

ischemic heart disease/stroke 局部缺血性心脏病／中风

cerebral ischemic stroke 脑梗

Meaning in English: Of or pertaining to the ischium, the hip-joint

Origin language: Ancient Greek ἰσχιόν (ischión), hip-joint, ischium

English examples:

ischial   adjective MEDICAL specialized UK /ˈɪs.ki.əl/ US /ˈɪs.ki.əl/ 坐骨的 relating to the ischium (= the large bone in the lower part of the hip)

ischiocondylar   adjective MEDICAL specialized UK /ˌɪs.ki.əʊˈkɒn.dɪ.lər/ US /ˌɪs.ki.oʊˈkɑːn.də.lɚ/ 坐骨的 relating to the ischium (= the large bone in the lower part of the hip)

ischiofemoral   adjective MEDICAL specialized UK /ˌɪs.ki.əʊˈfem.ər.əl/ US /ˌɪs.ki.oʊˈfem.ɚ.əl/ 坐骨股骨的 relating to the ischium (= the large bone in the lower part of the hip) and femur (= the long bone in the upper part of the leg)

an ischiofemoral ligament　　坐骨股韧带

ischiopubic adjective　MEDICAL　specialized UK /ˌɪs.ki.əʊˈpjuːbɪk/ US /ˌɪs.ki.oʊˈpjuː.bɪk/ 坐骨耻骨的 relating to the ischium and the pubic bone (= bones in the hip)

the ischiopubic region　坐骨耻骨区

ischium　　noun [C]　ANATOMY　specialized UK /ˈɪs.ki.əm/ US /ˈɪs.ki.əm/ plural ischia /ˈɪs.ki.ə/ 坐骨 the large bone in the lower part of the hip

Ischioanal fossa　noun [U] 坐骨肛窝 The ischioanal fossa (formerly called ischiorectal fossa) is the fat-filled wedge-shaped space located lateral to the anal canal and inferior to the pelvic diaphragm. It is somewhat prismatic in shape, with its base directed to the surface of the perineum and its apex at the line of meeting of the obturator and anal fasciae. 坐骨肛窝（以前称为坐骨直肠窝）是位于肛管外侧和盆膈下方的充满脂肪的楔形空间。 它的形状有点棱柱形，其基部指向会阴表面，其顶点位于闭孔和肛门筋膜的会合线上。

Prefix: it- very fashionable

Meaning in English: very fashionable

Origin language: Anglo-Saxon/ Latin

English examples:

it-　　4 prefix　informal UK /ɪt-/ US /ɪt-/ 时尚的；流行的（形容能引起普遍兴趣的某物或某人） used for describing things or people that are very fashionable, and everyone is interested in them, wants to have them, etc.

The design of this bag makes it the "it-bag" for this summer. 　这款包的设计使它成为了今夏的潮流。

Prefix: Italo- of or connected with Italy

Meaning in English: of or connected with Italy

Origin language: Anglo-Saxon/ Latin

English examples:

Italo- prefix UK /ɪt.ə.ləʊ-/ /ɪ.tæl.əʊ-/ US /ɪt.ə.loʊ-/ /ɪ.tæl.oʊ-/ 意大利的；与意大利相连的 of or connected with Italy

an Italo-German production   意德联合制作

JJJ
N/A

KKK
Prefix (Medical): kal/i (potassium)
Meaning in English: potassium

Origin language: Latin

English examples:

potassium   noun [U] UK /pəˈtæs.i.əm/ US /pəˈtæs.i.əm/ (symbol K) 钾 a silver-white chemical element that, when combined with other elements, is used in the production of soap, glass, and fertilizers (= substances that help plants to grow)

Prefix (Medical): karyo- nucleus
Meaning in English: nucleus

Origin language: Greek κάρυον, "nut"

English examples:

eukaryote   noun [C]   BIOLOGY   specialized /juːˈkær.i.əʊt/ /juːˈkær.i.oʊt/ 真核生物 a type of organism that has one or more cells each with a separate nucleus (= central part) containing chromosomes, which includes all animals and plants

prokaryotic adjective BIOLOGY specialized UK /prəʊ.kær.iˈɒt.ɪk/ US /proʊ.ker.iˈɑ ː.t̬ɪk/ 原核生物的 of or relating to single-cell organisms with no nucleus, such as bacteria

Prefix (Medical): kerat(o)- cornea (eye or skin)

Meaning in English: cornea (eye or skin)

Origin language: Greek

English examples:

keratin noun [U] BIOLOGY specialized UK /ˈker.ə.tɪn/ US /ˈker.ə.tɪn/ 角蛋白（一种坚韧、无色的天然蛋白质，是发、甲、蹄、角、羽毛等的主要组成物） a strong natural protein, the main substance that forms hair, nails, hoofs, horns, feathers, etc.

keratoconus noun [U] MEDICAL specialized UK /ˌke.rə.təˈkəʊ.nəs/ US /ˌker.ə.t̬əˈkoʊ.nəs/ 圆锥形角膜 an eye problem that changes the shape of the cornea (= the transparent outer covering of the eye) and affects the ability to see normally

In advanced cases of keratoconus, corneal transplant surgery is required. 严重圆锥形角膜需要做角膜移植。

Keratoscope noun [U] 角膜镜 A keratoscope, sometimes known as Placido's disk, is an ophthalmic instrument used to assess the shape of the anterior surface of the cornea. A series of concentric rings is projected onto the cornea and their reflection viewed by the examiner through a small hole in the centre of the disk. Wikipedia

Prefix: kilo- 1,000 times the stated unit

Meaning in English:

Origin language: Latin

English examples:

kilo- 2 prefix SCIENCE UK /ki:.ləʊ-/ US /ki:.loʊ-/ 千 1,000 times the stated unit

千瓦 kilowatt

千赫兹 kilohertz

kilo 1 noun [C] UK /ˈki:.ləʊ/ US /ˈki:.loʊ/ plural kilos A2 千克，公斤 a kilogram

kilobyte 1 noun [C] COMPUTING specialized UK /ˈkɪl.ə.baɪt/ US /ˈkɪl.ə.baɪt/ (abbreviation KB, Kb)

kilogram noun [C] UK /ˈkɪl.ə.græm/ US /ˈkɪl.ə.græm/ (written abbreviation kg) A2 千克，公斤 a unit of mass equal to 1,000 grams

kilohertz noun [C] UK /ˈkɪl.ə.hɜːts/ US /ˈkɪl.ə.hɝːts/ plural kilohertz (written abbreviation kHz) 千赫兹 a unit of measurement of radio waves that is equal to 1,000 hertz

kilojoule noun [C] PHYSICS specialized UK /ˈkɪl.əʊ.dʒuːl/ US /ˈkɪl.oʊ.dʒuːl/ (written abbreviation kJ) 千焦耳（1000 焦耳的能量或所作功的单位） a unit of measurement equal to 1,000 joules (= measure of energy or work done)

kilometre noun [C] UK (US kilometer) UK /ˈkɪl.əˌmiː.tər/ US /kɪˈlɑː.mə.tɚ/ (written abbreviation km) 千米，公里 A2 a unit of measurement equal to 1,000 metres

kilowatt noun [C] UK /ˈkɪl.ə.wɒt/ US /ˈkɪl.ə.wɑːt/ (written abbreviation kW) 千瓦 a unit of power equal to 1,000 watts

Prefix (Medical): kin(e)-, kin(o), kinesi(o)- movement

Meaning in English: movement, motion

Origin language: Greek κινέω

English examples:

kinaesthesia   noun [U] UK (US kinesthesia) UK /ˌkɪn.isˈθiː.zi.ə/ US /ˌkɪn.isˈθiː.zi.ə/ 动觉，（肌肉等的）运动感觉 the ability to know where the parts of your body are and how they are moving

kinesics   1 noun   SOCIAL SCIENCE   specialized /kɪˈniː.sɪks/ [U] 身势学，动作神态学 the study of how people use body movements when they are communicating with other people 2 noun   [plural]（与人交流时的）动作，身势 the movements of the body that people make when they are communicating with other people

kinesthetic   adjective 动觉的 US spelling of kinaesthetic

kinaesthetic   adjective 动觉的 connected with the ability to know where the parts of your body are and how they are moving:

kinesiologist   noun [C] UK /kɪˌniː.siˈɒl.ə.dʒɪst/ US /-ˈɑ l.ə.dʒɪst/ 人体运动学家 a person who studies the science of body movement

kinesiology   noun [U] UK /kɪˌniː.siˈɒl.ə.dʒi/ US /-ˈɑ l.ə.dʒi/ 人体运动学 the science of body movement

kinesiology tape   noun [U] UK /kɪˌniː.siˈɒl.ə.dʒi ˌteɪp/ /kɪˌniː.siˈ ɑ ː.lə.dʒi ˌteɪp/ (also informal K-tape) 肌内效运动贴布，机能运动贴布 a type of tape (= a long, narrow strip of material that is sticky on one side) that is stuck on injured parts of the body in order to support muscles and joints without affecting the body's range of movement

kinesthesia   noun [U] UK /ˌkɪn.isˈθiː.zi.ə/ US /ˌkɪn.isˈθiː.zi.ə/ US spelling of kinaesthesia （kinaesthesia 的美式拼写） the ability to know where the parts of your body are and how they are moving 动觉，（肌肉等的）运动感觉

Psychokinesis   念力 Psychokinesis, or telekinesis, is a claimed psychic ability allowing a person to influence a physical system without physical interaction. Psychokinesis experiments have historically been criticized for lack of proper controls and repeatability. Wikipedia

kinetic   adjective [before noun] UK /kɪˈnet.ɪk/ US /kɪˈneţ.ɪk/ specialized 运动的；运动引起的 involving or producing movement

kinetics   noun [U] UK /kɪˈnet.ɪks/ US /kɪˈneţ.ɪks/ specialized 动力学 the scientific study of forces on things that are moving

kinetic art   noun [U]   ART   specialized UK /kɪˌnet.ɪk ˈɑ:t/ /kɪˌneţ.ɪk ˈɑ:rt/ （雕塑等所表现出的）动态艺术 art that involves movement in some way, for example sculptures (= objects formed from clay, wood, etc.) with moving parts

kinetic energy   noun [U]   PHYSICS   specialized UK /kɪˌnet.ɪk ˈen.ə.dʒi/ US /kɪˌneţ.ɪk ˈen.ɚ.dʒi/ 动能 energy that an object or system has because it is moving

kinetics   noun [U]   PHYSICS   specialized UK /kɪˈnet.ɪks/ US /kɪˈneţ.ɪks/动力学 the scientific study of forces on things that are moving

kinetoscope   noun [C] UK /kɪnˈet.ə.skəʊp/ US /kɪnˈeţ.ə.skoʊp/ 活动物体的连续照片放映机（早期的电影放映机） an object containing a very small hole through which a person watched a film in the early days of film

Meaning in English: hollow

Origin language: Greek κοῖλος (koilos)

English examples:

Koilocyte   noun [U] 挖空细胞，也称为晕细胞 Koilocytes, also known as halo cells, are a type of epithelial cell that develops following a human papillomavirus (HPV) infection. Koilocytes are structurally different from other epithelial cells. For instance, their nuclei, which contain the cell's DNA, are an irregular size, shape, or color.

Meaning in English: humped

Origin language: LGreek κυφός

English examples:

kyphosis   noun [U]   MEDICAL   specialized UK /kaɪˈfəʊ.sɪs/ US /kaɪˈfoʊ.sɪs/ 驼背 (Google) a condition in which someone's spine (= the line of bones down their back) curves outwards too much

Kyphoscoliosis   noun [U] 脊柱侧凸 Kyphoscoliosis is a thoracic cage deformity that causes extrapulmonary restriction of the lungs and gives rise to impairment of pulmonary functions, as described earlier for restrictive lung diseases. The condition may be primary (idiopathic) or secondary to neuromuscular disease, spondylitis, or Marfan syndrome. (ScienceDirect); Kyphoscoliosis describes an abnormal curvature of the spine in both a coronal and sagittal plane. It is a combination of kyphosis and scoliosis. Wikipedia

Cyphosis   noun [U] 脊柱后凸 Kyphosis (Cyphosis) is curvature of the spine that causes the top of the back to appear more rounded than normal. Everyone has some degree of curvature in their spine. However, a curve of more than 45 degrees is considered excessive.

lordosis   noun [U]   MEDICAL   specialized UK /lɔːˈdəʊ.sɪs/ US
/lɔːrˈdoʊ.sɪs/ 脊柱前凸 (Google) a condition in which someone's spine (= the
line of bones down their back) curves inwards too much

LLL

Prefix (Medical): labi(o)- Of or pertaining to the lip
Meaning in English: Of or pertaining to the lip

Origin language: Latin (labium), lip

English examples:

bilabial   adjective phonetics specialized UK /ˌbaɪˈleɪ.bi.əl/ US
/ˌbaɪˈleɪ.bi.əl/（语音）双唇的 (of a sound) made using both lips

labial   1 adjective   specialized UK /ˈleɪ.bi.əl/ US /ˈleɪ.bi.əl/
PHONETICS 唇音的 Labial sounds are consonant sounds made with the two
lips.

/m/和/p/都是唇音。   /m/ and /p/ are labial sounds.

labial   2 MEDICAL relating to the lips 唇的

labial surgery   唇部手术

labial   3 MEDICAL 阴唇的 relating to the folds on the outside of the
female sex organs

labial herpes   生殖器疱疹

labial   noun [C] PHONETICS specialized 唇音 UK /ˈleɪ.bi.əl/ US
/ˈleɪ.bi.əl/ a consonant sound that is made with the two lips

bilabiate   having two lips   Prefix (Medical): labi(o)- Of or pertaining to the
lip

labiodental   adjective /ˌleɪbɪəʊˈdɛnt(ə)l/ PHONETICS 唇齿音 (of a
sound) made with the lips and teeth, for example f and v.

infralabial Adjective 1 (not comparable) (zoology) Below the lower lip; said of certain scales of reptiles and fishes.

labii noun [plural] MEDICAL specialized UK /ˈleɪ.bi.aɪ/ US /ˈleɪ.biˌaɪ/ （拉丁语，用于医学术语）唇 a Latin word meaning "of the labium" (= a lip or fold on the outside of the female sex organs), used in medical names and descriptions

Cleft lip and cleft palate 唇裂与腭裂；俗称兔唇或兔瓣嘴

cleft lip noun [C] UK /ˌkleft ˈlɪp/ US /ˌkleft ˈlɪp/ 唇裂，兔唇 an upper lip that does not join in the middle because it did not develop normally before birth

cleft palate ˡnoun [C] UK /ˌkleft ˈpæl.ət/ US /ˌkleft ˈpæl.ət/ 腭裂 èliè, an opening in the top of the mouth caused when a baby does not develop normally before it is born

labium 1 noun [C usually plural] UK /ˈleɪ.bi.əm/ US /ˈleɪ.bi.əm/ plural labia UK /ˈleɪ.bi.ə/ US labia 阴唇 folds on the outside of the female sex organs 2 noun ANATOMY specialized 唇，（身体上的）唇状组织 a lip or a structure in the body that looks like a lip

syllabic adjective LANGUAGE specialized UK /sɪˈlæb.ɪk/ US /sɪˈlæb.ɪk/ consisting of or relating to syllables:

disyllabic （单词）双音节的 (of a word) having two syllables

monosyllabic 单音节的 containing only one syllable

trisyllabic adjective LANGUAGE specialized UK /ˌtraɪ.sɪˈlæb.ɪk/ US /ˌtraɪ.sɪˈlæb.ɪk/ (of a word) having three syllables:

Prefix (Medical): lacrim(o)- tear

Meaning in English: tear

Origin language: Latin

English examples:

lachrymose adjective literary UK /ˈlæk.rɪ.məʊs/ US /ˈlæk.rɪ.moʊs/ lacrimous 悲伤的；爱哭的，容易落泪的 sad or likely to cry often and easily [GRE]

He is better known for his lachrymose ballads than hard rock numbers. 他的伤感民谣比他的硬摇滚乐更加广为人知。

lacrimal adjective MEDICAL specialized (also lachrymal) UK /ˈlæk.rɪ.məl/ US /ˈlæk.rə.məl/ 泪的 relating to tears from the eyes

lacrimalis adjective MEDICAL specialized UK /ˌlæk.rɪˈmɑːl.ɪs/ US /ˌlæk.rɪˈmæl.ɪs/ （拉丁语，用于医学用语）泪的 a Latin word meaning "lacrimal", used in the names of parts of the body connected with tears

Lacrimal canaliculi noun [C] 泪小管 The lacrimal canaliculi, (sing. canaliculus), are the small channels in each eyelid that drain lacrimal fluid, from the lacrimal puncta to the lacrimal sac. This forms part of the lacrimal apparatus that drains lacrimal fluid from the surface of the eye to the nasal cavity.

Canaliculitis noun [U] 小管炎 Canaliculitis is inflammation of the canaliculus.

lacrimal gland　　noun [C] 泪腺 The lacrimal gland is a bilobed, tear-shaped gland with the primary function of secreting the aqueous portion of the tear film, thereby maintaining the ocular surface. It is primarily located in the anterior, superotemporal orbit within the lacrimal fossa of the frontal bone.

Prefix (Medical): lact(i)-, lact(o)- milk

Meaning in English: milk

Origin language: Latin

English examples:

lactate　　verb [I]　BIOLOGY　specialized UK /læk'teɪt/ US /'læk.teɪt/ （妇女或雌性动物）泌乳，哺乳 (of a woman or female mammal) to produce milk

lactation　　noun [U]　BIOLOGY　specialized UK /læk'teɪ.ʃən/ US /læk'teɪ.ʃən/ 泌乳 the process in which a woman or female animal produces milk

Lactase　　noun [U] 乳糖酶 Lactase is an enzyme produced by many organisms. It is located in the brush border of the small intestine of humans and other mammals. Lactase is essential to the complete digestion of whole milk; it breaks down lactose, a sugar which gives milk its sweetness. Wikipedia

lacteal　　1 adjective UK /'læk.ti.əl/ US /'læk.ti.əl/ 乳的；产生乳汁的；乳汁状的 relating to, producing, or like milk

lactic　　adjective　BIOLOGY　specialized UK /'læk.tɪk/ US /'læk.tɪk/ 乳汁的，奶的 relating to milk

lactic acid　　noun [U] UK /ˌlæk.tɪk 'æs.ɪd/ US /ˌlæk.tɪk 'æs.ɪd/ 乳酸 an acid that exists in sour milk and is produced in muscles after a lot of exercise

lacto-vegetarian   noun [C] UK / ˌlæk.təʊ.vedʒ.ɪˈteə.ri.ən/ US /ˌlæk.toʊ.vedʒ.əˈter.i.ən/ 乳类素食者 a person who does not eat meat, fish, or eggs but does drink milk and eat some foods made from milk

ovo-vegetarian   noun [C] UK /ˌəʊ.vəʊ.vedʒ.ɪˈteə.ri.ən/ /ˌoʊ.voʊ.vedʒ.ɪˈter.i-/ （不吃鱼、肉和奶制品，但是吃蛋的）素食者 a person who does not eat meat, fish, or dairy products (= milk or foods made from milk) but does eat eggs

lactose intolerance   noun [U] UK /ˌlæk.təʊs ɪnˈtɒl.ər.əns/ US /ˌlæk.toʊs ɪnˈtɑː.lɚ.əns/ Medical Specialized 乳糖不耐症 the inability to digest lactose (= a substance in milk)

crusta lactea   noun [U] medical specialized UK /ˌkrʌs.tə ˈlæk.ti.ə/ US /ˌkrʌs.tə ˈlæk.ti.ə/ 乳痂（cradle cap 的医学名称） a medical name for cradle cap

galactic   adjective UK /gəˈlæk.tɪk/ US /gəˈlæk.tɪk/ 银河的；星系的 relating to the Galaxy or other galaxies

(Root: galact- Meaning in English: milk)

Galactorrhea   noun [U] 溢乳 Galactorrhea (guh-lack-toe-REE-uh) is a milky nipple discharge unrelated to the normal milk production of breast-feeding. Galactorrhea itself isn't a disease, but it could be a sign of an underlying problem. It usually occurs in women, even those who have never had children or after menopause.

stalactite   noun [C] UK /ˈstæl.ək.taɪt/ US /ˈstæl.ək.taɪt/ 钟乳石 a column of rock that hangs from the roof of a cave and is formed over a very long period of time by drops of water containing lime falling from the roof

Meaning in English: Of or pertaining to the abdomen-wall, flank

Origin language: Ancient Greek λαπάρā (lapárā), flank

English examples:

laparoscopic   adjective   MEDICAL   specialized UK /ˌlæp.ə.rəˈskɒp.ɪk/ US /ˌlæp.ɚ.əˈsk ɑ :p.ɪk/ 使用腹腔镜的 relating to laparoscopy (= the use of a long thin tube put into a cut made in the body in order to examine inside the body or do an operation)

laparoscopic surgery   腹腔镜手术

laparoscopy   noun [C or U]   MEDICAL   specialized UK /ˌlæp.əˈrɒs.kə.pi/ US /ˌlæp.əˈr ɑ :s.kə.pi/ 腹腔镜 the use of a long thin tube put into a cut made in the body in order to examine inside the body or do an operation

Typically, patients would prefer laparoscopy to an open surgery.   一般来说，与开腹手术相比，患者更倾向于接受腹腔镜手术。

laparotomy   noun [C or U]   MEDICAL   specialized UK /ˌlæp.əˈrɒt.ə.mi/ US /ˌlæp.əˈr ɑ :t̬.ə.mi/ 剖腹术 the act of making a cut through the wall of the abdomen, usually to examine the abdominal organs

removal of an ovarian tumor by laparotomy 通过剖腹术对卵巢肿瘤的切除

flank   noun [C] UK /flæŋk/ US /flæŋk/ flank noun [C] (BODY) （动物或人体的）胁腹 the area of the body between the ribs and the hips of an animal or a person

Meaning in English: Of or pertaining to the larynx, the lower throat cavity where the voice box is

Origin language: Ancient Greek λάρυγξ, λαρυγγ- (lárynx, laryng-), throat, gullet

English examples:

laryngeal adjective MEDICAL specialized UK /ləˈrɪn.dʒi.əl/ US /ləˈrɪn.dʒi.əl/ 喉的 relating to the larynx (= the organ that creates someone's voice)

laryngeal cancer 喉癌

laryngitis noun [U] UK /ˌlær.ɪnˈdʒaɪ.tɪs/ US /ˌler.ɪnˈdʒaɪ.t̬əs/ 喉炎 a painful swelling of the larynx, usually caused by an infection

laryngoscope noun [C] MEDICAL specialized UK /ləˈrɪŋ.gə.skəʊp/ US /ləˈrɪŋ.gə.skoʊp/ 喉镜，检喉镜 a device for examining the larynx (= the organ containing the muscles that create the human voice or animal sounds), or for putting a tube into the throat

用喉镜来查看会厌。 A laryngoscope is used to expose the epiglottis.

laryngoscopy noun [C or U] MEDICAL specialized UK /ˌlær.ɪŋˈgɒs.kə.pi/ US /ˌler.ɪŋˈgɒs.kə.pi/ 喉镜检查 an examination of the throat, including the parts that create the voice, using a long thin tube

医生让我做喉镜检查。 My doctor sent me for a laryngoscopy.

larynx noun [C] ANATOMY specialized UK /ˈlær.ɪŋks/ US /ˈler.ɪŋks/ plural larynxes or specialized larynges UK /lærˈɪn.dʒiːz/ US 喉，喉头 an organ in humans and animals between the nose and the lungs that contains the muscles that move very quickly to create the voice or animal sounds

Synonym

voice box noun [C usually singular] UK /ˈvɔɪs ˌbɒks/ US /ˈvɔɪs ˌbɑːks/ 喉，喉头 an organ that contains the muscles that move to create the voice

otolaryngology   noun [U]   MEDICAL   specialized UK /ˌəʊ.təʊ.lær.ɪŋˈɡɒl.ə.dʒi/ US /ˌoʊ.t̬oʊ.ler.ɪŋˈɡ ɑ ːlə.dʒi/ 耳鼻喉科 the study of diseases of the ear and throat

Prefix (Medical): latero- lateral

Meaning in English: lateral

Origin language: Latin

English examples:

anterolateral   adjective UK /ˌæn.tə.rəʊˈlæt.ər.əl/ US /ˌæn.tə.roʊˈlæt̬.ɚ.əl/ specialized 前外侧的 in front of and to one side of another part of the body

bilateral   adjective UK /ˌbaɪˈlæt.ər.əl/ US /ˌbaɪˈlæt̬.ɚ.əl/双边的，双方的 involving two groups or countries

contralateral   adjective medical specialized UK /ˌkɒn.trəˈlæt.ər.əl/ US /ˌk ɑ ːn.trəˈlæt̬.ɚ.əl/（身体）对侧的 on or affecting the opposite side of the body

lateral   1 adjective UK /ˈlæt.ər.əl/ US /ˈlæt̬.ɚ.əl/ [before noun] BIOLOGY, MEDICAL formal or specialized 侧面的；横向运动的 relating to the sides of an object or plant or to sideways movement

横向运动   lateral movement

lateral thinking   noun [U] UK /ˌlæt.rəl ˈθɪŋ.kɪŋ/ US /ˌlæt̬.ɚ.əl ˈθɪŋ.kɪŋ/ 水平思考，横向思维（指用想象力寻求解决问题的新办法） a way of solving a problem by thinking about it in a different and original way and not using traditional or expected methods

lateralis   adjective MEDICAL specialized UK /læt.əˈr ɑ ːl.ɪs/ US /ˌlæt.əˈræl.ɪs/（拉丁语，用于医学术语）侧的 a Latin word meaning "lateral"

(= relating to the sides of an object or to sideways movement), used in medical names and descriptions

Lateral pectoral nerve   noun [U] 胸外侧神经 The lateral pectoral nerve arises from the fifth through to the seventh cervical nerves (C5 - C7) and is the larger of the two pectoral nerves. It arises from the lateral cord or from the anterior divisions of the upper and middle trunks.

Prefix (Medical): lei(o)- smooth

Meaning in English: smooth

Origin language: Greek λεῖος

English examples:

leiomyoma   noun [C]   MEDICAL   specialized UK /ˌlaɪ.əʊ.maɪˈəʊ.mə/ US /ˌlaɪ.oʊ.maɪˈoʊ.mə/ 平滑肌瘤 a benign tumour (= one that is not likely to cause death) of muscle tissue, especially in the uterus (= the organ in a woman's body where a baby develops)

lei   noun [C] UK /ˈleɪ.i:/ US /ˈleɪ.i:/ plural leis （常戴在脖子上的）花环 a circle of flowers that is worn around the neck in Polynesia

Prefix (Medical): lept(o)- light, slender

Meaning in English: light, slender

Origin language: Greek λεπτός (leptos)

English examples:

antilepton noun [C] UK /ˌæn.tiˈlep.tɒn/ US /ˌæn.t̬iˈlep.tɑːn/反轻子 the antiparticle of a lepton

lepton   noun [C]   PHYSICS   specialized UK /ˈlep.tɒn/ US /ˈlep.tɑːn/ 轻子 any very small piece of matter that is influenced by the weak force. electrons, muons, and neutrinos are all leptons.

leptospirosis   noun [U]   MEDICAL   specialized UK
/ˌlep.təʊ.spɪˈrəʊ.sɪs/ US /ˌlep.toʊ.spəˈroʊ.sɪs/ 细螺旋体病（一种由细菌引起的传染病，损坏肝脏和肾脏，主要见于狗等牲畜） an infectious disease that damages the liver and kidneys, found mainly in dogs and farm animals and caused by bacteria

Prefix (Medical): leuc(o)-, leuk(o)- Denoting a white color

Meaning in English: Denoting a white color

Origin language: Ancient Greek λευκός (leukos), white, bright

English examples:

leucocyte   noun [C]   BIOLOGY   Medical Specialized UK specialized (US leukocyte) UK /ˈljuː.kə.saɪt/ US /ˈluː.kə.saɪt/ a white blood cell 白血球（同 white blood cell）

feline leukaemia   猫白血病

leucotomy   noun [C] UK UK /luːˈkɒt.ə.mi/ US /luːˈkɑː.t̬ə.mi/ 脑白质切断手术，脑叶切除手术（同 lobotomy） a lobotomy

leukaemia   noun [U] uk us leukemia UK /luːˈkiː.mi.ə/ US /luːˈkiː.mi.ə/ 白血病 a serious disease in which the body produces too many white blood cells

Prefix (Medical): lingu(a)-, lingu(o)- Of or pertaining to the tongue
Meaning in English: Of or pertaining to the tongue

Origin language: Latin (lingua), tongue

English examples:

bilingual   adjective UK /baɪˈlɪŋ.gwəl/ US /baɪˈlɪŋ.gwəl/能用两种语言的；两种语言的 C1 (of a person) able to use two languages equally well, or (of a thing) using or involving two languages

lingual   adjective   MEDICAL   specialized UK /ˈlɪŋ.gwəl/ US /ˈlɪŋ.gwəl/ 舌的 relating to the tongue

linguist   noun [C]   LANGUAGE, EDUCATION UK /ˈlɪŋ.gwɪst/ US /ˈlɪŋ.gwɪst/ 语言学家，语言学者；通晓数国语言的人 someone who studies foreign languages or can speak them very well, or someone who teaches or studies linguistics

linguistic   adjective UK /lɪŋˈgwɪs.tɪk/ US /lɪŋˈgwɪs.tɪk/ C1 语言的；语言学的 connected with language or the study of language

linguistics   noun [U] UK /lɪŋˈgwɪs.tɪks/ US /lɪŋˈgwɪs.tɪks/ (also linguistic science) 语言学 the scientific study of the structure and development of language in general or of particular languages

multilingual   adjective UK /ˌmʌl.tiˈlɪŋ.gwəl/ US /ˌmʌl.tiˈlɪŋ.gwəl/ 使用多种语言的；用多种语言表达的 (of people or groups) able to use more than two languages for communication, or (of a thing) written or spoken in more than two different languages

monolingual   adjective UK /ˌmɒn.əʊˈlɪŋ.gwəl/ US /ˌmɑːnoʊˈlɪŋ.gwəl/ 只使用一种语言的，单语的 speaking or using only one language

neurolinguistics   noun [U] UK /ˌnjʊə.rəʊ.lɪŋˈgwɪs.tɪks/ US /ˌnʊr.oʊ.lɪŋˈgwɪs.tɪks/ 神经语言学 the study of the relationship between language and the brain

sociolinguistic   adjective UK /ˌsəʊ.si.əʊ.lɪŋˈgwɪs.tɪk/ US /ˌsoʊ.si.oʊ.lɪŋˈgwɪs.tɪk/ 社会语言学的 connected with how language is used by different groups in society, or with the study of this

sublingual adjective   MEDICAL   specialized UK /ˌsʌbˈlɪŋ.gwəl/ US /ˌsʌbˈlɪŋ.gwəl/ 舌下的 under the tongue

trilingual adjective UK /ˌtraɪˈlɪŋ.gwəl/ US /ˌtraɪˈlɪŋ.gwəl/ 能讲三种语言的 able to speak three languages

Prefix (Medical): lip(o)- fat

Meaning in English: fat

Origin language: Latin

English examples:

atypical lipoma   noun [C] UK /eɪˌtɪp.ɪ.kəl lɪˈpəʊ.mə/ US /eɪˌtɪp.ɪ.kəl lɪˈpoʊ.mə/ specialized 非典型脂肪瘤 a soft mass of fat cells that grows under the skin and is found in the fat cell tissues on the back of the neck, shoulders, and back

Lipomas   noun [U] 脂肪瘤 Lipomas are soft, movable, subcutaneous nodules of adipocytes (fat cells); overlying skin appears normal.

liposome   noun [C]   MEDICAL   specialized UK /ˈlɪp.ə.səʊm/ US /ˈlɪp.ə.soʊm/ 脂质体（一种由脂质的人造微小脂囊，将药物、疫苗或其它物质携带到机体的特定细胞） an extremely small sac (= bag) made artificially from a type of lipid to carry a drug, vaccine, or other substance to particular cells in the body

liposuction noun [U] UK /ˈlɪp.əʊˌsʌk.ʃən/ US /ˈlaɪ.poʊˌsʌk.ʃən/ (informal lipo, /ˈlɪp.əʊ/ /ˈlaɪ.poʊ/) 吸脂术；脂肪抽吸术 an operation in which fat is sucked out from under the skin

Lipolysis   脂肪分解 Lipolysis is the metabolic pathway through which lipid triglycerides are hydrolyzed into a glycerol and three fatty acids. It is used to mobilize stored energy during fasting or exercise, and usually occurs in fat adipocytes. Wikipedia

Prefix (Medical): lith(o)- stone, calculus
Meaning in English: stone, calculus

Origin language: Greek λίθος

English examples:

lithograph noun [C] UK /ˈlɪθ.ə.grɑːf/ US /ˈlɪθ.oʊ.græf/ 平版印刷画，石版画 a picture printed using a stone or metal block on which an image has been drawn with a thick substance that attracts ink

megalith noun [C] UK /ˈmeg.ə.lɪθ/ US /ˈmeg.ə.lɪθ/ 巨石 a large stone, sometimes forming part of a group or circle, thought to have been important to people in the Stone Age for social or religious reasons

mesolithic adjective SCIENCE specialized /ˌmesəˈlɪθ.ɪk/ UK /ˌmes.əˈlɪθ.ɪk/ US /ˌmez.əˈlɪθ.ɪk/ 中石器时代的 relating to the middle part of the Stone Age (= the period when humans used tools and weapons made of stone)

monolith 1 noun [C] UK /ˈmɒn.ə.lɪθ/ US /ˈmɑː.nə.lɪθ/ [C] (STONE) （古人竖立的）独块巨石，独石柱 a large block of stone standing by itself that was put up by people in ancient times

Lithophyte 岩生植物 Lithophytes are plants that grow in or on rocks. They can be classified as either epilithic or endolithic; epilithic lithophytes grow on the surfaces of rocks, while endolithic lithophytes grow in the crevices of rocks. Lithophytes can also be classified as being either obligate or facultative. Wikipedia

the lithosphere noun [S] ENVIRONMENT specialized UK /ˈlɪθ.ə.sfɪər/ US /ˈlɪθ.ə.sfɪr/ （地球）岩石圈 the solid outer layer of the earth

Lithotripsy noun [U] 碎石术 Lithotripsy is a non-invasive procedure involving the physical destruction of hardened masses like kidney stones, bezoars or gallstones. The term is derived from the Greek words meaning "breaking stones". Wikipedia

Prefix: log(o)- speech

Meaning in English: speech

Origin language: Greek λόγος

English examples:

logograph noun [C] LANGUAGE specialized UK /ˈlɒg.ə.grɑːf/ US /ˈlɑː.goʊ.græf/ (also logogram, /ˈlɒg.ə.græm/ /ˈlɑː.goʊ.græm/) 语标，缩记符（如& 、@等）；非字母语言的字符 a symbol such as & or @ that stands for a word, or a character in a language that does not use the Roman alphabet (= the letters A to Z)

汉字相当于英文单词。 Chinese logographs are used as equivalents of English words.

logophile noun [C] formal UK /ˈlɒg.ə.faɪl/ US /ˈlɑː.g.ə.faɪl/ 爱好词语的人 a person who loves words and language

Prefix (Medical): lymph(o)- lymph

Meaning in English: lymph

Origin language: Latin

English examples: Greek λέμφος, λύμφη

lymph noun [U] UK /lɪmf/ US /lɪmf/ 淋巴液 a clear liquid that transports useful substances around the body, and carries waste matter, such as unwanted bacteria, away from body tissue in order to prevent infection

lymph gland   noun [C]   ANATOMY UK /ˈlɪmf ˌglænd/ US /ˈlɪmf ˌglænd/ (also lymph node) 淋巴腺，淋巴结 one of many small organs in the body that produce the white blood cells needed for the body to fight infection

lymph vessel   noun [C]   MEDICAL   specialized UK /ˈlɪmf ˌves.əl/ US /ˈlɪmf ˌves.əl/ (also lymphatic vessel) 淋巴管（淋巴液流通的细小管道，沿着淋巴管分布着淋巴腺） any of the thin tubes in the body through which lymph flows, and along which lymph glands are found

lymphatic   adjective MEDICAL   specialized UK /lɪmˈfæt.ɪk/ US /lɪmˈfæt̬.ɪk/ 淋巴液的 relating to lymph (= a liquid that transports useful substances around the body and carries waste matter away from body tissue)

lymphatic drainage/system/tissue   淋巴引流 / 系统 / 组织

lymphatics   noun [plural] MEDICAL   specialized UK /lɪmˈfæt.ɪks/ US /lɪmˈfæt̬.ɪks/ 淋巴系统 the system of tubes that transport lymph around the body

lymphedema   noun [U]   MEDICAL UK /lɪm.fəˈdiːmə/ US /ˌlɪm.fəˈdiːmə/ （lymphoedema 的美式拼写） US spelling of lymphoedema

lymphocyte   noun [C]   BIOLOGY   specialized UK /ˈlim.fə.saɪt/ US /ˈlim.fə.saɪt/ 淋巴细胞（一种杀死体内疾病和感染的白细胞，一些淋巴细胞还可以产生杀死有害细菌的抗体蛋白） a type of white blood cell involved in fighting disease and infection in the body, some of which produce antibodies (= proteins that attack and kill harmful bacteria)

lymphocytopenia   noun [U]   MEDICAL   specialized UK /ˌlɪm.fəʊ.saɪt.əˈpiːn.i.ə/ US /ˌlɪm.foʊ ˌsaɪ.t̬əˈpiː.ni.ə/ 淋巴细胞减少症 a condition in which the body does not have enough of a type of cell called a lymphocyte, which makes it more difficult for the body to fight infection

lymphoedema   noun [U]   MEDICAL   specialized (US lymphedema) UK /lɪm.fəˈdiːmə/ US /ˌlɪm.fəˈdiːmə/ 淋巴水肿 a condition in which body tissues become swollen because lymph cannot be carried away from them

Removing the lymph glands can sometimes lead to swelling known as lymphoedema.   移除淋巴腺有时候会造成水肿，称为淋巴水肿。

lymphoma   noun [U]   MEDICAL   specialized UK /lɪmˈfəʊ.mə/ US /lɪmˈfoʊ.mə/ 淋巴瘤 a cancer of the lymphatic system (= the system by which lymph in carried from tissues to the blood)

Prefix (Medical): lys(o)- dissolution

Meaning in English: dissolution

Origin language: Greek

English examples:

lysine   noun [U]   BIOLOGY   specialized UK /ˈlaɪ.siːn/ US /ˈlaɪ.siːn/ 赖氨酸 an amino acid that is necessary for growth and healthy bones

lysosomal disorder   noun [U]   MEDICAL   specialized UK /laɪ.səˈsəʊ.məl dɪˌsɔːd.ər/ US /ˌlaɪ.səˈsoʊ.məl dɪˌsɔːr.dɚ/ 溶酶体贮积症 a genetic condition in which the body cannot break down substances such as lipids, proteins, and carbohydrates

Lysosome   noun [U] 溶酶体 A lysosome is a membrane-bound cell organelle that contains digestive enzymes. Lysosomes are involved with various cell processes. They break down excess or worn-out cell parts. They may be used to destroy invading viruses and bacteria.

Prefix: Luso- relating to Portugal or the Portuguese language
Meaning in English: relating to Portugal or the Portuguese language

Origin language: Latin/Greek

English examples:

Luso- prefix /ˈluːsəʊ-/ UK /luːsəʊ-/ US /luːsoʊ-/ 葡萄牙的；葡萄牙语的 relating to Portugal or the Portuguese language

这一研究有关葡萄牙语美国文学，即身在北美的葡萄牙语作家的文学作品。
This is a study of Luso-American Literature, that is writings by Portuguese-speaking authors in North America.

MMM

Prefix: macro- large; relating to the whole of something, rather than its parts
Meaning in English:

Origin language: Greek μακρός

English examples:

macro- prefix UK /mæk.rəʊ-/ US /mæk.roʊ-/ 大的；宏观的 large; relating to the whole of something, rather than its parts

macrobiotic adjective UK /ˌmæk.rəʊ.baɪˈɒt.ɪk/ US /ˌmæk.roʊ.baɪˈɑː.t̬ɪk/ （食品）健康的，绿色的 Macrobiotic food is arranged into groups according to special principles, grown without chemicals, and thought to be very healthy.

macrocosm noun [C] UK /ˈmæk.rəʊˌkɒz.əm/ US /ˈmæk.roʊˌkɑː.zəm/ 宏观世界；整体 any large organized system considered as a whole, rather than as a group of smaller systems

macroeconomics　　　　noun [U]　FINANCE & ECONOMICS　specialized UK /ˌmæk.rəʊ.iːkəˈnɒm.ɪks/ US /ˌmæk.roʊ.e.kəˈnɑː.mɪks/ 宏观经济学 the study of financial systems at a national level

macroglobulinaemia　　noun [U]　MEDICAL　UK specialized (US macroglobulinemia) UK /ˌmæk.rəʊ.glɒb.jə.lɪˈniː.mi.ə/ US /ˈmæk.roʊ.glɑːb.jə.lɪˈniː.mi.ə/ 巨球蛋白血症 a condition in which the blood contains too many proteins, resulting in anaemia and an enlarged spleen, liver, and lymph nodes

macromolecule　　noun [C] UK /ˈmæk.rəʊˌmɒl.ɪ.kjuːl/ US /ˈmæk.roʊˌmɑː.lɪ.kjuːl/ 大分子，据分子 a large molecule, for example a protein

macrophage　　noun [C]　BIOLOGY　specialized UK /ˈmæk.rəˈfeɪdʒ/ US /ˈmæk.rəˌfeɪdʒ/ 巨噬细胞 a large white blood cell in the immune system that destroys bacteria and other harmful substances

macroscopic　　1 adjective UK /ˌmæk.rəˈskɒp.ɪk/ US /ˌmæk.rəˈskɑː.pɪk/ 肉眼可见的 large enough to be seen without using any devices that make things look larger

Prefix: mal- badly or wrongly
Meaning in English:

Origin language: Latin/Greek

English examples:

mal-　　　　prefix　formal UK /mæl-/ US /mæl-/ badly or wrongly 坏；不当；错误地

maladjusted　　adjective UK /ˌmæl.əˈdʒʌs.tɪd/ US /ˌmæl.əˈdʒʌs.tɪd/（通常指儿童）不适应社会环境的，适应不良的 A maladjusted person, usually a child, has been raised in a way that does not prepare them well for the demands of life, which often leads to problems with behaviour in the future.

maladroit　　adjective　formal UK /ˌmæl.əˈdrɔɪt/ US /ˌmæl.əˈdrɔɪt/ 不灵巧的，笨拙的；不熟练的 awkward in movement or unskilled in behaviour or action [GRE]

malaise　　1 noun [S or U]　formal UK /mælˈeɪz/ US /mælˈeɪz/ 身体不适；萎靡；心神不宁；（尤指对社会的）不满，无奈 a general feeling of being ill or having no energy, or an uncomfortable feeling that something is wrong, especially with society, and that you cannot change the situation [GRE]

malarkey　　noun [U]　informal UK /məˈlɑ:.ki/ US /məˈlɑ:r.ki/ 蠢行；蠢话；废话 silly behaviour or nonsense

malcontent　　noun [C] UK /ˈmæl.kən.tent/ US /ˈmæl.kən.tent/ literary 不满者；牢骚满腹者 a person who is not satisfied with the way things are, and who complains a lot and is unreasonable and difficult to deal with

malefactor　　noun [C]　formal UK /ˈmæl.ɪ.fæk.tər/ US /ˈmæl.ə.fæk.tɚ/ 作恶者，坏人；罪犯 a person who does bad or illegal things

malevolent　　adjective　literary UK /məˈlev.əl.ənt/ US /məˈlev.əl.ənt/ 恶意的；恶毒的；有害的 causing or wanting to cause harm or evil [GRE]

malfeasance　　noun [U]　LAW　specialized UK /mælˈfi:.zəns/ US /mælˈfi:.zəns/（尤指掌权者的）违法乱纪行为，渎职 an example of dishonest and illegal behaviour, especially by a person in authority

malformation   noun [C or U] UK /ˌmæl.fəˈmeɪ.ʃən/ US /ˌmæl.fɔːrˈmeɪ.ʃən/ 畸形（体）；变形（体） the condition of being wrongly formed, or a part of something, such as part of the body, that is wrongly formed

malfunction   1 verb [I]   formal UK /ˌmælˈfʌŋk.ʃən/ US /ˌmælˈfʌŋk.ʃən/ 运转不正常，发生故障 to fail to work or operate correctly

malice   noun [U] UK /ˈmæl.ɪs/ US /ˈmæl.ɪs/ 恶意，害人之心 the wish to harm or upset other people

malicious   1 adjective UK /məˈlɪʃ.əs/ US /məˈlɪʃ.əs/ C2 恶意的，恶毒的，意在伤人的 intended to harm or upset other people

malign   1 adjective   formal UK /məˈlaɪn/ US /məˈlaɪn/ 恶意的；邪恶的；有害的 causing or intending to cause harm or evil 2 verb [T often passive] UK /məˈlaɪn/ US /məˈlaɪn/ 诽谤，污蔑，中伤 to say false and unpleasant things about someone, or to criticize someone unfairly

malignancy   1 noun   MEDICAL   specialized UK /məˈlɪg.nən.si/ US /məˈlɪg.nən.si/ [U] 恶性；恶意 the state of being malignant

malignant   1 adjective UK /məˈlɪg.nənt/ US /məˈlɪg.nənt/ (DISEASE) （疾病或肿块）恶性的，致命的 A malignant disease or growth is likely to get worse and lead to death. [GRE]

malinger   1 verb [I]   disapproving UK /məˈlɪŋ.gər/ US /məˈlɪŋ.gɚ/ （为逃避工作）诈病，装病 to pretend to be ill in order to avoid having to work

Meaning in English: Of or pertaining to the breast

Origin language: Latin (mamma), breast; udder

English examples:

mammal   noun [C] UK /ˈmæm.əl/ US /ˈmæm.əl/ C1 哺乳动物 any animal of which the female feeds her young on milk from her own body. Most mammals give birth to live young, not eggs.

mammary adjective BIOLOGY specialized UK /ˈmæm.ər.i/ US /ˈmæm.ɚ.i/ 乳房的；乳腺的 relating to the breasts or milk organs

mammary gland noun [C] ANATOMY specialized UK US 乳腺 an organ in a woman's breast that produces milk to feed a baby, or a similar organ in a female animal

mammogram   noun [C] UK /ˈmæm.ə.græm/ US /ˈmæm.ə.græm/ (also mammograph,) 乳房 X 光片 an X-ray photograph of the breasts

mammograph   乳房 X 光片 an X-ray photograph of the breasts

mammography   noun [U] UK /məˈmɒg.rə.fi/ US /məˈm ɑ ː.grə.fi/ （检查肿瘤的）乳房 X 光造影检查 the use of X-ray photographs of the breasts to help discover possible cancers

Meaning in English: Of or pertaining to the hand

Origin language: Latin (manus), hand

English examples:

manual dexterity   noun [U] UK /ˌmæn.ju.əl dekˈster.ə.ti/ US /ˌmæn.ju.əl dekˈster.ə.t̬i/ 手的灵巧 someone's ability to use the hands to perform a difficult action skilfully and quickly so that it looks easy

manubrium   1 noun   ANATOMY   specialized UK /məˈnuː.bri.əm/ US /məˈnuː.bri.əm/ [C] plural manubria manubriums （身体内的）柄状的骨头 any bone in the body that is shaped like a handle 2 noun 胸骨柄 the wide upper bone of the breastbone

manufacture   1 verb [T] UK /ˌmæn.jəˈfæk.tʃər/ US /ˌmæn.jəˈfæk.tʃɚ/ [T] (PRODUCE) B2 （通常指工厂利用机械大量）制造，（批量）生产 to produce goods in large numbers, usually in a factory using machines

manus   noun [C]   MEDICAL   specialized UK /ˈmeɪ.nəs/ US /ˈmeɪ.nəs/ plural manus （拉丁语，用于医学术语）手 a Latin word meaning "hand" or "of the hand", used in medical names and descriptions

Prefix (Medical): mast(o)- Of or pertaining to the breast

Meaning in English: Of or pertaining to the breast

Origin language: Ancient Greek μαστός (mastós), breast, women's breast; man's pectoral muscle

English examples:

Mastodynia   乳痛 Mastodynia is the medical term describing the common symptom of breast pain, also labeled as mastalgia. This symptom can occur in both men and women, but it presents more often in women, with the severity of the pain varying from mild and self-limited to severe pain

gynaecomastia   noun [U]   MEDICAL   specialized (US gynecomastia) UK /ˌɡaɪ.nɪ.kəʊˈmæst.i.ə/ US /ˌɡaɪ.nə.koʊˈmæs.ti.ə/ 男性乳腺发育，男性乳房发育 the development of breast tissue in men

Gynaecomastia is usually harmless but emotionally upsetting.   男性乳房发育一般来说无害，但是令人恼火。

mastectomy 1 noun [C] UK /mæsˈtek.tə.mi/ US /mæsˈtek.tə.mi/ 乳房切除术 a medical operation to remove a woman's breast 2 noun 部分乳房切除 a partial mastectomy (= when part of the breast is removed)

a double mastectomy 双乳切除 (= when both breasts are removed)

mastitis noun [U] MEDICAL specialized UK /mæsˈtaɪ.tɪs/ US /mæsˈtaɪ.t̬əs/ 乳腺炎 painful swelling of the breast or the udder (= the part of a cow that produces milk), usually because of an infection

mastitis noun [U] MEDICAL specialized UK /mæsˈtaɪ.tɪs/ US /mæsˈtaɪ.t̬əs/ 乳腺炎 painful swelling of the breast or the udder (= the part of a cow that produces milk), usually because of an infection

mastoid 1 adjective MEDICAL specialized UK /ˈmæs.tɔɪd/ US /ˈmæs.tɔɪd/ 乳突骨 relating to the mastoid process (= part of the skull just behind the ear) 2 adjective 乳房状的；乳头状的 shaped like a breast or a nipple (= one of the two small darker parts that stick out from the breasts or chest)

Prefix: maxi- most, very large
Meaning in English:

Origin language: Latin/Greek

English examples:

maxi- prefix UK /mæk.si-/ US /mæk.si-/ 大部分，很大 most, very large

maxim noun [C] UK /ˈmæk.sɪm/ US /ˈmæk.sɪm/ 格言；基本原理；行为准则 a short statement of a general truth, principle, or rule for behaviour

maximal   adjective   SCIENCE   specialized UK /ˈmæk.sɪ.məl/ US /ˈmæk.sə.məl/ 最大的；最高的 largest or greatest

maximize   1 verb [T] (UK usually maximise) UK /ˈmæk.sɪ.maɪz/ US /ˈmæk.sə.maɪz/ C2 使最大化；使最重要 to make something as great in amount, size, or importance as possible

maximum   1 adjective UK /ˈmæk.sɪ.məm/ US /ˈmæk.sə.məm/ B1 最大 的；最高的；顶点的 being the largest amount or number allowed or possible

maximus   adjective   MEDICAL   specialized UK /ˈmæk.sɪ.məs/ US /ˈmæk.sə.məs/ 最大的（拉丁语，用于医学术语中）a Latin word meaning "largest", used in medical names and descriptions

Prefix (Medical): medull- bone marrow, marrow

Meaning in English: bone marrow, marrow

Origin language: Latin

English examples:

adrenal medulla   noun [C] UK   /əˌdriː.nəl medˈʌl.ə/ US   /əˌdriː.nəl məˈdʌl.ə/ specialized 肾上腺髓质 the inner part of the adrenal gland that produces adrenaline

medulla   noun [C]   MEDICAL   specialized UK /medˈʌl.ə/ US /məˈdʌl.ə/ （身体部分或器官）髓质，最内部分 the inner part of a body part or organ

medulla oblongata   noun [C usually singular] ANATOMY   specialized UK /meˌdʌl.ə ɒb.lɒŋˈɡ ɑ ː.tə/ US /məˌdʌl.ə ɑ ːb.l ɑ ːŋˈɡ ɑ ː.tə/ plural medullae oblongatae /-iː -iː/ /-iː -iː/ 延髓（大脑最下部，位于脊髓顶端，控制心跳、血压以及呼吸）the lowest part of the brain, positioned at the top of the spinal cord, that controls activities such as heartbeat, blood pressure , and breathing

medullary   adjective   MEDICAL   specialized UK /medˈʌl.ər.i/ US /məˈdʌl.ər.i/ 髓质的，最内部分的 relating to the medulla or middle of a body part

Medullary thyroid cancers often spread quickly.   甲状腺髓质癌通常扩散很快。

Prefix: mega- 1,000,000 times the stated unit

Meaning in English: 1,000,000 times the stated unit

Origin language: Greek

English examples:

mega-   2 prefix UK /me.gə-/ US /me.gə-/ (NUMBER) SCIENCE 兆，百万倍 1,000,000 times the stated unit

a megawatt 兆瓦

a megabyte 兆字节

megabyte   noun [C] UK /ˈmeg.ə.baɪt/ US /ˈmeg.ə.baɪt/ (written abbreviation MB) 兆字节，百万字节（计算机存储单位，相当于 1048576 字节） a unit used in measuring the amount of information a computer can store, with the value 1,048,576 bytes

megahertz   noun [C] UK /ˈmeg.ə.hɜːts/ US /ˈmeg.ə.hɜːts/ plural megahertz (written abbreviation MHz) 兆赫 a million hertz

megapixel   noun [C] UK /ˈmeg.ə.pɪk.səl/ US /ˈmeg.ə.pɪk.səl/ 兆像素（计算机、数码相机分辩率单位） one million pixels (= small points that form part of the image on a computer screen), used to measure the amount of detail in images made by a digital camera, computer screen, etc.

megaton   noun [C] UK /ˈmeg.ə.tʌn/ US /ˈmeg.ə.tʌn/ 百万吨级（相当于 100 万吨梯恩梯炸药的爆炸威力，用于计量爆炸威力、尤其是核武器

的爆炸威力） a unit that has the same value as the force produced by 1,000,000 tons of TNT (= an explosive), used for measuring the power of explosions, especially nuclear explosions

megawatt noun [C] UK /ˈmeg.ə.wɒt/ US /ˈmeg.ə.wɑːt/ 兆瓦，百万瓦特 a unit for measuring electric power, with the value of 1,000,000 watts

Prefix: mega- huge/big

Meaning in English: 1,000,000 times the stated unit

Origin language: Greek

English examples:

mega- 3 prefix (BIG/GOOD) informal 非常多的；巨大的 large in amount or size

He's mega-rich. 他非常富有。

megabucks noun [plural] informal UK /ˈmeg.ə.bʌks/ US /ˈmeg.ə.bʌks/ 大笔的钱 a very large amount of money

megacity noun [C] UK /ˈmeg.ə.sɪt.i/ US /ˈmeg.ə.sɪt̬.i/ 巨型城市（人口超过一千万的城市） a very large city, especially one with more than 10 million people living in it

megalith noun [C] UK /ˈmeg.ə.lɪθ/ US /ˈmeg.ə.lɪθ/ 巨石 a large stone, sometimes forming part of a group or circle, thought to have been important to people in the Stone Age for social or religious reasons

megalomania noun [U] UK /ˌmeg.əl.əˈmeɪ.ni.ə/ US /ˌmeg.əl.əˈmeɪ.ni.ə/ 夸大狂，自大狂；妄自尊大 an unnaturally strong wish for power and control, or the belief that you are very much more important and powerful than you really are

megalomaniac   noun [C] UK /ˌmeg.əl.əˈmeɪ.ni.æk/ US /ˌmeg.əl.əˈmeɪ.ni.æk/ 妄自尊大的人，夸大狂患者

megalopolis   noun [C] UK /ˌmeg.əˈlɒp.əl.ɪs/ US /ˌmeg.əˈlɑ ː.pəl.ɪs/ 大都市 an extremely large city or urban (= city) area where a lot of people live:

megaphone   noun [C] UK /ˈmeg.ə.fəʊn/ US /ˈmeg.ə.foʊn/ (UK also loudhailer) 喇叭，话筒，扩音器 a cone-shaped device that makes your voice louder when you speak into it, so that people can hear you although they are not near to you

megastar   noun [C] UK /ˈmeg.ə.st ɑ ːr/ US /ˈmeg.ə.st ɑ ːr/ 大名人；（尤指）超级明星，流行巨星 a very famous person, especially an actor or pop star

megastore   noun [C] UK /ˈmeg.ə.stɔːr/ US /ˈmeg.ə.stɔːr/ 大商店，大商场 a very large shop

Prefix (Medical): meg(a)-, megal(o)- (enlargement)

Meaning in English: enlargement

Origin language: Greek μέγας

English examples:

megalith   noun [C] UK /ˈmeg.ə.lɪθ/ US /ˈmeg.ə.lɪθ/ 巨石 a large stone, sometimes forming part of a group or circle, thought to have been important to people in the Stone Age for social or religious reasons

megalomania   noun [U] UK /ˌmeg.əl.əˈmeɪ.ni.ə/ US /ˌmeg.əl.əˈmeɪ.ni.ə/ 夸大狂，自大狂；妄自尊大 an unnaturally strong wish for power and control, or the belief that you are very much more important and powerful than you really are

megalomaniac   noun [C] UK /ˌmeg.əl.əˈmeɪ.ni.æk/ US /ˌmeg.əl.əˈmeɪ.ni.æk/ 妄自尊大的人，夸大狂患者

Prefix (Medical): melan(o)- black color

Meaning in English: black colo

Origin language: Ancient Greek μέλας, μελανο- (melas, melano-), black; dark

English examples:

melaena   noun [U]   MEDICAL   UK specialized (US melena) UK /məˈliː.nə/ US /məˈliː.nə/ 黑粪症 dark, solid body waste that contains blood as a result of bleeding in the upper part of the intestines

melancholia   noun [U]   old-fashioned or literary UK /ˌmel.əŋˈkəʊ.li.ə/ US /ˌmel.əŋˈkoʊ.li.ə/ 抑郁症 the condition of feeling unhappy or sad for no obvious reason

melancholic   adjective   formal UK /ˌmel.əŋˈkɒl.ɪk/ US /ˌmel.əŋˈkɑː.lɪk/ 忧郁的 expressing feelings of sadness

melancholy   1 adjective UK /ˈmel.əŋ.kɒl.i/ US /ˈmel.əŋ.kɑː.li/ 忧郁的，忧伤的 sad

melanin   noun [U] UK /ˈmel.ə.nɪn/ US /ˈmel.ə.nɪn/ 黑色素 a dark brown pigment (= substance that gives colour), found in eyes, skin, hair, feathers, etc. It helps to protect the skin against harmful light from the sun.

melanoma   noun [C]   MEDICAL   specialized UK /ˌmel.əˈnəʊ.mə/ US /ˌmel.əˈnoʊ.mə/ 黑色素瘤 a type of skin cancer that appears as a coloured mark or growth on the skin

melatonin   noun [U]   CHEMISTRY, BIOLOGY   specialized UK /mel.əˈtəʊ.nɪn/ US /mel.əˈtoʊ.nɪn/ 降黑素（体内的一种激素，能刺激肤色变化，与日常睡眠等生物节律有关） a hormone in the body that produces changes in skin colour and is involved in controlling biorhythms such as our sleep pattern

phaeomelanin   褐黑色素 Pheomelanin is comprised of benzothiazine units and contains sulfur. It is responsible for yellow and pink to red hues based on the amount present.

Prefix (Medical): mening(o)- membrane

Meaning in English: membrane

Origin language: Greek μῆνιγξ, μηνιγγ-

English examples:

meningeal   adjective   MEDICAL   specialized UK /menˈɪn.dʒi.əl/ US /məˈnɪn.dʒi.əl/ 脑脊膜的 relating to the meninges (= the three layers of tissue that surround the brain and spinal cord)

meningioma   noun [C]   MEDICAL   specialized UK /menˌɪn.dʒiˈəʊ.mə/ US /məˌnɪn.dʒiˈoʊ.mə/ 脑脊膜瘤 a brain tumour that grows from the meninges (= the three layers of tissue that surround the brain and spinal cord)

meningitis   noun [U] UK /ˌmen.ɪnˈdʒaɪ.tɪs/ US /ˌmen.ɪnˈdʒaɪ.t̬əs/ 脑脊膜炎 a serious infectious disease that causes the tissues around the brain and spinal cord to swell

meningocele   noun [C or U]   MEDICAL   specialized UK /menˈɪŋ.ɡə.siːl/ US /məˈnɪŋ.ɡəˌsiːl/ 脑脊膜膨出 a problem where part of the meninges (= the three layers of tissue that surround the brain and spiral cord) pushes through the skull or backbone, causing a raised area under the skin

meningococcal   adjective UK /məˌnɪn.dʒəˈkɒkəl/ US /məˌnɪŋ.ɡoʊˈk ɑ ːkəl/ 脑膜炎球菌的 caused by or relating to the bacteria involved in some forms of meningitis and some other similar infections

meninx   noun [C]   ANATOMY   specialized UK /ˈmen.ɪŋks/ US /ˈmi.nɪŋks/ plural meninges 脑脊膜中三层的任一层 one of the three layers of tissue that surround the brain and spinal cord

meniscus   1 noun [C]   specialized UK /məˈnɪs.kəs/ US /məˈnɪs.kəs/ plural menisci /-kaɪ/ meniscuses (BODY PART) ANATOMY 半月板（膝盖等关节处的软骨组织圆盘） a curved piece of cartilage inside a joint (= place where two bones are connected) of the body such as the knee   2 noun [C] (LIQUID) PHYSICS （表面张力形成的）弯液面 on a liquid, a surface that curves either out or in as a result of surface tension

Prefix (Medical): ment- mind

Meaning in English: mind

Origin language: Latin

English examples:

mental   1 adjective UK /ˈmen.təl/ US /-t̬əl/ B2 [before noun] 精神的；思想上的；心理的 relating to the mind, or involving the process of thinking

The family has a history of mental disorder. 这个家庭有精神失常的病史。

mental   2 adjective UK slang 疯癫的，不正常的 crazy

mental age noun [C usually singular] UK /ˌmen.təl ˈeɪdʒ/ US /ˌmen.t̬əl ˈeɪdʒ/ 智力年龄；心理年龄 A person's mental age is a measurement of their ability to think when compared to the average person's ability at that age.

Although Andrew is 25, he has a mental age of six.　　　虽然安德鲁已经 25 岁了，但智力年龄只有 6 岁。

mental arithmetic　　　noun [U] UK /ˌmen.təl əˈrɪθ.mə.tɪk/ US /ˌmen.t̬əl əˈrɪθ.mə.t̬ɪk/ 心算 calculations that you do in your mind, without writing down any numbers

mental block　　　noun [C] UK /ˌmen.təl ˈblɒk/ US /ˌmen.t̬əl ˈblɑːk/ 心理阻隔；思维阻断 If you have a mental block about something, you cannot understand it or do it because something in your mind prevents you.

He has a mental block about names - he just can't remember them.

他对名称的记忆有心理阻隔——他怎么也记不住。

mental cruelty　　　noun [U] UK /ˌmen.təl ˈkruː.əl.ti/ US /ˌmen.t̬əl ˈkruː.əl.t̬i/ 精神虐待 behaviour that makes another person suffer emotionally but does not involve physical violence

She divorced her husband on the grounds of mental cruelty.

她以受精神虐待为由与丈夫离了婚。

mental handicap noun [C usually singular] UK /ˌmen.təl ˈhæn.dɪ.kæp/ US /ˌmen.t̬əl ˈhæn.dɪ.kæp/ 学习障碍（learning difficulties 的旧称） old-fashioned for learning difficulties

learning difficulties　　　学习障碍

mental health　　　noun [U] UK /ˌmen.təl ˈhelθ/ US /ˌmen.t̬əl ˈhelθ/ 精神健康状态 the condition of someone's mind and whether or not they are suffering from any mental illness

Laughing is good for your mental health.　笑对你的精神状态有益。

mental health disorders　精神健康疾病

mental hospital　noun [C] UK /ˈmen.təl ˌhɒs.pɪ.təl/ US /ˈmen.t̬əl ˌhɑː.spɪ.t̬əl/ 精神病医院（psychiatric hospital 的旧称）　old-fashioned for psychiatric hospital

mental illness　noun [C or U] UK /ˌmen.təl ˈɪl.nəs/ US /ˌmen.t̬əl ˈɪl.nəs/ 精神病　an illness that affects the mind

mental note　noun UK /ˌmen.təl ˈnəʊt/ US /ˌmen.t̬əl ˈnoʊt/ 在脑子里记下 to make an effort to remember something

make a mental note of sth　在脑子里记下

I made a mental note of her address.　我将她的地址记在了心里。

mentality　noun [C usually singular] UK /menˈtæl.ə.ti/ US /menˈtæl.ə.t̬i/ C1 心态，心性，思想方法 a person's particular way of thinking about things

I can't understand the mentality of people who hurt animals.　我无法理解伤害动物的那些人究竟是什么心态。

He hopes that closer links between Britain and the rest of Europe will change the British mentality towards foreigners.　他希望英国与其他欧洲国家更为密切的关系可以改变英国人对外国人的心态。

mentally　adverb UK /ˈmen.təl.i/ US /ˈmen.t̬əl.i/ B2 心理上，精神上 connected with or related to the mind

mentally ill 患有心理疾病的

mentally defective adjective old-fashioned or offensive UK /ˌmen.təl.i dɪˈfek.tɪv/ US /ˌmen.təl.i dɪˈfek.tɪv/ 有心理缺陷的，有智力缺陷的 If you say that someone is mentally defective, you mean that they have low mental abilities because their brain is damaged due to an accident or illness, or has been damaged since birth.

mention 1 verb [T] UK /ˈmen.ʃən/ US /ˈmen.ʃən/ B1 提及，说起，谈到 to speak about something quickly, giving little detail or using few words 2 verb B1 谈及，提到 to refer to something or someone

mentor 1 noun [C] UK /ˈmen.tɔːr/ US /ˈmen.tɔːr/ 导师，指导者 a person who gives a younger or less experienced person help and advice over a period of time, especially at work or school [GRE]

Prefix (Medical): mero- part

Meaning in English: part

Origin language: Greek μέρος (meros), part

English examples:

Merocrine 美罗克林 Merocrine is a term used to classify exocrine glands and their secretions in the study of histology. A cell is classified as merocrine if the secretions of that cell are excreted via exocytosis from secretory cells into an epithelial-walled duct or ducts and then onto a bodily surface or into the lumen. Wikipedia

meroblastic 粒细胞 characterized by or being incomplete cleavage as a result of the presence of an impeding mass of yolk material (as in the eggs of birds) — compare holoblastic.

holoblastic 全胚层 characterized by complete cleavage that divides the whole egg into distinct and separate blastomeres — compare meroblastic.

Meaning in English: middle

Origin language: Ancient Greek μέσος (mesos), "middle"

English examples:

mesocolon   noun [C]   MEDICAL   specialized UK /ˌmes.əˈkəʊ.lɒn/ US /ˌmez.əˈkoʊ.lən/ 结肠系膜 the part of the mesentery (= the membrane that connects the bowel to the back wall of the abdomen) concerned with the large bowel

mesolithic   adjective   SCIENCE   specialized /ˌmesəˈlɪθ.ɪk/ UK /ˌmes.əˈlɪθ.ɪk/ US /ˌmez.əˈlɪθ.ɪk/ 中石器时代的 relating to the middle part of the Stone Age (= the period when humans used tools and weapons made of stone)

mesomorph   noun [C]   ANATOMY   specialized UK /ˈmes.ə.mɔːf/ US /-mɔːrf/体育型体质者，中胚层体型者 a person with a strong, triangular body and hard muscles

mesoderm   中胚层 The mesoderm is the middle layer of the three germ layers that develops during gastrulation in the very early development of the embryo of most animals. The outer layer is the ectoderm, and the inner layer is the endoderm. Mesoderm. Tissues derived from mesoderm.

Mesozoic   中生代 The Mesozoic Era, also called the Age of Reptiles and the Age of Conifers, is the second-to-last era of Earth's geological history, lasting from about 252 to 66 million years ago and comprising the Triassic, Jurassic and Cretaceous Periods. Wikipedia

meson   noun [C]   PHYSICS   specialized UK /ˈmiː.zɒn/ US /ˈmez. ɑ :n/ 介子 a very small piece of matter that contains a quark and an antiquark

mesophyll noun [U] BIOLOGY specialized UK /ˈmes.əʊ.fɪl/ US /ˈmez.oʊ.fɪl/ 叶肉（叶片进行光合作用部位） the part of a leaf between the two thin surface layers, containing the cells responsible for photosynthesis

mesmeric adjective literary UK /mezˈmer.ɪk/ US /mezˈmer.ɪk/ 令人着迷的，令人陶醉的 making you give your attention completely so that you cannot think of anything else [GRE]

music with a repetitive, slightly mesmeric quality 节奏重复、略让人着迷的音乐

mesmerism   令人着迷的，难以抗拒的：attracting [GRE]

mesmerize   1 verb (UK usually mesmerise) UK /ˈmez.mə.raɪz/ US /ˈmez.mə.raɪz/ 迷住；迷惑 [T often passive] to have someone's attention completely so that they cannot think of anything else [GRE]

我完全被表演迷住了。 I was completely mesmerized by the performance.

mesmerize   2 verb [T] old-fashioned for hypnotize 对…施催眠术 （hypnotize 过去的说法）

mesmerizing   adjective (UK usually mesmerising) UK /ˈmez.mə.raɪ.zɪŋ/ US /ˈmez.mə.raɪ.zɪŋ/ 吸引人的，迷人的 very attractive, in a mysterious way, making you want to keep looking [GRE]

He had the most mesmerizing blue eyes.   他有一双非常迷人的蓝眼睛。

Prefix: meta- involving change
Meaning in English: involving change

Origin language: Latin / Greek

English examples:

meta-　　　1 prefix UK /met.ə-/ US /ˌmet̬.ə-/ 有变化的 involving change
变形；变质 metamorphose (= to change into a completely different form)

metabolism　　　noun [C] UK /məˈtæb.əl.ɪ.zəm/ US /məˈtæb.əl.ɪ.zəm/
specialized 新陈代谢 all the chemical processes in your body, especially those
that cause food to be used for energy and growth

metabolic　adjective UK /met.əˈbɒl.ɪk/ US /ˌmet̬.əˈbɑ:.lɪk/ specialized 代谢
的，新陈代谢的 relating to metabolism (= the chemical processes within the
body required for life)

metabolite　noun [C] UK /məˈtæb.ə.laɪt/ US /məˈtæb.əˌlaɪt/ specialized 代
谢物 any substance involved in metabolism (= the chemical processes in the
body needed for life)

metabolize　　　verb [T]　BIOLOGY, MEDICAL　specialized (UK usually
metabolise) UK /məˈtæb.əl.aɪz/ US /məˈtæb.əl.aɪz/ （使）新陈代谢 to use
chemical processes in the body to turn food into energy, new growth, and waste
products

metabolic disorder　　　noun [C] UK /met.əˈbɒl.ɪk dɪˌsɔːd.ər/ US
/ˌmet̬.əˈbɑ:.lɪk dɪˌsɔːr.dɚ/ specialized （身体）代谢障碍 a problem affecting
the chemical processes by which the body reacts to changes inside and outside
the body

metacarpal　　　noun [C]　ANATOMY　specialized UK /ˌmet.əˈkɑ:.pəl/
US /ˌmet̬.əˈkɑ:r.pəl/ 掌骨 one of the five bones between the fingers and the
wrist

metacarpus   noun [C]   ANATOMY   specialized UK /ˌmet.əˈk ɑ :.pəs/ US /ˌmet̬.əˈk ɑ :r.pəs/ plural metacarpi 掌 the part of the hand between the wrist and the fingers

Prefix: meta- Beyond; outside the normal limits of something
Meaning in English: outside the normal limits of something

Origin language: Latin / Greek

English examples:

meta-   3 prefix 超出了一般的限制 outside the normal limits of something

metalanguage   元语言（用于描述其他语言的语言或符号集）(= a specialized form of language used for describing a language)

Meta   Meta Platforms, Inc., doing business as Meta and formerly known as Facebook, Inc., and TheFacebook, Inc., is an American multinational technology conglomerate based in Menlo Park, California. The company owns Facebook, Instagram, and WhatsApp, among other products and services. Wikipedia "Meta" 一词来自希腊语，意思是"Beyond"，表示未来主义的动机。

meta-analysis   noun [C or U]   MEDICAL   specialized UK /ˌme.tə.əˈnæl.ə.sɪs/ US /ˌmet̬.ə.əˈnæl.ə.sɪs/ 统合分析，整合分析 a research method that combines the results of several related studies to produce better results

metadata   noun [U or plural] UK /ˈmet.əˌdeɪ.tə/ US /ˈmet̬.əˌdeɪ.t̬ə/ /ˌmet̬.əˈdæ.t̬ə/ 元数据（用于解释或帮助理解信息的数据） information that is given to describe or help you use other information

metafiction   noun [U]   LITERATURE   specialized UK /ˈmet.əˌfik.ʃən/ US /ˈmet̬.əˌfik.ʃən/ 超小说（虚构人物事件，强调写作技巧）writing about imaginary characters and events in which the process of writing is discussed or described

Meaning in English: Pertaining to conditions or instruments of the uterus

Origin language: Ancient Greek μήτρᾱ (mētrā), womb, uterus

English examples:

endometrial　　adjective　MEDICAL　specialized UK /ˌen.dəʊˈmiː.tri.əl/ US /ˌen.doʊˈmiː.tri.əl/ 子宫内膜的 relating to the endometrium (= the lining of the uterus)

endometrial biopsy/cancer/polyp　　子宫内膜活组织检查/子宫内膜癌/子宫内膜息肉

endometriosis　　noun [U]　MEDICAL　specialized UK /ˌen.dəʊ.miː.triˈəu.sɪs/ US /ˌen.doʊ.miː.triˈou.sɪs/ 子宫内膜异位 a condition in which cells from the lining of the uterus grow outside the uterus

Doctors can treat endometriosis by controlling the levels of oestrogen in the body. 医生可以通过控制体内雌激素治疗子宫内膜异位。

endometrium　　noun [S]　MEDICAL　specialized UK /ˌen.dəʊˈmiː.tri.əm/ US /ˌen.doʊˈmiː.tri.əm/ 子宫内膜 the inside surface of the uterus (= the organ in which a baby develops)

Metrorrhagia　　noun [C] 崩漏 Metrorrhagia is abnormal bleeding between regular menstrual periods. Few data exist on the prevalence of metrorrhagia in adolescents. Common causes of metrorrhagia include pregnancy, use of certain contraceptives (especially Depo-Provera) and intrauterine devices, and STIs.

Meaning in English: very small

Origin language: Ancient Greek μικρός (mikros), small

English examples:

micro-   2 prefix   SCIENCE UK /maɪ.krəʊ-/ US /maɪ.kroʊ-/ micro- prefix (SMALL) 小的，微小的 very small

a microorganism   微生物

microbiology   微生物学

microbe   noun [C]   BIOLOGY   specialized UK /ˈmaɪ.krəʊb/ US /ˈmaɪ.kroʊb/ 微生物；（尤指致病的）细菌 a very small living thing, especially one that causes disease, that can only be seen with a microscope

microbiology   noun [U] UK /ˌmaɪ.krəʊ.baɪˈɒl.ə.dʒi/ US /ˌmaɪ.kroʊ.baɪˈɑː.lə.dʒi/ 微生物学 the study of very small living things, such as bacteria

microblog   noun [C] UK /ˈmaɪ.krəˌblɒg/ US /ˈmaɪ.kroʊˌblɑːg/ 微博客 a blog in the form of a short message for anyone to read, sent especially from a mobile phone

microbrew   noun [C] mainly US UK /ˈmaɪ.krə.bruː/ US /ˈmaɪ.krə.bruː/ 微酿啤酒，小酒厂酿制的啤酒 a beer made in a microbrewery

microbrewery   noun [C] mainly US UK /ˈmaɪ.krəʊˌbruː.ər.i/ US /ˈmaɪ.kroʊˌbruː.ɚ.i/ （采用传统方法酿造并以前店后厂方式经营的）小啤酒厂 a small company that makes beer, usually using traditional methods, and often has a restaurant where its beer is served

microbusiness   noun [C]   ECONOMICS   specialized UK /ˈmaɪ.krəʊˌbɪz.nɪsˌ/ US /-kroʊ-/ 微型企业 a very small company, especially a family-owned company employing only a few people

microchip   noun [C] UK /ˈmaɪ.krəʊ.tʃɪp/ US /ˈmaɪ.kroʊ.tʃɪp/ 集成电路片，芯片（同 chip）a chip noun(COMPUTER PART)

microcircuit   noun UK /ˈmaɪ.krəʊˌsɜː.kɪt/ US /ˈmaɪ.kroʊˌsɜː.kɪt/ 集成电路（同 integrated circuit） an integrated circuit

microcosm   noun [C or U] UK /ˈmaɪ.krəʊˌkɒz.əm/ US /ˈmaɪ.kroʊˌkɑː.zəm/ 缩影；微观世界 a small place, society, or situation that has the same characteristics as something much larger

microcredit   noun [U] ECONOMICS UK /ˈmaɪ.krəʊˌkred.ɪt/ US /ˈmaɪ.kroʊˌkred.ɪt/ 微型信贷 a very small amount of money lent to a person or group, especially in order to make it possible for people in poor countries to start businesses

microdot   noun [C] UK /ˈmaɪ.krəʊ.dɒt/ US /-kroʊ.dɑːt/微点 a piece of text or an image that has been reduced in size to fit onto a very small circular object

microeconomics   noun [U] UK /ˌmaɪ.krəʊ.iː.kəˈnɒm.ɪks/ US /ˌmaɪ.kroʊ.iː.kəˈnɑː.mɪks/微观经济学 the study of the economic problems of businesses and people and the way particular parts of an economy behave

microelectronics   noun [U] UK /ˌmaɪ.krəʊˌɪl.ekˈtrɒn.ɪks/ US /ˌmaɪ.kroʊ.ɪˌlekˈtrɑː.nɪks/ 微电子学 the science and technology involved in the making and using of very small electronic parts

microfibre   noun [C] UK (US microfiber) UK /ˈmaɪ.krəʊˌfaɪ.bər/ US /ˈmaɪ.kroʊˌfaɪ.bɚ/ 微纤维 a soft, light material made from very thin artifical threads

micromanage   verb [T]   often disapproving UK /ˈmaɪ.krəʊˌmæn.ɪdʒ/ US /ˈmaɪ.kroʊˌmæn.ɪdʒ/ 细节管理 to control every part of a situation, even small details

micrometer   noun [C] UK /maɪˈkrɒm.ɪ.tər/ US /maɪˈkrɑː.mə.t̬ɚ/ 测微计，千分尺 a device used for making very exact measurements or for measuring very small things

micron   noun [C] UK /ˈmaɪ.krɒn/ US /ˈmaɪ.krɑːn/ 微米，百万分之一米 one millionth of a metre

micropower   noun [U] UK /ˈmaɪ.krəʊˌpaʊər/ US /ˈmaɪ.kroʊˌpaʊ.ɚ/ (also microgeneration,) 微能源（通过私人设备、阳光、风力提供所需热、电） the use of your own equipment and the sun, wind, etc. to produce all the heat and power that you need

micropyle   noun [C]   BIOLOGY specialized UK /ˈmaɪ.krəʊ.paɪl/ US /ˈmaɪ.kroʊ.paɪl/ 株孔；卵膜孔 a very small opening in the cover of a plant's ovule (= the part that contains the female sex cell)

microscope   noun [C] UK /ˈmaɪ.krə.skəʊp/ US /ˈmaɪ.krə.skoʊp/ 显微镜 a device that uses lenses to make very small objects look larger, so that they can be scientifically examined and studied

microscopy   noun [U]   SCIENCE specialized UK /maɪˈkrɒs.kə.pi/ US /maɪˈkrɑː.skə.pi/ 显微镜学（显微镜的使用、设计或生产） the use, design, or production of microscopes

microsecond   noun [C] UK /ˈmaɪ.krəʊˌsek.ənd/ US /ˈmaɪ.kroʊˌsek.ənd/ 微秒，百万分之一秒 one millionth of a second

microsite   noun [C] UK /ˈmaɪ.krəˌsaɪt/ US /ˈmaɪ.krəˌsaɪt/ 微型网站 a small website, usually one advertising a particular product or service for a company

microsurgery   noun [U] UK /ˌmaɪ.krəʊˈsɜː.dʒər.i/ US /ˌmaɪ.kroʊˈsɜː.dʒər.i/ 显微手术 operations on very small areas of a body, for example nerve fibres (= structures like threads) or the small tubes that carry blood

microvascular   adjective   MEDICAL   specialized UK /ˌmaɪ.krəʊˈvæs.kjə.lər/ US /ˌmaɪ.kroʊˈvæs.kjə.lə/ 毛细血管的 relating to the smallest blood vessels

microwave   1 noun [C] UK /ˈmaɪ.krə.weɪv/ US /ˈmaɪ.kroʊ.weɪv/ (also microwave oven) 微波炉 an electric oven that uses waves of energy to cook or heat food quickly

Prefix: mid- the middle of
Meaning in English: middle

Origin language: Anglo-Saxon

English examples:

mid-   2 prefix UK /mɪd-/ US /mɪd-/ 在...中间，在...中部 the middle of

mid-March   3 月中旬

mid-afternoon   下午 3 点左右

He's in his mid-thirties.   他三十五六岁。

He stopped (in) mid-sentence.   他话说了一半停了下来。

mid-afternoon   noun [U or C] UK /ˌmɪdˌɑːf.təˈnuːn/ US /ˌæf.tə.təˈnuːn/ 下午中段，下午 3 点左右 the part of the afternoon half way between 12 o'clock and the time when you last see the sun

344 | P a g e

mid-air   noun [U] UK /ˌmɪdˈeər/ US /ˌmɪdˈer/ a point in the air, not on the ground 空中，半空中

mid-morning   adjective [before noun] UK /ˌmɪdˈmɔː.nɪŋ/ US /ˌmɪdˈmɔːr.nɪŋ/ 上午 10 时左右的，半晌午的 in the middle of the morning

mid-table   1 adjective, adverb UK /ˌmɪdˈteɪ.bəl/ US /ˌmɪdˈteɪ.bəl/ （足球联赛中）排名中间的 in a safe position half way between the top and bottom clubs in a football league (= group of teams who play each other)

middle   1 noun UK /ˈmɪd.əl/ US /ˈmɪd.əl/ A2 [S] 中部，中间；中央；当中 the central point, position, or part

middle class   noun [S, + sing/pl verb] UK /ˌmɪd.əl ˈklɑːs/ US /ˌmɪd.əl ˈklæs/ (also the middle classes) 中产阶级 a social group that consists of well-educated people, such as doctors, lawyers, and teachers, who have good jobs and are neither very rich nor very poor

middle finger   noun [C] UK /ˌmɪd.əl ˈfɪŋ.gər/ US /ˌmɪd.əl ˈfɪŋ.gɚ/ 中指 the longest finger on the hand

middle school   1 noun [C] UK /ˈmɪd.əl ˌskuːl/ US /ˈmɪd.əl ˌskuːl/ （英国 9 至 14 岁儿童入学的）中学 in parts of the UK, a school for children between the ages of about nine and 14 2 noun （美国 11 至 14 岁儿童入学的）中学 in parts of the US, a school for children between the ages of about 11 and 13

middle-aged   1 adjective UK /ˌmɪd.əlˈeɪdʒd/ US /ˌmɪd.əlˈeɪdʒd/ B1 中年的 in middle age 2 disapproving 具有中年人特点的；谨慎无热情的 too careful and not showing the enthusiasm, energy, or style of someone young

middle-of-the-road   adjective UK /ˌmɪd.əl.əv.ðəˈrəʊd/ US /ˌmɪd.əl.əv.ðəˈroʊd/ 温和路线的；多数人能接受的，为大众所喜爱的 used to describe a person, organization, opinion, or type of entertainment that is not extreme and is acceptable to or liked by most people

middleman   1 noun [C] UK /ˈmɪd.əl.mæn/ US /ˈmɪd.əl.mæn/ plural -men UK /-men/ US 经销商；中间商 a person who buys goods from the company that has produced them and makes a profit by selling them to a shop or a user

middling   adjective   informal UK /ˈmɪd.əl.ɪŋ/ US /ˈmɪd.əl.ɪŋ/ 中等的；二流的；普通的，一般的 medium or average; neither very good nor very bad

Prefix: milli- mille- 0.001 or one thousandth of the stated unit

Meaning in English: 0.001 or one thousandth of the stated unit

Origin language: Latin

English examples:

milli-   prefix   SCIENCE UK /mɪl.ɪ-/ US /mɪl.ɪ-/ 毫，千分之一 0.001 or one thousandth of the stated unit

milliampere   noun [C] UK /ˌmɪl.iˈæm.peər/ US /ˌmɪl.iˈæm.pɪr/ 毫安（电流单位） a unit for measuring small electric currents, equal to an ampere divided by 1,000

milligram   noun [C] (UK also milligramme) UK /ˈmɪl.ɪ.græm/ US /ˈmɪl.ɪ.græm/ (written abbreviation mg) 毫克 a unit of mass that is equal to 0.001 grams

millilitre   noun [C] UK (US milliliter) UK /ˈmɪl.ɪˌliː.tər/ US /ˈmɪl.əˌliː.t̬ɚ/ (written abbreviation ml) 毫升 a unit of volume that is equal to 0.001 litres

millimetre   noun [C] UK (US millimeter) UK /ˈmɪl.ɪˌmiː.tər/ US /ˈmɪl.əˌmiː.t̬ɚ/ (written abbreviation mm) B1 毫米 a unit of length that is equal to 0.001 metres

millenary   noun mil·le·na·ry | \ ˈmi-lə-ˌner-ē , mə-ˈle-nə-rē \ plural millenaries 1: a group of 1000 units or things

Prefix: mini- smaller or less important

Meaning in English: small (From the Latin word miniature… Modern generations shortened miniature to mini-.)

Origin language: Latin

English examples:

mini-   2 prefix UK /mɪn.i-/ US /mɪn.i-/ （同类中）小型的，重要性较低的 smaller or less important than a normal example of the same thing

mini system   1 noun [C] UK /ˈmɪn.i ˌsɪs.təm/ US /ˈmɪn.i ˌsɪs.təm/ 小型音响 a very small set of electronic equipment for playing recorded sound

mini-break   noun [C] UK UK /ˈmɪn.i.breɪk/ US /ˈmɪn.i.breɪk/ 短假 a very short holiday

mini-golf   noun [U] UK ➔ miniature golf （在小型场地上的）迷你高尔夫球，袖珍高尔夫球（同 miniature golf）

miniature   1 adjective [before noun] UK /ˈmɪn.ə.tʃər/ US /ˈmɪn.i.ə.tʃɚ/ C2 微型的；小型的；微小的 used to describe something that is a very small copy of an object

miniature golf   noun [U] (UK also mini-golf, crazy golf) （在小型场地上玩儿的）迷你高尔夫球，袖珍高尔夫球 a type of golf game played for entertainment on a small course (= playing area), where players try to hit balls into holes that each have different features and obstacles (= objects that block the way)

miniaturization   noun [U] (UK usually miniaturisation) UK /ˌmɪn.ə.tʃər.aɪˈzeɪ.ʃən/ US /ˌmɪn.i.ə.tʃɚ.əˈzeɪ.ʃən/ 小型化，微型化 the process of making something very small using modern technology

minibar   noun [C] UK /ˈmɪn.i.bɑːr/ US /ˈmɪn.i.bɑːr/ 迷你吧（酒店客房内放有饮料的小冰箱） a small fridge in a hotel bedroom, with drinks inside

minibus   noun [C] UK /ˈmɪn.i.bʌs/ US /ˈmɪn.i.bʌs/ 小型公共汽车；中巴车 a small bus in which there are seats for about ten people

minimal   adjective UK /ˈmɪn.ɪ.məl/ US /ˈmɪn.ə.məl/ C1 极小的；极少的 very small in amount

minimalist   1 adjective UK /ˈmɪn.ɪ.məl.ɪst/ US /ˈmɪn.ə.məl.ɪst/ (SIMPLE) ART, ARCHITECTURE, THEATRE & FILM 极简抽象派艺术的，极简抽象派风格的，简约主义的 belonging or relating to a style in art, design, and theatre that uses the smallest range of materials and colours possible, and only very simple shapes or forms

minimize   1 verb [T] (UK usually minimise) UK /ˈmɪn.ɪ.maɪz/ US /ˈmɪn.ə.maɪz/ C1 使降到最低限度；使减到最少 to reduce something to the least possible level or amount

minimum   1 noun [C usually singular] UK /ˈmɪn.ɪ.məm/ US /ˈmɪn.ə.məm/ plural minimums or specialized minima (written abbreviation min.) B1 最小值；最少量；最低限度 the smallest amount or number allowed or possible

miniskirt   noun [C] UK /ˈmɪn.iˌskɜːt/ US /ˈmɪn.i.skɝːt/ (also mini) 超短裙 a very short skirt

minivan   noun [C] US UK /ˈmɪn.i.væn/ US /ˈmɪn.i.væn/ (UK people carrier) 小型货车 a large, high car that can carry more people than a normal car

Prefix: mis- bad or badly/ wrong or wrongly

Meaning in English: bad or badly/ wrong or wrongly

Origin language: Latin

English examples:

mis-   prefix UK /mɪs-/ US /mɪs-/ （用于动词，或由动词衍生出来的词前）错误地，不良地 added to the beginning of a verb or word formed from a verb, to show that the action referred to by the verb has been done wrongly or badly

misaddress   verb [T] UK /ˌmɪs.əˈdres/ US /ˌmɪs.əˈdres/ （在信件或包裹上）写错地址 to put the wrong address on a letter or parcel

misadventure   noun [C]   literary UK /ˌmɪs.ədˈven.tʃər/ US /ˌmɪs.ədˈven.tʃɚ/ 不幸事故；不幸遭遇；厄运 an accident or bad luck

misanthrope   noun [C] UK /ˈmɪs.ən.θrəʊp/ US /ˈmɪs.ən.θroʊp/ (also misanthropist,) 厌恶人类者；遁世者 someone who dislikes and avoids other people

misanthropic   adjective UK /ˌmɪs.ənˈθrɒp.ɪk/ US /ˌmɪs.ənˈθrɑː.pɪk/ 厌恶人类的；遁世的，不与他人交往的 not liking other people [GRE]

misapprehension noun [C or U] UK /ˌmɪs.æp.rɪˈhen.ʃən/ US /ˌmɪs.æp.rəˈhen.ʃən/ 误解，误会 a failure to understand something, or an understanding or belief about something that is not correct [GRE]

misbehave   1 verb [I] UK /ˌmɪs.bɪˈheɪv/ US /ˌmɪs.bɪˈheɪv/ [I] (PERSON) C1 举止失礼；行为不端 to behave badly

miscalculate   1 verb [I or T] UK /mɪsˈkæl.kjə.leɪt/ US /mɪsˈkæl.kjə.leɪt/ 误算；（把…）算错 to calculate an amount wrongly

miscarriage   noun [C or U] UK /ˈmɪsˌkær.ɪdʒ/ US /ˈmɪsˌker.ɪdʒ/ 流产 an early, unintentional end to a pregnancy when the baby is born too early and dies because it has not developed enough

mischance   noun [C or U]   formal UK /ˌmɪsˈtʃɑːns/ US /ˌmɪsˈtʃæns/ 厄运，坏运气；不幸 bad luck or an unlucky event

mischief   1 noun UK /ˈmɪs.tʃɪf/ US /ˈmɪs.tʃɪf/ [U] （尤指儿童的）恶作剧，淘气，捣蛋 behaviour, especially a child's, that is slightly bad but is not intended to cause serious harm or damage

mischievous   1 adjective UK /ˈmɪs.tʃɪ.vəs/ US /ˈmɪs.tʃə.vəs/ （人、行为等）爱恶作剧的，好捣乱的，顽皮的，淘气的 behaving in a way, or describing behaviour, that is slightly bad but is not intended to cause serious harm or damage [GRE]

misconceived adjective UK /ˌmɪs.kənˈsiːvd/ US /ˌmɪs.kənˈsiːvd/ 设想错误的；计划不周的；判断失误的 badly planned because of a failure to understand a situation and therefore unsuitable or unlikely to succeed

misconception noun [C] UK /ˌmɪs.kənˈsep.ʃən/ US /ˌmɪs.kənˈsep.ʃən/ 误解，错误的想法 an idea that is wrong because it has been based on a failure to understand a situation

misconduct 1 noun [U] UK /ˌmɪsˈkɒn.dʌkt/ US /ˌmɪsˈkɑːn.dʌkt/ [U] (BEHAVIOUR) 不端行为；失职；滥用职权 unacceptable or bad behaviour by someone in a position of authority or responsibility

misconstrue verb [T] formal UK /ˌmɪs.kənˈstruː/ US /ˌmɪs.kənˈstruː/ 误解…的意思（或意图） to form a false understanding of the meaning or intention of something that someone does or says [GRE]

miscount verb [I or T] UK /ˌmɪsˈkaʊnt/ US /ˌmɪsˈkaʊnt/ 数错，算错 to reach a total that is not correct when counting

miscreant 1 noun [C] formal UK /ˈmɪs.kri.ənt/ US /ˈmɪs.kri.ənt/ 恶棍，无赖；歹徒 someone who behaves badly or does not obey rules [GRE]

misdeed noun [C] formal UK /ˌmɪsˈdiːd/ US /ˌmɪsˈdiːd/ 违法行为；罪行；不端行为 an act that is criminal or bad

misdemeanour noun [C] UK (US misdemeanor) UK /ˌmɪs.dɪˈmiː.nər/ US /ˌmɪs.dɪˈmiː.nɚ/ 不端行为，不检点的举止 an action that is slightly bad or breaks a rule but is not a crime [GRE]

misdirect   1 verb [T] UK /ˌmɪs.daɪˈrekt/ /ˌmɪs.dɪˈrekt/ US /ˌmɪs.daɪˈrekt/ /ˌmɪs.dɪˈrekt/ 将…送错地方；把…瞄错方向 to send something to the wrong place or aim something in the wrong direction

miserable   1 adjective UK /ˈmɪz.ər.ə.bəl/ US /ˈmɪz.ɚ.ə.bəl/ (UNHAPPY) B1 痛苦的；可怜的 very unhappy 2 adjective B2 令人难受的，令人痛苦的 unpleasant and causing unhappiness

miserly   1 adjective disapproving UK /ˈmaɪ.zəl.i/ US /ˈmaɪ.zɚ.li/ (PERSON) 守财奴似的；吝啬鬼似的；吝啬的，小气的 like or typical of a miser [GRE]

misfortune   noun [C or U] UK /ˌmɪsˈfɔː.tʃuːn/ US /ˌmɪsˈfɔːr.tʃən/ C1 不幸；厄运；不幸事故；灾难 bad luck, or an unlucky event [GRE]

misgiving   noun [C or U] UK /ˌmɪsˈɡɪv.ɪŋ/ US /ˌmɪsˈɡɪv.ɪŋ/ （对未来事件的）疑虑，担忧 a feeling of doubt or worry about a future event

misgovern   verb [T] UK /ˌmɪsˈɡʌv.ən/ US /ˌmɪsˈɡʌv.ɚn/ 对（国家）管理不当 to govern a country badly

misguided   adjective UK /ˌmɪsˈɡaɪ.dɪd/ US /ˌmɪsˈɡaɪ.dɪd/ 被误导的；被引入歧途的；判断失误的 unreasonable or unsuitable because of being based on bad judgment or on wrong information or beliefs

mishandle   verb [T] UK /ˌmɪsˈhæn.dəl/ US /ˌmɪsˈhæn.dəl/ 对…处理不当 to deal with something without the necessary care or skill

mishap   noun [C or U] UK /ˈmɪs.hæp/ US /ˈmɪs.hæp/ C2 厄运；不幸事故 bad luck, or an unlucky event or accident [GRE]

mishear   verb [I or T] UK /ˌmɪsˈhɪər/ US /ˌmɪsˈhɪr/ misheard | misheard 听错，误听 to fail to hear someone's words correctly or in the way that was intended and to think that something different was said

misinform   verb [T] UK /ˌmɪs.ɪnˈfɔːm/ US /ˌmɪs.ɪnˈfɔːrm/ C1 误报；误传 to tell someone information that is not correct

misinterpret   verb [T] UK /ˌmɪs.ɪnˈtɜː.prət/ US /ˌmɪs.ɪnˈtɜː.prət/ C2 误解；误释 to form an understanding that is not correct of something that is said or done

misjudge   1 verb [T] UK /ˌmɪsˈdʒʌdʒ/ US /ˌmɪsˈdʒʌdʒ/ 错误地判断；对…判断不公；错看 to form an opinion or idea about someone or something that is unfair or wrong

mislead   verb [T] UK /ˌmɪsˈliːd/ US /ˌmɪsˈliːd/ misled C1 误导；使…产生错误的想法；把…引入歧途 to cause someone to believe something that is not true

misleading   adjective UK /ˌmɪsˈliː.dɪŋ/ US /ˌmɪsˈliː.dɪŋ/ B2 误导的；引入歧途的；让人产生错误观念的 causing someone to believe something that is not true

mismanage   verb [T] UK /ˌmɪsˈmæn.ɪdʒ/ US /ˌmɪsˈmæn.ɪdʒ/ 对…管理不善；对…处置不当 to organize or control something badly

mismatch   1 verb [T] UK /ˌmɪsˈmætʃ/ US /ˌmɪsˈmætʃ/ 使错配；使不适当地在一起 to put together people or things that are unsuitable for each other

misogynist 1 noun [C] UK /mɪˈsɒdʒ.ən.ɪst/ US /mɪˈsɑː.dʒən.ɪst/ 厌恶女人者，嫌忌女人者 a man who hates women or believes that men are much better than women

misandry noun [U] UK /mɪˈsæn.dri/ US /ˈmɪs.æn.dri/ 厌恶男人，憎恨男人 feelings of hating men

misplace verb [T] UK /ˌmɪsˈpleɪs/ US /ˌmɪsˈpleɪs/ C2 随意搁置；乱放（而一时找不到） to lose something temporarily by forgetting where you have put it

misrepresent verb [T] UK /ˌmɪs.rep.rɪˈzent/ US /ˌmɪs.rep.rɪˈzent/ 不如实地叙述（或说明）；误传；歪曲；诈称 to describe falsely an idea, opinion, or situation, often in order to get an advantage

mistaken adjective UK /mɪˈsteɪ.kən/ US /mɪˈsteɪ.kən/ C1 错误的；弄错的 wrong in what you believe, or based on a belief that is wrong

mistime verb [T] UK /ˌmɪsˈtaɪm/ US /ˌmɪsˈtaɪm/ 在不当的时候做；选错…的时机 to do something at the wrong moment with the result that it is unsuccessful or has an unwanted effect

mistreat verb [T] UK /ˌmɪsˈtriːt/ US /ˌmɪsˈtriːt/ 虐待 to treat a person or animal badly, cruelly, or unfairly

misunderstand verb [I or T] UK /ˌmɪs.ʌn.dəˈstænd/ US /ˌmɪs.ʌn.dɚˈstænd/ misunderstood | misunderstood B2 误解；曲解 to think you have understood someone or something when you have not

misuse   1 verb [T] UK /ˌmɪsˈjuːz/ US /ˌmɪsˈjuːz/ C1 错用，误用；滥用；盗用 to use something in an unsuitable way or in a way that was not intended

Prefix: mono- one; single

Meaning in English: one; single

Origin language: Greek μονός

English examples:

mono-   4 prefix UK /mɒn.əʊ-/ US /mɑː.noʊ-/ 单，一，单一 one; single

monochrome   1 adjective UK /ˈmɒn.ə.krəʊm/ US /ˈmɑː.nə.kroʊm/ (COLOUR) 黑白的；单色的 using only black, white, and grey, or using only one colour [GRE]

monogamy   noun [U] UK /məˈnɒg.ə.mi/ US /məˈnɑː.gə.mi/ 一夫一妻制 the fact or custom of having a sexual relationship or marriage with only one other person at a time

monograph   noun [C] UK /ˈmɒn.ə.grɑːf/ /ˈmɒn.ə.græf/ US /ˈmɑː.nə.græf/ 专论，专题文章；专著 a long article or a short book on a particular subject

monolingual   adjective UK /ˌmɒn.əʊˈlɪŋ.gwəl/ US /ˌmɑː.noʊˈlɪŋ.gwəl/ 只使用一种语言的，单语的 speaking or using only one language

monolith   1 noun [C] UK /ˈmɒn.ə.lɪθ/ US /ˈmɑː.nə.lɪθ/ [C] (STONE)（古人竖立的）独块巨石，独石柱 a large block of stone standing by itself that was put up by people in ancient times

monolithic adjective disapproving UK /ˌmɒn.əˈlɪθ.ɪk/ US /ˌmɑ:.nəˈlɪθ.ɪk/ 庞大的；大一统的 too large, too regular, or without interesting differences, and unwilling or unable to be changed

monologue 1 noun [C] (US also monolog) UK /ˈmɒn.əl.ɒg/ US /ˈmɑ:.nə.lɑ:g/ （一个人的）滔滔不绝的话，长篇大论 a long speech by one person [GRE]

monopolize 1 verb [T] (UK usually monopolise) UK /məˈnɒp.əl.aɪz/ US /məˈnɑ:.pəl.aɪz/ [T] (BUSINESS)垄断；包办；实行…的专卖 in business, to control something completely and to prevent other people having any effect on what happens

monopoly noun [C or S] UK /məˈnɒp.əl.i/ US /məˈnɑ:.pəl.i/ C2 垄断（机构）；专卖；独占 (an organization or group that has) complete control of something, especially an area of business, so that others have no share

monosyllabic 1 adjective UK /ˌmɒn.ə.sɪˈlæb.ɪk/ US /ˌmɑ:.noʊ.sɪˈlæb.ɪk/ (PERSON) disapproving 话少而无礼的；寡言少语的 saying very little in a way that is rude or unfriendly

monosyllable noun [C] LANGUAGE specialized UK /ˈmɒn.əˌsɪl.ə.bəl/ US /ˈmɑ:.noʊˌsɪl.ə.bəl/ 单音节词 a word that contains only one syllable

monotheism noun [U] RELIGION UK /ˌmɒn.əʊˈθi:.ɪ.zəm/ US /ˌmɑ:.noʊˈθi:.ɪ.zəm/ 一神论 the belief that there is only one god

monotone noun [U] UK /ˈmɒn.ə.təʊn/ US /ˈmɑ:.nə.toʊn/ 单音调 a sound that stays on the same note without going higher or lower

monotonous adjective UK /məˈnɒt.ən.əs/ US /məˈnɑː.t̬ən.əs/ C1 单调乏味的；毫无变化的 not changing and therefore boring [GRE]

monotony noun [U] UK /məˈnɒt.ən.i/ US /məˈnɑː.t̬ən.i/ (also monotonousness,) 单调乏味；毫无变化 a situation in which something stays the same and is therefore boring

Prefix (Medical): mon(o)- single

Meaning in English: single

Origin language: Greek μονός

English examples:

monoclonal adjective BIOLOGY specialized UK /ˌmɒn.əˈkləʊ.nəl/ US /ˌmɑː.nəˈkloʊ.nəl/ 单克隆的 relating to a group of cells that originally come from a single cell

monoclonal gammopathy of unknown significance noun [U] MEDICAL specialized UK /mɒn.əˌkləʊ.nəl gæmˌɒp.ə.θi əv ʌn.nəʊn sɪgˈnɪf.ɪ.kəns/ US /ˌmɑː.nəˈkloʊ.nəl gæmˈɑː.pə.θi əv ˈʌnˌnoʊn sɪgˈnɪf.ə.kəns/ (abbreviation MGUS); (benign monoclonal gammopathy); (monoclonal gammopathy of undetermined significance) 意义不明的单克隆丙种球蛋白 a condition in which the body produces high levels of an abnormal protein found in the blood, called paraprotein. The condition does not usually cause any symptoms but in a few cases may lead to the development of multiple myeloma (= cancer in the plasma cells in bone marrow).

monocyte disorder noun MEDICAL specialized UK /ˈmɒn.əʊ.saɪt dɪˌsɔː.dəz/ US /ˈmɑː.noʊ.saɪt dɪˌsɔːr.dɚz/ 单核细胞失调 one of various problems that affect monocytes (= a type of white blood cell important for protecting the body against disease)

monomer noun [C] CHEMISTRY specialized UK /ˈmɒn.ə.mər/ US /ˈmɑː.nə.mɚ/ 单体 a chemical substance whose basic molecules can join together to form polymers

mononucleosis noun [U] mainly US UK /ˌmɒn.əʊˌnjuː.kliˈəʊ.sɪs/ US /ˌmɑː.noʊˌnuː.kliˈoʊ.sɪs/ (informal mono); (UK usually glandular fever) 腺热 an infectious disease that has an effect on particular glands and makes you feel weak and sick for a long time

Infectious mononucleosis   传染性腺热 Infectious mononucleosis, also called "mono," is a contagious disease. Epstein-Barr virus (EBV) is the most common cause of infectious mononucleosis, but other viruses can also cause this disease. It is common among teenagers and young adults, especially college students.

monosaccharide noun [C] CHEMISTRY specialized UK /ˌmɒn.əʊˈsæk.ər.aɪd/ US /ˌmɑː.noʊˈsæk.ə.raɪd/ 单糖（一种结构简单的碳水化合物，如葡萄糖、果糖，其分子无法进一步分解）a simple type of carbohydrate, such as glucose and fructose, formed of molecules that cannot be broken down into any simpler form

monosodium glutamate   noun [U] UK /ˌmɒn.əˌsəʊ.di.əm ˈgluː.tə.meɪt/ US /ˌmɑː.nəˌsoʊ.di.əm ˈgluː.t̬ə.meɪt/ (abbreviation MSG) 谷氨酸单钠盐，味精 a chemical that is sometimes added to food to improve the taste

monounsaturated   adjective CHEMISTRY, FOOD & DRINK specialized UK /ˌmɒn.əʊ.ʌnˈsætʃ.ər.eɪ.tɪd/ US /ˌmɑː.noʊ.ʌnˈsætʃ.ə.reɪ.t̬ɪd/ 单不饱和的（其化学结构只有一个双键，据信单不饱和油脂，如橄榄油，比饱和油脂更健康）with a chemical structure that contains one double bond. Monounsaturated fat, for example olive oil, is thought to be healthier than saturated fat.

Compare

polyunsaturated （脂肪或油脂）多重不饱和的 Polyunsaturated fat or oil has a chemical structure that does not easily change into cholesterol (= a substance containing a lot of fat that can cause heart disease) because it contains several double bonds.

saturated fat 饱和脂肪 a type of fat found in meat, eggs, milk, cheese, etc. that is thought to be bad for your health

unsaturated （脂肪或油）不饱和的 Unsaturated fat or oil is either monounsaturated or polyunsaturated, found in plants, vegetable oil, and fish, and thought to be better for your health than saturated fat.

monozygotic adjective BIOLOGY specialized UK /ˌmɒn.əʊ.zaɪˈɡɒt.ɪk/ US /ˌmɑː.noʊ.zaɪˈɡɑː.t̬ɪk/ 单卵的（单卵分裂发育而成的双胞胎，即同卵双生） Monozygotic twins (= two babies born to the same mother at the same time) develop from just one egg.

monozygotic adjective BIOLOGY specialized UK /ˌmɒn.əʊ.zaɪˈɡɒt.ɪk/ US /ˌmɑː.noʊ.zaɪˈɡɑː.t̬ɪk/ 单卵的（单卵分裂发育而成的双胞胎，即同卵双生） Monozygotic twins (= two babies born to the same mother at the same time) develop from just one egg.

Prefix (Medical): morph(o)- form, shape
Meaning in English: form, shape

Origin language: Greek μορφή

English examples

morph verb [I or T] UK /mɔːf/ US /mɔːrf/ （使）图像变形；将（图像）进行合成处理；演变(YAO) to gradually change one image into another, or combine them, using a computer program

morphine   noun [U] UK /ˈmɔː.fiːn/ US /ˈmɔːr.fiːn/ 吗啡 a drug made from opium, used to stop people from feeling pain or to make people feel calmer

morphological   adjective UK /ˌmɔː.fəˈlɒdʒ.ɪ.kəl/ US /ˌmɔːr.fəˈlɑː.dʒɪ.kəl/ BIOLOGY   specialized 形态学的 relating to the scientific study of the structure and form of animals and plants

morphology   noun [U] UK /mɔːˈfɒl.ə.dʒi/ US /mɔːrˈfɑː.lə.dʒi/ specialized 形态学 biology the scientific study of the structure and form of animals and plants

Prefix: multi- many/ much

Meaning in English: many/ much

Origin language: Latin

English examples:

multi-   prefix UK /mʌl.ti-/ US /mʌl.ti-/ /mʌl.taɪ-/ 多个，许多

a multi-faith society   宗教信仰多元化的社会

a multi-coloured skirt (= a skirt with many colours)五彩缤纷的裙子

a multi-vitamin pill   复合维生素药片

multi-ethnic   adjective UK /ˌmʌl.tiˈeθ.nɪk/ US /ˌmʌl.tiˈeθ.nɪk/ 由不同种族组成的；涉及不同种族的 consisting of, or relating to various different races

multicellular   adjective BIOLOGY   specialized UK /ˌmʌl.tiˈsel.jə.lər/ US /ˌmʌl.tiˈsel.jə.lɚ/ 多细胞的 A multicellular organism is made of many cells.

multicoloured   adjective UK (US multicolored) 多种色彩的 having many different colours

multicultural   adjective UK /ˌmʌl.tiˈkʌl.tʃər.əl/ US /ˌmʌl.tiˈkʌl.tʃɚ.əl/ 多元文化的；融合多种文化的 including people who have many different customs and beliefs

multidimensional   adjective UK /ˌmʌl.ti.daɪˈmen.ʃən.əl/ US /ˌmʌl.ti.daɪˈmen.ʃən.əl/ 多元的，多方面的，有众多特点的 having many different features

multidisciplinary   adjective UK /ˌmʌl.ti.dɪs.əˈplɪn.ər.i/ US /ˌmʌl.tiˈdɪs.ə.plɪ.ner.i/ 结合多种学科的；（涉及）多种学科的 involving different subjects of study in one activity

multifaceted   adjective UK /ˌmʌl.tiˈfæs.ɪ.tɪd/ US /ˌmʌl.tiˈfæs.ɪ.t̬ɪd/ 多方面的，多元的 having many different parts

multifarious   adjective   formal UK /ˌmʌl.tɪˈfeə.ri.əs/ US /ˌmʌl.tɪˈfer.i.əs/ 多种类的，各式各样的 of many different types

multilateral   adjective UK /ˌmʌl.tiˈlæt.ər.əl/ US /ˌmʌl.tiˈlæt̬.ɚ.əl/ 多国（或多方）参加的，多国（或多方）间的 involving more than two groups or countries

multilingual   adjective UK /ˌmʌl.tiˈlɪŋ.gwəl/ US /ˌmʌl.tiˈlɪŋ.gwəl/ 使用多种语言的；用多种语言表达的 (of people or groups) able to use more than two languages for communication, or (of a thing) written or spoken in more than two different languages

multinational   1 adjective UK /ˌmʌl.tiˈnæʃ.ən.əl/ US /-t̬i-/ 多国的；（企业）在多国经营的，跨国的 involving several different countries, or (of a business) producing and selling goods in several different countries

multiparty　　　adjective [before noun]　POLITICS UK /ˌmʌl.tiˈpɑ :.ti/ US /ˌmʌl.tiˈpɑ :r.ţi/ 多党派的 involving several political parties

multiple　　1 adjective UK /ˈmʌl.tɪ.pəl/ US /ˈmʌl.tə.pəl/ 多个的；多种的 C1 very many of the same type, or of different types

multiple-choice　　adjective [before noun] UK /ˌmʌl.tɪ.pəlˈtʃɔɪs/ US /ˌmʌl.tə.pəlˈtʃɔɪs/ 多项选择的；由多项选择题组成的 A multiple-choice test or question is one in which you are given a list of answers and you have to choose the correct one.

multiply　　　verb [I or T] UK /ˈmʌl.tɪ.plaɪ/ US /ˈmʌl.tə.plaɪ/ 大幅增加；乘，使相乘 to increase very much in number, or (in mathematics) to add a number to itself a particular number of times

multiplicity　　　noun [U]　formal UK /ˌmʌl.tɪˈplɪs.ə.ti/ US /ˌmʌl.tə ˈplɪs.ə.ţi/ 多种多样，多样性 a large number or wide range (of something)

multipurpose　　adjective UK /ˌmʌl.tiˈpɜː.pəs/ US /ˌmʌl.tiˈpɜː.pəs/ 多用途的；多功能的 A multipurpose tool, etc. can be used in several different ways.

multiracial　　　adjective UK /ˌmʌl.tiˈreɪ.ʃəl/ US /ˌmʌl.tiˈreɪ.ʃəl/ 多种族的 involving people of several different races

multistorey　　　1 adjective UK (US multistory) UK /ˌmʌl.tiˈstɔː.ri/ US /ˌmʌl.tiˈstɔːr.i/ 多层的 A multistorey building has several floors.

multitasking   1 noun [U] UK /ˌmʌl.tiˈtɑ:s.kɪŋ/ US /ˌmʌl.tiˈtæs.kɪŋ/ [U] (PERSON) 同时做多件事 a person's ability to do more than one thing at a time

multitude   noun formal UK /ˈmʌl.tɪ.tʃuːd/ US /ˈmʌl.tə.tuːd/ 许多，众多 a large number of people or things

multitudinous   adjective UK /ˌmʌl.tɪˈtjuː.dɪ.nəs/ US /-təˈtuː-/ literary 众多；大量；(YAO) consisting of many things or parts:

Prefix (Medical): muscul(o)- muscle

Meaning in English: muscle

Origin language: Latin

English examples:

muscle   1 noun UK /ˈmʌs.əl/ US /ˈmʌs.əl/ (BODY PART) B2 [C or U] 肌肉 one of many tissues in the body that can tighten and relax to produce movement

muscle in   informal 强行挤入 to force your way into a situation and make certain you are included, although you are not wanted

muscle-bound   adjective disapproving UK /ˈmʌs.əl.baʊnd/ US /ˈmʌs.əl.baʊnd/ 肌肉僵硬粗大的 used to describe someone who has very large muscles that make it difficult to move normally

muscle-flexing   noun [U] UK /ˈmʌs.əlˌflek.sɪŋ/ US /ˈmʌs.əlˌflek.sɪŋ/ 军事（或政治）实力的显示 a public show of military or political power that is intended to worry an opponent

muscled   adjective /ˈmʌs.əld/ /ˈmʌs.əld/ 肌肉发达的；强健的 having a lot of well-developed muscles

muscleman   noun [C] UK /ˈmʌs.əl.mæn/ US /ˈmʌs.əl.mæn/ plural -men UK /-men/ US 肌肉发达的人，强壮的男子 a man who has very large muscles as a result of doing special exercises to improve them

muscly   adjective UK informal UK /ˈmʌs.li/ US /ˈmʌs.li/ 肌肉发达的；强健的 having a lot of well-developed muscles

muscular   1 adjective UK /ˈmʌs.kjə.lər/ US /ˈmʌs.kjə.lɚ/ (BODY) 肌肉的 related to muscles

muscular contractions   肌肉收缩

muscular pain   肌肉疼痛

having well-developed muscles 肌肉发达的；强壮的

muscular dystrophy   noun [U] UK /ˌmʌs.kjə.lə ˈdɪs.trə.fi/ US /ˌmʌs.kjə.lɚ ˈdɪs.trə.fi/ 肌肉萎缩 a serious disease in which a person's muscles gradually become weaker until walking is no longer possible

muscularis   noun [S] MEDICAL specialized UK /mʌs.kjəˈl ɑ ː.rɪs/ US /ˌmʌs.kjəˈler.ɪs/ 肌层 the layer of muscle surrounding a hollow organ

musculature   noun [U] UK /ˈmʌs.kjə.lə.tʃər/ US /ˈmʌs.kjə.lə.tʃɚ/ 肌肉系统 the position and structure of the muscles

By looking at the bones of this animal, we can discover quite a lot about its musculature.   通过观察这种动物的骨骼，我们可以了解其肌肉系统的不少特点。

musculi   noun [C] ANATOMY specialized UK /ˈmʌs.kjə.laɪ/ US /ˈmʌs.kjə.laɪ/ （拉丁语，用于医学术语）肌肉的 a Latin word meaning "of the muscle", used in medical names and descriptions

musculocutaneous   adjective   MEDICAL   specialized UK
/ˌmʌs.kjə.ləʊ.kjuːˈteɪ.ni.əs/ US /ˌmʌs.kjəˌloʊ.kjuːˈteɪ.ni.əs/ 肌皮的 relating to
or supplying the muscles and the skin

musculoskeletal   adjective   MEDICAL   specialized UK
/ˌmʌs.kjə.ləʊˈskel.ɪ.təl/ US /ˌmʌs.kjə.loʊˈskel.ə.təl/ 肌肉与骨骼的 relating to
the muscles and skeleton and including bones, joints, tendons, and muscles

the musculoskeletal system   肌肉骨骼系统

a musculoskeletal injury   肌肉骨骼受伤

musculus   noun [C]   MEDICAL   specialized UK /ˈmʌs.kjə.ləs/ US
/ˈmʌs.kjə.ləs/ （拉丁语，用于医学术语）肌肉的 a Latin word meaning
"muscle", used in medical names and descriptions

Prefix: must- something that is so good, you must do it, have it, or see it
Meaning in English: something that is so good, you must do it, have it, or see it

Origin language: Latin / Greek

English examples:

must-   7 prefix   informal UK /mʌst-/ US /mʌst-/ 必须要做 / 有 / 看的
something that is so good, you must do it, have it, or see it

a must-do, must-have, must-see, etc. 必须要做 / 有 / 看的 something that is
so good, you must do it, have it, or see it

The cashmere scarf is this season's must-have.   羊绒围巾是本季的必备品。

It's a moderately entertaining film but it's certainly not a must-see.   这部电
影娱乐性还不错，但肯定不是非看不可的。

must-have   adjective [before noun] UK /ˈmʌst.hæv/ US /ˈmʌst.hæv/ 必备的 A must-have object is something that many people want to own.

must-read   noun [C] UK /ˌmʌstˈriːd/ US /ˌmʌstˈriːd/ 必读的（东西） something that many people want to read or that a particular group of people should read

Prefix (Medical): my(o)- Of or relating to muscle

Meaning in English: Of or relating to muscle

Origin language: Ancient Greek μῦς, μυ- (mys, my-), muscle; mouse; mussel

English examples:

cardiomyopathy noun [U] medical specialized UK /ˌkɑː.di.əʊ.maɪˈɒp.ə.θi/ US /ˌkɑːr.di.oʊ.maɪˈɑːp.ə.θi/ 心肌病 a disease in which the muscle of the heart is much thicker, bigger, or stiffer than normal

leiomyoma   noun [C] MEDICAL specialized UK /ˌlaɪ.əʊ.maɪˈəʊ.mə/ US /ˌlaɪ.oʊ.maɪˈoʊ.mə/ 平滑肌瘤 a benign tumour (= one that is not likely to cause death) of muscle tissue, especially in the uterus (= the organ in a woman's body where a baby develops)

Electromyography   肌电图 Electromyography (EMG) measures muscle response or electrical activity in response to a nerve's stimulation of the muscle. The test is used to help detect neuromuscular abnormalities. During the test, one or more small needles (also called electrodes) are inserted through the skin into the muscle.

myocardial   adjective MEDICAL specialized UK /ˌmaɪ.əʊˈkɑː.di.əl/ US /ˌmaɪ.oʊˈkɑːr.di.əl/ 心肌的 relating to the muscle tissue of the heart

myocardial infarction   心肌梗塞

myocardial ischaemia   心肌缺血

myocardial infarction   noun [C]   MEDICAL   specialized UK /maɪ.ə͵k ɑ :.di.əl ɪnˈf ɑ :k.ʃən/ US /maɪ.ə͵k ɑ :r.di.əl ɪnˈf ɑ :r:k.ʃən/ 心肌梗塞 a heart attack

myocarditis   noun [U]   MEDICAL   specialized UK /͵maɪ.əʊ.k ɑ :ˈdaɪ.tɪs/ US /͵maɪ.oʊ.k ɑ :rˈdaɪ.təs/ 心肌炎 inflammation of the inner muscular layer of the heart, usually caused by a viral infection

myocardium   noun [U]   ANATOMY   specialized UK /͵maɪ.əˈk ɑ :.di.əm/ US /͵maɪ.əˈk ɑ :r.di.əm/ 心肌 the muscle that forms the walls of the heart

myoclonus noun [U]   MEDICAL   specialized UK /͵maɪ.əˈkləʊ.nəs/ US /maɪˈ ɑ :.klə.nəs/ 肌阵孪 sudden short movements of a muscle or group of muscles that you cannot control

Myokymia 肌纤维抽搐 (Google) Myokymia of the lid is a unilateral and uncontrollable lid twitch or tic that is not caused by disease or pathology. Myokymia is thought to be brought on by stress and other similar issues and resolves on its own with time. It usually involves the lower eyelid and is self-limiting to a few days or a week.

myopathy   noun [U or C]   MEDICAL   specialized UK /maɪˈɒp.ə.θi/ US /maɪˈ ɑ :.pə.θi/ 肌病 a disease of the muscles:

Myositis   肌炎 Myositis means inflammation of the muscles that you use to move your body. An injury, infection, or autoimmune disease can cause it. Two specific kinds are polymyositis （多发性肌炎） and dermatomyositis （皮肌炎）. Polymyositis causes muscle weakness, usually in the muscles closest to the trunk of your body.

myotome   A myotome （肌节）is the group of muscles that a single spinal nerve innervates. Similarly a dermatome （皮节）is an area of skin that a single nerve innervates. In vertebrate embryonic development, a myotome is the part of a somite that develops into muscle.

myoblast   noun [C] 成肌细胞 Myoblasts are the embryonic precursors of myocytes (also called muscle cells).

Myogenesis   noun [C] 肌生成 Myogenesis is the formation of skeletal muscular tissue, particularly during embryonic development. Muscle fibers generally form through the fusion of precursor myoblasts into multinucleated fibers called myotubes. Wikipedia

Prefix (Medical): myc(o)- fungus

Meaning in English: fungus

Origin language: Greek μύκης, μυκητ-

English examples:

mycology   noun [U] UK /maɪˈkɒl.ə.dʒi/ US /maɪˈk ɑ ː.lə.dʒi/ 真菌学 the scientific study of fungi

Ascomycetes   子囊菌门 Ascomycetes are 'spore shooters'. They are fungi which produce microscopic spores inside special, elongated cells or sacs, known as 'asci', which give the group its name. Asexual reproduction is the dominant form of propagation in the Ascomycota, and is responsible for the rapid spread of these fungi into new areas.

Mycoplasma pneumoniae bacteria   肺炎支原体细菌 Mycoplasma pneumoniae bacteria commonly cause mild infections of the respiratory system (the parts of the body involved in breathing). The most common illness caused by these bacteria, especially in children, is tracheobronchitis (chest cold). Lung infections caused by M. pneumoniae are sometimes referred to as "walking pneumonia" since symptoms are generally mild. Sometimes M. pneumoniae can cause more serious lung infections that require care in a hospital though.

Onychomycosis   甲癣; 甲真菌病,俗称臭甲、灰指甲 Onychomycosis (tinea unguium) is a fungal infection of the fingernails or toenails that causes discoloration, thickening, and separation from the nail bed. Onychomycosis is fungal infection of the nail plate, nail bed, or both. The nails typically are deformed and discolored white or yellow. Diagnosis is by appearance, wet mount, culture, polymerase chain reaction, or a combination. Treatment, when indicated, is with oral terbinafine or itraconazole. Onychomycosis occurs in 10% of the general population but is more common in older adults; the prevalence is 20% in those older than 60 years and 50% in those older than 70 years.

Prefix (Medical): myel(o)- Of or relating to bone marrow

Meaning in English: Of or relating to bone marrow

Origin language: Ancient Greek μυελόν (myelon), marrow; bone-marrow

English examples:

agnogenic myeloid metaplasia   noun [U] UK /æg.nəˌdʒen.ɪk ˌmaɪ.ə.lɔɪd met.əˈpleɪ.ʒə/ US /æg.nəˌdʒen.ɪk ˌmaɪ.ə.lɔɪd met.əˈpleɪ.ʒə/ also myelofibrosis specialized 特发性髓样化生 a condition in which scar tissue grows in the bone marrow so that not enough blood cells are produced for the body

myelin   noun [U]   ANATOMY   specialized UK /ˈmaɪə.lɪn/ US /ˈmaɪə.lɪn/ 髓磷脂（含大量脂肪，特别是在脑神经周围形成保护层，保障脑神经有效发出信号） a substance containing a lot of fat that forms a covering around nerves, especially those in the brain, protecting them and helping them to send signals effectively

The myelin sheath around the neuron is damaged. 神经元周围的髓鞘遭到破坏。

myelin damage   noun [U]   MEDICAL   specialized UK /ˈmaɪə.lɪn ˌdæm.ɪdʒ/ US /ˈmaɪə.lɪn ˌdæm.ɪdʒ/ 髓鞘损伤 damage to the fatty substance that covers nerves

myelocele   noun [C or U]   MEDICAL   specialized UK /ˈmaɪ.ə.ləʊˌsiːl/ US /ˈmaɪ.ə.loʊˌsiːl/ 脊髓突出 a place where the spinal cord sticks out through a defect in the spine, or the act of doing this

myelofibrosis   noun MEDICAL specialized UK /ˌmaɪ.ə.ləʊ.faɪˈbrəʊ.sɪs/ US /ˌmaɪ.ə.loʊ.faɪˈbroʊ.sɪs/ (also agnogenic myeloid metaplasia) 骨髓纤维化，骨髓纤维变性 a condition in which scar tissue grows in the bone marrow so that not enough blood cells are produced for the body

myeloma   noun [C or U]   MEDICAL   specialized UK /maɪ.əˈləʊ.mə/ US /ˌmaɪ.əˈloʊ.mə/ 骨髓瘤 cancer of the plasma cells in the bone marrow of the large bones of the body that will result in death if not treated

She was diagnosed with multiple myeloma when fractures in her vertebrae were found.   当她的脊椎被发现有裂缝时，她被诊断出患有多发性骨髓瘤。

myelomeningocele   noun [U]   MEDICAL   specialized UK /ˌmaɪ.ə.ləʊ.menˈɪŋ.gə.siːl/ US /ˌmaɪ.ə.loʊ.menˈɪŋ.gə.siːl/ 脊髓脊膜突出 a condition in which the backbone and spinal canal do not close before birth. It is a type of spina bifida.

amyelia   先天性脊髓缺失 congenital absence of the spinal cord.

myeloblast   A type of immature white blood cell that forms in the bone marrow. Myeloblasts become mature white blood cells called granulocytes (neutrophils, basophils, and eosinophils). Enlarge. Blood cell development.

myelogenous   Having to do with, produced by, or resembling the bone marrow

myeloid   Having to do with or resembling the bone marrow.

agnogenic myeloid metaplasia noun [U]   MEDICAL   specialized UK /æg.nə͵dʒen.ɪk ͵maɪ.ə.lɔɪd met.ə'pleɪ.ʒə/ US /æg.nə͵dʒen.ɪk ͵maɪ.ə.lɔɪd met.ə'pleɪ.ʒə/ (also myelofibrosis) 特发性髓样化生 a condition in which scar tissue grows in the bone marrow so that not enough blood cells are produced for the body

Myelopoiesis   In hematology, myelopoiesis in the broadest sense of the term is the production of bone marrow and of all cells that arise from it, namely, all blood cells. Wikipedia

Myeloblast   noun [C] 成髓细胞 (MY-eh-loh-blast) A type of immature white blood cell that forms in the bone marrow. Myeloblasts become mature white blood cells called granulocytes (neutrophils, basophils, and eosinophils). The myeloblast is a unipotent stem cell which differentiates into the effectors of the granulocyte series. It is found in the bone marrow. 一种在骨髓中形成的未成熟白细胞。 成髓细胞变成成熟的白细胞，称为粒细胞（中性粒细胞、嗜碱性粒细胞和嗜酸性粒细胞）。 成髓细胞是一种单能干细胞，可分化为粒细胞系列的效应物。 它存在于骨髓中。

poliomyelitis   Polio 脊髓灰质炎，小儿麻痹症, or poliomyelitis, is a disabling and life-threatening disease caused by the poliovirus. The virus spreads from person to person and can infect a person's spinal cord, causing paralysis

Prefix (Medical): myring(o)- eardrum

Meaning in English: eardrum

Origin language: Latin myringa

English examples:

Myringotomy   noun [C] 鼓膜切开术 A myringotomy is a surgical procedure in which an incision is created in the eardrum to relieve pressure

caused by excessive buildup of fluid, or to drain pus from the middle ear.
Wikipedia

Prefix (Medical): myx(o)- mucus
Meaning in English: mucus 粘液

Origin language: Greek μύξα

English examples:

Myxoma　　noun [C] 粘液瘤；粘液瘤 Myxoma is a noncancerous tumor that arises from connective tissue, which is tissue that connects and supports other tissues all over the body. Most frequently, myxomas are found in the heart and are referred to as cardiac myxomas, which are the most common type of primary cardiac tumors in adults.

myxomatosis　　noun [U] UK /ˌmɪk.sə.məˈtəʊ.sɪs/ US /ˌmɪk.sə.məˈtoʊ.sɪs/ （通常致兔子死亡的）黏液瘤病 an infectious disease of rabbits that usually kills them

Myxedema　　noun [C] 粘液性水肿 Myxedema is another term for severely advanced hypothyroidism. It's a condition that occurs when your body doesn't produce enough thyroid hormone. The thyroid is a small gland that sits right at the front of your neck. It releases hormones that help your body regulate energy and control a wide variety of functions. 粘液性水肿是严重晚期甲状腺功能减退症的另一个术语。 当您的身体不能产生足够的甲状腺激素时，就会出现这种情况。 甲状腺是一个小腺体，位于您的脖子前面。 它释放激素，帮助您的身体调节能量并控制各种功能。

NNN

Prefix: nano- one billionth of the stated unit
Meaning in English:

Origin language: Latin / Greek

English examples:

nano-   prefix   SCIENCE   specialized UK /næn.əʊ-/ US /næn.oʊ-/ 十亿分之一的 one billionth of the stated unit

nanocomputer   noun [C] UK /ˈnæn.əʊ.kəmˌpjuː.tər/ US /ˈnæn.oʊ.kəmˌpju.t̬ɚ/ 纳米计算机（零部件小到只能通过显微镜才能看到）a computer with electronic parts that are so small that they can only be seen using a microscope

a nanosecond   纳秒（十亿分之一秒）

nanogram   noun [C]   SCIENCE   specialized UK /ˈnæn.ə.græm/ US /ˈnæn.əˌgræm/ 毫微克，纳克 0.000,000,001 of a gram

nanometre   noun [C] UK (US nanometer) UK /ˈnæn.əʊˌmiː.tər/ US /ˈnæn.oʊˌmiː.t̬ɚ/ 毫微米，纳米 0.000,000,001 of a metre

nanosecond   noun [C] UK /ˈnæn.əʊˌsek.ənd/ US /ˈnæn.oʊˌsek.ənd/ 毫微秒，纳秒 0.000,000,001 seconds

nanotechnology   noun [U] UK /ˌnæn.əʊ.tekˈnɒl.ə.dʒi/ US /ˌnæn.oʊ.tekˈnɑː.lə.dʒi/ 纳米技术（指通过控制原子的组合排列开发制造微型器具的学科） an area of science that deals with developing and producing extremely small tools and machines by controlling the arrangement of separate atoms

Prefix (Medical): narc(o)- numb, sleep

Meaning in English: numb, sleep

Origin language: Greek νάρκη

English examples:

narcissism noun [U] PSYCHOLOGY disapproving UK /ˈnɑː.sɪ.sɪ.zəm/ US /ˈnɑːr.sə.sɪ.zəm/ （对容貌和能力的）自我陶醉，孤芳自赏，自恋 too much interest in and admiration for your own physical appearance and/or your own abilities [GRE]

narcissist noun [C] PSYCHOLOGY UK /ˈnɑː.sɪ.sɪst/ US /ˈnɑːr.sə.sɪst/ 自我陶醉者，自恋者 someone who has too much admiration for himself or herself

narcissistic personality disorder noun [C or U] PSYCHOLOGY specialized UK /nɑː.sɪˌsɪs.tɪk pɜː.sənˈæl.ə.ti dɪˌsɔːd.ər/ US /ˌnɑːr.sɪˈsɪs.tɪk ˌpɜː.səˈnæl.ə.ţi dɪˌsɔːr.dɚ/ 自恋型人格异常 a personality disorder in which someone has too much admiration for himself or herself and too much concern with his or her own importance

narcissus noun [C] UK /nɑːˈsɪs.əs/ US /nɑːrˈsɪs.əs/ plural narcissi narcissuses or narcissus 水仙花 a yellow, white, or orange flower, similar to a daffodil

narcolepsy noun [U] UK /ˈnɑː.kə.lep.si/ US /ˈnɑːr.kə.lep.si/ Medical Specialized 发作性睡病，嗜睡病 a medical condition that makes you go to sleep suddenly and when you do not expect it

narcosis noun nar·co·sis | \ när-ˈkō-səs \ plural narcoses\ när-ˈkō-ˌsēz \ 药物引起的昏迷、嗜睡或无意识状态 a state of stupor, unconsciousness, or arrested activity produced by the influence of narcotics or other chemical or physical agents — compare NITROGEN NARCOSIS

narcotic 1 noun [C] UK /nɑːˈkɒt.ɪk/ US /nɑːrˈkɑːţ.ɪk/ mainly US 毒品 （如海洛因或可卡因） an illegal drug such as heroin or cocaine Prefix (Medical): narc(o)- numb, sleep 2 MEDICAL specialized 催眠药；麻醉剂 a drug that makes you want to sleep and prevents you feeling pain 3 adjective UK /nɑːˈkɒt.ɪk/ US /nɑːrˈkɑːt̬ɪk/ 催眠药；麻醉剂 relating to drugs that make you want to sleep and prevent pain

Prefix (Medical): nas(o)- Of or pertaining to the nose

Meaning in English: Of or pertaining to the nose

Origin language: Latin (nāsum), nose

English examples:

aurinasal   耳鼻的 relating to the ear and nose.

nasal   1 adjective UK /ˈneɪ.zəl/ US /ˈneɪ.zəl/ 鼻的 related to the nose

nasal passages   鼻道

nasal congestion   鼻塞

the nasal cavity   鼻腔

a nasal spray   鼻腔喷剂

nasalis   noun ANATOMY specialized UK /neɪˈzɑː.lɪs/ US /neɪˈzæl.ɪs/ 鼻肌 one of the three muscles of the nose

nasalization   noun [U] PHONETICS specialized (UK usually nasalisation) UK /ˌneɪ.zəl.aɪˈzeɪ.ʃən/ US /ˌneɪ.zəl.əˈzeɪ.ʃən/ 鼻音化 the effect on a speech sound when air escapes through the nose

nasi   adjective MEDICAL specialized UK /ˈneɪ.zaɪ/ US /ˈneɪ.zaɪ/ （拉丁语，用于医学术语）鼻的 a Latin word meaning "of the nose", used in medical names and descriptions

compare:

nasi goreng noun [U] UK /ˌnaː.zi gəˈreŋ/ US /ˌnæz.i gəˈreŋ/ （加入各色的肉粒和蔬菜粒的）印尼炒饭 an Indonesian rice dish with pieces of meat and vegetables added

Prefix: near- "almost"

Meaning in English: combines with adjectives and nouns to mean "almost"

Origin language: Latin / Greek

English examples:

near-　　　7 prefix UK /nɪər-/ US /nɪr-/ （与形容词和名词连用）几乎，差不多 combines with adjectives and nouns to mean "almost"

We had a near-disaster this morning in the car!　　我们今天上午险些出了车祸！

She was near-hysterical by the time I arrived there. 我到那儿的时候，她近乎歇斯底里了。

nearly　　　adverb UK /ˈnɪə.li/ US /ˈnɪr.li/ A2 几乎，差不多，将近 almost, or not completely

near miss　　1 noun [C usually singular] UK /ˌnɪə ˈmɪs/ US /ˌnɪr ˈmɪs/ [C usually singular] (HIT) (also near thing) 几乎击中；几乎相撞 a situation in which something almost hits something else 2 noun [C usually singular] (HAPPEN) 功亏一篑 an attempt to do or achieve something that fails although it almost succeeds

near the knuckle　　　UK informal 近乎下流，近乎猥亵 about sex and therefore likely to offend people

near thing　　　noun [S] UK UK /ˌnɪə ˈθɪŋ/ US /ˌnɪr ˈθɪŋ/ 险胜，侥幸取胜 a situation in which you almost failed to achieve something and only just succeeded

near-death experience   noun [C] UK /ˌnɪəˌdeθ ɪkˈspɪə.ri.əns/ US /ˌnɪrˌdeθ ɪkˈspɪr.i.əns/ 濒死体验 an experience described by some people who have been close to death, in which the person feels as if they have left their body and are watching themselves from above

Prefix (Medical): necr(o)- death

Meaning in English: death

Origin language: Greek νεκρός

English examples:

Necrotizing fasciitis   noun [C] 坏死性筋膜炎，又称食肉菌感染或噬肉菌感染（Flesh-eating disease） Flesh-eating bacteria (necrotizing fasciitis) is a rare infection of the skin and tissues below it. It can be deadly if not treated quickly. Necrotizing fasciitis spreads quickly and aggressively in an infected person. It causes tissue death at the infection site and beyond.

necromancy   noun [U] UK /ˈnek.rə.mæn.si/ US /ˈnek.rə.mæn.si/ 通灵术，（招亡魂问卜的）巫术；妖术 the act of communicating with the dead in order to discover what is going to happen in the future, or black magic (= magic used for bad purposes)   necr- Meaning in English: dead

Necromimesis   一个人认为自己已经死去的病态状态 a pathological state in which a person believes himself or herself to be dead   mim- Meaning in English: repeat

necrophilia   noun [U] UK /ˌnek.rəˈfɪl.i.ə/ US /ˌnek.rəˈfɪl.i.ə/ 恋尸癖 being sexually attracted to dead bodies, or sexual activity with dead bodies

necrophiliac   noun [C] UK /ˌnek.rəˈfɪl.i.æk/ US /ˌnek.rəˈfɪl.i.æk/ 恋尸癖者 a person who is sexually attracted to or has sex with dead bodies

necropolis noun [C] UK /nekˈrɒp.əl.ɪs/ US /nekˈrɑ·.əl.ɪs/ 古冢，古代坟场 an ancient cemetery (= piece of ground where people are buried)

necrophobia 死尸恐惧症 Necrophobia is a specific type of phobia that involves a fear of dead things and things that are associated with death. A person with this type of phobia may be afraid of dead bodies as well as things such as coffins, tombstones, and graveyards.

necrosis noun [U] MEDICAL specialized UK /ˈnek.rəʊ.sɪs/ US /neˈkroʊ.sɪs/ （细胞组织）坏死 death of cell tissues

necrotic adjective MEDICAL specialized UK /nekˈrɒt.ɪk/ US /-ˈrɑ·.t̬ɪk/ （细胞组织）坏死的 (of cell tissues) dying

Prefix: neo- new or recent, or in a modern form

Meaning in English: new or recent, or in a modern form

Origin language: Latin / Greek

English examples:

neo- prefix UK /niː.əʊ-/ US /niː.oʊ-/ 新的；最近的；新型的 new or recent, or in a modern form

neo-fascist 新法西斯主义的

neo-Nazi 新纳粹党人

neo-realist cinema 新现实主义电影

neoclassical adjective UK /ˌniː.əʊˈklæs.ɪ.kəl/ US /ˌniː.oʊˈklæs.ɪ.kəl/ specialized 新古典主义的 made in a style that is based on the art and building designs of ancient Greece and Rome

neocolonialism   noun [U] UK /ˌniː.əʊ.kəˈləʊ.ni.əl.ɪ.zəm/ US /ˌniː.oʊ.kəˈloʊ.ni.əl.ɪ.zəm/新殖民主义 political control by a rich country of a poorer country that should be independent and free to govern itself

neocon   noun [C] UK /ˈniː.əʊ.kɒn/ US /ˈniː.oʊ.kɑ ːn/ informal 新保守主义派（一些倡导使用军事力量的美国共和党人，neo-conservative 的缩写） abbreviation for neo-conservative: in the US, someone who is a Republican and thinks that the US should use its military power

neoliberal   adjective   FINANCE & ECONOMICS UK /ˌniː.əʊˈlɪb.ər.əl/ US /ˌniː.oʊˈlɪb.ər.əl'/ 新自由主义的（支持增加市场自由度，减少政府干预和花费，降低税收） supporting a large amount of freedom for markets, with little government control or spending, and low taxes

neolithic   adjective   SCIENCE   specialized UK /ˌniː.əˈlɪθ.ɪk/ US /ˌniː.oʊˈlɪθ.ɪk/ 新石器时代的 relating to the period when humans used tools and weapons made of stone and had just developed farming

neologism   noun [C]   LANGUAGE   formal UK /niˈɒl.ə.dʒɪ.zəm/ US /niˈɑ ːlə.dʒɪ.zəm/ 新词；新语汇；旧词新义 a new word or expression, or a new meaning for an existing word

neonatal   adjective [before noun] UK /ˌniː.əʊˈneɪ.təl/ US /ˌniː.oʊˈneɪ.təl/ 新生儿的；新生期的 of or for babies that were born recently

neonate   noun [C]   MEDICAL   specialized UK /ˈniː.əʊ.neɪt/ US /ˈniː.əˌneɪt/ 不足四周的婴儿 a baby who is less than four weeks old

neophyte   noun [C]   formal UK /ˈniː.ə.faɪt/ US /ˈniː.oʊ.faɪt/ 新手；初学者 someone who has recently become involved in an activity and is still learning about it [GRE]

Meaning in English: Of or pertaining to the kidney

Origin language: Ancient Greek νεφρός (nephrós), kidney

English examples:

nephrogenic systemic fibrosis   noun [U]   MEDICAL   specialized UK /nef.rəˌdʒen.ɪk sɪˌstem.ɪk faɪˈbrəʊ.sɪs/ US /ˌnef.rəˈdʒen.ɪk sɪˈstem.ɪk faɪˈbroʊ.sɪs/ 肾源性系统性纤维化 a condition in which there are many areas of thick, hard skin that usually affect the kidneys but may also affect the heart and lungs

nephrologist   noun [C]   MEDICAL   specialized UK /nɪˈfrɒl.ə.dʒɪst/ US /nɪˈfr ɑ :.lə.dʒɪst/ 肾病学家, 治疗肾病的专家 a doctor or scientist who specializes in nephrology

nephrology   noun [U]   MEDICAL   specialized UK /nɪˈfrɒl.ə.dʒi/ US /nɪˈfr ɑ :.lə.dʒi/ 肾病学 the area of science and medicine that is concerned with the kidneys

nephron   noun [C]   MEDICAL   specialized UK /ˈnef.rɒn/ US /ˈnef.r ɑ :n/肾元，肾单位 a basic unit of the kidney

肾脏中含有几百万个被称为肾元的过滤单位。   The kidneys contain millions of tiny filtering units called nephrons.

nephron-sparing surgery   noun [U or C]   MEDICAL   specialized UK /ˌnef.rɒnˌspeə.rɪŋ ˈsɜː.dʒər.i/ US /ˌnef.r ɑ :nˌsper.ɪŋ ˈsɜː.dʒər.i/ 保留肾单位手术 an operation to remove of a kidney tumour by removing only part of the kidney

nephropathy   noun [U]   MEDICAL   specialized UK /nɪˈfrɒp.ə.θi/ US /nɪˈfrɑː.p.ə.θi/肾病 kidney disease

在同时患有肾病的糖尿病人身上心力衰竭很常见。   Heart failure is common in diabetic patients with nephropathy.

Prefix (Medical): nerv- Of or pertaining to nerves and the nervous system

Meaning in English: Of or pertaining to nerves and the nervous system

[Uncommon as a root: neuro- mostly always used]

Origin language: Latin (nervus), tendon; nerve; Cognate with the Greek νευρον (neuron)

English examples:

nerve   1 noun UK /nɜːv/ US /nɝːv/ (BODY) C2 [C] 神经 a group of long, thin fibres (= structures like threads) that carry information or instructions between the brain and other parts of the body

the optic nerve	视神经
a spinal nerve	脊神经
nerve damage	神经损伤
nerve fibres	神经纤维

nerve cell   noun [C]   BIOLOGY UK /ˈnɜːv ˌsel/ US /ˈnɝːv ˌsel/ 神经元 a cell that carries information between the brain and other parts of the body

nerve agent   noun [C or U] UK /ˈnɜːv ˌeɪ.dʒənt/ US /ˈnɝːv ˌeɪ.dʒənt/ （用作武器的）神经毒剂 a poisonous substance that damages the nervous system of the body, used as a weapon

nerve centre   noun [C] UK (US nerve center) UK /ˈnɜːv ˌsen.tər/ US /ˈnɝːv ˌsen.tɚ/ 中枢；核心；控制中心 a place from which an organization or activity is controlled or managed

nerve-racking   adjective (also nerve-wracking) UK /ˈnɜːvˌræk.ɪŋ/ US /ˈnɝːvˌræk.ɪŋ/ 伤脑筋的；使人心烦的 Something that is nerve-racking is difficult to do and causes a lot of worry for the person involved in it.

nerveless   adjective UK /ˈnɜːv.ləs/ US /ˈnɝːv.ləs/ 沉着的；镇定自若的 calm and confident about something difficult that you are doing

nervous   1 adjective UK /ˈnɜː.vəs/ US /ˈnɝː.vəs/ (WORRIED) B1 担心的；紧张不安的 worried and anxious 2 adjective (BODY) 神经的；神经系统的 relating to the nerves

nervous breakdown   noun [C usually singular] UK /ˌnɜː.vəs ˈbreɪk.daʊn/ US /ˌnɝː.vəs ˈbreɪk.daʊn/ 神经失常；神经衰弱 a period of mental illness, usually without a physical cause, that results in anxiety, difficulty in sleeping and thinking clearly, a loss of confidence and hope, and a feeling of great sadness

He suffered a nervous breakdown in his twenties.   他二十多岁的时候曾患神经衰弱。

nervous system   noun [C usually singular] UK /ˈnɜː.vəs ˌsɪs.təm/ US /ˈnɝː.vəs ˌsɪs.təm/ 神经系统 An animal's or person's nervous system consists of its brain and all the nerves in its body that together make movement and feeling possible by sending messages around the body.

nervously   adverb UK /ˈnɜː.vəs.li/ US /ˈnɝː.vəs.li/ B2 担忧地，焦虑地 feeling or showing that you are worried and anxious

He looked nervously over his shoulder, making sure no one else was listening.他紧张地回头望了一下，以确定没有其他人在听。

nervousness   noun [U] UK /ˈnɜː.vəs.nəs/ US /ˈnɝː.vəs.nəs/ C1 担忧，焦虑 a feeling of worry and anxiety

There is growing nervousness about the possibility of a war. 担心爆发战争的紧张情绪不断加剧。

nervus   noun   MEDICAL   specialized UK /ˈnɜː.vəs/ US /ˈnɝː.vəs/ plural nervi （拉丁语，用于医学用语）神经 a Latin word meaning "nerve" or "group of nerves", used in medical names and descriptions

nervy   adjective UK UK /ˈnɜː.vi/ US /ˈnɝː.vi/ 紧张不安的 worried

I'm always nervy before an exam.   我在考试前总是很紧张。

Prefix: neur(o)- relating to nerves

Meaning in English: relating to nerves

Origin language: Latin / Greek

English examples:

neur(o)-   prefix UK /njʊə.rəʊ-/ US /nʊr.oʊ-/ 神经的；神经系统的 relating to nerves

neuroscience   神经系统科学

A neurotransmitter is a chemical that nerve cells use to communicate with each other and with muscles. 神经传递素是神经细胞用来在相互之间及向肌肉组织传递信号的化学物质。

neural   **adjective** [before noun] UK /ˈnjʊə.rəl/ US /ˈnʊr.əl/ 神经的；神经系统的 involving a nerve or the system of nerves that includes the brain

neural network   noun [C] UK /ˌnjʊə.rəl ˈnet.wɜːk/ US /ˌnʊr.əl ˈnet.wɝːk/ 类神经网络（一种模拟人脑运作机制的电脑系统或程序） a computer system or a type of computer program that is designed to copy the way in which the human brain operates

Neural networks can learn solutions to difficult problems.　　类神经网络能学习如何解决问题的办法。

neurodegenerative　adjective　MEDICAL　specialized　UK /ˌnjʊə.rəʊ.dɪˈdʒen.ə.rə.tɪv/ US /ˌnʊr.oʊ.dɪˈdʒen.ə.rə.t̬ɪv/ 神经组织退化的 involving the nerves gradually stopping working

neurodegenerative disease　　神经退行性疾病

neuroendocrine　adjective　MEDICAL　specialized UK /ˌnjʊə.rəʊˈen.də.krɪn/ US /ˌnʊr.oʊˈen.də.krɪn/ 神经内分泌的 relating to the release of hormones into the bloodstream after being stimulated by a nerve

a neuroendocrine cell　　神经内分泌细胞

a neuroendocrine tumour　　神经内分泌肿瘤

neurolinguistics　noun [U] UK /ˌnjʊə.rəʊ.lɪŋˈgwɪs.tɪks/ US /ˌnʊr.oʊ.lɪŋˈgwɪs.tɪks/ 神经语言学 the study of the relationship between language and the brain

neurologic　adjective　MEDICAL　specialized UK /ˌnjʊə.rəˈlɒdʒ.ɪk/ US /ˌnʊr.əˈl ɑ:dʒ.ɪk/ 神经学的；神经病学的 relating to neurology (= the study of the nervous system)

a neurologic examination　　神经学检查

neurologic symptoms　　神经病学症状

neurological　adjective UK /ˌnjʊə.rəˈlɒdʒ.ɪ.kəl/ US /ˌnʊr.əˈl ɑ:.dʒɪ.kəl/ 神经的；神经系统的 relating to nerves

neurological disease/damage　神经疾病 / 神经损伤

Alzheimer's disease is a neurological disorder.　　阿兹海默症是一种神经疾病。

neurologist   noun [C]   MEDICAL UK /njʊəˈrɒl.ə.dʒɪst/ US /nʊˈr ɑ :.lə.dʒɪst/ 神经病学家；神经科医生 a doctor who studies and treats diseases of the nerves

neurology   noun [U] UK /njʊəˈrɒl.ə.dʒi/ US /nʊˈr ɑ :.lə.dʒi/ 神经学；神经病学 the study of the structure and diseases of the brain and all the nerves in the body

neuromuscular   adjective MEDICAL specialized UK /ˌnjʊə.rəʊˈmʌs.kjə.lər/ US /ˌnʊr.oʊˈmʌs.kjə.lə-/ 神经肌肉的 relating to the nerves that control muscles

a neuromuscular disorder   神经肌肉障碍

neuron   noun [C]   BIOLOGY (UK also neurone) UK /ˈnjʊə.rɒn/ US /ˈnʊr. ɑ :n/ 神经元，神经细胞 a nerve cell that carries information between the brain and other parts of the body

neuronal   adjective MEDICAL specialized UK /njʊəˈrəun.əl/ US /nʊˈroʊ.nəl/ 神经元的，神经细胞的 relating to a nerve cell or a neuron (= a basic unit of a nerve cell)

The drugs increase neuronal activity as a treatment for Alzheimer's disease.

这些药物通过增加神经元活动来治疗阿兹海默症。

neuropathic   adjective MEDICAL specialized UK /ˌnjʊə.rəˈpæθ.ɪk/ US /ˌnʊr.əˈpæθ.ɪk/ 神经病的 relating to diseases of the nervous system

neuropathic pain   神经性疼痛

neuroscience   noun [U] UK /ˌnjʊə.rəʊˈsaɪəns/ US /ˌnʊr.oʊ-/ 神经科学 the scientific study of the nervous system and the brain

Thanks to advances in neuroscience, we now know that adult brains can grow and change. 由于神经科学的进展，我们现在知道成人大脑会继续增长和变化。

neuroscientist   noun [C] UK /ˌnjʊə.rəʊˈsaɪən.tɪst/ /ˌnʊr.oʊ-/ 神经科学家 a scientist who studies the nervous system and the brain

Neuroscientists are able to record the firing of a single nerve cell.   神经科学家能够记录单个神经元发出的信号。

neurosis   noun [C or U] UK /njʊəˈrəʊ.sɪs/ US /nʊˈroʊ.sɪs/ plural neuroses 神经官能症，神经症 a mental illness resulting in high levels of anxiety, unreasonable fears and behaviour and, often, a need to repeat actions for no reason

If you want my opinion, I think she's suffering from some form of neurosis.

如果你想听听我的意见，我认为她患有某种神经官能症。

She's obsessively clean - it's almost become a neurosis with her.   她有洁癖——几乎到了神经过敏的程度。

neurosurgeon   noun [C]   MEDICAL   specialized UK /ˈnjʊə.rəʊˌsɜː.dʒən/ US /ˈnʊr.oʊˌsɜː.dʒən/ 神经外科医生 a doctor who performs operations involving the brain or nerves

neurosurgery   noun [U or C]   MEDICAL   specialized UK /ˌnjʊə.rəʊˈsɜː.dʒər.i/ US /ˌnʊr.oʊˈsɜː.dʒər.i/ 神经外科手术 operations on any part of the nervous system including the brain, spinal cord, and individual nerves

neurosurgical   adjective   MEDICAL   specialized UK /ˌnjʊə.rəʊˈsɜː.dʒɪ.kəl/ US /ˌnʊr.oʊˈsɜː.dʒɪ.kəl/ 神经外科手术的 relating to operations on the nervous system

neurotic   1 adjective UK /njʊəˈrɒt.ɪk/ US /nʊˈr ɑ ː.t̬ɪk/ 神经过敏的，神经质的 behaving strangely or in an anxious (= worried and nervous) way, often because you have a mental illness

neurotic behaviour/tendencies   神经质的行为 / 倾向

She's neurotic about her weight - she weighs herself three times a day.

她对自己的体重有些神经过敏——每天要称 3 次体重。

neurotic   2 noun [C] UK /njʊəˈrɒt.ɪk/ US /nʊˈr ɑ ː.t̬ɪk/ 神经过敏者，神经质者；神经官能症患者 someone who behaves strangely, often because they have a mental illness

neuroticism   noun [U] UK /njʊəˈrɒt.ɪ.sɪ.zəm/ US /nʊˈr ɑ ː.t̬ə.sɪ.zəm/ 神经过敏，神经质 the condition of often feeling worried and nervous, often because of a mental illness

Researchers found that high levels of neuroticism were linked to lower life expectancy.   研究者发现高度神经过敏症与低预期寿命有相关性。

neurotransmitter   noun [C] UK /ˌnjʊə.rəʊ.trænzˈmɪt.ər/ US /ˌnʊr.oʊ.trænsˈmɪt.ə/ 神经传递素（神经细胞用来在相互之间及向肌肉组织传递信号的化学物质） a chemical that carries messages between neurons or between neurons and muscles

neurovascular   adjective   MEDICAL   specialized UK /ˌnjʊə.rəʊˈvæs.kjə.lər/ US /ˌnʊr.oʊˈvæs.kjə.lə/ 神经血管的 relating to the nerves and blood vessels

If the problem is severe enough, the neurovascular bundle of nerves to the arm can become compressed.   如果问题很严重的话，手臂的血管神经束会受压迫。

Neurofibromatosis   神经纤维瘤 Neurofibromatoses are a group of genetic disorders that cause tumors to form on nerve tissue. These tumors can develop anywhere in the nervous system, including the brain, spinal cord and nerves.

There are three types of neurofibromatosis: neurofibromatosis 1 (NF1), neurofibromatosis 2 (NF2) and schwannomatosis.

bilateral acoustic neurofibromatosis noun [U] medical specialized UK /baɪˌlæt.ər.əl əˌkuː.stɪk njʊə.rəʊ.faɪ.brə.məˈtəʊ.sɪs/ US /baɪˈlæt̬.ɚ.əl əˈkuː.stɪk ˈnʊr.oʊˌfaɪ.brə.məˈtoʊ.sɪs/ (also neurofibromatosis Type 2) 双侧听神经纤维瘤 a genetic condition in which a person develops acoustic neuromas (= tumours that affect the nerve that runs from the inner ear to the brain) that eventually lead to loss of the ability to hear and difficulties with balance

bilateral acoustic schwannoma noun [C or U] medical specialized UK /baɪˌlæt.ər.əl əˌkuː.stɪk ʃw ɑ ːˈnəʊ.mə/ US /baɪˌlæt̬.ɚ.əl əˌkuː.stɪk ʃw ɑ ːˈnoʊ.mə/ (also acoustic neuroma) 双侧听神经鞘瘤 a growth on a nerve in the brain that interrupts information being sent from the inner ear to the brain causing problems with hearing and balance

Prefix: new- recent or recently

Meaning in English: recent or recently

Origin language: Latin / Greek

English examples:

new- 7 prefix UK /njuː-/ US /nuː-/ 最近的；最近地 recent or recently

newly adverb UK /ˈnjuː.li/ US /ˈnuː.li/ B2 最近，新近 recently

new broom noun [C] UK /ˌnjuː ˈbruːm/ US /ˌnu ˈbruːm/ （往往带来很多变革的）新上任者 someone who has just started to work for an organization and intends to make a lot of changes

new girl/boy 1 noun [C] mainly UK UK /ˈnjuː ˌɡɜːl/ US /ˈnuː ˌɡɝːl/ 刚上学的孩子，（小学）新生 a child who has recently started going to a school

2 noun 新手；新成员 someone who has recently become involved with an activity or organization

new media noun [plural] UK /ˌnjuːˈmiː.di.ə/ US /ˌnuːˈmiː.di.ə/ 新媒体（指利用计算机或因特网提供资讯或娱乐的产品和服务）products and services that provide information or entertainment using computers or the internet, and not by traditional methods such as television and newspapers

newborn adjective [before noun] UK /ˈnjuː.bɔːn/ US /ˈnuː.bɔːrn/ 新生的 recently born

newbuild noun [C] UK UK /ˈnjuːˌbɪld/ US /ˈnuːˌbɪld/ 新建房 a house or other building that has been built recently

newcomer noun [C] UK /ˈnjuːˌkʌm.ər/ US /ˈnuːˌkʌm.ɚ/ 新来者；新手 someone who has recently arrived in a place or recently become involved in an activity

newfangled adjective UK /ˌnjuːˈfæŋ.gəld/ US /ˌnuːˈfæŋ.gəld/ disapproving 新奇的；新式的；新花样的 recently made for the first time, but not always an improvement on what existed before

newfound adjective UK /ˈnjuː.faʊnd/ US /ˈnuː.faʊnd/ （素质或能力）新获得的 a newfound quality or ability has started recently

newlywed noun [C usually plural] UK /ˈnjuː.li.wed/ US /ˈnuː.li.wed/ 新婚者 someone who has recently married

Prefix: non- "not" or "the opposite of" to adjectives and nouns
Meaning in English: not

Origin language: Latin

English examples:

non- prefix UK /nɒn-/ US /nɑːn-/ （与形容词和名词连用）无，不，非 used to add the meaning "not" or "the opposite of" to adjectives and nouns

non-sexist 无性别歧视的

non-racist 无种族歧视的

non-addictive adjective UK /ˌnɒn.əˈdik.tɪv/ US /ˌnɑːn.əˈdik.tɪv/ （药物）不致瘾的 A non-addictive drug does not make people who take it want to take more of it regularly.

non-alcoholic adjective UK /ˌnɒn.æl.kəˈhɒl.ɪk/ US /ˌnɑːn.ælkəˈhɑːlɪk/ （饮料）不含酒精的 A non-alcoholic drink does not contain alcohol.

non-aligned adjective UK /ˌnɒn.əˈlaɪnd/ US /ˌnɑːn.əˈlaɪnd/ （国家）不结盟的 If a country is non-aligned, it does not support or depend on any powerful country or group of countries.

non-believer noun [C] UK /ˌnɒn.bɪˈliː.vər/ US /ˌnɑːn.bɪˈliː.vɚ/ 无信仰者 a person who has no religious beliefs

non-binding adjective 无法律约束力的 not legally necessary to obey or follow

non-bio adjective uk UK /ˌnɒnˈbaɪ.əʊ/ US /ˌnɑːnˈbaɪ.oʊ/ (also non-biological,) （洗衣粉或洗衣液）不含酶的 Non-bio washing powder or liquid does not contain enzymes (= special chemical substances) to help clean clothes.

non-combatant   noun [C] UK /ˌnɒnˈkɒm.bə.tənt/ US /ˌnɑːnˈkɑːm.bə.t̬ənt/ （尤指军队中的）非战斗人员 a person, especially in the armed forces, who does not fight in a war, for example a priest or a doctor

non-communicable   adjective   formal UK /ˌnɒn.kəˈmjuː.nɪ.kə.bəl/ US /ˌnɑːn.kəˈmjuː.nə.kə.bəl/ 无法在人与人之间传播的 that cannot be passed from one person to another

non-consensual   adjective   LAW   formal or specialized UK /ˌnɒn.kɒnˈsen.sju.əl/ US /ˌnɑːn.kɑːnˈsen.sju.əl/ 没有获得所有参与者同意的 without the willing agreement of all the people involved

non-custodial   1 adjective law specialized UK /ˌnɒn.kʌsˈtəʊ.di.əl/ US /ˌnɑːn.kʌsˈtoʊ.di.əl/ (PUNISHMENT) （判决）无需入狱的 (of a punishment) that does not involve a person being sent to prison 2 adjective (PARENT) （对非成年孩子）无监护权的 not having custody of a child (= the legal right to care for him or her)

non-dairy   adjective UK /ˌnɒnˈdeə.ri/ US /ˌnɑːnˈder.i/ 非乳制的；不含奶的 containing nothing that is made from cow's milk

non-event   noun [C usually singular]   informal UK /ˌnɒn.ɪˈvent/ US /ˌnɑːn.ɪˈvent/ （尤指不如预期的）令人扫兴之事 a disappointing occasion that was not interesting, especially one that was expected to be exciting and important

non-existent   adjective UK /ˌnɒn.ɪɡˈzɪs.tənt/ US /ˌnɑːn.ɪɡˈzɪs.tənt/ C1 不存在的 Something that is non-existent does not exist or is not present in a particular place.

non-fat　adjective UK /ˌnɒnˈfæt/ US /ˌnɑːnˈfæt/ （食物）脱脂的，不含脂肪的 Non-fat food contains no fat.

non-fatal　adjective　formal UK /ˌnɒnˈfeɪ.təl/ US /ˌnɑːnˈfeɪ.t̬əl/ （疾病、受伤、事故等）非致命的 A non-fatal illness, injury, or accident does not cause death.

non-invasive　adjective　MEDICAL　specialized UK /ˌnɒn.ɪnˈveɪ.sɪv/ US /ˌnɑːn.ɪnˈveɪ.sɪv/ 非入侵性的 relating to any medical test or treatment that does not cut the skin or enter any of the body spaces

non-negotiable　1 adjective UK /ˌnɒn.nəˈɡəʊ.ʃə.bəl/ US /ˌnɑːn.nəˈɡoʊ.ʃi.ə/ (NOT DISCUSSED) 无商量余地的 Something that is non-negotiable cannot be changed by discussion.

non-partisan　adjective UK /ˌnɒnˌpɑː.tɪˈzæn/ /ˌnɒnˈpɑː.tɪ.zæn/ US /ˌnɑːnˈpɑːr.t̬ə.zən/ 非党派的 not a member of or connected with a group or political party

non-payment　noun [U] UK /ˌnɒnˈpeɪ.mənt/ US /ˌnɑːnˈpeɪ.mənt/ 无力支付；未付 a failure to pay money that is owed

non-profit　adjective UK /ˌnɒnˈprɒf.ɪt/ US /ˌnɑːnˈprɑː.fɪt/ (also not-for-profit) （机构）非营利性的 not intended to make a profit, but to make money for a social or political purpose or to provide a service that people need

non-proliferation noun [U] UK /ˌnɒn.prə.lɪf.ərˈeɪ.ʃən/ US /ˌnɑːn.prə.lɪf.əˈreɪ.ʃən/ （尤指对核武器或化学武器的）不扩散，防止扩散 the controlling of the spread and/or amount of something, especially nuclear or chemical weapons

non-racist adjective UK /ˌnɒnˈreɪ.sɪst/ US /ˌnɑːnˈreɪ.sɪst/ 无种族歧视的 not influenced by a person's race

non-renewable 1 adjective UK /ˌnɒn.rɪˈnjuː.ə.bəl/ US /ˌnɑːn.rɪˈnuː.ə.bəl/ 不可再生的 existing in limited quantities that cannot be replaced after they have all been used

non-returnable adjective UK /ˌnɒn.rɪˈtɜː.nə.bəl/ US /ˌnɑːn.rɪˈtɜː.nə.bəl/ 不可退还的 Something that is non-returnable cannot be returned.

non-smoker noun [C] UK /ˌnɒnˈsməʊ.kər/ US /ˌnɑːnˈsmoʊ.kɚ/ 不抽烟的人 a person who does not smoke

non-specific adjective MEDICAL specialized UK /ˌnɒn.spəˈsɪf.ɪk/ US /ˌnɑːn.spəˈsɪf.ɪk/ （疾病或症状）非特异的 A non-specific disease or condition does not result from any one particular cause.

non-stop adjective, adverb UK /ˌnɒnˈstɒp/ US /ˌnɑːnˈstɑːp/ 不停顿的；不间断的 without stopping or without interruptions

non-surgical 1 adjective UK /ˌnɒnˈsɜː.dʒɪ.kəl/ US /ˌnɑːnˈsɜː.dʒɪ.kəl/ 非手术的 used to describe a medical treatment that does not involve cutting open the body

non-toxic adjective UK /ˌnɒnˈtɒk.sɪk/ US /ˌnɑːnˈtɑːk.sɪk/ 非毒性的 not poisonous or not containing poisonous substances

non-traditional adjective 非传统的 different from what was considered usual or typical in the past

non-vegetarian   adjective UK /ˌnɒn.vedʒ.ɪˈteə.ri.ən/ US /ˌnɑːn.vedʒ.əˈter.i.ən/ 非素食餐的；非素食者的 used to refer to a meal that contains meat, or a person who eats meat

non-verbal   adjective UK /ˌnɒnˈvɜː.bəl/ US /ˌnɑːnˈvɜː.bəl/ 非言语的 not using spoken language

Body language is a potent form of non-verbal communication. 肢体语言是一种有效的非言语交流方式。

non-violence   noun [U] UK /ˌnɒnˈvaɪə.ləns/ US /ˌnɑːnˈvaɪə.ləns/ （尤指为推动政治变革而采取的）非暴力（政策） a situation in which someone avoids fighting or using physical force, especially when trying to make political change

nonchalant   adjective UK /ˈnɒn.ʃəl.ənt/ US /ˌnɑːn.ʃəˈlɑːnt/ 若无其事的；漠不关心的；毫不在乎的 behaving in a calm manner, often in a way that suggests you are not interested or do not care [GRE]

nondescript   1 adjective UK /ˈnɒn.dɪ.skrɪpt/ US /ˈnɑːn.dɪ.skrɪpt/ 平常的；平庸的；平淡无奇的 very ordinary, or having no interesting or exciting features or qualities [GRE]

nonentity   1 noun UK /ˌnɒnˈen.tɪ.ti/ US /ˌnɑːˈnen.tə.ţi/ [C] disapproving 没有个性（或想法、影响）的人；无足轻重的人 a person without strong character, ideas, or influence [GRE]

nonsense   1 noun UK /ˈnɒn.səns/ US /ˈnɑːn.sens/ B2 [S or U] 愚蠢的想法；谬论；胡扯；胡闹 an idea, something said or written, or behaviour that is silly or stupid

Meaning in English: normal

Origin language: Latin

English examples:

Normocapnia   noun [C] 正常碳酸血症或正常碳酸 Normocapnia or normocarbia is a state of normal arterial carbon dioxide pressure, usually about 40 mmHg. Wikipedia

OOO

Prefix: oct- eight

Meaning in English: eight

Origin language: Latin/ Greek

English examples:

octagon   noun [C] UK /ˈɒk.tə.gən/ US /ˈɑ:k.tə.gɑ:n/ 八边形；八角形 a flat shape with eight sides

octahedron   noun [C]   MATHEMATICS   specialized UK /ˌɒk.təˈhiː.drən/ US /ˌɑ:k.təˈhiː.drən/ plural octahedrons or octahedra UK /-drə/ US   八面体（八个面均为等同的正三角形的棱锥体） a solid shape whose eight sides are triangles of equal size

octode   noun oc·tode | \ ˈäkˌtōd \ plural -s 八极管: a vacuum tube with eight electrodes comprising a cathode, an anode, a control grid, and five additional electrodes that are usually grids

octangular   adjective oc·tan·gu·lar | \ (')äk¦taŋgyələ(r) \ : 八角形 OCTAGONAL

octennial   /ɒkˈtɛnɪəl/ adjective recurring every eight years；lasting for or relating to a period of eight years octopus   noun [C] UK /ˈɒk.tə.pəs/ US /ˈɑ:k.tə.pəs/ 章鱼 a sea creature with a soft, oval body and eight tentacles (= long parts like arms)

Meaning in English: Of or pertaining to the eye

Origin language: Latin (oculus), the eye

English examples:

ocular   adjective MEDICAL specialized UK /ˈɒk.jə.lər/ US /ˈɑ:.kjə.lə/ 眼睛的；视力的 of or related to the eyes or sight

oculist   noun [C] UK /ˈɒk.jə.lɪst/ US /ˈɑ:.kjə.lɪst/ 眼科医师，眼科专家（ophthalmologist 的旧称） old-fashioned for ophthalmologist

oculomotor   adjective MEDICAL specialized UK /ˈɒk.jə.ləˌməʊ.tər/ US /ˌɑ:k.jə.loʊˈmoʊ.tə/ 眼球运动的 relating to the movement of the eyeball

oculus   noun [C] MEDICAL specialized UK /ˈɒk.jə.ləs/ US /ˈɑ:k.jə.ləs/ plural oculi （拉丁语，用于医学术语）眼 a Latin word meaning "eye", used in medical names and descriptions

Meaning in English: Of or pertaining to teeth

Origin language: Ancient Greek ὀδούς, ὀδοντ- (odoús, odont-), tooth

English examples:

orthodontics   noun [U] MEDICAL specialized UK /ˌɔ:.θəˈdɒn.tɪks/ US /ˌɔ:r.θoʊˈdɑ:n.tɪks/ 正牙治疗，口腔正畸 the job or activity of correcting the position of teeth and dealing with and preventing problems of the teeth

orthodontist   noun [C]   MEDICAL   specialized UK /ˌɔː.θəˈdɒn.tɪst/ US /ˌɔːr.θoʊˈdɑːn.tɪst/ 正牙医生 a person whose job is to correct the position of the teeth

odontology   noun odon·tol·o·gy | \ (ˌ)ō-ˌdän-ˈtä-lə-jē \   正牙，牙科学 a science dealing with the teeth, their structure and development, and their diseases

Prefix (Medical): oesophago-, (-oesophageal) BrE- gullet

Meaning in English:

Origin language: Greek οἰσοφάγος

English examples:

esophageal   adjective UK /ɪˌsɒf.əˈdʒi.əl/ US /ɪˌsɑːf.əˈdʒi.əl/ US spelling of oesophageal （oesophageal 的美式拼写）食道的，食管的

oesophageal   adjective   MEDICAL   UK specialized (US esophageal) UK /ɪˌsɒf.əˈdʒi.əl/ US /ɪˌsɑːf.əˈdʒi.əl/ 食道的，食管的 relating to the oesophagus (= the tube that takes food from the mouth to the stomach)

oesophageal cancer   食道癌

esophagitis   noun [U] /ɪˌsɒf.əgˈaɪ.tɪs/ US /ɪˌsɑːf.əˈdʒaɪ.ţəs/ （oesophagitis 的美式拼写） US spelling of oesophagitis 食道炎

oesophagitis   noun [U]   MEDICAL   UK specialized (US esophagitis) UK /ɪˌsɒf.əˈdʒaɪ.tɪs/ US /ɪˌsɑːf.əˈdʒaɪ.ţəs/ 食道炎 inflammation of the oesophagus (= the tube that takes food from the mouth to the stomach)

吞咽时疼痛可能是严重的食道炎造成的。   Pain on swallowing may be due to severe oesophagitis.

esophagus noun [C] UK /ɪˈsɒf.ə.gəs/ US /ɪˈsɑː.fə.gəs/
（oesophagus 的美式拼写） US spelling of oesophagus 食道，食管

oesophagus noun [C] ANATOMY UK specialized (US esophagus)
UK /ɪˈsɒf.ə.gəs/ US /ɪˈsɑː.fə.gəs/ plural oesophagi oesophaguses 食道，食管
the tube in the body that takes food from the mouth to the stomach

gastroesophageal adjective MEDICAL specialized UK
/ˌgæs.trəʊ.ɪ.sɒf.əˈdʒi.əl/ US /ˌgæs.troʊ.ɪˌsɑː.f.əˈdʒiː.əl/ （拉丁语，用于医学
术语）胃食管的 relating to the stomach and oesophagus (= the tube through
which food passes to the stomach)

gastroesophageal cancer 胃食管癌

Gastroenterology 肠胃病学 Gastroenterology is the branch of medicine
focused on the digestive system and its disorders. Diseases affecting the
gastrointestinal tract, which include the organs from mouth into anus, along the
alimentary canal, are the focus of this speciality. Physicians practicing in this
field are called gastroenterologists. Wikipedia; Gastroenterology is the study of
the normal function and diseases of the esophagus, stomach, small intestine,
colon and rectum, pancreas, gallbladder, bile ducts and liver.

gastroesophageal reflux disease noun [U] MEDICAL specialized UK
/gæs.trəʊ.ɪ.sɒf.əˌdʒi.əl ˈriː.flʌks dɪˌziːz/ US /ˈgæs.troʊ.ɪˌsɑː.f.əˈdʒi.əl ˈriː.flʌks
dɪˌziːz/ (US abbreviation GERD); (UK abbreviation GORD) 胃食道逆流 a
chronic disease where stomach acid goes up into the oesophagus (= the tube
through which food passes to the stomach) causing inflammation and pain

Prefix (Medical): ole- small or little
Meaning in English: small or little

Origin language: Latin

English examples:

oleaginous   adjective formal UK /ˌəʊ.liˈædʒ.ɪ.nəs/ US /ˌoʊ.liˈædʒ.ə.nəs/ 甜言蜜语的；油嘴滑舌的；花言巧语的 extremely polite, kind, or helpful in a false way that is intended to bring some advantage to yourself

oleosity   The state or quality of being oily or fat; fatness.

olecranon noun [C] ANATOMY specialized UK /əʊˈlek.rə.nɒn/ US /oʊˈlek.rəˌn ɑ ːn/鹰嘴，肘突 the end part of the ulna (= a long thin bone in the lower arm) at the elbow

The olecranon forms the point of the elbow. 肘突是手肘的尖点。

Olestra   noun [U] trademark UK /əʊˈles.trə/ US /oʊˈles.trə/ 蔗糖聚酯，油脂取代物 a brand name for an artificially produced substance that replaces fat in some foods

Prefix (Medical): olig(o)- having little, having few
Meaning in English: Denoting something as 'having little, having few'

Origin language: Ancient Greek ὀλίγος (oligos), few

English examples:

oligarch   noun [C] UK /ˈɒl.ɪ.g ɑ ː.k/ US /ˈ ɑ ː.lɪ.g ɑ ːrk/ 寡头政治家；寡头统治集团成员 one of the people in an oligarchy

oligarchy   noun [C or U, + sing/pl verb] UK /ˈɒl.ɪ.g ɑ ː.ki/ US /ˈ ɑ ː.lɪ.g ɑ ːr.ki/ 寡头统治（的政府）；寡头统治集团 (government by) a small group of powerful people

oligopoly   noun [C] UK /ˌɒl.ɪˈgɒp.əl.i/ US /ˌ ɑ ː.lɪˈg ɑ ː.pəl.i/ 寡头垄断 a situation in which a small number of organizations or companies has control of an area of business, so that others have no share

Oligotrophy noun [U] 寡养生物; 贫营养 An oligotroph is an organism that can live in an environment that offers very low levels of nutrients. They may be contrasted with copiotrophs, which prefer nutritionally rich environments. Oligotrophs are characterized by slow growth, low rates of metabolism, and generally low population density. Environments where oligotrophs can be found include the deep oceans.Wikipedia

copiotrophs noun [U] 富营养型生物; 富营养型 A copiotroph is an organism found in environments rich in nutrients, particularly carbon. They are the opposite to oligotrophs, which survive in much lower carbon concentrations. Copiotrophic organisms tend to grow in high organic substrate conditions. For example, copiotrophic organisms grow in Sewage lagoons. Wikipedia

Prefix: omni- everywhere or everything

Meaning in English: all

Origin language: Latin

English examples:

omni- prefix UK /ɒm.nɪ-/ US / ɑ :m.nɪ-/ 到处，遍及；一切 everywhere or everything

omnibus 1 noun [C] UK /ˈɒm.nɪ.bəs/ US /ˈ ɑ :m.nə.bəs/ [C] (SEVERAL PARTS) （若干已发表作品的）选集，汇编 a book consisting of two or more parts that have already been published separately

omnidirectional adjective ELECTRONICS, MEDIA specialized UK /ˌɒm.nɪ.daɪˈrek.ʃən.əl/ US /ˌ ɑ :m.nɪ.dɪˈrek.ʃən.əl/ （天线）全方向的 used to describe an antenna (= a piece of electronic equipment that connects radio or computer networks) that can receive or send signals in all directions

omnificent   adjective. 无所不能的，万能的 creating all things; having unlimited powers of creation.

omnificence   无所不能，万能 unlimited in creative power.

omnipotent   adjective   formal UK /ɒmˈnɪp.ə.tənt/ US /ɑːmˈnɪp.ə.tənt/ 全能的，万能的，无所不能的 having unlimited power and able to do anything

omnipotence   noun   om·nip·o·tence | \ äm-ˈni-pə-tən(t)s \ 1: the quality or state of being omnipotent 2: an agency or force of unlimited power

omnipresent   adjective   formal UK /ˌɒm.nɪˈprez.ənt/ US /ˌɑːm.nɪˈprez.ənt/ 无所不在的，遍及各处的 present or having an effect everywhere at the same time

omniscient   adjective   formal UK /ɒmˈnɪs.i.ənt/ US /ɑːmˈnɪʃ.ənt/ 无所不知的，全知的 having or seeming to have unlimited knowledge

omnivore   noun [C] UK /ˈɒm.nɪ.vɔːr/ US /ˈɑːm.nɪ.vɔːr/ 杂食动物 an animal that is naturally able to eat both plants and meat

omnishambles   noun [C usually singular] UK /ˈɒm.nɪˌʃæm.bəlz/ US /ˈɑːm.nɪˌʃæm.bəlz/ uk informal （因为组织糟糕和严重错误导致的）各方面都很糟糕的局面 a situation that is bad in many different ways, because things have been organized badly and serious mistakes have been made

Prefix (Medical): om(o)- Of or pertaining to the shoulder
Meaning in English: Of or pertaining to the shoulde

Origin language: Ancient Greek ὦμός (ōmos), shoulder

English examples:

omohyoid adjective MEDICAL specialized UK /ˌəʊ.məʊˈhaɪ.ɔɪd/ US /ˌoʊ.moʊˈhaɪ.ɔɪd/ 肩胛舌骨的 relating to the shoulder and the hyoid bone (= a bone in the front of the neck)

Omophorion 护身符 In the Eastern Orthodox and Eastern Catholic liturgical tradition, the omophorion is the distinguishing vestment of a bishop and the symbol of his spiritual and ecclesiastical authority. Wikipedia

Omoplate noun [C] 肩胛骨 the shoulder blade

Prefix (Medical): omphal(o)- navel, the umbilicus
Meaning in English: Of or pertaining to the navel, the umbilicus

Origin language: Ancient Greek ὀμφαλός (omphalós), navel, belly-button

English examples:

omphalectomy 脐带切除术 Umbilectomy, also referred to as omphalectomy, is a surgical procedure wherein the umbilicus or the belly button is removed typically due to large umbilical hernias. Who Should Undergo and Expected Results. Umbilectomy is not a commonly conducted surgical procedure and is typically indicated for large umbilical hernias

umbilicus noun [C] ANATOMY specialized UK /ʌmˈbɪl.ɪ.kəs/ US /ʌmˈbɪl.ə.kəs/ plural umbilici umbilicuses 脐 the small, round part in the middle of the belly that is left after the umbilical cord (= the long tube of flesh joining the baby to its mother) has been cut at birth

Prefix (Medical): onco- tumor, bulk, volume
Meaning in English: tumor, bulk, volume

Origin language: Greek ὄγκος

English examples:

oncogene   noun [C]   BIOLOGY, MEDICAL   specialized UK /ˈɒŋ.kəʊ.dʒiːn/ US /ˈɑːn.kə.dʒiːn/ （致）癌基因 a gene that is present in every cell and causes a healthy cell to become cancerous under particular conditions

oncology   noun [U] UK /ɒŋˈkɒl.ə.dʒi/ US /ɑːnˈkɑː.lə.dʒi/ 肿瘤学 the study and treatment of tumours (= masses of cells) in the body

Prefix (Medical): onych(o)- Of or pertaining to the nail (of a finger or toe)

Meaning in English: Of or pertaining to the nail (of a finger or toe)

Origin language: Ancient Greek < ὄνυξ, ὀνυχο- (ónyx, ónycho-), nail; claw; talon

English examples:

Onychomycosis   noun [C] 甲癣; 甲真菌病,俗称臭甲、灰指甲 Onychomycosis (tinea unguium) is a fungal infection of the fingernails or toenails that causes discoloration, thickening, and separation from the nail bed. Onychomycosis is fungal infection of the nail plate, nail bed, or both. The nails typically are deformed and discolored white or yellow. Diagnosis is by appearance, wet mount, culture, polymerase chain reaction, or a combination. Treatment, when indicated, is with oral terbinafine or itraconazole. Onychomycosis occurs in 10% of the general population but is more common in older adults; the prevalence is 20% in those older than 60 years and 50% in those older than 70 years.

Onychophagia   noun [C] 食甲癣 Onychophagia is the clinical name for fingernail biting. It is a common stress-related or nervous habit in children and adults. It involves biting off the nail plate, and sometimes the soft tissues of the nail bed and the cuticle as well.

Prefix (Medical): oo- an egg, a woman's egg, the ovum

Meaning in English: Of or pertaining to the an egg, a woman's egg, the ovum

Origin language: Ancient Greek ᾠόν, ᾠo- (ōón, ōo-), egg, ovum

English examples:

oology   noun [U]   BIOLOGY   specialized UK /əʊˈɒl.ə.dʒi/ US /oʊˈɑ:.lə-/ 鸟卵学；鸟卵收藏 the study or collecting of eggs, especially birds' eggs

Oogenesis   noun [U] 卵子生成 Oogenesis is the process of formation of female gametes. Oogenesis is the type of gametogenesis through which ova, also called the female gametes are formed and the produced female gamete is known as an ovum.

Prefix (Medical): oophor(o)- Of or pertaining to the woman's ovary

Meaning in English: Of or pertaining to the woman's ovary

Origin language: Neoclassical Greek ᾠοφόρον (ōophóron), ovary, egg-bearing

English examples:

Oophorectomy   noun [C] 卵巢切除术 Oophorectomy, historically also called ovariotomy is the surgical removal of an ovary or ovaries. The surgery is also called ovariectomy, but this term is mostly used in reference to animals, e.g. the surgical removal of ovaries from laboratory animals. Wikipedia

Prefix (Medical): ophthalm(o)- Of or pertaining to the eye

Meaning in English: Of or pertaining to the eye

Origin language: Ancient Greek ὀφθαλμός (ophthalmós), the eye

English examples:

ophthalmic   adjective   MEDICAL   specialized UK /ɒpˈθæl.mɪk/ US / ɑ:fˈθæl.mɪk/ 眼科的 relating to ophthalmology (= the scientific study of eyes and their diseases)

ophthalmic optician   noun [C] UK UK /ɒpˌθæl.mɪk ɒpˈtɪʃ.ən/ US / ɑ:fˌθæl.mɪk ɑ:pˈtɪʃ.ən/ 验光师；配镜师（同 optician） an optician

ophthalmologist noun [C]   MEDICAL UK / ˌɒf.θælˈmɒl.ə.dʒɪst/ US /ˌɑ:f.θælˈmɑ:.lə.dʒɪst/ 眼科医师，眼科专家 a doctor who treats eye diseases

optician 1 noun [C] UK UK /ɒpˈtɪʃ.ən/ US /ɑ:pˈtɪʃ.ən/ (UK also ophthalmic optician); (US optometrist) 验光师；配镜师 someone whose job is examining people's eyes and selling glasses or contact lenses to correct sight problems

ophthalmic optician   验光师；配镜师

optometrist   验光师；配镜师

optometrist noun [C] US UK /ɒpˈtɒm.ə.trɪst/ US /ɑ:pˈtɑ:.mə.trɪst/ (UK optician) 验光师；配镜师 someone whose job is examining people's eyes and selling glasses or contact lenses to correct sight problems

ophthalmology noun [U] UK /ˌɒf.θælˈmɒl.ə.dʒi/ US /ˌɑ:f.θælˈmɑ:.lə.dʒi/ 眼科学 the scientific study of eyes and their diseases

Prefix (Medical): optic(o)- Of or relating to chemical properties of the eye

Meaning in English: Of or relating to chemical properties of the eye

Origin language: Middle French (optique) < Greek ὀπτικός (optikós); Cognate with Latin oculus, relating to the eye

English examples:

optician 1 noun [C] UK UK /ɒpˈtɪʃ.ən/ US /ɑ:pˈtɪʃ.ən/ (UK also ophthalmic optician); (US optometrist) 验光师；配镜师 someone whose job is examining people's eyes and selling glasses or contact lenses to correct sight problems 2 nounUS (UK dispensing optician) 眼镜销售员 a person whose job is fitting and selling glasses and contact lenses to correct sight problems, but who does not examine people's eyes

Opticochemical Pertaining both to optics and to chemistry.

Meaning in English: Of or pertaining to the mouth

Origin language: Latin (ōs, or-), mouth

English examples:

oracular adjective formal UK /ɒrˈæk.jə.lər/ US /ɔːrˈæk.jə.lɚ/ 神谕似的，天书般的，晦涩难懂的 mysterious and difficult to understand, but probably wise

oral 1 adjective UK /ˈɔː.rəl/ US /ˈɔːr.əl/ (SPOKEN) B2 口头的；口述的 spoken and not written 2 adjective (MOUTH) 口的；口服的；口腔的 of, taken by, or done to the mouth

oral hygiene 口腔卫生

oral contraceptives 口服避孕药

oral surgery 口腔手术

Meaning in English: testis

Origin language: Greek ὄρχις (orkhis, orkhi-)

English examples:

cryptorchidism noun [U] UK /ˈkrɪp.tɔː.kɪd.ɪz.əm/ US /krɪpˈtɔːr.kɪˌdɪz.əm/ specialized 隐睾症 a condition in which a man's scrotum (= a bag of skin near the penis) contains only one testicle (= round sex organ) or no testicles

Orchiectomy noun [U] 睾丸切除术 Orchiectomy is a surgical procedure in which one or both testicles are removed. The surgery is performed as treatment for testicular cancer, as part of surgery for transgender women, as management for advanced prostate cancer, and to remove damaged testes after testicular torsion. Wikipedia

Orchiectomy   noun [U] 睾丸切除术 Orchiectomy is a surgical procedure in which one or both testicles are removed. The surgery is performed as treatment for testicular cancer, as part of surgery for transgender women, as management for advanced prostate cancer, and to remove damaged testes after testicular torsion. Wikipedia

Prefix (Medical): orth(o)- Denoting something as straigh or correct

Meaning in English: Denoting something as straigh or correct

Origin language: Ancient Greek ὀρθός (orthos), straight, correct, normal

English examples:

orthodontics   noun [U]   MEDICAL   specialized UK /ˌɔː.θəˈdɒn.tɪks/ US /ˌɔːr.θoʊˈd ɑ ːn.tɪks/ 正牙治疗，口腔正畸 the job or activity of correcting the position of teeth and dealing with and preventing problems of the teeth

orthodontist   noun [C]   MEDICAL   specialized UK /ˌɔː.θəˈdɒn.tɪst/ US /ˌɔːr.θoʊˈd ɑ ːn.tɪst/ 正牙医生 a person whose job is to correct the position of the teeth

odontology   noun odon·tol·o·gy | \ (ˌ)ō-ˌdän-ˈtä-lə-jē \   正牙，牙科学 a science dealing with the teeth, their structure and development, and their diseases

orthodox   adjective UK /ˈɔː.θə.dɒks/ US /ˈɔːr.θə.d ɑ ːks/ C2 （信仰、观点或活动）正统的，传统的，普遍接受的 (of beliefs, ideas, or activities) considered traditional, normal, and acceptable by most people

orthodox treatment/methods 传统的疗法 / 方法

orthodox medicine   noun [U] UK /ˌɔː.θə.dɒks ˈmed.ɪ.sən/ US /ˌɔːr.θə.d ɑ ːks ˈmed.ɪ.sən/ 正统医学 the use of drugs and operations to cure illness

orthoepy   noun [U] LANGUAGE specialized UK /ɔːˈθəʊ.ɪ.pi/ US /ɔːrˈθoʊ.ə.pi/ 标准发音，准确发音 correct pronunciation

orthognathic   adjective MEDICAL specialized UK /ˌɔː.θɒgˈnæθ.ɪk/ US /ˌɔːr.θ ɑ ːgˈnæθ.ɪk/ 正颌学的 relating to moving the position of the jaw (= either of the two bones in your body in which the teeth are held)

orthognathic surgery/treatment   正颌外科手术/治疗

orthopaedic   adjective [before noun] MEDICAL UK specialized (US orthopedic) UK /ˌɔː.θəˈpiː.dɪk/ US /ˌɔːr.θəˈpiː.dɪk/ 整形的，矫形的 relating to orthopaedics

an orthopaedic surgeon/specialist/hospital   矫形外科医生 / 专家 / 医院

designed to prevent or treat bone injuries   用于矫形的

an orthopaedic mattress   矫形床垫

orthopaedic shoes   矫形鞋

orthopaedics   noun [plural] MEDICAL UK specialized (US orthopedics) UK /ˌɔː.θəˈpiː.dɪks/ US /ˌɔːr.θəˈpiː.dɪks/ 矫形外科（学），整形外科（学） the treatment or study of bones that have not grown correctly or that have been damaged

orthostatic   adjective MEDICAL specialized UK /ˌɔː.θəʊˈstæt.ɪk/ US /ˌɔːr.θəˈstætˌɪk/ 直立的 relating to standing up straight

Orthotics   又称矫形支架、骨科支架（英语：Orthopedic brace）Orthotics is a medical specialty that focuses on the design and application of orthoses. An orthosis is "an externally applied device used to influence the structural and functional characteristics of the neuromuscular and skeletal system". Wikipedia

orthosis 矫形支架、骨科支架 An orthosis is the correct term for an externally applied device that is designed and fitted to the body to achieve one or more of the following goals: Control biomechanical alignment. Correct or accommodate deformity. Protect and support an injury. Assist rehabilitation.

Prefix (Medical): ossi- bone

Meaning in English: bone

Origin language: Latin

English examples:

ossicle   noun [C] MEDICAL specialized UK /ˈɒs.ɪ.kəl/ US /ˈɑ:s.ɪ.kəl/ 小骨；骨状的 a small bone or structure that is similar to a bone

The auditory ossicles are small bones in the middle ear. 听小骨是中耳内的小骨。

ossification   1 noun [U] UK /ˌɒs.ɪ.fɪˈkeɪ.ʃən/ US /ˌɑ:s.ə.fəˈkeɪ.ʃən/ [U] (OF IDEAS) （习惯或思想的）僵化 the process of habits or ideas becoming fixed and unable to change

the ossification of his thought processes as he grew older   随着年纪增长他思想的越发僵化

ossification   2 noun [U] (IN BODY) MEDICAL specialized 骨化 the process of becoming hard and changing into bone

ossify   1 verb UK /ˈɒs.ɪ.faɪ/ US /ˈɑ:.sə.faɪ/ (IDEAS) [I or T] formal disapproving （使）（习惯或思想）僵化；（使）固定不变 If habits or ideas ossify, or if something ossifies them, they become fixed and unable to change.

Years of easy success had ossified the company's thinking and it never faced up to the challenge of the new technology.

多年来轻易取得的成功让这家公司变得思维僵化，从不直面新技术带来的挑战。

ossify 2 verb (BODY) [I] MEDICAL specialized （身体组织）骨化
If body tissue ossifies, it becomes hard and changes into bone.

Prefix (Medical): ost(e)-, oste(o)- bone
Meaning in English: bone

Origin language: Greek ὀστέον

English examples:

osteoarthritis noun [U] UK /ˌɒs.ti.əʊ.ɑːˈθraɪ.tɪs/ US /ˌɑː.sti.oʊ.ɑːrˈθraɪ.t̬əs/ 骨关节炎 a disease that causes pain and stiffness in the joints (= places where two bones are connected)

osteoclast noun os·te·o·clast | \ ˈä-stē-ə-ˌklast \ 破骨细胞 any of the large multinucleate cells closely associated with areas of bone resorption

osteochondroma noun [C or U] MEDICAL specialized UK /ˌɒs.ti.əu.kɒnˈdrəʊ.mə/ US /ˌɑːs.ti.oʊ.kɑːnˈdroʊ.mə/ 骨软骨瘤 a type of growth or tumour that is found on bones but is not harmful

osteology noun [U] MEDICAL specialized UK /ˌɒs.tiˈɒl.ə.dʒi/ US /ˌɑːs.tiˈɑː.lə.dʒi/ 骨学，骨骼学 the scientific study of bones

osteomyelitis noun [U] MEDICAL specialized UK /ˌɒs.ti.əu.maɪ.əˈlaɪ.tɪs/ US /ˌɑːs.ti.oʊˌmaɪ.əˈlaɪ.t̬əs/ 骨髓炎 a type of serious bone infection

juvenile osteomyelitis 少儿骨髓炎

osteomyelitis of the jaw 颌骨骨髓炎

osteopath   noun [C] UK /ˈɒs.ti.ə.pæθ/ US /ˈɑː.sti.oʊ.pæθ/ 按骨医生，整骨医生，骨疗医师 a person who is trained to treat injuries to bones and muscles using pressure and movement

osteopathy   noun [U] UK /ˌɒs.tiˈɒp.ə.θi/ US /ˌɑː.stiˈɑː.pə.θi/ 按骨术，整骨术；骨疗学 the treatment of injuries to bones and muscles using pressure and movement

osteoporosis   noun [U] UK /ˌɒs.ti.əʊ.pəˈrəʊ.sɪs/ US /ˌɑː.sti.oʊ.pəˈroʊ.sɪs/ 骨质疏松（症） a disease that causes the bones to become weaker and easily broken; Osteoporosis is a disease that weakens bones to the point where they break easily—most often, bones in the hip, backbone (spine), and wrist. Osteoporosis is called a "silent disease" because you may not notice any changes until a bone breaks. All the while, though, your bones had been losing strength for many years. Wikipedia

Osteomalacia   骨软化症 Osteomalacia is softening of the bones. It most often occurs because of a problem with vitamin D, which helps your body absorb calcium. Your body needs calcium to maintain the strength and hardness of your bones. In children, the condition is called rickets.

osteotomy   noun [C or U]   MEDICAL   specialized UK /ˌɒs.tiˈɒt.ə.mi/ US /ˌɑːs.tiˈɑːt̬.ə.mi/ 骨切开术，截骨术 an operation in which bones are cut by a doctor

Prefix (Medical): ot(o)- Of or pertaining to the ear

Meaning in English: Of or pertaining to the ear

Origin language: Ancient Greek οὖς, ὠτ- (ous, ōt-), the ear

English examples:

otolaryngology   noun [U]   MEDICAL   specialized UK /ˌəʊ.təʊ.lær.ɪŋˈɡɒl.ə.dʒi/ US /ˌoʊ.toʊ.ler.ɪŋˈɡɑː.lə.dʒi/ 耳鼻喉科 the study of diseases of the ear and throat

otology　　　noun [U] 耳科 Otology is a branch of medicine which studies normal and pathological anatomy and physiology of the ear as well as their diseases, diagnosis and treatment. Wikipedia

Otopathy　　noun [U] 耳病 A disease of the ear

Prefix: out- "not central"

Meaning in English:

Origin language: Latin / Greek

English examples:

out-　　　29 prefix UK /aʊt-/ US /aʊt-/ prefix (NOT CENTRAL) （用于给名词和形容词加上"非中心的"之意） used to add the meaning "not central" to nouns and adjectives

the outskirts of town 　　市郊 (= the areas that form the edge of the town)

out-of-town　　　1 adjective [before noun] UK /ˌaʊt.əvˈtaʊn/ US /ˌaʊt̬.əvˈtaʊn/ （商店或其他服务设施）城外的，市郊的，郊野的 in a place outside the main part of a town 2 adjective 来自外地的访客 / 商人 an out-of-town visitor/businessman

outer　　　adjective [before noun] UK /ˈaʊ.tər/ US /ˈaʊ.t̬ɚ/ B2 远离中心的；外围的 at a greater distance from the centre

outlying　　　adjective [before noun] UK /ˈaʊt̬ˌlaɪ.ɪŋ/ US /ˈaʊt̬ˌlaɪ.ɪŋ/ 远离城镇的；远离中心的；边远的 far away from main towns and cities, or far from the centre of a place

Prefix: out- "going further" or "being better than"

Meaning in English: "going further" or "being better than"

Origin language: Latin / Greek

English examples:

out- 30 prefix (FURTHER) （用于给动词加上"超越"或"胜过"之意） used to add the meaning "going further" or "being better than" to verbs

She doesn't drink or smoke and I'm sure she'll outlive (= live longer than) us all 她烟酒不沾，我想她肯定比我们都要活得长久。

out-and-out adjective [before noun] UK /ˌaʊt.ənd'aʊt/ US /ˌaʊtˌənd'aʊt/ 彻头彻尾的，十足的，完完全全的 complete or in every way; used to emphasize an unpleasant quality of a person or thing

outclass verb [T] UK /ˌaʊt'klɑːs/ US /ˌaʊt'klæs/ 大大高出，超过，胜过 to be much better than someone or something

outdistance verb [T] UK /ˌaʊt'dɪs.təns/ US /ˌaʊt'dɪs.təns/ （在赛跑中）远远超过，遥遥领先于；（大大）优于 to be faster in a race than other competitors, or (more generally) to be much better than someone

outdo verb [T] UK /ˌaʊt'duː/ US /ˌaʊt'duː/ outdid | outdone 胜过，超越；优于 to be, or do something, better than someone else

outermost adjective [before noun] UK /'aʊ.tə.məʊst/ US /'aʊ.tɚ.moʊst/ 最外层的；（距中心）最远的 at the greatest distance from the centre

outgrow 1 verb [T] UK /ˌaʊt'grəʊ/ US /ˌaʊt'groʊ/ outgrew | outgrown [T] (SIZE) 长得比···大；长得太大（而不再需要） to grow bigger than or too big for something

outgrowth　1 noun [C] UK /ˈaʊt.ɡrəʊθ/ US /ˈaʊt.groʊθ/ BIOLOGY specialized 长出物；旁枝 a growth on the outside of an animal or plant [GRE]

outgun　1 verb [T] UK /ˌaʊtˈɡʌn/ US /ˌaʊtˈɡʌn/ -nn- （因武器数量多而）胜过，超过，打赢 to win a war or fight by having more weapons than the other side 2 verb 打败，战胜（某人或球队）to beat a person or team by using greater skill

outlandish　adjective　disapproving UK /ˌaʊtˈlæn.dɪʃ/ US /ˌaʊtˈlæn.dɪʃ/ 稀奇古怪的；不寻常的；难以接受的 strange and unusual and difficult to accept or like [GRE]

outlast　verb [T] UK /ˌaʊtˈlɑːst/ US /ˌaʊtˈlæst/ 比…活得长；比…持续时间长 to live or exist, or to stay energetic and determined, longer than another person or thing

outlive　verb [T] UK /ˌaʊtˈlɪv/ US /ˌaʊtˈlɪv/ 比…活得长；比…待续时间长 to live or exist longer than someone or something

outmanoeuvre　verb [T] UK (US outmaneuver) UK /ˌaʊt.məˈnuː.vər/ US /ˌaʊt.məˈnuː.vɚ/ 智胜；比（对手）技高一筹 to cleverly get an advantage over someone, especially a competitor [GRE]

outmoded　adjective　disapproving UK /ˌaʊtˈməʊ.dɪd/ US /ˌaʊtˈmoʊ.dɪd/ 过时的；废弃的；无用的 no longer modern, useful, or necessary [GRE]

outnumber　verb [T] UK /ˌaʊtˈnʌm.bər/ US /ˌaʊtˈnʌm.bɚ/ C1 在数量上超过，比…多 to be greater in number than someone or something

outplay verb [T] UK /ˌaʊtˈpleɪ/ US /ˌaʊtˈpleɪ/ （在比赛中）比…打得好，战胜，击败 to play a game more cleverly and successfully than another person or team

outright adverb UK /ˌaʊtˈraɪt/ US /ˌaʊtˈraɪt/ 彻底，完全；立刻；当场 completely or immediately

outrun 1 verb [T] UK /ˌaʊtˈrʌn/ US /ˌaʊtˈrʌn/ present participle outrunning | past tense outran | past participle outrun 比…跑得快（或远） to move faster or further than someone or something 2 verb 发展得比…快；超过，胜过 to develop faster or further than something

outscore verb [T] mainly US UK /ˌaʊtˈskɔːr/ US /ˌaʊtˈskɔːr/ （在比赛中）得分超过 to score more points than another player or team in a competition

outshine verb [T] UK /ˌaʊtˈʃaɪn/ US /ˌaʊtˈʃaɪn/ outshone | outshone 胜过；比…更优异，比…更出色 to be much more skilful and successful than someone

outsize adjective [before noun] UK /ˈaʊt.saɪz/ US /ˈaʊt.saɪz/ （尤指衣服）超过标准尺寸的，特大号的 (especially of clothing) much larger than usual

They specialize in outsize clothes. 他们专营特大号服装。

outsmart verb [T] UK /ˌaʊtˈsmɑːt/ US /ˌaʊtˈsmɑːrt/ to outwit （智力上）超过，胜过；智胜（同 outwit）

outsold UK /ˌaʊtˈsəʊld/ US /ˌaʊtˈsoʊld/ past simple and past participle of outsell （outsell 的过去式及过去分词）

outstanding   1 adjective UK /ˌaʊtˈstæn.dɪŋ/ US /ˌaʊtˈstæn.dɪŋ/ (EXCELLENT) B2 优秀的；卓越的；出众的 clearly very much better than what is usual

outstay   verb UK /ˌaʊtˈsteɪ/ US /ˌaʊtˈsteɪ/ （在某处）呆得太久而变得不受欢迎 to continue to stay in a place although other people want you to leave

outstrip   verb [T] UK /ˌaʊtˈstrɪp/ US /ˌaʊtˈstrɪp/ -pp- （在数量、程度或成就上）超过，胜过 to be or become greater in amount, degree, or success than something or someone

outvote   verb [T usually passive] UK /ˌaʊtˈvəʊt/ US /ˌaʊtˈvoʊt/ 得票超过，以多数票胜过 to defeat someone by winning a greater number of votes

outweigh   verb [T] UK /ˌaʊtˈweɪ/ US /ˌaʊtˈweɪ/ C1 比⋯更重要；重于；大于 to be greater or more important than something else [GRE]

The benefits of this treatment far outweigh any risks.   这种治疗方法的好处远远大于任何风险。

outwit   verb [T] UK /ˌaʊtˈwɪt/ US /ˌaʊtˈwɪt/ -tt- (also outsmart) （智力上）超过，胜过；智胜 to get an advantage over someone by acting more cleverly and often by using a trick

Prefix: out- "out of" or "away from"

Meaning in English: "out of" or "away from"

Origin language: Latin / Greek

English examples:

out- 31 prefix (AWAY FROM) （用于给名词和形容词加上"向外"或"离开"之意） used to add the meaning "out of" or "away from" to nouns and adjectives

She turned away from their outstretched hands (= hands held out). 她转身不理睬他们伸出的手。

out-of-body experience noun [C] 灵魂出窍的体验，出体体验 an experience in which you feel as if you have left your own body and can see it from the outside, usually from above

out-of-court adverb [before noun], adjective UK /ˌaʊt.əvˈkɔːt/ US /ˌaʊt.əvˈkɔːrt/ 庭外和解的（地） agreed without involving a trial in a law court

out-of-pocket adjective [before noun] UK /ˌaʊt.əvˌpɒk.ɪt ɪkˈspen.sɪz/ US /ˌaʊt.əvˌpɑː.kɪt ɪkˈspen.sɪz/ （为他人工作时）垫付的费用；实付费用 used about money that you have to spend yourself rather than having it paid for you, for example by your employer or insurance company

out-of-the-way adjective [before noun] 偏僻的 far from places where many people live or usually go

outburst noun [C] UK /ˈaʊt.bɜːst/ US /ˈaʊt.bɜːst/ （尤指愤怒情绪的）爆发，迸发 a sudden forceful expression of emotion, especially anger

outcast noun [C] UK /ˈaʊt.kɑːst/ US /ˈaʊt.kæst/ 受排斥的人；被社会（或集体）抛弃的人；流浪者 a person who has no place in their society or in a particular group, because the society or group refuses to accept them

outcome noun [C usually singular] UK /ˈaʊt.kʌm/ US /ˈaʊt.kʌm/ C1 结果，后果；效果 a result or effect of an action, situation, etc.

outcrop   noun [C] UK /ˈaʊt.krɒp/ US /ˈaʊt.krɑ:p/ (US also outcropping, US /-ɪŋ/ UK) 露出地面的岩石（或岩层） a large rock or group of rocks that sticks out of the ground

outcry   noun [C] UK /ˈaʊt.kraɪ/ US /ˈaʊt.kraɪ/ 呐喊；大声疾呼；强烈抗议 a strong expression of anger and disapproval about something, made by a group of people or by the public

outdated   adjective UK /ˌaʊtˈdeɪ.tɪd/ US /ˌaʊtˈdeɪ.t̬ɪd/ 过时的，陈旧的 old-fashioned and therefore not as good or as fashionable as something modern

outdoor   1 adjective [before noun] UK /ˈaʊtˌdɔːr/ US /ˈaʊtˌdɔːr/ B1 户外的，室外的，露天的 existing, happening, or done outside, rather than inside a building

outflow   noun [C] UK /ˈaʊt.fləʊ/ US /ˈaʊt.floʊ/ 外流；流出 a movement away from a place

outgoing   1 adjective UK /ˌaʊtˈgəʊ.ɪŋ/ US /ˈaʊt.goʊ.ɪŋ/ (FRIENDLY) C1 approving UK /ˌaʊtˈgəʊ.ɪŋ/ US /ˈaʊt.goʊ-/ （人）开朗的，外向的，友好的，爱交际的 (of a person) friendly and energetic and finding it easy and enjoyable to be with others 2 adjective (LEAVING) C2 [before noun] UK /ˈaʊtˌgəʊ.ɪŋ/ US /-ˌgoʊ-/ 离开的；即将离职的，即将卸任的；即将结业的 leaving a place, or leaving a job

outline   1 noun [C] UK /ˈaʊt.laɪn/ US /ˈaʊt.laɪn/ [C] (SHAPE) C2 轮廓，略图，外形 the main shape or edge of something, without any details

outlook 1 noun UK /ˈaʊt.lʊk/ US /ˈaʊt.lʊk/ (FUTURE SITUATION) C1 [S] 前景；展望 the likely future situation

output noun [U] UK /ˈaʊt.pʊt/ US /ˈaʊt.pʊt/ C2 （人、机器、工厂、国家等的）产量 an amount of something produced by a person, machine, factory, country, etc.

outrage 1 noun UK /ˈaʊt.reɪdʒ/ US /ˈaʊt.reɪdʒ/ [U] 愤慨，义愤 a feeling of anger and shock 2 noun C2 [C] 暴行；（道义上）难以接受的事情；骇人听闻的行为 a shocking, morally unacceptable, and usually violent action

outrageous 1 adjective UK /ˌaʊtˈreɪ.dʒəs/ US /ˌaʊtˈreɪ.dʒəs/ 骇人的；无耻的；无法接受的 B2 shocking and morally unacceptable

outreach 1 noun [U] UK /ˈaʊt.riːtʃ/ US /ˈaʊt.riːtʃ/ 扩大（医疗或其他）服务范围，外展服务 an effort to bring services or information to people where they live or spend time

outside 1 adjective, adverb, preposition UK /ˌaʊtˈsaɪd/ /ˈaʊt.saɪd/ US /ˌaʊtˈsaɪd/ /ˈaʊt.saɪd/ A1 在外面（的），在室外（的）；在…外面（的）not inside a building

outsider 1 noun [C] UK /ˌaʊtˈsaɪ.dər/ US /ˌaʊtˈsaɪ.dɚ/ [C] (NOT MEMBER) 局外人；外来者；外部的人 a person who is not involved with a particular group of people or organization or who does not live in a particular place

outsource verb [I or T] UK /ˈaʊt.sɔːs/ US /ˈaʊt.sɔːrs/ 外包；（将…）交外办理 If a company outsources, it pays to have part of its work done by another company.

outspoken   adjective UK /ˌaʊtˈspəʊ.kən/ US /ˌaʊtˈspoʊ.kən/ 直言不讳的；坦率的，直率的 expressing strong opinions very directly without worrying if other people are offended

outspread   adjective UK /ˌaʊtˈspred/ US /ˌaʊtˈspred/ 伸开的，展开的 spread as far as possible

outstretched   adjective UK /ˌaʊtˈstretʃt/ US /ˌaʊtˈstretʃt/ 展开的，伸出的 reaching out as far as possible

outward   1 adjective UK /ˈaʊt.wəd/ US /ˈaʊt.wəd/ (ON OUTSIDE) [before noun] 外表的，外面的 relating to how people, situations, or things seem to be, rather than how they are inside

outwith   adverb, preposition Scottish English UK /ˌaʊtˈwɪθ/ US /ˌaʊtˈwɪθ/ 在…之外 outside

Prefix (Medical): ovari(o)- Of or pertaining to the ovaries

Meaning in English: Of or pertaining to the ovaries

Origin language: Latin (ōvarium), ovary

English examples:

ovarian   adjective UK /əʊˈveə.ri.ən/ US /oʊˈver.i.ən/ 卵巢的；与卵巢有关的 of or relating to the ovaries or an ovary

ovarian cancer   卵巢癌

an ovarian cyst   卵巢囊肿

Ovarian follicle   noun [U] 卵泡 An ovarian follicle is a roughly spheroid cellular aggregation set found in the ovaries. It secretes hormones that influence stages of the menstrual cycle.

ovary   noun [C] UK /ˈəʊ.vər.i/ US /ˈoʊ.vər.i/ （女性或雌性动物的）卵巢；（雌性植物的）子房 either of the pair of organs in a woman's body that produce eggs, or the part of any female animal or plant that produces eggs or seeds

Ovariectomy   noun [C] 卵巢切除术 Oophorectomy, historically also called ovariotomy is the surgical removal of an ovary or ovaries. The surgery is also called ovariectomy, but this term is mostly used in reference to animals, e.g. the surgical removal of ovaries from laboratory animals. Wikipedia

Prefix: over- too much or more than usual

Meaning in English: too much or more than usual

Origin language: Anglo-Saxon

English examples:

over-   25 prefix UK /əʊ.vər-/ US /oʊ.və-/ (TOO MUCH) 太，过分 too much or more than usual

The children got over-excited (= too excited).   孩子们兴奋过头了。

over-egg the pudding   UK 画蛇添足 to spoil something by trying too hard to improve it

overact   verb [I or T]   disapproving UK /ˌəʊ.vəˈrækt/ US /ˌoʊ.vəˈækt/ 过火地表演（角色）；演得过于夸张 to make your voice and movements express emotions too strongly when acting in a play, etc.

overreact   verb [I] UK /ˌəʊ.və.riˈækt/ US /ˌoʊ.və.riˈækt/ 反应过激，反应过火（尤指愤怒或恐惧） to react in an extreme, especially an angry or frightened, way

overate　　UK /ˌəʊ.vəˈret/ /ˌəʊ.və.reɪt/ US /ˌoʊ.vəˈeɪt/ past simple of overeat（overeat 的过去式）

overawe　　verb [T usually passive] UK /ˌəʊ.vəˈrɔː/ US /ˌoʊ.vəˈɑː/ 使胆怯；使畏惧；吓住 to cause someone to feel a mixture of respect and fear

overbalance　　verb [I] mainly UK UK /ˌəʊ.vəˈbæl.əns/ US /ˌoʊ.vəˈbæl.əns/ 失去平衡 to lose balance and therefore fall or nearly fall

overbearing　　adjective　disapproving UK /ˌəʊ.vəˈbeə.rɪŋ/ US /ˌoʊ.vəˈber.ɪŋ/ 专横的；傲慢的；盛气凌人的 too confident and too determined to tell other people what to do, in a way that is unpleasant [GRE]

overbid　　verb [I or T] UK /ˌəʊ.vəˈbɪd/ US /ˌoʊ.vəˈbɪd/ present participle overbidding | past tense and past participle overbid 出价过高；出价高于 to offer more money than someone in an attempt to buy something, or to offer too much money in an attempt to buy something

overblown　　adjective　disapproving UK /ˌəʊ.vəˈbləʊn/ US /ˌoʊ.vəˈbloʊn/ 夸张的；过分渲染的 bigger or more important or impressive than it should be

overburden　　verb [T often passive] UK /ˌəʊ.vəˈbɜː.dən/ US /ˌoʊ.vəˈbɜː.dən/ 使不堪重负；使负担过重；使装载过多 to make someone or something work too hard or carry, contain, or deal with too much

overcharge　　verb [I or T] UK /ˌəʊ.vəˈtʃɑːdʒ/ US /ˌoʊ.vəˈtʃɑːrdʒ/ （向某人）索价过高；多收（某人）钱 to charge someone either more than the real price or more than the value of the product or service

overcome   1 verb UK /ˌəʊ.vəˈkʌm/ US /ˌoʊ.vɚˈkʌm/ overcame | overcome (DEAL WITH) B2 [I or T] 克服；战胜；攻克；解决 to defeat or succeed in controlling or dealing with something

overcook   verb [T often passive] UK /ˌəʊ.vəˈkʊk/ US /ˌoʊ.vɚˈkʊk/把…煮过了头，把…煮得太熟（或太久） to cook food for longer than necessary, reducing its quality as a result

overcrowded   adjective UK /ˌəʊ.vəˈkraʊ.dɪd/ US /ˌoʊ.vɚˈkraʊ.dɪd/ C1 过分拥挤的；拥挤不堪的 containing too many people or things

overdeveloped   adjective UK /ˌəʊ.və.dɪˈvel.əpt/ US /ˌoʊ.vɚ.dɪˈvel.əpt/ 过度发展的；过于发达的；发育过度的 having developed too much

overdo   verb [T] UK /ˌəʊ.vəˈduː/ US /ˌoʊ.vɚˈduː/ overdid | overdone C1 把…做得过头（或过火） to do something in a way that is too extreme

overdone   adjective UK /ˌəʊ.vəˈdʌn/ US /ˌoʊ.vɚˈdʌn/ （尤指肉）煮得太老的，烹制得太久的 (especially of meat) cooked too long

overdose   1 noun [C] UK /ˈəʊ.və.dəʊs/ US /ˈoʊ.vɚ.doʊs/ (informal OD) （一次用药的）过量，超剂量 too much of a drug taken or given at one time, either intentionally or by accident

overdraft   noun [C] UK /ˈəʊ.və.drɑːft/ US /ˈoʊ.vɚ.dræft/ 透支额 C1 an amount of money that a customer with a bank account is temporarily allowed to owe to the bank, or the agreement that allows this

overdressed   adjective UK /ˌəʊ.vəˈdrest/ US /ˌoʊ.vɚˈdrest/ 穿得过于正式的；穿着过于讲究的 wearing clothes that are too formal or special for a particular occasion

overdrive   noun [U] UK /ˈəʊ.və.draɪv/ US /ˈoʊ.vɚ.draɪv/ 超速运转；加倍努力；过度操劳 a state of great activity, effort, or hard work

overdue   adjective UK /ˌəʊ.vəˈdʒuː/ US /ˌoʊ.vɚˈduː/ 过期的；延误的；迟的 not done or happening when expected or when needed; late

overestimate   verb [I or T] UK /ˌəʊ.vəˈres.tɪ.meɪt/ US /ˌoʊ.vɚˈes.tə.meɪt/ C1 过高估计；过高评价 to think that something is or will be greater, more extreme, or more important than it really is

overflow   1 verb UK /ˌəʊ.vəˈfləʊ/ US /ˌoʊ.vɚˈfloʊ/ (TOO FULL) C2 [I or T] （液体）溢出，泛滥 When a liquid overflows, it flows over the edges of a container, etc. because there is too much of it.

overgrown   1 adjective UK /ˌəʊ.vəˈgrəʊn/ US /ˌoʊ.vɚˈgroʊn/ (COVERED) 草木丛生的；枝繁叶茂的；（植物）蔓生的 covered with plants that are growing thickly and in an uncontrolled way

overhaul   verb [T] UK /ˈəʊ.və.hɔːl/ US /ˈoʊ.vɚ.h ɑ :l/ 彻底检修，大修；改造；改进 to repair or improve something so that every part of it works as it should

overindulge   verb [I or T] UK /ˌəʊ.və.rɪnˈdʌldʒ/ US /ˌoʊ.vɚ.ɪnˈdʌldʒ/ （尤指在吃喝上）过分放纵，太纵情 to allow yourself or someone else to have too much of something enjoyable, especially food or drink

overweight   1 adjective UK /ˌəʊ.vəˈweɪt/ US /ˌoʊ.vɚˈweɪt/ B2 肥胖的 fat

Meaning in English:

Origin language: Anglo-Saxon

English examples:

over- 26 prefix (MORE THAN) 在…以上，超过 more than
a club for the over-50s 50 岁以上人士参加的俱乐部

over the hill often humorous 过了巅峰期；年老不中用 used for
describing someone who is old and no longer useful or attractive

over the odds UK informal （价钱）超出所值的 more than something is
really worth

over the top UK informal (abbreviation OTT) C2 太过头；太过分 too
extreme and not suitable, or demanding too much attention or effort, especially
in an uncontrolled way

over your head 无法理解 too difficult or strange for you to understand

overage adjective UK /ˌəʊ.vəˈreɪdʒ/ US /ˌoʊ.vɚˈeɪdʒ/ 超过年龄的 older
than a particular age and therefore no longer allowed to do or have particular
things

overbook verb [I or T] UK /ˌəʊ.vəˈbʊk/ US /ˌoʊ.vɚˈbʊk/ 超额订出，超
额预订（机位、客房等）to sell more tickets or places for an aircraft, holiday,
etc. than are available

overload 1 verb [T] UK /ˌəʊ.vəˈləʊd/ US /ˌoʊ.vɚˈloʊd/ C1 使超载，使负荷过重 to put too many things in or on something

override 1 verb UK /ˌəʊ.vəˈraɪd/ US /ˌoʊ.vɚˈraɪd/ overrode | overridden (NOT ACCEPT) [T] （拥有必要权威的人）否决，推翻，撤销，使无效 (of a person who has the necessary authority) to decide against or refuse to accept a previous decision, an order, a person, etc. [GRE]

oversleep verb [I] UK /ˌəʊ.vəˈsliːp/ US /ˌoʊ.vɚˈsliːp/ overslept | overslept 睡过头，睡得过久 to sleep for longer than you intended to and so wake up late

overstate verb [T] UK /ˌəʊ.vəˈsteɪt/ US /ˌoʊ.vɚˈsteɪt/ 把…讲得过分，夸大 to describe or explain something in a way that makes it seem more important or serious than it really is

overwhelm 1 verb UK /ˌəʊ.vəˈwelm/ US /ˌoʊ.vɚˈwelm/ (FORCE) （用武力）制服，击败，征服 [T] to defeat someone or something by using a lot of force [GRE]

overwhelming 1 adjective UK /ˌəʊ.vəˈwel.mɪŋ/ US /ˌoʊ.vɚ-/ 难以抵挡的；无法抗拒的 C1 difficult to fight against

overwork 1 verb [I or T] UK /ˌəʊ.vəˈwɜːk/ US /ˌoʊ.vɚˈwɜːk/ （使）劳累过度，（使）工作太累 to (cause someone to) work too much

overworked 1 adjective UK /ˌəʊ.vəˈwɜːkt/ US /ˌoʊ.vɚˈwɜːkt/ C1 工作过度的，过分劳累的 having to work too much

overwrought   adjective UK /ˌəʊ.vəˈrɔːt/ US /ˌoʊ.vəˈrɑːt/ 过度烦乱的，过度紧张的，过度焦虑的；神经质的 in a state of being upset, nervous, and worried [GRE]

Prefix: over- across

Meaning in English:

Origin language: Anglo-Saxon

English examples:

over-   27 prefix (ACROSS) across （越）过；从一边到另一边

Of course, the overland route is much slower than going by air. 当然，走陆路比坐飞机要慢多了。

over the counter   1 （买药）不用处方，在药店购买 Drugs that are bought over the counter are bought in a shop without first visiting a doctor

over-the-counter   1 adjective UK /ˌəʊ.və.ðəˈkaʊn.tər/ US /ˌoʊ.və.ðəˈkaʊn.tə/ (MEDICINE) （药品）非处方的，无需处方也可买到的 An over-the-counter drug is bought from a shop without the person who buys it having visited a doctor first. 2 adjective (SHARES) FINANCE & ECONOMICS   specialized 场外交易，柜台交易 used to describe shares that are traded directly between dealers (= people and organizations that buy and sell for others), rather than on a stock market

overcast   adjective UK /ˈəʊ.və.kɑːst/ /ˌəʊ.vəˈkɑːst/ US /ˈoʊ.və.kæst/ 阴天的，多云的；布满阴云的 with clouds in the sky and therefore not bright and sunny

overcoat   noun [C] UK /ˈəʊ.və.kəʊt/ US /ˈoʊ.və.koʊt/ 大衣，长大衣 a long thick coat worn in cold weather

overland   adjective, adverb UK /ˈəʊ.və.lænd/ US /ˈoʊ.vɚ.lænd/ （旅行）横跨陆地（的）；从陆路（的） (of travel) across the land in a vehicle, on foot, or on a horse; not by sea or air

overlap   1 verb UK /ˌəʊ.vəˈlæp/ US /ˌoʊ.vɚˈlæp/ -pp- [I or T] （与…）交叠，（与…）部分重叠，叠盖 to cover something partly by going over its edge; to cover part of the same space 2 C2 [I] （活动、课程或时间）相互重叠，有共同之处 If two or more activities, subjects, or periods of time overlap, they have some parts that are the same.

overnight   1 adjective, adverb UK /ˌəʊ.vəˈnaɪt/ US /ˌoʊ.vɚˈnaɪt/ (TIME OF DAY) B1 一夜间（的）；在夜间（的），在晚上（的） for or during the night

overseas   adjective, adverb UK /ˌəʊ.vəˈsiːz/ US /ˌoʊ.vɚˈsiːz/ B2 在海外（的）；从国外来（的）；到国外（的） in, from, or to other countries

overtime   1 adverb, noun [U] UK /ˈəʊ.və.taɪm/ US /ˈoʊ.vɚ.taɪm/ B2 加班地 (time spent working) after the usual time needed or expected in a job

Prefix: over- above (HIGHER POSITION)

Meaning in English:

Origin language: Anglo-Saxon

English examples:

over- **above**   29 prefix (HIGHER POSITION) 悬于…之上；突出于…之上

She was knocked off her bicycle by an overhanging branch.   她被一根垂下来的树枝撞下了自行车。

over my dead body   只要我还有一口气就不能那样做；除非我死了 If you say something will happen over your dead body, you mean that you will do everything you can to prevent it.

overall   adverb [before noun], adjective UK /ˌəʊ.vəˈrɔːl/ US /ˌoʊ.vəˈɑːl/ B2 总的（来说）；全面的（地）；包括一切的（地） in general rather than in particular, or including all the people or things in a particular group or situation

overarching   adjective [before noun]   formal UK /ˌəʊ.vəˈrɑːtʃɪŋ/ US /ˌoʊ.vəˈɑːr.tʃɪŋ/ 首要的；包罗万象的，支配一切的 most important, because of including or affecting all other areas

overboard   adverb UK /ˈəʊ.və.bɔːd/ /ˌəʊ.vəˈbɔːd/ US /ˈoʊ.və.bɔːrd/ C2 从船上落入水中 over the side of a boat or ship and into the water

overhang   1 verb [T] UK /ˌəʊ.vəˈhæŋ/ US /ˌoʊ.vəˈhæŋ/ overhung | overhung [T] (STICK OUT) 凸出于…之上；悬于…之上；悬垂，悬挂 to stick out over something at a lower level

overhead   1 adjective, adverb UK /ˈəʊ.və.hed/ US /ˈoʊ.və.hed/ 在头顶上（的）；在空中（的） above your head, usually in the sky

overhear   verb [I or T] UK /ˌəʊ.vəˈhɪər/ US /ˌoʊ.vəˈhɪr/ overheard | overheard C2 无意中听到，偶然听到 to hear what other people are saying without intending to and without their knowledge

overlook   1 verb [T] UK /ˌəʊ.vəˈlʊk/ US /ˌoʊ.vəˈlʊk/ [T] (VIEW) B2 眺望；（尤指）俯瞰，俯视 to provide a view of, especially from above

oversee   verb [T] UK /ˌəʊ.vəˈsiː/ US /ˌoʊ.vɚˈsiː/ present participle overseeing | past tense oversaw | past participle overseen 监督；监察；监管 to watch or organize a job or an activity to make certain that it is being done correctly

overshadow   1 verb [T often passive] UK /ˌəʊ.vəˈʃæd.əʊ/ US /ˌoʊ.vɚˈʃæd.oʊ/ 使黯然失色；使相形见绌；使蒙上阴影 to cause someone or something to seem less important or less happy [GRE]

overstep   verb [T] UK /ˌəʊ.vəˈstep/ US /ˌoʊ.vɚˈstep/ -pp- 超越，逾越 （可以接受的或正确的限度） to go further than what is considered acceptable or correct

overtake   1 verb UK /ˌəʊ.vəˈteɪk/ US /ˌoʊ.vɚˈteɪk/ overtook | overtaken (GO PAST) C1 [T] （数量或程度上）大于，超过 to go past something by being a greater amount or degree

overtax   1 verb [T] UK /ˌəʊ.vəˈtæks/ US /ˌoʊ.vɚˈtæks/ [T] (MONEY) 对…征税过重，对…课税过多 to demand too much tax from someone or to put too much tax on goods

overturn   1 verb UK /ˌəʊ.vəˈtɜːn/ US /ˌoʊ.vɚˈtɜːn/ (GO UPSIDE DOWN) [I or T] 打翻，弄翻；（使）倾覆；（使）翻倒 to (cause to) turn over

overview   noun [C] UK /ˈəʊ.və.vjuː/ US /ˈoʊ.vɚ.vjuː/ C1 概述；概观 a short description of something that provides general information about it, but no details

Prefix (Medical): ovo-, ovi-, ov- Of or pertaining to the eggs, the ovum

Meaning in English: Of or pertaining to the eggs, the ovum

Origin language: Latin (ōvum), egg, ovum

English examples:

oviduct noun [C] ANATOMY specialized UK /ˈəʊ.vɪ.dʌkt/ US /ˈoʊ.vɪ.dʌkt/ （女性或雌性动物的）输卵管 a tube inside an animal that an egg passes through as it leaves the ovary (= organ that produces eggs)

ovulate verb [I] UK /ˈɒv.jə.leɪt/ US /ˈɑ:.vjuː.leɪt/ （女性或雌性动物）排卵，产卵 (of a woman or female animal) to produce an egg from which a baby can be formed

ovulation noun [U] UK /ˌɒv.jəˈleɪ.ʃən/ US /ˌɑ:.vjuːˈleɪ.ʃən/ 排卵 the time when a woman or female animal produces an egg

ovule noun [C] BIOLOGY specialized UK /ˈɒv.juːl/ US /ˈɑ:.vjuːl/ 胚珠（植物子房中的一部分，产生雌性生殖细胞，受精后变成种子） a part inside the ovary (= organ that produces eggs) of a plant that contains the female sex cell and develops into a seed when that cell is fertilized

ovum noun [C] BIOLOGY specialized UK /ˈəʊ.vəm/ US /ˈoʊ.vəm/ plural ova

Ovogenesis noun [U] 卵子生成 Oogenesis, ovogenesis, or oögenesis is the differentiation of the ovum into a cell competent to further develop when fertilized. It is developed from the primary oocyte by maturation. Oogenesis is initiated in the embryonic stage. Wikipedia

Prefix (Medical): oxo- (oxi-)- addition of oxygen

Meaning in English: addition of oxygen

Origin language: Greek ὀξύς

English examples:

oxidative adjective   CHEMISTRY, MEDICAL   specialized UK /ɒkˈsɪd.ə.tɪv/ US /ˈɑ:k.sɪˌdeɪ.tɪv/ 氧化的 An oxidative chemical reaction adds oxygen to the tissues of the body.

oxidative damage   氧化损伤

Stress cardiomyopathy is associated with increased oxidative stress.   应激性心肌病和氧化应激程度增加有关。

oxide noun [C or U] UK /ˈɒk.saɪd/ US /ˈɑ:k.saɪd/ 氧化物 a chemical combination of oxygen and one other element

iron oxide   氧化铁

an oxide of copper 一种铜的氧化物

oxidize 1 verb [I or T] (UK usually oxidise) UK /ˈɒk.sɪ.daɪz/ US /ˈɑ:k.sə.daɪz/ 氧化；生锈 If a substance oxidizes, it combines with oxygen and loses hydrogen to form another substance, and if something oxidizes a substance, it causes it to do this.

Iron oxidizes to form rust.   铁氧化形成铁锈。

When you heat fat, it oxidizes easily. 脂肪在燃烧时迅速氧化。

oxidize 2 verb （使）氧化 If a chemical element oxidizes, it loses electrons (= very small pieces of matter with negative electrical charge) and if you oxidize it, you cause it to do this.

Prefix (Medical): oxy- sharp, acid, acute, oxygen
Meaning in English: sharp, acid, acute, oxygen

Origin language: Greek ὀξύς

English examples:

oxygen noun [U] UK /ˈɒk.sɪ.dʒən/ US /ˈɑ:k.sɪ.dʒən/ (symbol O) B2 氧，氧气 a chemical element that is a gas with no smell or colour. Oxygen forms a large part of the air on earth, and is needed by animals and plants to live.

oxygen bar   noun [C] UK /ˈɒk.sɪ.dʒən ˌbɑːr/ US /ˈɑːk.sɪ.dʒən ˌbɑːr/ 提供吸氧服务的场所，氧吧（顾客付费吸入纯净的、有益健康的氧气，有助于放松） a place where you pay to breathe pure oxygen in order to improve your health and help you relax

oxygen debt   noun [C]   BIOLOGY   specialized UK /ˈɒk.sɪ.dʒən ˌdet/ US /ˈɑːk.sɪ.dʒən ˌdet/ 氧债（运动时身体消耗的额外氧气，需要在运动后恢复） the extra oxygen that the body uses during exercise, which must be replaced when resting

oxygen mask   noun [C] UK /ˈɒk.sɪ.dʒən ˌmɑːsk/ US /ˈɑːk.sɪ.dʒən ˌmæsk/ 氧气面具，氧气罩 a piece of equipment that can be put over a person's nose and mouth to supply them with oxygen

oxygen tank   noun [C] UK /ˈɒk.sɪ.dʒən ˌtæŋk/ US /ˈɑːk.sɪ.dʒən ˌtæŋk/ 氧气罐（充满氧气的容器，帮助病人或潜水者呼吸） a container with oxygen inside it, used for helping people to breathe, for example when they are very ill, or when they are diving underwater

oxygen tent   noun [C] UK /ˈɒk.sɪ.dʒən ˌtent/ US /ˈɑːk.sɪ.dʒən ˌtent/ （输氧用的）氧幕 a clear covering put over the head and upper body of a person who is ill to provide oxygen to help them breathe

oxygenate   verb [T]   CHEMISTRY UK /ˈɒk.sɪ.dʒə.neɪt/ US /ˈɑːk.sɪ.dʒə.neɪt/ 给…加氧；给…供氧（或输氧） to add oxygen to something

oxygenation   noun [U]   CHEMISTRY UK /ˌɒk.sɪ.dʒənˈeɪ.ʃən/ US /ˌɑːk.sɪ.dʒəˈneɪ.ʃən/ 氧合，加氧 the process of adding oxygen to something

oxyhaemoglobin   noun [U]   BIOLOGY   UK specialized (US oxyhemoglobin) UK /ˌɒk.siˌhiː.məˈɡləʊ.bɪn/ US /ˌɑːk.siˌhiː.məˈɡloʊ.bɪn/ 氧合血红蛋白（红细胞中鲜红的血红素在血液循环到肺部时与氧结合） the bright red form of haemoglobin (= substance in red blood cells) that contains oxygen

oxymoronic   adjective   LANGUAGE   specialized UK /ˌɒk.sɪ.məˈrɒn.ɪk/ US /ˌɑːk.sɪ.mɔːˈrɑː.nɪk/ 矛盾修辞法的，逆喻的 (of two words used together) having, or seeming to have, opposite meanings:

More Related Products 更多相关书籍和课程

KDP- Edeo & Legoo Mandarin Publications List 2021 September Issue 方正教育最新书籍及课程

- ➢ PDF eBook and Paperback.

- ➢ FREE @ https://1salesforce.com/OwDodnxXgcMhyHT or https://bit.ly/3grHNcJ

Edeo & Legoo Mandarin Publications List 2021 September Issue 方正教育最新书籍及课程- Share the best we know and what we know the best! 分享最好的给你！For Hardcopy or Paperback books at best price with reduced postage, please visit: Our Amazon Kindle Author Central page: http://bit.ly/david-amazon-kdp, using ISBN or ASIN to search the book, // Amazon KDP ISBN: 9798487909367; Amazon KDP Hard Cover ISBN: 9798487986344 Google book: GGKEY:YZFH7P68J8T Apple Store Link: http://books.apple.com/us/book/id1588419012

英语也可这样学 Learn English can be fun like this!

KDP- Decoding Greek and Latin roots in English

➢ Decoding Greek and Latin roots in English 探源英语词根，轻松扩大英语词汇 - Expand English Vocabulary in Unique Smart Way! Part 1 out of 4 Version 2022 .

➢ PDF eBook and Paperback.

- ➢ ☐   Best Price and Details @ https://1salesforce.com/products/decoding-greek-and-latin-roots-in-english-part-1-2 OR https://bit.ly/3xOxM1a

- ➢ ☐   For Hardcopy or Paperback books at best price with reduced postage, please visit: Our Amazon Kindle Author Central page: http://bit.ly/david-amazon-kdp, using ISBN or ASIN to search the book, // Amazon KDP ISBN: 9798838321763; Amazon KDP Hard Cover ISBN: 9798838328915 Or // Google book: GGKEY:NBTF117DUFP Apple Store Link: http://books.apple.com/us/book/id6443026215 // Kobo bookId=7af11251-8039-4b3f-b815-4f75c6f6182a

KDP- PSAT/NMSQT 5000 English Vocabulary According CEFR C1 C2

- ➢ PDF eBook and Paperback.

- ➢ Best Price and Details @ https://bit.ly/3CGE0BP http://edeo.biz/29567

- ➢ PSAT/NMSQT 5000 English Vocabulary According CEFR C1 C2, PSAT/NMSQT 考试英语 5000 词汇- The latest and most complete reference for your success 最新、最完整词汇参考 For Hardcopy or Paperback books at best price with reduced postage, please visit: Our Amazon Kindle Author Central page: http://bit.ly/david-amazon-kdp, using ISBN or ASIN to search the book, // Amazon KDP ISBN: 9798455631870 BLOCKED;

  Amazon KDP Hard Cover ISBN: 9798455657269 BLOCKED; Google book: GGKEY:G35BQ83URU5 Apple ID: 1581048431

KDP- ACT 5000 English Vocabulary According CEFR C1 C2 美国大学测验英语词汇

- ➢ PDF eBook and Paperback.

- ➢ Best Price and Details @ http://edeo.biz/29492

- ➢ For Hardcopy or Paperback books at best price with reduced postage, please visit: Our Amazon Kindle Author Central page: http://bit.ly/david-amazon-kdp, using ISBN or ASIN to search the book, // Amazon KDP ISBN: 9798548898388; Amazon KDP Hard Cover ISBN: 9798548913401 Google book: GGKEY:390FBZCWNYN Apple ID:1579472399
http://edeo.biz/00000

KDP- Edeo & Legoo Mandarin Publications List 2021 July Issue 方正教育最新书籍及课程

- ➢ PDF eBook and Paperback.

- ➢ FREE @ http://edeo.biz/29464

Edeo & Legoo Mandarin Publications List 2021 July Issue 方正教育最新书籍及课程- Share the best we know and what we know the best! 分享最好的给你！ For Hardcopy or Paperback books at best price with reduced postage, please visit: Our Amazon Kindle Author Central page: http://bit.ly/david-amazon-kdp, using ISBN or ASIN to search the book, // Amazon KDP ISBN: 9798547569258; Amazon KDP Hard Cover ISBN: 9798547588549 Google book: GGKEY:ZP8ULBLSHBP Apple ID:1579219478

KDP- GMAT English Vocabulary V2021, GMAT 研究生管理科入学考试英语词汇

- ➢ PDF eBook and Paperback.

- ➢ Best Price and Details @ http://edeo.biz/29454

GMAT English Vocabulary V2021, GMAT 研究生管理科入学考试英语词汇- 2500 Vocabulary According GMAT past papers 最新、最完整词汇参考 For Hardcopy or Paperback books at best price with reduced postage, please visit: Our Amazon Kindle Author Central page: http://bit.ly/david-amazon-kdp, using ISBN or ASIN to search the book, // Amazon KDP ISBN: 9798547219955; Amazon KDP Hard Cover ISBN: 9798547236716 Google book: GGKEY:HEFYH6ZEKF4 Apple ID:1579174285

KDP- SAT Chinese Grammar 2021 Edition 汉语水平考试规范性语法

➤ PDF eBook and Paperback.

➤ Best Price and Details @ http://edeo.biz/29402

SAT Chinese Grammar 2021 Edition 汉语水平考试规范性语法 - The latest and most complete grammar by referring SAT and HSK Syllabus 最新、最完整语法参考 For Hardcopy or Paperback books at best price with reduced postage, please visit: Our Amazon Kindle Author Central page: http://bit.ly/david-amazon-kdp, using ISBN or ASIN to search the book, // Amazon KDP ISBN: 9798545124824; Amazon KDP Hard Cover ISBN: 9798545137008 Google book: GGKEY:D7WH73PC7L4 Apple ID:1578648747

KDP- TOEFL English Vocabulary 5000, TOEFL 托福考试英语词汇- Classified English Vocabulary According CEFR V2021 (欧盟语言标准) 分级英语词汇

➤ PDF eBook and Paperback.

➤ Best Price and Details @ http://edeo.biz/29262

For Hardcopy or Paperback books at best price with reduced postage, please visit: Our Amazon Kindle Author Central page: http://bit.ly/david-amazon-kdp, using ISBN 9798533775168 or ASIN to search the book, //

KDP- TOEIC 5000 English Vocabulary, TOEIC 多益考试英语词汇 - Classified English Vocabulary According CEFR (欧盟语言标准) 分级英语词汇

- ➢ PDF eBook and Paperback.

- ➢ Best Price and Details @ http://edeo.biz/29303

For Hardcopy or Paperback books at best price with reduced postage, please visit: Our Amazon Kindle Author Central page: http://bit.ly/david-amazon-kdp, using ISBN or ASIN to search the book, // Amazon KDP ISBN: 9798538544950 Amazon KDP Hard Cover ISBN: 9798538557080 Google book: GGKEY:UHP1SH22SA3 Apple Book ID: Apple ID:1576854172

KDP- SAT 5000 English Vocabulary V2021, SAT 赛达考试英语词汇 - Classified English Vocabulary According CEFR (欧盟语言标准) 分级英语词汇

- ➢ PDF eBook and Paperback.

- ➢ Best Price and Details @ http://edeo.biz/29288

For Hardcopy or Paperback books at best price with reduced postage, please visit: Our Amazon Kindle Author Central page: http://bit.ly/david-amazon-kdp, using ISBN or ASIN to search the book, // Amazon KDP ISBN: 9798537153092, Amazon KDP Hard Cover ISBN: 9798537164937 Google book: GGKEY:U1AXNXPE1J1 Apple ID:1576480846

KDP- IELTS English Vocabulary 5000 Version 2021, 雅思考试英语词汇 - Classified English Vocabulary According CEFR (欧盟语言标准) 分级英语词汇

- ➢ PDF eBook and Paperback.

➢ Best Price and Details @ http://edeo.biz/29275

For Hardcopy or Paperback books at best price with reduced postage, please visit: Our Amazon Kindle Author Central page: http://bit.ly/david-amazon-kdp, using ISBN or ASIN to search the book, // Amazon KDP ISBN: 9798534826388 Amazon KDP Hard Cover ISBN: 9798534835137 Google book: GGKEY:6AA0FDSL23T Apple Book ID:1576050813

Kobo bookId=11c5a801-78c3-4a4b-a3e1-ea543c7b9db2 Apple ID:1576050813 http://edeo.biz/29275

KDP- Edexcel IGCSE in English as a Second Language (ESL) , Edexcel IGCSE 英语词汇 (二语) - Classified English Vocabulary According CEFR (欧盟语言标准) 分级英语词汇

➢ PDF eBook and Paperback.

➢ Best Price and Details @ http://edeo.biz/29256

For Hardcopy or Paperback books at best price with reduced postage, please visit: Our Amazon Kindle Author Central page: http://bit.ly/david-amazon-kdp, using ISBN 9798533313957   or ASIN to search the book, //

KDP- C2 Proficiency (CPE) 3000 English Vocabulary C2 精通级 3000 英语词汇 Version 2021 -- Classified English Vocabulary According CEFR (A1, A2, B1, B2, C1, C2) (欧盟语言标准)分级英语词汇

➢ PDF eBook and Paperback.

- ➢ Best Price and Details @ http://edeo.biz/13227   (Newly Updated)

For Hardcopy or Paperback books at best price with reduced postage, please visit: Our Amazon Kindle Author Central page: http://bit.ly/david-amazon-kdp, using ISBN 9798530920707 or ASIN to search the book, //

KDP- C1 Advanced (CAE) 2100 English Vocabulary C1 高级 2100 英语词汇 Version 2021 -- Classified English Vocabulary According CEFR (A1, A2, B1, B2, C1, C2) (欧盟语言标准)分级英语词汇

- ➢ PDF eBook and Paperback.

- ➢ Best Price and Details @ http://edeo.biz/13218 (Newly Updated)

For Hardcopy or Paperback books at best price with reduced postage, please visit: Our Amazon Kindle Author Central page: http://bit.ly/david-amazon-kdp, using ISBN 9798530261008 or ASIN to search the book, //

KDP- B2 First (FCE) 3800 English Vocabulary B2 中高级 3800 英语词汇 Version 2021 -- Classified English Vocabulary According CEFR (A1, A2, B1, B2, C1, C2) (欧盟语言标准)分级

- ➢ PDF eBook and Paperback.

- ➢ Best Price and Details @ http://edeo.biz/13205 (Updated)

For Hardcopy or Paperback books at best price with reduced postage, please visit: Our Amazon Kindle Author Central page: http://bit.ly/david-amazon-kdp, using ISBN 9798529699553 or ASIN to search the book

KDP- B1 Preliminary (PET) 2800 English Vocabulary B1 中级 2800 英语词汇 Version 2021 -- Classified English Vocabulary According CEFR (A1, A2, B1, B2, C1, C2) (欧盟语言标准)分级

- ➢ PDF eBook and Paperback.

- ➢ Best Price and Details @ http://edeo.biz/13198 (Updated)

For Hardcopy or Paperback books at best price with reduced postage, please visit: Our Amazon Kindle Author Central page: http://bit.ly/david-amazon-kdp, using ISBN 9798529286562 or ASIN to search the book, //

KDP- A2 Flyers (YLE Flyers) 1540 English Vocabulary A2 初级 1540 英语词汇 Version 2021

- ➢ PDF eBook and Paperback.

- ➢ Best Price and Details @ http://edeo.biz/13189 (Updated)

For Hardcopy or Paperback books at best price with reduced postage, please visit: Our Amazon Kindle Author Central page: http://bit.ly/david-amazon-kdp, using ISBN 9798529191873 or ASIN to search the book, //

KDP- A1 Movers (YLE Movers) 780 Vocabulary 入门级 780 个词汇

- ➢ PDF eBook and Paperback.

- ➢ Best Price and Details @ http://edeo.biz/13119

For Hardcopy or Paperback books at best price with reduced postage, please visit: Our Amazon Kindle Author Central page: http://bit.ly/david-amazon-kdp, using ISBN 9798647023728 or ASIN to search the book, //

KDP- GRE English Vocabulary 2500 大师级必胜 GRE 词汇- Advance Level English Vocabulary According GRE past papers 分级英语词汇

- ➢ PDF eBook and Paperback.

- ➢ Best Price and Details @ http://edeo.biz/13234 (Updated)

For Hardcopy or Paperback books at best price with reduced postage, please visit: Our Amazon Kindle Author Central page: http://bit.ly/david-amazon-kdp, using ISBN 9798647067463 or ASIN to search the book, //

Udemy[3]-Test English Vocabulary Level According CEFRL A1-C2 V2020-05
- ➢ Online Video Course

- ➢ Best Price and Details @ https://www.udemy.com/course/test-english-vocabulary-level-according-cefrl-a1-c2-v2020-05/?referralCode=D02D9EEBF0DAEB3F2774

Quiz[4]-Test Your English Vocabulary Level in 10 Minutes Flash Cards
- ➢ Online Practice Test and Quiz

- ➢ Best Price and Details @ https://www.udemy.com/course/test-your-english-vocabulary-level-in-10-minutes-flash-cards/?referralCode=718D1D2EA23BF47AFE70

KDP[5]-英语词汇-A1 入门级 780 个词汇 A1 - Beginner Level English Vocabulary
- ➢ PDF eBook and Paperback.

- ➢ Best Price and Details @ http://edeo.biz/13119

- ➢ For Hardcopy or Paperback books at best price with reduced postage, please visit: Our Amazon Kindle Author Central page: http://bit.ly/david-amazon-kdp, using ISBN or ASIN to search the book, A1 - Beginner Level English Vocabulary (欧盟语言标准) 分级英语词汇-A1 入门级 780 个词汇 - Classified English Vocabularies According CEFRL A1, A2, B1, B2, C1, C2 780 Vocabularies // Kindle eBook LIVE Submitted on May 19, 2020 $6.99 USD ASIN: B088SZK72X KINDLE

---

[3] Udemy: Online Video Courses hosted in Udemy, lifetime access
[4] Quiz: Online Quiz, auto grading and explanations, hosted on Udemy, lifetime access
[5] KDP: Amazon Kindle Books, ebook and Paperback.

EBOOK ACTIONS // Paperback DRAFT Last modified on June 4, 2020 ISBN: 9798647023728

KDP-英语词汇 A2 初级 1540 个词汇 A2 CEFRL- Beginner Level English Vocabularies

➢ PDF eBook and Paperback.

➢ Best Price and Details @ http://edeo.biz/13189

➢ For Hardcopy or Paperback books at best price with reduced postage, please visit: Our Amazon Kindle Author Central page: http://bit.ly/david-amazon-kdp, using ISBN or ASIN to search the book, A2 - Beginner Level English Vocabularies (欧盟语言标准)分级英语词汇-A2 初级 1540 个词汇- Classified English Vocabularies According CEFRL A1, A2, B1, B2, C1, C2 1540 Vocabularies //Kindle eBook LIVE Submitted on May 19, 2020 $8.99 USD ASIN: B088TK3NTD // Paperback DRAFT Last modified on June 4, 2020 ISBN: 9798647032959

KDP-英语词汇-B1 中级 2800 个词汇 B1 - Intermediate Level English Vocabularies

➢ PDF eBook and Paperback.

➢ Best Price and Details @ http://edeo.biz/13198

➢ For Hardcopy or Paperback books at best price with reduced postage, please visit: Our Amazon Kindle Author Central page: http://bit.ly/david-amazon-kdp, using ISBN or ASIN to search the book, 英语词汇-B1 中级 2800 个词汇 B1 - Intermediate Level English Vocabularies (欧盟语言标准)分级- Classified English Vocabularies According CEFRL A1, A2, B1, B2, C1, C2 2800 Vocabularies // Kindle eBook LIVE Submitted on May 19, 2020 $12.99 USD ASIN: B088TPTDWK // Paperback DRAFT PAPERBACK ACTIONS ISBN: 9798647038678

➢ PDF eBook and Paperback.

➢ Best Price and Details @ http://edeo.biz/13205

➢ For Hardcopy or Paperback books at best price with reduced postage, please visit: Our Amazon Kindle Author Central page: http://bit.ly/david-amazon-kdp, using ISBN or ASIN to search the book, 英语词汇 B2 中高级 3800 个词汇 B2 - Intermediate Level English Vocabularies (欧盟语言标准)分级-- Classified English Vocabularies According CEFRL A1, A2, B1, B2, C1, C2 3800 Vocabularies // Kindle eBook LIVE Submitted on May 19, 2020 $15.00 USD ASIN: B088TQTBPH // Paperback DRAFT Last modified on June 4, 2020 ISBN: 9798647049889

➢ PDF eBook and Paperback.

➢ Best Price and Details @ http://edeo.biz/13218

➢ For Hardcopy or Paperback books at best price with reduced postage, please visit: Our Amazon Kindle Author Central page: http://bit.ly/david-amazon-kdp, using ISBN or ASIN to search the book, 分级英语词汇-C1 高级 2100 个词汇 CEFRL C1 - Advance Level English Vocabularies (欧盟语言标准)分级英语词汇-C1 高级 2100 个词汇- Classified English Vocabularies According CEFRL A1, A2, B1, B2, C1, C2 2100 Vocabularies // Kindle eBook LIVE Submitted on May 19, 2020 $12.00 USD ASIN: B088TR9KW4 // Paperback DRAFT Last modified on June 4, 2020 ISBN: 9798647057587

KDP-分级英语词汇-C2 精通级 3000 个词汇 CEFRL C2 - Advance Level English Vocabularies

➢ PDF eBook and Paperback.

➢ Best Price and Details @ http://edeo.biz/13227

➢ For Hardcopy or Paperback books at best price with reduced postage, please visit: Our Amazon Kindle Author Central page: http://bit.ly/david-amazon-kdp, using ISBN or ASIN to search the book, 分级英语词汇-C2 精通级 3000 个词汇 CEFRL C2 - Advance Level English Vocabularies (欧盟语言标准)- Classified English Vocabularies According CEFRL A1, A2, B1, B2, C1, C2 3000 Vocabularies, Kindle eBook LIVE Submitted on May 19, 2020 $15.00 USD ASIN: B088TRQRTY //Paperback DRAFT Last modified on June 4, 2020 ISBN: 9798647062086

KDP-大师级必胜 GRE 词汇 GRE English Vocabulary 2500 分级英语词汇

➢ PDF eBook and Paperback.

➢ Best Price and Details @ http://edeo.biz/13234

➢ For Hardcopy or Paperback books at best price with reduced postage, please visit: Our Amazon Kindle Author Central page: http://bit.ly/david-amazon-kdp, using ISBN or ASIN to search the book, 大师级必胜 GRE 词汇 GRE English Vocabulary 2500 分级英语词汇 - - Advance Level English Vocabularies According GRE past papers; // Kindle eBook LIVE Submitted on May 19, 2020 $18.00 USD ASIN: B088TSMJJH // Paperback DRAFT Last modified on June 4, 2020 PAPERBACK ACTIONS ISBN: 9798647067463；

[iiii] Reference 1: https://www.msdmanuals.com/professional/eye-disorders/eyelid-and-lacrimal-disorders/canaliculitis

Reference 2: https://www.genome.gov/genetics-glossary

Reference 3: https://dictionary.cambridge.org/dictionary/

Printed in Great Britain
by Amazon

58012802R00249